I0816746

A HISTORY OF FIREWORKS
FROM THEIR ORIGINS TO THE PRESENT DAY

A HISTORY OF FIREWORKS

FROM THEIR ORIGINS TO THE PRESENT DAY

JOHN WITHINGTON

REAKTION BOOKS

In memory of my lovely wife
Anne Clements, 1950–2021

Published by
Reaktion Books Ltd
Unit 32, Waterside
44–48 Wharf Road
London N1 7UX, UK
www.reaktionbooks.co.uk

First published 2024

Printed and bound in Great Britain by TJ Books Ltd, Padstow, Cornwall

A catalogue record for this book is available from the British Library

ISBN 978 1 78914 935 7

CONTENTS

Introduction

When I was growing up in Manchester in the 1950s, fireworks meant Bonfire Night (and that is what we would call it, rather than Guy Fawkes Night or Fireworks Night). I have no recollection of seeing them at private celebrations such as birthdays or weddings, or even on New Year's Eve. If I remember rightly, they made an appearance in October, a couple of weeks before the great day, in newsagents, and were sold singly or in selection boxes. Bangers, I recall, were a penny each (that's an old penny, just over 0.4p) and gloried in names like 'Little Devil'. Their sharp reports would punctuate the days running up to 5 November as boys threw them in the street. Especially intimidating were rip-raps, which looked like tightly folded-up little snakes and gave a bang every few seconds, flying off each time in random directions at about ankle height. My mother thought they were a waste of money, and made sure our, or rather her and my father's, hard-earned cash was invested in more picturesque fireworks.

While the bangers banged, the streets would resound to cries of 'Penny for the Guy!' as children tried to raise money to buy fireworks by parading their effigies of Guy Fawkes. The Guy would be made from an old shirt or jumper, an old pair of trousers and a retired pillowcase for the head, all stuffed with newspaper, plus a hat and a mask, ideally one that was a bit scary, to round off the outfit. Then, on a trolley, or in an old pram or a wheelbarrow, it would be trundled to some suitable vantage point with plenty of passing footfall.

The night itself would begin indoors with sparklers by the fire. It was November, don't forget. Even if the sparks landed on your hands, arms or legs, they didn't hurt, and, perhaps more important, they never seemed to set fire to the rug either. As you got more confident, you could use your sparkler to write in the air, though the letters didn't hang around for long. Outside, the bonfire was waiting. There weren't a lot of trees in the neighbourhood, so it was usually made up of bits of wood that people wanted to get rid of – boxes, decaying planks, pensioned-off furniture. Sitting on top, as the last thing to be consumed, was the Guy. The first bonfire I remember was at a relative's, whose house had the great advantage of being on a cobbled street – a much better grounding for a blaze than the new-fangled asphalt roads on the housing estate where we lived. When we did start having bonfires at home, we used the back garden.

Food was another essential part of the Bonfire Night ritual. Jacket potatoes – cooked in the bonfire, then eaten from a gloved hand – toffee apples, treacle toffee and parkin, a rich ginger and treacle cake. Once the fire was lit, it was time for my dad, my uncle or my grandad to 'light the blue touchpaper and retire' – the standard instruction on fireworks. This was a job for grown-ups. We often seemed to start with a Roman candle, which gave out flurries of sparks in changing colours. Fountains spewed out a more continuous rain of light. A Catherine wheel would be nailed to a post to whirl around, and rockets would climb from milk bottles into the night sky. Big fires lit in the midst of high-density housing with no emergency services in attendance, fireworks lying around ready to be ignited by any random spark, rockets fired from bottles: it all sounds like a series of accidents waiting to happen, but I don't recall any. I do remember that the walk to school the next morning would be marked by dead rockets and the air scented with bonfire smoke.

A few minutes' walk from our house was Belle Vue – a zoo, a speedway track, a boating lake, an amusement park, a ballroom (where, as a teenager, I would see the Rolling Stones), and every year the scene of ambitious firework displays usually featuring some great feat of British arms, such as Wolfe's victory at Quebec. But I don't recall ever attending a big public display of that kind, nor do I ever remember seeing fireworks on television. For me in those days, they were a small-scale, back-garden, family-and-friends phenomenon. It was only later in life that I saw grand shows, such as the annual 'fires of Torello' on Italy's Amalfi coast, caught quite by accident one September, or the New Year's Eve display in Madeira's capital, Funchal. Living in north London, in the last few years, I've found a vantage point from which to enjoy in reasonable comfort London's New Year's Eve spectaculars, which would have been unimaginable in the back gardens of my childhood.

NOTE. As the companies of the famous fireworks families of Brock and Pain operated under a variety of names, I have simply referred to them throughout as 'Brocks' and 'Pains'.

I
From Origins to Guy Fawkes

Once upon a time, long, long ago in China, someone threw a piece of bamboo on a fire. Now the thing about bamboo is that, unlike wood, it is not usually solid. Its stalks, or culms, are hollow but broken up by internal nodes, which means that when they are heated up, the air inside each section expands rapidly, and they explode. So the piece of bamboo on the fire went off with a loud bang. Our ancient Chinese friend threw on another stalk, the same thing happened again, and everyone laughed. The firework, or at least the firecracker, was born! Or something like that. Perhaps it happened sometime during the Han dynasty, which stretched for two hundred years on either side of Christ's birth, or maybe at some other time or somewhere else in Asia, or in one of the other four continents where bamboo grows. Or did the firecracker's birth occur in some quite different way? Perhaps appropriately, the truth is lost in the smoke of history.

A Cradle in China

What is clear is that in China these natural firecrackers soon proved themselves useful as well as entertaining. The Chinese *Book of the Spiritual and Strange*, probably written around AD 290 but possibly drawing on earlier sources and stories, relates: 'Deep in the mountains of the west there exist human-like creatures more than 10 ft. tall. They go naked and catch frogs and crabs to eat. They are not shy of men.'[1] Indeed, so unshy were these mysterious 'mountain men' that they would commandeer fires lit by humans to cook their prey, and even steal salt to improve its flavour. The book noted that the creatures were able to take on forms other than humanoid, and that if you were rash enough to attack one, you ran the risk of being infected with a fever. So instead, 'people cast lengths of bamboo on the fire, which explode and leap out of it, thereby scaring' the mountain men away. It is said that for centuries, no self-respecting Chinese traveller would leave home without a stash of natural bamboo firecrackers. As to what exactly these mysterious mountain creatures were, some suggested they might be apes, while others, pointing to their taste for cooked food, took the view they were more likely to be primitive humans. And the 'ten feet tall' bit? Perhaps it was just a graphic way of saying they were big and frightening.

The ancient Chinese believed firecrackers could also be used to scare off evil spirits. *Annual Folk Customs of the States of Ching and Chhu*, written about AD 550, says that on New Year's Day, as soon as people got up, 'bamboo crackers are let off with big bangs in all the courtyards to frighten away the mountain spirits and evil demons.'[2] But the writer warns that, although this practice may be acceptable among the lower orders, it ought to be 'superfluous for rulers and officials'. Be that as it may, the custom survived. Nearly five hundred years later, another author wrote that each family would explode around ten sticks of bamboo every New Year's Eve, while at the end of the sixteenth century a scholar named Feng Ying Ching noted: 'bamboo is exploded in fires throughout the night until morning, in order to shake and arouse the Yang of the spring, and to remove and dissipate all evil influences.'[3] Indeed, natural firecrackers were still being used this way into the twentieth century.

Gunpowder Explodes onto the Scene

The next, and perhaps most important, step change in the development of fireworks was the invention of gunpowder. Here again, the Chinese generally get the credit, though some have put forward the claims of the Indians, the Arabs, the Greeks or even the English. As early as AD 142, a Chinese alchemist named Wei Boyang was writing about experiments with a mixture of three powders that would 'fly and dance' violently when heated.[4] He did not name the ingredients, but some believe he was referring to what we now call gunpowder, although even if he was, it does not necessarily mean he was the inventor. About AD 300, another Chinese alchemist, Ko Hung, referred to mixing sulphur and saltpetre (potassium nitrate), and around 350 years after that, the alchemist and practitioner of traditional medicine Sun Ssu-Mo suggested adding the charred pods of the soap-bean tree, which would have provided charcoal.

One theory is that the discovery of gunpowder was an accident, because its ingredients – sulphur, charcoal and saltpetre – were commonly found in the kitchen. (Sulphur was an ingredient in ancient medicines, while saltpetre was used as a substitute for salt and in the curing of meat.) Did some saltpetre or sulphur fall on the embers of a fire by accident, and revive them? Did someone then have the bright idea of mixing sulphur, charcoal and saltpetre as a way of giving a fire more oomph? Anyway, the mixture became known as 'black powder' or 'fire chemical'. Charcoal is the primary fuel, with the sulphur acting as the secondary fuel but also playing an important catalytic role by reducing the temperature at which the mixture ignites. The saltpetre releases oxygen, which allows the black powder to go on burning in a sealed container. But it is possible that the three substances were put together for a quite different reason, by alchemists searching for the 'elixir of life', which would bestow the gift of immortality. We know saltpetre was being included in elixirs from at least the second century AD, and that it was used to treat skin diseases. A book entitled *Classified Essentials of the Mysterious Tao of the True Origin of Things*, probably written about AD 850, listed more than thirty recipes for elixirs and warned of their dangers, noting that some alchemists heated up a brew that included sulphur, saltpetre and honey, 'so that their hands and faces have been burnt, and even the whole house where they were working burned down'.[5] Incidentally, gunpowder continued to be used as a medicine until at least the eighteenth century. In 1749 Britain's *Gentleman's Magazine* reported that a woman who had 'relapsed into a certain fever' took a 'remedy much in vogue among the soldiers' – gunpowder in brandy. This was 'quickly followed by her death'.[6]

The first use of gunpowder in war may have been by the Chinese at the great naval battle of Langshan Jiang in 919 during one of the country's many civil wars, while the first known written formulae for the mixture appeared in a Chinese military handbook in 1044 (though it may also have appeared in earlier works that have since been lost). It offered three versions, but not what is now regarded as the most effective proportions for the ingredients: 75 parts saltpetre to 15 parts charcoal and 10 parts sulphur. The highest amount of saltpetre found in any of the handbook's recipes was 50 per cent, and they included many other ingredients – eleven more in one and thirteen in another – including such things as oil, beeswax and pitch. This means they would burn quite happily without the gunpowder trio, and suggests they were incendiary rather than explosive. (Alchemists were not privy to the principles of modern chemistry, so their recipes often involved throwing in a bit of this and a bit of that, including ingredients such as human sperm.) As early as 975, Chinese soldiers may have been shooting fire arrows tipped with gunpowder, and soon there were reports of the mixture being wrapped in paper 'in a lump like a pomegranate' before being sealed with pine resin and attached to an arrow's shaft.[7] The archer lit a fuse just before firing. By then the Chinese were also flinging pots of gunpowder from catapults, and by 1083 they had developed an industry to produce weapons on a huge scale: one commander got a delivery of a quarter of a million gunpowder-tipped arrows. But these weapons were using the incendiary properties of gunpowder when they landed rather than exploiting its potential pyrotechnic power to propel them.

The Chinese tried to keep their discovery secret, but information leaked out. They claimed this happened through treachery. In 1126 Jurchen tribesmen from Manchuria captured the Chinese city of Kaifeng, and 'a certain Li' is said to have revealed gunpowder's mysteries to them. Even more formidable than the Jurchen were the Mongols, who, as they extended their conquests into the Middle East, recruited Arab and Muslim advisers to help them in their assault on China. By the late thirteenth century these advisers had taken knowledge of gunpowder back to their own countries, although as Islamic armies had been fighting against the Chinese since the mid-eighth century, it is possible they had already learned about the 'fire chemical'. In the end, black powder could not save China, and by 1279 the Mongols had conquered the whole country.

Europe may have originally acquired knowledge of gunpowder from Italian merchants. Soon after 1260, the Venetian Pietro Vilioni became the first of them to reach Mongol-ruled Iran, while the father and uncle of Marco Polo were in China the same decade. We know there were Mongol ambassadors in Genoa in 1269, although, according to Chinese tradition, it was a Mongol gunner who carried knowledge of the 'fire chemical' to the West. Around 1300 a manuscript appeared entitled *Liber Ignium ad Comburendos Hostes* or *The Book of Fires for Burning the Enemy*. Probably compiled by Jewish scholars in Spain, it detailed various recipes for gunpowder, including the obligatory odd ingredients such as ink and onion juice.

Away from the clash of arms, the Chinese discovered at some point that if they packed their bamboo firecrackers with black powder, they could get a bigger bang. In the city of Liuyang, the centre of China's

Eighteenth-century view of Marco Polo in Tartar costume.

fireworks industry today, stands a huge statue of a local monk named Li Tian, who is credited with inventing the artificial firecracker sometime from the seventh to the tenth century. He became revered for saving Hunan province from the floods and droughts that plagued it, because his gunpowder-boosted firecrackers were believed to scare off the evil spirits that caused them. Every year on 18 April, the Chinese offer sacrifices to his memory. In the thirteenth century, Europe heard from Marco Polo (some revisionist historians now question whether Polo himself ever went to China, and say he may just have been recycling other travellers' tales) about what he took to be the power of natural bamboo firecrackers, relating that if they were thrown on a campfire, 'they burn with such a dreadful noise that it can be heard for ten miles at night, and anyone who was not used to it could easily go into a swoon and even die.'[8] So, he said, people put cotton wool in their ears, while horses had to have their ears and eyes covered and all four feet fettered.

But some modern experts have questioned whether natural firecrackers could make such a din, and have suggested that Polo, or whoever told him the story, must have heard the bang from a bamboo stalk packed with black powder. By this time, the Chinese had also begun to make firecrackers by packing the mixture in paper tubes, which were often red, as the colour was thought particularly effective in deterring spirits. These firecrackers got a mention in 1267 from the English monk, scientist and philosopher Roger Bacon, who described a 'children's toy . . . no bigger than one's thumb' that gave out a sound 'exceeding the roar of strong thunder and a flash brighter than the most brilliant lightning', which could be found in 'diverse parts of the world'.[9] Bacon also wrote about gunpowder, but was often cryptic regarding the recipe.

Saltpetre, potassium nitrate, is formed as waste products containing nitrogen, such as urine, break down. The action of bacteria produces nitrate ions, made up of oxygen and nitrogen, which can combine with potassium occurring naturally in the environment. In parts of China and in India, the chemical was found in the soil, though the Chinese also scraped it from caves and walls. Those soaked in urine, such as in stables or latrines, were the most productive. The Chinese seem to have

Nineteenth-century depiction of a Roger Bacon experiment.

identified the chemical as distinct from other nitrates such as calcium as early as the fourth century BC, but finding enough, particularly enough that was sufficiently pure for gunpowder, involved a cumbersome process and soon became a headache. As with gunpowder, they tried to ban its export, but Muslim scientists had learned how to extract it and incorporate it into gunpowder by the late thirteenth century, calling it 'Chinese snow'.

In Europe's chillier countries, there was much less saltpetre in the soil, so the inhabitants were restricted to wall scrapings, and what they got often contained more nitrates of calcium (sometimes known as 'wall saltpetre') and magnesium than of potassium. These had the major disadvantage that they absorbed water easily, making any gunpowder that contained them ineffective. In 1378 the continent's first artificial bed for farming saltpetre was opened in Nuremberg, but just as in China, it involved a lengthy, painstaking process. Every 100 kilograms of earth might yield as little as 1 kilogram of saltpetre, though this was better than scrapings from walls and floors, where 100 kilograms normally boiled down to about 330 grams of the chemical. Farmers in particular were not keen on handing the raw material over to the authorities, as saltpetre represented a rare source of fertilizer, so all over Europe, governments would give their agents power to dig up ground or enter property to seize the precious stuff. In 1477 Louis XI of France authorized saltpetre commissioners to force entry into any building where they thought it might be found, and in 1625 Charles I of England would issue a proclamation preventing anyone from hindering any 'saltpetre-man' going about his 'necessary and important' business.

Meanwhile, gunpowder making was getting more sophisticated, with some limited economies of scale as gunpowder mills opened. The first we know of was at Augsburg in Germany in 1340. These were not real factories, more just a bringing together of individual craftsmen. Still, the price of the mixture fell by half in Europe between 1380 and 1420. England's first gunpowder mill would open at Rotherhithe in 1555. For gunpowder to work, the three key components have to be pulverized so they can be thoroughly mixed, and in fifteenth-century Europe an important advance was made. Traditionally, the sulphur, charcoal and saltpetre had been ground separately before being mixed together and then ground again for several hours, but in a new process called 'corning', water was added during the final stages of mixing the ingredients to make a paste. This was then forced through a sieve, creating granules that were left to dry. These granules produced a bigger explosion, though if they got too big, performance seemed to fall away.

Greek Fire

There used to be a theory that long before gunpowder appeared, the Greeks must have latched on to the secrets of pyrotechnics, the evidence being their weapon 'Greek fire', which could burn while floating on water. The Byzantine Empire deployed it in naval battles from the 670s as they defended their territory against the growing threat from the Arabs. It was invented by a Jewish architect named Kallinikos, who had fled from Syria. 'Greek fire' achieved an almost mythical status because its recipe was kept a state secret, and has remained a mystery to this day. Some have suggested there might have been several versions. Ejected through tubes or siphons under pressure, it probably included pitch, sulphur, naphtha, a highly volatile petroleum, and perhaps quicklime. It used to be thought that it also contained gunpowder or saltpetre, but this idea is now generally rejected. The concoction could not be put out with water, and had to be extinguished with sand or a mild acid, such as urine or vinegar. It played a decisive role in the Battle of Cyzicus against a Saracen fleet off Constantinople in 673, but it could not prevent the gradual withering away of the empire until Constantinople itself fell in the fifteenth century. It may be that both the Byzantines and their enemies tended to exaggerate its effectiveness. The Arabs adopted a similar weapon and it was probably from them that the Chinese acquired enough knowledge to develop their own version, known as 'fierce fire oil'.

Chinese Fireworks Get More Exciting

In China, gunpowder added noise to firecrackers, but what about the visual element of fireworks? We know the Chinese were already using smoke in warfare, for concealment or as a weapon, with irritants such as mustard added, four centuries before Christ. By the time of the Han dynasty, it looks as though they were also able to colour the smoke. The ancient Chinese name for fireworks, *yen huo*, actually means 'smoke-fires'. As early as the fifth century AD, there were stories of a monk in Nanking curing people's disabilities by generating fire that was 'redder than ordinary fire and also more ethereal', leading to theories that he had stumbled on some natural ore of strontium, compounds of which are still used today to colour fireworks red.[10] It is believed that by the seventh century the Chinese were using iron filings to create silvery spangles in smoke.

Early in the twelfth century, Emperor Huizong went to see a great entertainment put on by the army. A contemporary account recorded: 'Suddenly a noise like thunder was heard, the setting off of exploding crackers, and then the fireworks began.' Dancers in strange costumes moved through clouds of coloured smoke during a series of acts with names like 'the dancing judge of the ghosts', and each change was punctuated by the noise of firecrackers.[11] By around this time, the emperor's subjects could buy fireworks from street sellers, who did a roaring trade thanks to Li Tian's famed success in driving out the evil spirits of Hunan. Pyrotechnics were soon in great demand for weddings, celebrations of births, funerals and festivals such as New Year, and there was

Modern Chinese statue of Li Tian.

new technology. Someone worked out how to twist paper into a long string, making a fuse, which you could light, instead of having to throw a firecracker onto a fire. Then came the idea of blocking off one end of the tube, which made the firecracker race off in all directions, spouting flames and sparks and behaving a bit like a rocket on the ground, what would become known in England as a rip-rap. In China, they were 'ground rats', and were also used in war to confuse enemy soldiers and terrify horses. The Chinese developed a weapon called a 'water melon bomb', which would release up to sixty ground rats when it exploded.

By all accounts, Huizong was delighted by his early twelfth-century firework display, but in 1264 the empress dowager Gong Sheng was not amused by a show held in her honour by Emperor Lizong. According to an account written about 25 years later, a firework 'of the "ground rat" type, went straight to the steps of the throne of the Empress-Mother, and gave her quite a fright. She stood up in anger, gathered her skirts around her, and stopped the feast.' The emperor was very worried and arrested the officials responsible for organizing the event. At dawn the next day he went to apologize to his mother, but she said: 'Probably it was an unintentional mistake, and it can be forgiven,' although according to other versions, the great lady was less philosophical, and ground rats were banned at court.[12]

In addition to basic firecrackers, ground rats and rockets, an account of life in Hangchow about 1150 reported that there were now firecrackers 'in the shape of fruits or men or other things, and between them there were fuses so arranged that when you lit one it set off hundreds of others, some were like . . . comets, others again shooting along the surface of the water, or flying like kites'.[13] The Chinese also developed wheels that span and standing fountains that would throw out showers of sparks. (Modern fountains are cones or cylinders with nozzles from which sparks are ejected up to 6 metres into the air, a bit like a volcano erupting. Conical fountains usually produce the same effect right through their performance, while cylinders often contain a number of fountains fused to go off one after another, so the effects change. More recently, fountains have started to appear with novelty features, such as smiley faces that light up on the case. Some just give out coloured smoke and are used in the daytime.) Different kinds of fireworks – fountains, firecrackers, rockets – were put into a very popular device known as the 'dragon', a big wooden framework covered in paper scales, which seemed to breathe fire as the fireworks shot from its mouth. A fifteenth-century

Modern fountain, 2012.

poem talks about a 'pear-tube', something like a Roman candle, which shot out sparks of different colours forming a shape like the flowers of pear-trees. At the end of the sixteenth century in Fukien province, the scholar Feng Ying Ching described 'a single bomb', from which 'there burst forth all sorts of sparks and flowers, ground rats, "water rats" etc. Hundreds of them are strung together inside one tube and come out at the same time. One man holds [the fuse] and sets them all off, which is a very wonderful technique.'[14]

Rockets Take Off

The principle of the rocket is fairly simple. You compact pyrotechnic mixture in a tube and close the top, but leave an opening at the bottom, and the force exerted on the closed end will keep pushing it away from the open end so the rocket ascends into the sky, with the stick guiding it. A Chinese official named Wan-Hu decided they were his passport to space, so he sat in a chair equipped with two kites and powered by 47 rockets. Then 47 assistants lit the 47 fuses and retired smartly. There was a huge explosion, and when the smoke cleared there was no sign of the chair or Wan-Hu. With the exploit being dated at anything between 2000 BC and AD 1500, and Wan-Hu's name apparently translating to something like 'crazy fox', it seems reasonable to wonder whether this episode belongs more to the realm of legend than history, but the intrepid bureaucrat did get a crater on the moon named after him.

As we saw, eleventh-century recipes for gunpowder included less saltpetre than modern ones, but these low-saltpetre or low-nitrate versions, though less powerful, had their uses, notably in rockets, which would have had their cases blown apart by the full-blooded mixture. It is difficult to be sure when the Chinese first started using rockets, because the same word, *huo chien*, was sometimes used to mean a fire arrow, where propulsion was provided fully or partly by the bow string. Some believe genuine rockets made their first appearance on a battlefield in 1206 when the Jurchen were besieging Hsiangyang, with the Chinese defenders firing bamboo sticks about 1.2 metres long. Each was powered by a thick paper tube filled with gunpowder bound to the bamboo near the top of the stick, where there was an iron or steel arrowhead smeared with poison. It is said that in 1232 rocket barrages repeatedly drove back attacks on the city of Kaifeng by Mongol cavalry, though Kaifeng fell the following year. The Chinese discovered that a rocket could fly further if they attached a small iron weight to the end of the stick, and that the gunpowder would burn more evenly if they made a cavity through the middle. By around 1250, rockets were capable of travelling about 500 metres. The fuel was given the name of 'flying gunpowder'. Its exact recipe is not known, but it would have to have been about 60 per cent saltpetre to reach the happy medium of providing sufficient power without blowing the tube to bits.

As so often happens in human history, war was the great spur for innovation. The Chinese developed a weapon known as the 'fire-lance', a firework around 50 or 60 centimetres long compared by some to a big Roman candle. Attached to the end of a pole held by a soldier, it created a primitive flamethrower, hurling fire for about five minutes into the face of the enemy. Sometimes the Chinese replaced the head of an arrow with a fire-lance, lit by a fuse and timed to ignite when it was above their adversaries. They also experimented with different arrow shapes to find the most aerodynamic, adding wings or a wooden body shaped like a bird. By the mid-fourteenth century they had made multi-stage rockets. The main one carried a cluster of smaller ones, and as it was about to burn out, a series of fuses automatically ignited the smaller rockets, sending them off in a swarm.

The problem with rockets, which was to bedevil them in the military arena for centuries, was their inaccuracy. They could go haywire if the gunpowder was mixed in slightly wrong proportions, or was packed unevenly, or if the shape of the tube was not quite right. To try to overcome this drawback, the Chinese used multiple launchers made of wood, bamboo or basketry that could hold up to two hundred rockets, each in its own compartment, and fire them in one go, in the hope that some at least would find their target.

Rockets also seem to have appeared in Europe by the thirteenth century. After being on the receiving end against the Chinese, the Mongols had developed their own version. Some believe they used them at the Battle of Legnica in Poland in 1241, in which they heavily defeated a European army. The Moors are supposed to have fired them on the Iberian peninsula by the end of that decade, while the Europeans themselves were deploying them before the close of the next century, as they made an appearance during the war between the Genoese and the Venetians in 1380. Rockets were also used by the French in the latter stages of the Hundred Years War against England, and gunpowder found its way to Korea where by 1388 soldiers were using rockets or *singijeons*.

Hwacha (firecart) capable of dispatching a hundred fire arrows.

The biggest were 50 centimetres long and would be fired from hand-held guns. The Koreans also shot rockets or fire arrows from a *hwacha* (fire-cart), a two-wheeled conveyance carrying a box similar to the Chinese multiple launcher. It was used against invaders from Japan in the last decade of the sixteenth century.

During this time, guns were also advancing but, like rockets, they posed considerable technical problems. You needed an explosion powerful enough to fling out a projectile, but not so strong that it would shatter the barrel. There is some evidence that the Chinese had developed them by the early twelfth century, though the first known specimen dates back to 1288. Within the next half-century, China was making them on a considerable scale, from hand weapons to cannons, and by 1324 they had reached Europe. The Moors used cannons in Spain, while the first mention of them being deployed by Europeans comes in 1326, when the government of Florence ordered the making of iron shot for cannons. Later, guns were used by the French during a raid on Southampton in 1338 at the start of the Hundred Years War.

India's Early Fireworks

Gunpowder seems to have been known in India, with which China had a long trading history, from around the mid-thirteenth century, while rockets were probably being used in war there by the mid-fifteenth. Certainly the Mughal emperor Akbar the Great ordered 16,000 for a siege in 1572. By then fireworks had long been providing entertainment. It is said that 3,000 cartloads were set off to welcome an envoy of the Mongol emperor to Delhi in 1258. Some historians argue that soon royal courts across the country were being treated to complex and sophisticated displays. We know that in 1443 fireworks were used at the Mahanavami festival, which celebrates the triumph of good over evil, at the court of the Vijayanagar king in southern India. The ambassador of the great Central Asian Timurid Empire described 'all the various kinds of pyrotechny and squibs . . . which were exhibited'.[15] (Squibs, sometimes called serpents or fizgigs, produced a hissing sound followed by a bang, a quick, bright burst of flame and a powerful smell from the detonation of the gunpowder. They flew off in unpredictable directions, rather like rockets that did not have sticks to give them stability.) A few decades later, the Italian traveller Ludovico di Varthema, visiting Vijayanagara, noted that its elephants were prone to stampede because 'this race of people are great masters of making fireworks and these animals have a great dread of fire.'[16] (Varthema also said that by the first decade of the sixteenth century, there were 'excellent masters of the art of making fireworks' on the Indonesian island of Sumatra.)

Sanskrit formulae for fireworks appeared in the early sixteenth century, sometimes including exotic items like cows' urine, and there is evidence of pyrotechnics featuring at the dedications of temples as well as at weddings and other festive occasions. Duarte Barbosa, brother-in-law of the great Portuguese explorer Magellan, described a wedding in Gujarat in about 1518 where the bride and bridegroom were entertained with 'firing of bombs and rockets in plenty'. Around 1609 the Sultan of Bijapur gave 80,000 rupees for fireworks as part of a lavish dowry for the marriage of a courtier's daughter. Meanwhile, they had also been used for propaganda, with Akbar the Great, when he was only thirteen, creating an effigy of one of his enemies, filling it with fireworks and then setting it alight. In 1633 an English traveller named Peter Mundy described a great display featuring huge puppets shaped like 'great elephants, whose bellies were full of squibs, crackers, etc., giants with wheels in their hands then a rank of monsters, then of turrets, then of artificial trees and other inventions, all full of rockets'.[17]

Fireworks Come to Europe

The puzzle of how pyrotechnics came to Europe is shrouded in as much historical smoke as the questions of who invented them and who invented gunpowder. We know Roger Bacon encountered a basic firework in the mid-thirteenth century, while some have asserted that Marco Polo brought examples back from China in 1295, if, of course, he ever went to China. Certainly the Italians seemed to take the lead. They are generally credited with inventing exploding shells, which appear to have first been used by the Venetians in a battle in 1376, though some argue the Chinese may have started firing cast-iron shells filled with gunpowder around the same time. Either way, shells would develop into the mainstay of modern pyrotechnic displays. The Italians also experimented with slower-burning explosive mixtures that produced showers of radiant sparks and used them to create the forerunners of many modern fireworks, such as sparklers. We also owe the word 'rocket' to the Italians, who in the late fourteenth century started describing fire arrows propelled by gunpowder as *rochetta*. Perhaps the first recorded firework display in Europe was at Vicenza in 1379. Outside the bishop's palace during a Pentecostal mystery play, 'there was a flash and a loud thunderclap.' Then a model dove representing the Holy Spirit flew down a string emitting sparks: 'Almost all fell to the ground in terror and amazement, beseeching God in hymns and chants that the promised Holy Spirit should descend upon them according to the prophecies.' Churches had always been places of spectacle, with pictures of angels, demons and the fiery mouth of hell. Fireworks added a fresh dimension. By the fifteenth century Italy had a number of pyrotechnic schools training experts, and an eyewitness described fireworks enlivening a celebration of the Annunciation in Florence in 1439 with 'a noise of uninterrupted thunder . . . rising up again in flames and rebounding once more, so that the whole church was filled with sparks'.[18]

What sounds like an even more elaborate display is described by Vanuzzio Biringuccio, who was for a time director of the pope's arsenal, in his book *Pirotechnia* (1540). The 'ingenious and beautiful' event, held in Florence and Siena every year on the feasts of St John and of Our Lady of the Assumption, featured great wooden and papier-mâché wheels covered in painted human and animal figures filled with rockets, squibs and crackers that were raised over the town square on ropes.[19] As the wheel, or girandola, span on top of a pole, fireworks linked by fuses went off, making it similar to a horizontal Catherine wheel. Sparks flew in all directions, and spectators had to watch out. Later, rockets were added to a girandola so it climbed into the air like a flying saucer. The Spanish have their own version of the girandola, known as *una corona de subir y bajar* – a rising and falling crown. This is also a wheel that soars into the sky, whirling and throwing out sparks. It falls, then rises again as though attached to a giant rubber band. (The traditional Catherine wheel was a spiral tube filled with pyrotechnic powder that was nailed to a post, and then span when the powder was lit. It was named after St Catherine of Alexandria, a fourth-century Christian martyr sentenced by the Roman emperor Maxentius to be broken on the wheel. Legend has it that angels broke the wheel, so Maxentius had her beheaded instead. More recent versions are made of plastic and fitted with pyrotechnic driver tubes that set the wheel spinning while it flings out sparks, sometimes whistling or screeching. There are smaller types called 'pinwheels', while more elaborate ones are made by attaching fireworks to a piece of wood between 1.2 and 1.5 metres long, so that when it spins, it creates coloured wheels of fire.)

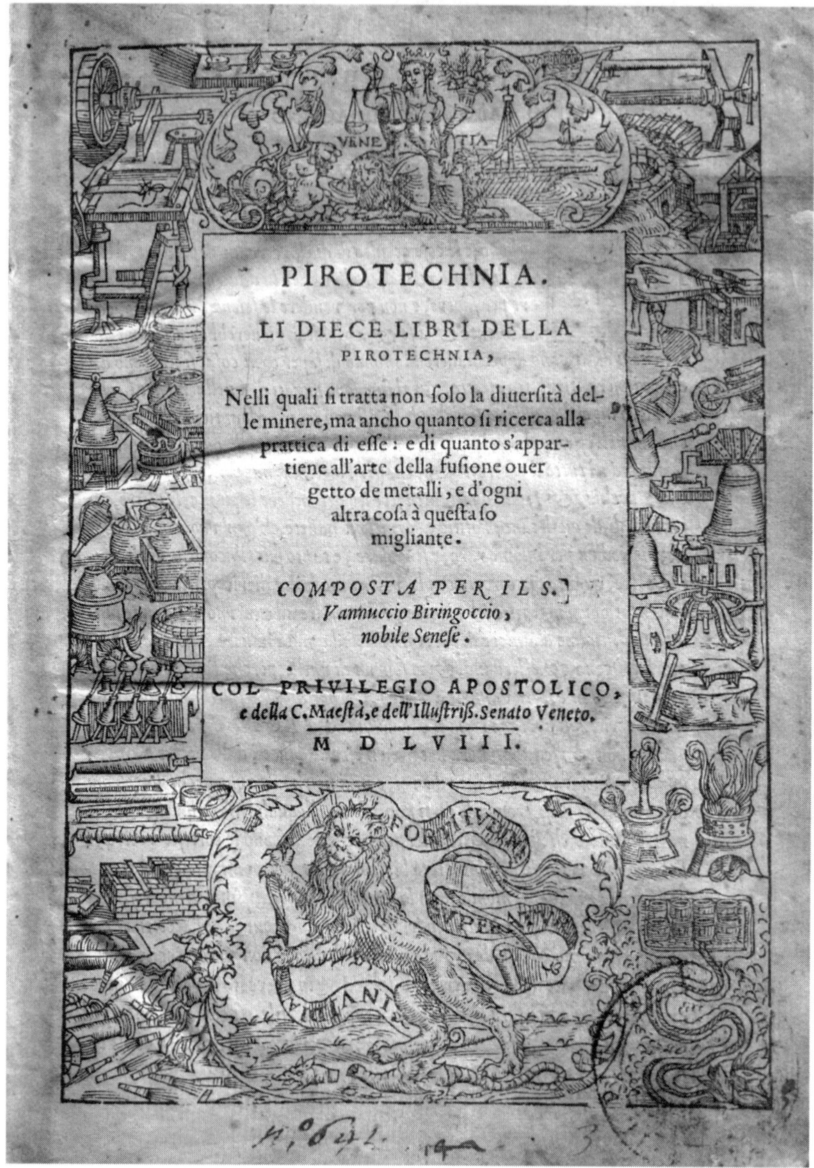

PIROTECHNIA.

LI DIECE LIBRI DELLA PIROTECHNIA,

Nelli quali ſi tratta non ſolo la diuerſità delle minere, ma ancho quanto ſi ricerca alla prattica di eſſe: e di quanto s'appartiene all'arte della fuſione ouer getto de metalli, e d'ogni altra coſa à queſta ſomigliante.

COMPOSTA PER IL S. Vannuccio Biringoccio, nobile Seneſe.

COL PRIVILEGIO APOSTOLICO, e della C. Maeſtà, e dell'Illuſtriſs. Senato Veneto.

M D L V I I I.

Edition of Biringuccio's *Pirotechnia*, 1558.

Confusingly, the name *girandola* was also applied to the finale of a spectacular event in Rome. Firework displays in the Eternal City are first mentioned in a diary in 1410, while from 1471, every June the papacy sponsored festivals at the ancient Castel Sant'Angelo fortress on the Tiber on the eve of the Feast of Saints Peter and Paul, and whenever a new pope was elected. Michelangelo was supposed to have designed some of these events. By Biringuccio's time, they had become an awesome demonstration of papal power and perhaps the most famous pyrotechnic spectacle in Europe. First the castle walls were lit with row upon row of lanterns and candles 'as far as the eye can reach'. Then a gun was fired, and up shot fireballs that were 'like stars, finally bursting', while the climax was a great volley of rockets, so in the end, 'nothing can be seen but smoke and fire,' and it was like 'the fire imagined in hell'. One of the earliest engravings of the scene by Giovanni Ambrogio Brambilla in 1579 shows crowds of mainly male spectators. He wrote: 'it seems as if the whole city is on fire,' and that when the rockets 'burst in the air in the shapes of stars it appears as if the sky has opened'. During the finale, it felt 'as if all the air in the world is filled with fireworks, and all the stars in the heavens are falling to earth – a thing truly stupendous, and marvellous to behold'.[20]

This would have been powerfully symbolic because at the end of the Bible, in the Book of Revelation, when 'the stars of heaven fell unto the earth,' it was one of the signs of the Second Coming of Christ. Recipes for pyrotechnic 'stars' began to appear in the sixteenth century. They were sent up in the caps at the top of rockets, and when the rocket reached its highest point, a small charge would burst the cap open and throw out the stars, which would fall as if from heaven. (Stars are small pellets of pyrotechnic mixture about 3 or 4 centimetres across, held together by

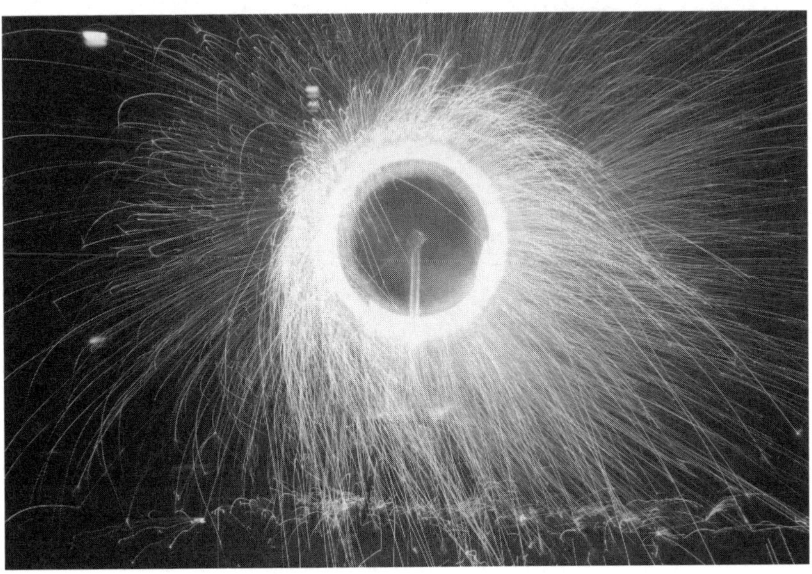

Catherine wheel in the Netherlands, 2014.

a binding, such as dextrin, which also acts as a fuel. In Roman candles, which stand on the ground, there are alternate layers of compacted gunpowder and single stars, so the stars come out one at a time, rising to a height of up to 15 metres, and often produce different effects. Sometimes sawdust is used to separate the stars, which are lit by a fuse running down the inside of the case.) These rockets were perhaps the first fireworks developed purely as spectacle, earlier ones having been festive versions of military fireworks. The link between fireworks and stars gained added significance because this was an age when astrology was highly influential.

Giovanni Ambrogio Brambilla,
The Girandola at the Castel Sant'Angelo, Rome, 1579, etching.

Scoppio del Carro, or 'explosion of the cart', Florence, 2019.

One pyrotechnician drew up a calendar of propitious times for making fireworks.

The Castel Sant'Angelo continued to work its magic, with another observer in 1664 writing that the scores of rockets, all launched at the same time, 'resemble, by their quantity, velocity, and murmuring, a swarm of bees driven from their hive ... Scattered across the sky, they are transformed into shining gold flames resembling a great vase of gilded flowers ... finally falling to earth like the purest stars.'[21] Even the normally restrained neoclassical architect Robert Adam would be bowled over in 1755, gushing: 'It exceeded for beauty, invention, and grandeur anything I had ever seen or indeed could conceive.' He compared the multiple rockets to 'a wheatsheaf in the air, each one of which gives a crack and sends out a dozen burning balls like stars'. Adam said they seemed to spread across the landscape for a mile, as 'crowds of people, coaches and horses swarmed on all sides.'[22] In 1818 the English travel writer Charlotte Ann Eaton considered the display was part of 'one of the most brilliant spectacles in the world', opening with a 'tremendous explosion that represented the raging eruption of a volcano. Red sheets of fire seemed to blaze upwards into the glowing heavens, and then to pour down their liquid streams upon the earth.' This was followed by 'every varied device that imagination could figure' so that 'the reflection in the depth of the calm clear waters of the Tiber was scarcely less beautiful than the spectacle itself, and the whole ended in a tremendous burst of fire, that, while it lasted, almost seemed to threaten conflagration to the world.'[23] In the 1880s the girandola would be banned as too dangerous, only to be revived this century in a new location with stricter safety standards.

Another famous Italian firework festival is the Scoppio del Carro, or 'explosion of the cart', which still happens every Easter in Florence and has become a big tourist attraction. Its origins lay in 1099 when the Crusaders took Jerusalem, and a Florentine soldier was said to have been the first man to raise a Christian banner above the city. Sometime between 1513 and 1521 pyrotechnics were incorporated into the proceedings, and, just as at Vicenza, a dove featured. Nowadays oxen crowned with flowers pull a cart carrying a pagoda full of fireworks into the square outside the cathedral. (The cart in use today dates from the eighteenth century.) A wire is stretched from the cart into the building, and after Mass, the archbishop lights a line rocket inside a model dove, which flies down the wire out of the cathedral into the cart and sets off the fireworks. The air fills with bangs, sparks and smoke, while a pinwheel twirls on the top of the cart. Legend has it that if everything works like clockwork, it is a good omen for the coming year. If something goes wrong, a bad harvest and other misfortunes can be expected. It is said that pyrotechnicians who failed to deliver were sometimes put to death, or at the very least had their fee withheld. So, understandably, they sometimes hedged their bets. A witness to the ceremony in the early twentieth century said the dove exploded halfway through its journey but the fireworks went off anyway, because an electrical fuse had been secreted in the cart as insurance. Line rockets would become a favourite method of ignition.

In the Middle Ages, Italy was divided into lots of separate independent states, giving it a plethora of royal courts, and by the late fifteenth century many were putting on private firework displays. From the 1480s the Este family in Ferrara used pyrotechnics to enhance mystery plays and comedies, and gradually the fireworks became an attraction in their own right, with crowds of rich and poor turning out to enjoy them as a climax to church festivals or courtly pageants. In 1569 a tournament by the moat of Este Castle provided a location for '*girandolas* spinning with frequent bangs and roars' and 'endless multicoloured flames flickering through the air, creating strange shapes so that the whole sky was alight'. The audience considered it 'wonderful to see so many different fireworks', and the prestige of the prince was no doubt suitably enhanced.[24] In addition to Michelangelo, some of Italy's and the world's greatest artists were involved with displays in this era. According to his biographer Vasari, Leonardo da Vinci created a great lion that would walk a few steps, then roar, at which point a flurry of birds and flowers would burst out of its chest in an effect created largely by fireworks. Vasari maintained this work ranked 'with any of the great accomplishments by this Master Artist'.[25]

Until the nineteenth century Germany too was a collection of small states, loosely ruled by the Holy Roman Emperor, and it also became a hotbed of firework activity. The first recorded display was in 1506 when 350 rockets were let off from a barge on Lake Constance in honour of

Etching by Lorenz Müller from 1635 showing a fireworks display in Nuremberg.

Emperor Maximilian I – confirmation perhaps that the Germans, like the Romans with their Castel Sant'Angelo displays, had spotted how reflections in water could enhance fireworks. A German favourite also seen in Italy was the mock battle – often a celebration of some real victory. These might be naval tussles on water, or they might feature soldiers running about on a stage or in a field hurling rockets and fireballs. Real or mock castles were often used as backdrops. Nuremberg was the headquarters of arms manufacturing for the emperor, and soon became an important centre for fireworks, with a display, for example, held in 1535 to celebrate Charles V's capture of Tunis from the Turks. A contemporary woodcut shows rockets flying in all directions.

By then, Europe was assembling a shelf-full of instructional firework books. *The Book of Fires for Burning the Enemy* may have been compiled by scholars, but most of these early works were by military men. The German *Feuerwerchbuch* (*c.* 1420) was written by an anonymous gunner and concentrated on military pyrotechnics, as did one of its successors, the *Buch von den probierten Künsten* (*c.* 1530), literally *Book of the Arts Practised*, written by Franz Helm of Cologne, who had fought with Charles V's artillery, though he also included some recipes that could be used for peaceful fireworks. Around the same time, Biringuccio observed that fireworks were expensive and 'endured no longer than the kiss of a lover for his lady, if as long . . . and thus should be reserved only for very special occasions of rejoicing'.[26] A burgeoning fireworks literature there may have been, but it did not give away too many trade secrets, and recipes were jealously guarded. Many practitioners preferred never to write them down, instead committing them to memory to be passed down the generations by word of mouth. It made sense to protect these secrets for commercial advantage or even national security, but there was another motive. Some spectators were terrified because fireworks were a phenomenon they could not understand, so they provided a way of maintaining the superiority of those in the know over the poor benighted masses. In his twenty-volume survey of scientific knowledge, *Natural Magic* (1589), the Neapolitan scholar Giambattista della Porta wrote of pyrotechnics: 'there is nothing in the world that more frights and terrifies the minds of men.'[27] He added: 'If you would have your works appear more wonderful, you must not let the cause be known.'[28] Not surprisingly, fireworks became part of the repertoire of many magicians.

One possible indication of pyrotechnics' growing popularity is the way writers began to compare natural phenomena to them. We have seen how they were used to mimic stars, and by the late sixteenth century they were being enlisted to imitate other celestial wonders. The great German astronomer Johannes Kepler likened comets and meteors to them, while in *A goodly gallery with a most pleasant prospect, into the garden of natural contemplation, to behold the natural causes of all kind of meteors* (that is only the first section of the title), the English Puritan theologian William Fulke wrote that those seen in the sky over London in 1560 were 'like squibs that are cast into the air, saving that they move more swiftly than any squibs'.[29] The mystery and awe surrounding fireworks would have been enhanced by the fact that comets, meteors and other astronomical marvels were often seen as portents of great events.

Early Fireworks in England

The first tentative record we have of a firework display in England is at the coronation of Henry VII's wife, Elizabeth of York, in 1487. This was a very important occasion because it was designed to mark the end of the enmities of the Wars of the Roses, after which the victorious Lancastrian king Henry VII (founder of the Tudor dynasty) married his Yorkist bride. The grand celebration involved the Lord Mayor of London's procession of barges, at the head of which was one 'garnished and apparelled above all others [that] carried a dragon spouting flames'.[30] In those days, dragons had powerful associations. They could be seen as symbols of sin or even of Satan himself. So if a ruler could be associated with the idea of overcoming this dreadful creature, that burnished his image as someone who could defeat evil and the foes of Christianity. And, of course, a fire-breathing dragon provided a perfect vehicle for pyrotechnics. They were featured on the tops of castles, emerging from caves, fighting with other creatures or sailing through the air. The airborne effect was achieved by flying dragon figures full of pyrotechnic mixture on wooden frames like kites, or using line rockets to power them back and forth on ropes stretched between high points as flames belched from them. In 1520 Henry VII's son and successor Henry VIII tried, unsuccessfully, to make a lasting peace with the French king Francis I by putting on a hyper-lavish celebration at the Field of the Cloth of Gold near Calais. Included in the eighteen days of feasts, tournaments, masquerades and religious services was the 'appearance in the air of a great salamander or dragon, artificially constructed; it was four fathoms [7.3 metres] long, and seemed to be filled with fire . . . Many were greatly

Nineteenth-century portrayal of 'Green Men' from Joseph Strutt's *The Sports and Pastimes of the People of England* (1801).

frightened thereby, thinking that it must be a comet or some monster or portent, as nothing could be seen to support it.'[31]

Royal occasions did not come much bigger than Anne Boleyn's coronation in 1533. Henry VIII had been courting her desperately for years as he tried to extricate himself from his marriage to Catherine of Aragon, removing England from the Roman Catholic Church in the process. In three years, it would all end in tears – for Anne at least, as Henry had her beheaded – but for the coronation, no expense was spared. The festivities went on for four days, and featured a no-doubt popular fountain that dispensed free wine to all-comers. As with Elizabeth of York, there was an aquatic procession, including a great red pyrotechnic dragon as well as 'terrible monstrous wild men casting fire and making a hideous noise'.[32] This is the first reference to important figures in the development of fireworks in England: 'wild men', later known as 'Green Men'. Two would feature in a procession to Chester Races on St George's Day in 1610, clad in 'green ivy . . . with black hair and black beads, very ugly to behold, and garlands upon their heads, with great clubs in their hands, with fireworks to scatter'.[33]

Contemporary illustrations show Green Men carrying 'fire clubs' that spill out sparks as they advertise firework displays or clear a path for processions. They were also said to have performed as jesters during the inevitable longueurs during a show while fireworks were being prepared. It was a job that carried plenty of opportunities for getting injured or even killed when pyrotechnics went wrong. The Green Man became an important feature of the pageant whenever the Lord Mayor of London went on the water, and two characters in George Whetstone's play *The History of Promos and Cassandra* (1578), a tale of urban lowlife, appear 'apparelled like green men at the mayor's feast with clubs of fireworks'.[34] The Pyrotechnics Guild International still uses a green man as its logo, and members say 'Stay green' to each other. There are claims that the traditional English 'Green Man' pub sign pays homage to these harbingers of fireworks, but others believe the hostelries are honouring an ancient fertility symbol.

In Henry VIII's time, most fireworks were set off during daylight hours, and at some point, probably in the early 1540s, the king brought over two Dutchmen to help with firing them from mortars, suggesting England was lagging behind continental countries. Mortars, which had probably first been deployed in war in the early fifteenth century, are still widely used in firework displays. The Dutch duo came from the realms of the Emperor Charles V, then the most powerful man in the world, whose domains, in addition to the Netherlands, included Spain, Austria, much of Italy and the Spanish Empire of the Americas. By the 1530s he had recruited into his forces 'fire-workers', who applied pyrotechnic technology to war. It is likely they were also in charge of fireworks at victory celebrations, confirming the relationship between pyrotechnics and the military that would last for centuries. Another hint that the Europeans had the lead around this time comes from the sixteenth-century Scottish chronicler Robert Lindsay, who described the festivities at King James v of Scotland's marriage to Madeleine de Valois, the French king's daughter, in Paris in 1537. Although the use of fireworks in Scotland had been first mentioned in 1507 when 'fireballs' featured in a royal tournament at Edinburgh Castle, James v appeared mightily impressed by the work of 'profound necromancers' who could conjure up 'fowls flying in the air spouting fire'.[35] Perhaps this was what motivated the king to stump up the then substantial sum of £57 6*s* 1*d* (about £25,000 at today's prices) for fireworks to celebrate his marriage to his second wife, Mary of Guise, in 1540. (Madeleine had died of tuberculosis while still in her teens.)

Fireworks got a big boost in England when the daughter of Henry viii and Anne Boleyn, Elizabeth i, became queen. She loved them, and would create the post of 'Fire Master of England', what we would probably now call the 'Fireworks Tsar'. In his exhaustive survey *The Sports and Pastimes of the People of England from the Earliest Period* (1801), the antiquary Joseph Strutt wrote that fireworks were 'little spoken of prior to the reign of Elizabeth, and seem to have been of a very trifling nature'.[36] The Virgin Queen's first encounter with pyrotechnics probably came when she visited Warwick Castle in August 1572. Ambrose Dudley, Earl of Warwick and Master-General of the Ordnance, put on a big display by the River Avon, erecting two canvas forts and recruiting a cast of two hundred or more for a mock siege with fireworks. According to a contemporary account, 'The wild fire falling into the river Avon would for a time lie still and then again rise and fly abroad, casting many flashes and flames, whereat the Queen's Majesty took great pleasure.' But for less distinguished spectators, who 'understood it not', it was 'strange' or even 'terrifying'; particularly, presumably, the climax. One of the forts fell when 'a dragon flying casting out huge flames and squibs' ignited it, but then unfortunately 'a ball' hit a nearby house, setting it ablaze. A certain Henry Cooper lived there, and he and his wife were burned to death in their bed. 'Another house or two adjoining' were also set alight, and according to our contemporary informant, it was a wonder the damage was no worse, because 'the fire balls and squibs' flew right over the castle and 'into the midst of the town to the great peril and fear of the inhabitants'.[37] Elizabeth organized a whip-round that raised £25 for those whose houses had been burned down.

In July 1575 the queen attended an even bigger display. She was the guest of the Earl of Warwick's younger brother, Robert Dudley, Earl of Leicester, at Kenilworth Castle. Leicester was her closest confidant and a long-time suitor, and the twelve-day extravaganza featured dancing, hunting, bear-baiting and other delights. Elizabeth's arrival, we are told, was greeted by fireworks that could be seen 20 miles away, but Leicester's Italian pyrotechnics expert had been persuaded to drop his plan to fire live cats and dogs into the air. There were two displays while the queen was present. A minor court official named Robert Laneham described one of them: 'a blaze of burning darts flying to and fro, beams of stars coruscant [brilliant], streams and hail of fire sparks, lightnings of wildfire on the water; and on the land, flight and shot of thunder-bolts', so that 'the heavens thundered, the waters surged and the earth shook; and for my part, hardy as I am, it made me vengeably afraid.'[38] Another eyewitness also remembered fireworks on the water: 'when all men thought they had been quenched, they would rise and mount out of the water again and burn furiously until they were utterly consumed.'[39] (Water fireworks could simply be buoyed up with blocks of wood or papier-mâché bowls. More elaborate effects involved 'skimmers', stickless rockets that would skim the surface of the water, sometimes diving beneath.) The event was seen by some as Leicester's final bid for the queen's hand. If so, however much the fireworks delighted her, it failed. He went on to marry someone else, and she, as we all know, never married at all.

Another fireworks display Elizabeth attended sixteen years after her visit to Kenilworth demonstrates, according to some, that the pyrotechnic arts in England had progressed during the interval. This time she was a guest of the Earl of Hertford at Elvetham in Hampshire. The high jinks lasted for a mere four days, but for the occasion, the earl had created an artificial pond with three islands, including a fort, a 'Ship Isle' and a snail-mount that could turn into a flaming monster. A banquet accompanied the fireworks display, while

> a castle of fireworks of all sorts played in the Fort. Answerable to that, there was in the Snail-mount a globe of all manner of fireworks as big as a barrel. When these were spent on either side, there were many running rockets on lines, which passed between the Snail-mount and the castle in the Fort. On either side were many fire wheels, pikes of pleasure, and balls of wildfire which burned in the water.[40]

Contemporary engraving of the Gunpowder Plotters.
Fawkes is third from the right.

During Elizabeth's reign, England began to contribute to Europe's firework library. In 1562 Peter Whitehouse wrote a supplement for Machiavelli's *The Art of War* in which he discussed their military use, detailing, for example, how they could be attached to pikes, though William Bourne in his book *Inventions or Devices* (1578) declared he 'never knew any good service' done by fireworks as a weapon and that it was best to reserve them solely for pleasure, or for inspiring wonder.[41] Bourne explained how artificial birds could be made to 'fly by art . . . which the common people would marvel at, thinking that it is done by enchantment'.[42] Ten years later, Cyprian Lucar, who had translated three Italian volumes on gunnery, backed fireworks as weapons, which 'may be shot out of great pieces of artillery or thrown out of men's hands', but said they could have another military application: illumination. If they were fired from a mortar, they would 'give so great a light' that any members of the enemy skulking nearby would be revealed.[43] Lucar also described how they could be used in triumphs and celebrations.

Gunpowder, Treason and Plot

Early in the seventeenth century came the event that had perhaps more effect than any other on the history of fireworks in Britain. As we saw, Henry VIII discarded Roman Catholicism so he could discard his wife, Catherine of Aragon, but plenty of people in England were not prepared to jettison Roman Catholicism, and some were ready to die before they would abandon it. One such was Guy Fawkes, a Yorkshireman who had been fighting in the Spanish army against Protestant rebels in the Netherlands. In 1604 he was recruited by Robert Catesby, a member of the Catholic gentry and an incorrigible spinner of plots against the Crown, who had twice been imprisoned. His latest scheme was to blow up the Houses of Parliament at the state opening on 5 November 1605, killing the Protestant king James I, his queen and his eldest son, as well as MPs and peers. In the resulting chaos, a Catholic uprising was to restore the country to the true faith. The problem was that the explosion would kill not only Protestants but Catholics too, and one Catholic lord received an anonymous letter warning him to steer clear of Parliament on the appointed day. He showed it to the authorities, and late on 4 November 1605, they mounted a search of the cellars beneath the Palace of Westminster.

Guy Fawkes had the dangerous job of lighting the fuse for the explosion, and just before midnight the search party discovered him with 36 barrels of gunpowder hidden beneath piles of firewood. So it was Fawkes whose name would go down in history to be forever uttered in the same breath as 'Gunpowder Plot', and Fawkes whose effigy would be burned on bonfires. Incidentally, one firework company, Pains, still claims to have been the firm that sold Fawkes his gunpowder! Anyway, by the evening of 5 November, bonfires were being lit all over London to celebrate the failure of the conspiracy. Up in Staffordshire, Catesby still tried to foment rebellion, but was killed in a shoot-out with the king's forces. Eight of the conspirators, including Fawkes, were sentenced to death, but the Yorkshireman managed to jump from the ladder leading up to the scaffold and die instantly of a broken neck, so cheating the executioner, though his body was still quartered. There was such relief that king and country had been spared the dreadful fate Catesby's team had planned for them that less than three months after the event, Parliament passed an act decreeing annual thanksgivings across the nation every 5 November. It was not repealed until 1859.

2
From Guy Fawkes to an Explosion of Colour

James I's narrow escape from the Gunpowder Plot did not put him off fireworks. The following year, his brother-in-law, Christian IV of Denmark, came to London on a visit and, as a thank you for James's hospitality, he showcased the best of Danish fireworks for his host. At this time, Denmark was regarded as being way ahead of England in pyrotechnics. Christian's father, Frederick II, had been a great enthusiast. The first recorded display in Denmark had been put on in 1559 for his coronation, and he had a book on pyrotechnics specially printed for his son. Christian carried on the royal tradition, even making fireworks himself, and his coronation in 1596 had featured a dragon and 'a crocodile with gaping jaws' along with 16,000 fireworks and 300 rockets.[1] The London display was put on by the artillery masters of the Danish fleet. English spectators commented on its orderliness, noting that the fireworks 'very methodically ... continued burning and cracking for the space of three-quarters of an hour'.[2] The one downside was that it had to be put on in the early afternoon so the fleet could catch the tide for home, which meant the 'brightness of the sun ... dimmed the brightness' of the fireworks. Still, the display was impressive enough for James to ask Christian to leave one of his experts behind, and that Christmas, the king of England put on a show of his own 'contrived by a Dane, two Dutchmen' and others.[3]

James also mounted a major display on the Thames in 1613, watched by 'many thousands', to mark the marriage of his daughter Elizabeth to a German prince. Four fireworkers ran operations on barges, while on shore, William Hammond, the Master-Gunner of England, took charge of a 'most strange battle' between a firework dragon and a pyrotechnic St George on horseback, who, after a quarter of an hour, emerged victorious as the dragon roared and 'burst in pieces'. Next came rockets that flew so high, it appeared 'Art hath exceeded Nature.' After that, from 'a hill of earth' on the water, there emerged another firework like 'a hunted Harte', which raced along the river chased by 'hunting-hounds made of fire' just as if this was a real hunting scene on land.[4] Finally to round things off, there was a mock sea battle. By this time it was reckoned the English court might spend up to £1,000 on a display, approaching £250,000 in today's money, to pay for the fireworks themselves, as well as the scenery built and painted by numerous artisans and labourers. According to a *History of Colleges in and around London* (1611), the city had many 'men very skilful in the art of pyrotechny and fireworks'.[5] Even so, the assessment of Alan Brock of the great firework dynasty in *A History of Fireworks* (1949) was that except perhaps in terms of 'showmanship and theatrical invention', the 1613 display showed 'little real advance' on the one seen by Queen Elizabeth at Warwick forty years before.[6]

Rival Schools and Theories

By now, two schools of pyrotechnics had emerged in Europe: the Southern, dominated by the Italians, and the Northern, led by the Germans. Their fireworks were much the same, though some say the North was slightly ahead technically. The key differences were in presentation. As we saw, the big firework displays in Italy often celebrated saints' days or other religious festivals. Elaborate gilded architectural facades, transparent in parts, were erected and the fireworks let off inside them, creating apparently miraculous effects. Often beautifully constructed and more impressive than the pyrotechnics themselves, they might be embellished with allegorical figures, flowers, lamps and pictures. Known as 'temples' or 'machines', they were sometimes worked on by eminent artists such as the Italian sculptor and architect Gianlorenzo Bernini. The predominantly Protestant North, perhaps partly because of hostility to Roman Catholicism, took a different approach, shunning artifice to avoid giving any impression of the miraculous. In Nuremberg, Augsburg and Frankfurt, members of fireworkers' guilds would lay out their creations on the ground in orderly lines for other members to inspect before setting them off. Although structures such as mock castles or perhaps a giant Cupid for a wedding might be built from scaffolding, they were less elaborate and very much a supporting act for the pyrotechnics themselves. As the show was about to begin, the structure was swung open,

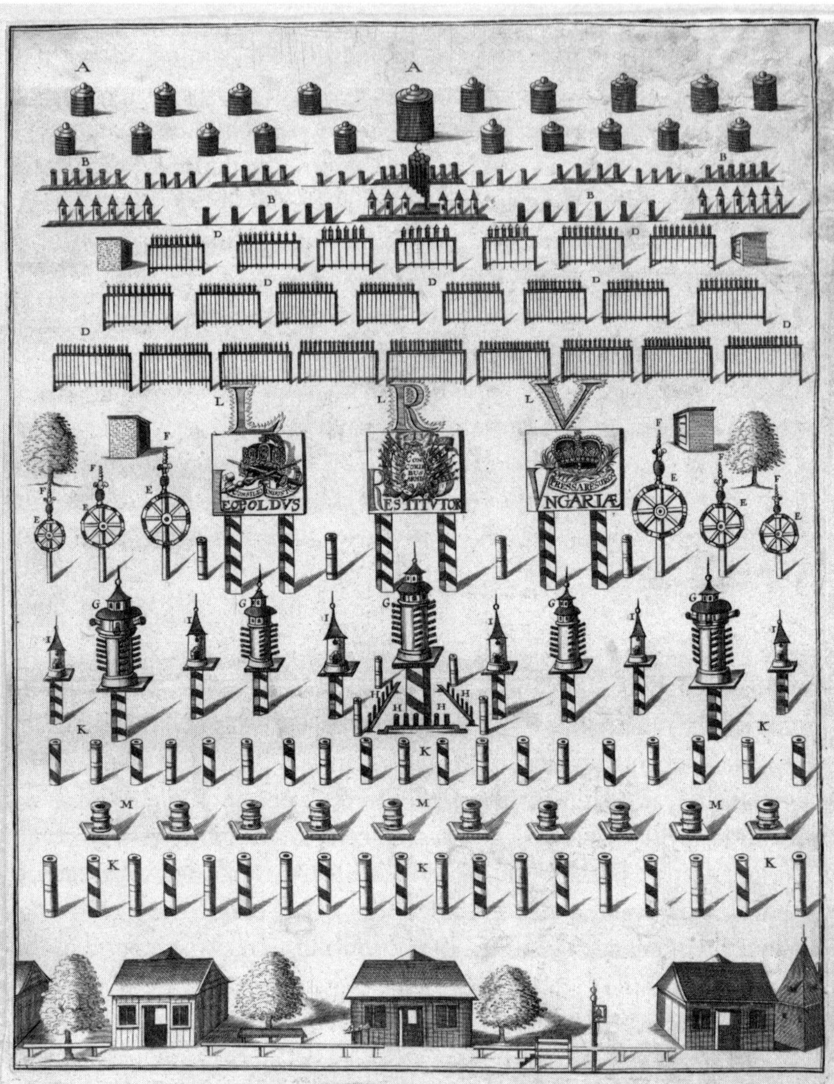

Plan for a fireworks display in honour of the Holy Roman Emperor Leopold I, Nuremberg, 1686.

like a great trunk, before the fireworks were let off. The Northerners were also happy to use real buildings and landscape features to enhance the impact of the fireworks. Illustrations of southern European displays from this period tend to show the specially constructed structures in great detail, but represent the fireworks with a few vague squiggles, while those of the Northern school depict the fireworks with meticulous accuracy, sometimes showing them laid out before the show in daylight and then the actual display by night.

The rival camps could be quite sniffy about each other. The Spanish artilleryman Diego Ufano, in his *Tratada de Artilleria* (1612), sneered at the 'simple fireworks supported on wooden frameworks' he saw in Flanders, comparing them unfavourably with the 'magnificent spectacles' put on in Italy.[7] But some have argued that the two styles were by no means so distinct; that elements of both could be seen in both regions, and that the rival schools in the end effectively merged, amalgamating the best features of each, thanks to the efforts of experts such as Kazimierz Siemienowicz, Lieutenant-General of the Ordnance to the King of Poland, who wrote a classic work on pyrotechnics, *The Great Art of Artillery* (1650). His approach involved 'machines' that were less intricate, but elaborate enough to be an attraction in their own right. They were often made from a wooden framework covered with papier-mâché from which hidden fireworks would send out sparks and stars. Tall obelisks were popular with both schools, often as the focal point of the event.

In 1635 the first book in English to deal solely with recreational fireworks appeared: John Babington's *Pyrotechnia; or, a Discourse of Artificial Fire-works,* essentially a do-it-yourself guide. The writer, who describes himself as an 'inferior gunner' in the service of Charles I, explains that he had had plenty of experience in using pyrotechnics 'against an enemy in the field', but thanks to 'the halcyon days of peace and tranquillity, which through the goodness of God we have so long enjoyed', he could now concentrate on those that served 'only for delight'.[8] Sadly, just four years after the book was published, Britain would be plunged into a dozen years of civil war. The author provided more explicit instructions than any offered by earlier writers. He also described epic productions to delight 'a Prince or some great person', providing designs for coats of arms, ships and mermaids as well as St George and the dragon:

> you must make a hollow trunk through the body of each figure, for a great line to pass through, and likewise for a smaller line

> to draw them to and from each other . . . so that as you turn that wheel, the George and dragon will run furiously at each other; and when you please you may cause them to make a retreat, and come again divers times.[9]

Babington's book seems to have been the first to describe a Roman candle – 'a trunk of fire which shall cast forth divers fire balls'.[10] Alan Brock argues this suggests it was invented in Britain, because its first appearance in any overseas pyrotechnic literature came more than a century later, though the name 'Roman candle' may have first been used as late as 1769. As to why it is called a *Roman* candle, there are various explanations. One suggests it refers to a torture Emperor Nero inflicted on Christians – covering their bodies in pitch or some other inflammable material, then setting fire to them. According to another, the reference is to a Roman carnival at which each reveller carried a candle they tried to keep alight while putting out those of other merrymakers, creating an effect of candles constantly being extinguished and then relit. Another English gunner, Robert Norton, had already given instructions in *The Gunners Dialogue* (1628) for making a flying fiery dragon from whalebone, wood, paper and Muscovy glass, a cheaper, naturally occurring substitute for glass. The monster was to be suspended from pulleys and moved by rockets. Over in France, in his book *La Pyrotechnie* (1630), Jean Appier Hanzelet also recommended whalebone for making a sun using two 'ribs laid in a cross, tying stars to the four ends with brass wire'.[11] If you attached rockets to the ribs, it made them spin, producing a swirling circle of light.

In France as in Britain, senior military people tended to take charge of big displays for royal births, marriages and triumphs, but also for the court theatre and ballet. One for the visit of King Louis XIII and his wife to Lyon in 1623 featured scenery based on astrological signs and a huge artificial lion with fire bursting from its jaws. Like many firework displays, it had a clear allegorical objective: to show how 'our king, who, travelling through the cities of his realm like the king of the planets through the signs of the zodiac, has at last arrived at . . . the sign of the lion'.[12] Five years later, a leading artillery light, Horace Morel, celebrated Louis' victory over Protestant rebels at La Rochelle by putting on a pyrotechnic display in Paris featuring great figures that portrayed Perseus saving Andromeda from the sea monster. The people watched from the banks of the Seine while the court enjoyed the spectacle from the balconies and windows of the Louvre. Fireworks continued to be a way of dividing the sophisticated classes from those not in the know. At La Rochelle in 1629, a hundred 'thunderbolts' were set off at a display where 'naïve bystanders . . . were stunned and frightened and . . . thrown about pell-mell. The Court alone remained still and undaunted, being well acquainted with the vanity and ostentation of these diversions.'[13]

Seventeenth-century allegories were constructed with great care and packed with meaning. Siemienowicz gave a comprehensive guide to the etiquette of firework displays, with tips on how to honour kings, as well as setting out the correct ways of celebrating occasions such as weddings, saints' days and victories. At coronations, he advised the Wheel of Fortune should feature to remind monarchs of the 'incertitude of prosperity'.[14] But those in on the hidden meanings were conscious that a lot of people might not be. So when a display was put on to celebrate the election of Ferdinand III as Holy Roman Emperor in 1637, he insisted 'that each night programmes be distributed, the contents of which would reveal to the eyes the artifice and aim of the *macchina*'.[15] A century later, in his *Traité des feux d'artifice pour le spectacle* (1747), the French military engineer, mathematician and spy Amédée-François Frézier took a similar view: 'One must take pains to instruct by means of printed explanations distributed to the public.' Without this, 'the wit that one employs is a waste of time for the majority of spectators.'[16] The eighteenth-century French playwright Jean-Louis de Cahuzac instructed pyrotechnists: 'all

Display at Nuremberg in 1648 to celebrate the end of the Thirty Years War, which cost up to 8 million lives across Central Europe. Etching print.

spectacles represent something . . . The movement of the most brilliant rocket, if it does not have a fixed aim, displays nothing but a trail of fire that vanishes into thin air.' Fireworks featuring only 'the play of different colours, movements, and brilliant effects . . . no matter how cleverly designed, will never amount to anything more than the frivolous charms of paper cut-outs'.[17]

England: The Reign of Beckman

King Charles II of England would have understood all about the 'incertitude of prosperity'. During the Civil War, his father was executed, and he had to flee the country in disguise with a price on his head. He then spent a decade as a wandering exile before he was finally restored to the throne in 1660. The firework display on the Thames to celebrate his coronation the following year was directed by a Swedish soldier of fortune, Martin Beckman, who was injured by an explosion during the preparations and got £100 in compensation. History does not record whether the Wheel of Fortune featured in the display. After being locked up in the Tower for a time as a suspected Dutch spy, Beckman would be appointed Firemaster of England and reign supreme over British pyrotechnics until his death in 1702, living in the Tower as a resident rather than a prisoner. It was there in 1671 that he wrestled Colonel Thomas Blood to the ground, so preventing him from stealing the crown jewels. The Swede's great skill was in building papier-mâché structures – obelisks, pillars, pyramids or sometimes figures of men – and filling them with fireworks. He raised the standard of public displays in Britain to a new level.

One observer described the show celebrating the coronation of Charles II's younger brother and successor, the Catholic James II, in 1685 as 'wonderful and stupendous'.[18] Again it was on the Thames (Beckman loved using water reflections) and guests tucked into a banquet while they watched. The display featured an artificial sun and rockets soaring and exploding around 12-metre pyramids, with allegorical figures such as Father Thames astride a dolphin leading a long line of cygnets, meant to symbolize the nation's hope that the king would produce lots of heirs. Beckman was praised for incorporating the best elements of the Northern and Southern fireworks schools, but there were a couple of mishaps. A pile of the king's silverware was stolen, and the writer John Aubrey, while considering the fireworks 'stately', wrote that some 'took

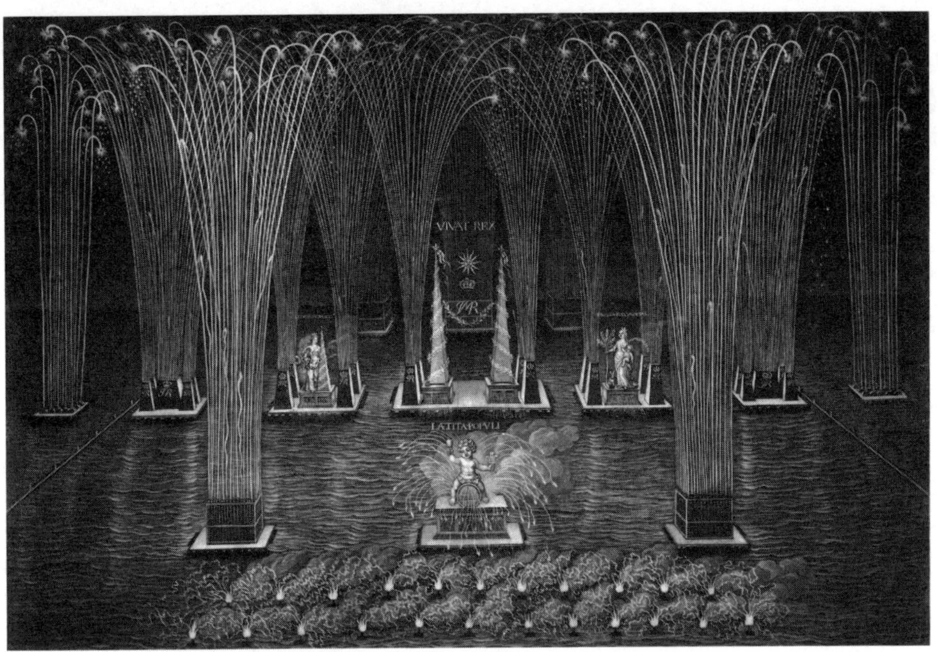

Martin Beckman's display to celebrate the birth of James II's son, 1688.

fire all together, and it was so dreadful, that several spectators leap'd into the River, choosing rather to be drown'd than burn'd'.[19] But James himself seemed pleased enough, because he knighted Beckman, the first firemaster to receive this honour. Soon, though, the Swede was having to show his political skills. In June 1688 he put on a display on the Thames to celebrate the birth of the king's son, featuring among other things a cupid riding on a barrel and emitting fireworks to 'the continued shouts and huzzas of the people', according to a contemporary account. The diarist John Evelyn seems mainly to have been unfavourably impressed by the price tag, remarking that the fireworks 'had cost some thousands of pounds . . . but were spent too soon, for so long a preparation'.[20] A year later, Beckman was mounting another event, this time to welcome King William III, who had just deposed James in the Glorious Revolution. The Swede held on to the favour of the new king, and in 1697 he was appointed 'Comptroller of the Fireworks as well as for war as for triumph' and put in charge of 'all firemasters [and] fireworkers'.[21]

England: Fireworks at the Grass Roots

Big displays might be growing ever more ambitious, but what about ordinary people? Were they indulging in their own pyrotechnics? When Guy Fawkes was apprehended he allegedly had a 'fire work' in his pocket to light the gunpowder, so it was natural that they quickly became part of the 5 November celebrations, as seems to have happened in Dorchester by 1607. Because of their endorsement of Protestant heroics, Bonfire Night celebrations even survived the Puritans, who suppressed plenty of other things that might fall under the category of 'fun' after the Roundheads defeated the Cavaliers in the English Civil Wars. We have a good account of the display put on in London in 1647 for Parliament and the London militia. Held 'in commemoration of God's great mercy in delivering this kingdom from the hellish plots of papists', it featured a firewheel, fireballs burning in water, and fireboxes that sent out multiple rockets to symbolize popish spirits attacking Protestant England.[22] The traditional rhyme

> Remember, remember, the Fifth of November,
> Gunpowder treason and plot.

is believed to have originated in the seventeenth century. There were various versions, generally including some virulently anti-Catholic sentiments. One called for 'A rope, a rope to hang the Pope.' The great poet John Milton is sometimes claimed to have been the author. This seems unlikely, though Milton did write a Latin poem commemorating 5 November when he was an undergraduate at Cambridge, expressing his gratitude that God had 'thwarted the Papists'.[23] At the other great university city, Oxford, 5 November was soon being associated with hooliganism. In 1657 the master of Jesus College was woken by a squib that had been thrown through his window.

Of jumping crackers, John Bate had noted in his *The Mysteries of Nature and Art* (1635): 'it is well known that every boy can make these'; while in 1661, Samuel Pepys writes in his diary of 'seeing the boys in their streets flying their crackers'.[24] Five years later, he and his friends and family celebrated an English victory over the Dutch with 'an abundance of serpents and rockets' and were 'flinging our fireworks' until midnight.[25] (According to Babington's description, serpents 'will first appear like so many stars, and when the stars are spent . . . they will run wriggling to and fro like Serpents, and after a while they will give so many reports, which will give great content'.[26]) That was the year of the Great Fire of London, and not surprisingly, the conflagration put a damper on firework making in the City of London. A local law passed two months after it laid down 'that no person whatever be permitted, at any time, to make, or cause to be made, any sort of fire-works ... except such persons only as shall be thereunto appointed by his majesty, or other lawful authority'.[27] Instead of stopping firework production in the City, this drove it underground. The distinguished twentieth-century firework maker the Reverend Ron Lancaster observed: 'the legislation was not, nor could be, adequately enforced and only served to drive manufacturers to work in more and more dangerous conditions in back kitchens.'[28] Among those defying it were Protestants who fled France in 1685 after Louis XIV revoked the religious toleration they had enjoyed. Many skilled silk weavers settled in Spitalfields in London's East End, and some made fireworks in the evening after they had finished their day jobs. The rule put the authorities in the embarrassing situation of using illegally produced fireworks for many official displays, and it also probably encouraged manufacturing outside the Square Mile.

Effigies were being burned on 5 November by 1670, but not generally, it seems, of Guy Fawkes. In 1677 Londoners set fire to a figure of a pope whose belly was filled with live cats 'who squalled most hideously as soon as they felt the fire'.[29] And it was not just the foiling of the Gunpowder Plot that was celebrated; every year bonfires were also lit to mark another red-letter date in the Protestant calendar, Queen's Day, 17 November, the anniversary of Elizabeth I's accession. One account of the event in the City of London in 1678 said the numerous 'volleys of squibs ... might have been a cure for deafness'. Like Guy Fawkes Night, Queen's Day often provided an excuse for a raucous anti-Catholic jamboree.

In 1679 tension was high as elements in Parliament were trying to exclude the future James II from the line of succession, and the day was celebrated with a procession featuring friars, Jesuits, bishops, cardinals and priests whose robes were decorated with skulls and skeletons, and an effigy of the pope with 'bloody consecrated daggers for murdering Protestant kings and princes ... faithfully accompanied' by the Devil. The spectators, supposedly numbering 200,000, were 'diverted with variety of excellent fire-works' until the pope's effigy was thrown on to a 'very great bonfire'. The same evening there were bonfires in 'most streets of London'.[30] When MPs failed to get James excluded, Protestant mobs got even more agitated. In 1682 the authorities tried to persuade the Lord Mayor of London to ban the Good Queen Bess celebrations, fearing they would turn into a riot, but to no avail. The following year the Horse Guards and the Trained Bands, the City's militia, did halt the event.

Nor can James have been thrilled with the way the first Guy Fawkes Night of his reign went in 1685, because the following day his government forbade 'making any Bonfires or other Public Fire-Works' without express official permission, to try to foil 'the evil designs of people disaffected to the government, who commonly make use of such occasions to turn those meetings into riots and tumults'.[31] This rule seems to have been no more effective than the one banning fireworks manufacture in the City. The authorities may have been as worried by general hooliganism as by raucous anti-popish sentiment, because even after James was overthrown by the impeccably Protestant William III, who incidentally had landed in England on 5 November, an Act of Parliament of 1695 said anyone making fireworks could be fined £5, while miscreants setting them off in the street faced being sent 'to the house of correction ... to be set and kept to hard labour' for a month.[32] Officially, this law remained in force for 150 years, but the pleasure gardens that used fireworks so extensively over that time never had any problems getting supplies, and the rule was more honoured in the breach than the observance to such a degree that the authorities had to put a notice in the press in 1778 to remind people about it. That did not work either, because in 1814, having heard that a London firework maker named William Swift was allegedly 'supplying boys or any person who applied indiscriminately with these dangerous commodities', the powers-that-were dispatched an undercover shopper to expose him. Once the purchase was made, officers 'forced their way in' and searched Swift's premises, finding 'concealed in closets and other parts' nearly 20,000 fireworks, a stash 'large enough to have spread ruin through the neighbourhood, had they by accident exploded'. Still, the court noted that Swift was 'respectable' and 'a man of property' and declared their objective was not 'to punish the defendant with severity but only to inform him and others acting like him' that the law was still in force even if 'it had not lately been acted upon.'[33]

The arrival of the Hanoverian dynasty in 1714 seemed to seal the triumph of Protestantism, though there would be Roman Catholic Jacobite rebellions for the next three decades, and it took some of the anti-popery sting out of the great firework nights of 5 and 17 November, though not everywhere. Lewes in Sussex had history because Queen

Bonfire Night, Windsor, 1776, aquatint print.

'Bloody' Mary had burned ten local Protestants at the stake there in 1557, the biggest of her infamous human bonfires as she tried to turn England back to Rome. In 1785 the traditional bonfire celebrations in the town, which featured home-made fireworks called 'squibs and rousers', degenerated into a riot, causing bitter divisions in the local community. In other places, the nights turned into opportunities for general hooliganism or the settling of scores. In Kettering in 1766, the target was a local farmer considered to be charging too much for his produce:

> a dreadful fire broke out . . . occasioned by the boys throwing squibs . . . The common people, instead of joining to extinguish the flames, called out tauntingly to a farmer whose ricks were on fire, 'Now farmer, will you sell your wheat at seven and sixpence a strike?'

Across the country, a moral panic arose about 'greasy rogues' and 'bonfire boys' who tried to extract money from passers-by, while magistrates voiced fears about 'depredations and disorders' as 'blackguards' and mobs of 'idle fellows' took over the streets.[34] Even where religious tension waned, there was always politics. One of 5 November's signal features was its versatility, as revellers burned effigies of whichever hate figure happened to be in vogue, with Guy Fawkes still seeming to take a back seat. A farce written in 1718 talks about 'the pope, devil, Pretender' and others being consumed by the flames, but there is no mention of the Gunpowder Plotter.[35] (The Pretender was James II's Catholic son, who claimed the throne of England.) In 1785 William Pitt the Younger went on the fire after introducing an unpopular tax, while three years later it was his great rival, Charles James Fox. Still, by 1790, *The Times* was writing about boys 'begging for money to burn Guy Faux [sic]' in a way that suggested it was a fairly well-established custom.[36]

The same year, the newspaper expressed the wish that 'constables and other officers of the peace' would get tough with anyone 'found throwing squibs, crackers or other dangerous combustibles': a 'most pernicious practice' that had caused a woman to miscarry when a squib was thrown into her coach, while 'timber yards and houses have been set on fire.' Besides, pickpockets frequented bonfires, and among boys asking for pennies for their Guy, there were usually 'two or three striplings belonging to the light-fingered society'.[37] In spite of Bonfire Night's links with trouble, in the eighteenth century many British towns held official celebrations – the mayor of Guildford's accounts for 1704 and 1706 both had entries for 'wine on Gunpowder Treason'[38] – but fear that bonfires would damage property diluted official enthusiasm for them. Then, when the two-decade-long war between Britain and Revolutionary France broke out in the 1790s, worries about disorder grew. For eleven of the years between 1795 and 1815, Guildford prohibited fireworks, although in 1803 somebody threw one through the mayor's window. Sometimes fireworks were allowed on other dates to celebrate British victories, but after 1805 Guildford also forbade this practice, and following a lot of damage on 5 November 1827, the town banned the use of fireworks for the Bonfire Nights of 1828 and 1829.

Fireworks on the Continent

The year after Charles II's coronation fireworks, Louis XIV of France, the 'Sun King' and perhaps the most powerful man in the world, was invited to the ultimate housewarming party by his finance minister, Nicolas Fouquet. By this time France was probably the global, or at least the European, leader in pyrotechnics. The 6,000 guests were treated to a prodigious banquet and a ballet with fireworks. The show was masterminded by the Venetian Giacomo Torelli, who had also put on events for the king. Instead of party bags, guests were sent home with presents such as horses and diamond tiaras. Unfortunately for Fouquet, the young king started wondering where all the money had come from and then clapped the finance minister in irons for misuse of public funds. Torelli tumbled from favour, and Louis recruited another pyrotechnic Italian, Gaspare Vigarani, and his sons with the promise of virtually unlimited budgets. Vigarani had cut his teeth on celebrated displays for the Este family, with 'machines' featuring, among other things, floating clouds and wave machines that earned him the nickname 'the great sorcerer' and made him famous across Europe. He had also built fortifications and improved canals for the family. Now at Versailles, he pulled out all the stops for Louis. In 1664 he provided the climax to 'The Pleasures of the Enchanted Isle', a three-day festival that had featured music by Lully and comedies by Molière, with a pyrotechnic battle between three sea monsters and the eruption by fireworks of an artificial island.

For a time at Versailles, fireworks even announced noon: a sundial in the king's garden was equipped with a magnifying glass so that when the sun reached the right height, its beams ignited a charge that sent a maroon up into the sky. (A maroon is a firework that gives out a flash and a single loud bang, taking its name from *marron*, French for chestnut, because of the pop chestnuts make when they are being roasted.) Louis also loved to entertain his mistresses with pyrotechnic displays.

As befitted an 'enlightened despot', the Sun King's contemporary, Peter the Great, Tsar of Russia, had a mission to modernize his country, and was not afraid of getting his hands dirty in the process. He came to work in London's Deptford Dockyard to learn the trade secrets of shipbuilding and develop an industry in Russia, and he took a similar hands-on approach to fireworks, which Russians had been setting off since the sixteenth century. Major displays, such as one lasting five hours to mark the birth of his son in 1690, he liked to fire himself. He also built a new pyrotechnic laboratory and came up with his own recipes.

The tsar was a rough diamond. While he was working at Deptford, he stayed in a house owned by the diarist John Evelyn, who sorrowfully recorded that Peter and his entourage used portraits for target practice and wrecked a whole inventory of fixtures and fittings, including eight beds. Not surprisingly, Peter was particularly fond of loud fireworks. At his son's birthday binge, a large rocket fell back to earth and killed a Russian nobleman, but the tsar insisted the show must go on. In 1693 he put on a huge display in lancework of Hercules prising open the jaws of a lion. (Lancework is made up of 'lances': small fireworks, each about the size of a stick of chalk and filled with a slow-burning composition, linked together by a fast-burning fuse. They are fixed end-on to a frame so the design is picked out in firework dots. When the lances are lit, they can show a message, such as 'Good Night', a portrait, a building or object, or a tableau with moving parts.) Then in 1699 he ordered that New Year should be celebrated by fireworks in Moscow's Red Square. Russia's new pyrotechnic laboratories made 'rockets, various balls packed with stars and projected with mortars, and candles', but also huge 'plans' said to be 90 metres long and 45 metres high – background scenery for displays composed of pictures and mottos, designed by professors from the Academy of Sciences.[39] They were based on Western European culture, and were therefore often a bit obscure for the Russian aristocracy who made up the audience, so the academics would supply explanatory notes.

Russia also imported overseas talent. The fireworker Mikhail Danilov gave a glowing description of a display masterminded by the Italian Giuseppe Sarti at the Moscow opera house during the 1750s which 'consisted of various changing figures, burning one after the other with great order and accuracy' and 'rockets of white fire, with moving wheels and fountains'.[40]

Asia and America

Exciting though the new developments in Russia might have been, in 1712 Peter the Great had ordered the Russian commissar in Beijing to 'obtain and dispatch the secret of the composition' of Chinese fireworks. His ambassador reported that China made 'such fireworks that no one in Europe has ever seen', and brought back some rockets that the tsar himself tested.[41] The Scottish physician and traveller John Bell, who made a number of journeys to China on Peter's behalf, records that the Chinese emperor claimed to have made 'many improvements' to fireworks himself, bringing them to 'their present perfection'.[42] So was Europe still behind the inventors of the firework? China remained a mysterious land, and it is hard to come up with a definitive answer. Some experts argue that a compilation of military devices and explosives, the *Wu Pei Chih*, which appeared in the 1620s, demonstrated that in the field of military pyrotechnics the Chinese were still out in front, but that Europe had moved ahead in entertainment and display. A similar view came from the seventeenth-century German Jesuit scholar Athanasius

Kircher, who wrote an encyclopaedia of China. He maintained that although 'they had the invention of gun-powder before us,' the Chinese were relatively 'unskilled in fireworks'.[43] But by the second half of the seventeenth century, there was a burgeoning vogue in the courts of Europe for chinoiserie. Did that nudge opinion back in the direction of Peter the Great's ambassador? Certainly, by 1696 another Jesuit, Louis Le Comte, was asserting that the Chinese made 'the finest fireworks in the world', and in 1751 the Sir John Oldcastle pleasure gardens in London put on a firework display 'in the Chinese manner' paid for by 'some gentlemen curious of seeing the New Fire Works'.[44] According to Chao Hsüeh-min's *Outline of Pyrotechnics*, written about that time, manufacturing in China was subject to very strict rules. Some would not be out of place in modern safety regulations, such as banning smoking in the powder room, while forbidding 'noisy talk' in order to 'soothe' the 'soul of the powder' might be seen as having benefits like helping the workers to concentrate. Other provisions sound more esoteric. Firework manufacture must not, for example, be done in a house of mourning, though if the deceased was someone outside the immediate family, then it was all right so long as a piece of red silk was hung in the compounding room. Women must not handle powder, because if they do, 'the crackers will change into fountains and vice versa.'[45]

China certainly appears to have played an important role in the development of fireworks in Japan. A fifteenth-century diary refers to a memorial service at Shojokein Temple in Kyoto's imperial palace in 1447, after which 'some kind of arts by fire was performed and because it was so splendid like a shooting star', an award was made to those responsible 'who seemed to be Chinese'.[46] The Japanese word for firework, *hanabi* (fire-flower), first appears in literature in 1613, referring to a show put on by an emissary of King James I of England for the shogun, who was said to be so impressed that he sanctioned their sale in Japan. English go-betweens were credited with playing an important role in building links with Chinese firework merchants, and until 1659 it is said that all fireworks set off in Japan came from China. In that year an itinerant farmer named Yaheh set up the Kagiya company, which still exists, in Edo, now Tokyo. He began simply by stuffing pieces of cane and reed with gunpowder, but by the eighteenth century Japan was developing children's fireworks, such as *senko-hanabi*, which were like sparklers, and *nezumi-hanabi*, an echo of Chinese 'ground rats' that ran spinning across the floor. Edo became the country's firework manufacturing centre – not particularly convenient, as more than a million people lived in closely packed houses built of paper and wood with thatched roofs, making any fire devastating. It was in 1717, 58 years after his arrival in Edo, that Yaheh sent up his first aerial firework as an offering to the water god of the Sumida river. It was dubbed 'tiger tail' because of the thick trail of sparks it left behind as it rose in the sky. After this, *hanabi* on the river became a regular ritual. In 1733 plague and famine were sweeping the land, and the shogun got one of Yaheh's successors as head of the Kagiya firm to stage a huge display at the Ryogoku festival on the Sumida to dispel the evil spirits believed to be responsible. The fete became a popular annual event. Today there is a firework museum close to the spot.

By the eighteenth century pyrotechnics had become obligatory at Diwali celebrations organized by Indian rulers. The five-day festival of lights, held in October or November, features the burning of giant effigies, sometimes more than 30 metres high, filled with fireworks. They depict legendary villains, such as the demon king Narakasura, who held captive 16,000 women until the Hindu god Krishna freed them.

Meanwhile, Europeans were alive to the possibilities of fireworks as propaganda. In 1790 an English 'artist' described only as 'Karar' put on a display for the Nawab of Lucknow. He spent six months preparing, and on the appointed day, on a square pillar, he set up a 'statue of fireworks'. He asked the guests to start the show by firing their guns at it, but they kept missing. Since it was getting late, Karar set them off himself. The display was 'spectacular' and went on for quite a time, featuring fireworks that flew high in the sky and then, as they fell, 'were transformed into hooded serpents'. Others 'produced hundreds of fish, which fell down on earth like stars', while 'from another firework arose a mosque.' As the show was drawing to a close, up went two rockets, one of which turned into a sun and the other a moon. The finale was 'a sun-like fire flower which went on whirling in the sky producing bright letters'.[47] The nawabs present were delighted and rewarded Karar handsomely. According to Athanasius Kircher, the Jesuits used fireworks to overawe local people. He gave recipes for 'fiery rain', 'fiery fountains' and other pyrotechnics to colonial and religious missions, explaining that Indigenous people 'usually take as wonders and omens all the things whose reason they cannot understand'.[48]

America is generally considered to have had its first taste of fireworks in 1608, via Captain John Smith, the English soldier and explorer who was supposedly saved from death by Pocahontas. He wrote in his

General History of Virginia that on the evening of 24 July 1608 he and his comrades used them to impress the locals: 'we fired a few rockets, which flying in the air so terrified the poor savages that they supposed nothing impossible we attempted; and desired to assist us.'[49] But there are suggestions that pyrotechnics may have made an earlier transatlantic appearance. The English mathematician and writer on gunnery Thomas Harriot, visiting Virginia in 1585, reported that he had used 'wildfire works' along with other wonders such as guns and compasses to overawe the Native Americans. Were these 'wildfire works' fireworks of some kind? Certainly Harriot writes that local people 'thought they were rather the works of gods than of men'.[50] After Smith's exploits, the first engineer-in-chief of New France, Jean Bourdon, performed a firework display for the native Huron in Quebec featuring rockets, serpents and wheels fired from a small artificial castle. Watching Jesuits noted how the Huron were told 'the French were more powerful than demons, that they commanded fire; and that if they wished to burn the villages of their enemies they soon could do it.'[51]

The War of Independence provided as big a boost for pyrotechnics in America as the Gunpowder Plot did in England. On 3 July 1776, the day before the Declaration of Independence, John Adams, who would become the United States' second president, wrote to his wife that the next day would be 'the most memorable . . . in the history of America. I am apt to believe that it will be celebrated by succeeding generations as the great anniversary festival,' to be marked with parades, bonfires and what he called 'illuminations', in other words fireworks, 'from one end of the continent to the other, from this time forward forevermore'.[52] On that first 4 July the war was still being fought, and the celebrations were pretty muted, with a couple of dozen rockets being set off in Philadelphia. The following year, despite continued hostilities, the city of the Liberty Bell put on a much bigger show, including, according to the *Virginia Gazette*, 'a grand exhibition of fireworks, which began and concluded with thirteen rockets on the commons, and the city was beautifully illuminated'.[53] Boston and other cities rejoiced too, and the tradition of fireworks on 4 July was firmly established. By 1783 ordinary folk were starting to hold their own celebrations, with a Philadelphia merchant advertising 'a large and curious assortment of fireworks' for sale.[54] Enterprising American politicians also started using pyrotechnic displays to entice people to come and listen to their speeches.

A European Peace Treaty Brings the Biggest Display Yet

While Indigenous peoples were being baffled and intimidated by fireworks, in Europe, scientists were starting to probe their secrets. Sir Isaac Newton owned a copy of Bate's *The Mysteries of Nature and Art* with its many pyrotechnic recipes, and experiments with fireworks were soon being conducted at the Royal Society, the world's oldest independent scientific academy, set up by Charles II in 1660. John Evelyn described a 'wonderful' experiment conducted by a Dr Slayer in 1685 which produced 'divers suns and stars of real fire, perfectly globular, on the sides of the glass, and which there stuck like so many constellations, burning most vehemently, and resembling stars and heavenly bodies'.[55] Some scientists believed that if we could find a way of imitating natural phenomena, that would make it easier to understand them. In 1734 the physician and chemist Peter Shaw opined: 'Many natural Phenomena, such as Earthquakes, Thunder, Lightning, Volcanoes, the Aurora Borealis . . . are imitable and explicable by chemical Experiments . . . and explosive Powers.'[56]

After Martin Beckman's death in 1702, official displays in England seem to have entered the doldrums, with none to celebrate Queen Anne's succession that year, though spectacular shows were seen in the Netherlands to mark a military success and in Italy for a royal wedding. There was a major display from a raft of barges 120 metres long on the Thames to celebrate the Peace of Utrecht in 1713, when expense does seem to have been an object, with some of the props probably recycled from the celebration of the Peace of Ryswick in 1697. (The Peace of Ryswick brought a close to one of the seemingly endless wars between England and France in this era, the Nine Years War. But hostilities were up and running again four years later for the War of the Spanish Succession, which was ended by the Peace of Utrecht.) Still, even if there was nothing much new in the scenery, experts say the list of fireworks suggests a good deal of progress had been made since 1697, certainly in terms of variety, with '1500 great and small Rockets; 5 large water Pyramids; 4 water fountains' and many fireworks that 'swam' on the water, including 'large and small bees' swarms'.[57] But the 1713 show may have been a flash in the pan. There was no firework display for the coronation of George I the following year or for his successor, George II, in 1727, and indeed it was more than twenty years into his reign before the next notable one came along.

Across Europe, though, it was a different story. The development of better fuses made it easier to let off lots of fireworks at once, enabling more spectacular shows, so increasingly they became an accepted accompaniment to big royal or national events. Philip v of Spain, for example, was greeted by a grand display when he visited Frankfurt in 1741. France, though its military power was now on the wane, was still the pyrotechnic leader. For the marriage of Louis xv's eldest daughter to Philip v's son a couple of years earlier, it put on not one but two enormous displays. Five Ruggieri brothers from Bologna, already famous in Italy, were enticed by open chequebooks. They fired their first display at Versailles on 26 August 1739, featuring a 330-metre-long 'machine' with a classic facade representing the 'Palace of Hymen'. Three days later, the City of Paris, at its own expense, covered 800 metres of the Seine, allowing a temple and a bandstand to be put up in the middle of the river around which dragons and 'water fireworks' kept up a non-stop show. Louis xv's famous mistress Madame de Pompadour went off fireworks when a spark set her hat ablaze at another Ruggieri extravaganza, but the Italians were nothing if not ambitious and their exploits allegedly included sending rats and mice up by rocket and having them drift back to earth by mini-parachute. They planned to try the same trick with a small boy, but the police put a stop to it.

In 1749 another time-out in the wars between Britain and France, the Treaty of Aix-la-Chapelle, which ended the War of the Austrian Succession, brought the biggest fireworks jamboree yet across Europe. The Hague erected a huge 'machine' on water with great whirling wheels of fireworks and Dublin a 'magnificent' Temple of Peace, but it was in France and Britain that the kitchen sink was truly thrown in. The British government had set up a 'laboratory' at Woolwich to make pyrotechnics and ammunition in 1695. By now it had become the Royal Laboratory and was under a civilian comptroller, though the Chief Firemaster was still a military man, Capt. Thomas Desaguliers. It was given an order for £8,000 worth of fireworks, about £1.8 million at today's prices, while an Italian, the Cavalieri Servandoni, was hired to create a 'temple' for London's Green Park. Servandoni had won an international reputation with his design work at the Paris Opera and for royal weddings on the Continent. The government also imported Italian pyrotechnicians – a Ruggieri, Gaetano, along with Giuseppe Sarti, who had worked for the Russian royal family. The fireworks would be 'principally performed' under the joint control of Ruggieri and Sarti, but 'all various parts of the great work' would be under the direction of the comptroller and the firemaster.[58] This rather complicated command structure turned out to be a recipe for confusion.

It took more than five months to build the 'machine' of timber covered with canvas, which was 125 metres long, more than 33 metres high and featured, according to the official programme, artificial flowers, statues, allegorical pictures and inscriptions, among other things. The display sounds quite sophisticated, including 'Stars of six Points', fixed suns and a 'Sun moved by double Fires', plus cascades and 12-metre-high pyramids of gerbs. (A gerb is a kind of fountain. The name is derived from the French word *gerbe*, meaning a wheatsheaf, reflecting the shape the firework made in the sky. They could also be used to provide power, and would play an important part in displays at Crystal Palace in the nineteenth century as they turned three great firewheels.) More than 10,600 rockets were to be fired, but the highlight would be a 'regulated' piece that featured 'mutations' and changed appearance a dozen times, culminating in 'a Royal brilliant Wheel' 9 metres in diameter.[59]

George II took a special interest in the celebrations, as he was entitled to. During the war, he had earned the distinction of being the last King of England to lead his troops into battle. They won. At seven o'clock in the evening of 27 April, along with assorted nobility, he made a tour of the 'machine'. At half past eight, he handed out purses of gold to those who had worked on the show, then took his seat in the royal box, while a rocket signalled the start. The king had commissioned George Frideric Handel to compose his famous *Music for the Royal Fireworks* for the

Contemporary print of the 1749 London celebrations for the Treaty of Aix-la-Chapelle.

The Duke of Richmond's display to celebrate the Treaty of Aix-la-Chapelle, 1749.

occasion. A public rehearsal of the piece six days before at the Vauxhall Pleasure Gardens was said to have attracted 12,000 people, even though it was arranged at just two days' notice, and caused a traffic jam lasting for hours on London Bridge. (Some modern historians have suggested the attendance was actually more like 3,500.) The composer had wanted his music performed by a conventional orchestra of string and wind instruments with percussion, but the king insisted on having it played only by 'war-like instruments', dispensing with the string section. The music was also spiced up by the firing of a hundred brass cannons.

'Peace' was the big message of the show, but behind the scenes the forces of harmony were in retreat. The British and Italian contingents disagreed about the best way of lighting the fireworks – trails of gunpowder or quick-match, a length of cotton wick impregnated with an inflammable mixture such as gunpowder and starch. Some had been dampened by April showers, and were reluctant to light at all. The confused chain of command meant there were half a dozen people all firing off orders at the same time, and in the chaos an explosion set fire to and severely damaged the machine. The Cavalieri Servadoni was so enraged he drew his sword on the Comptroller of the Royal Laboratory. The Italian was disarmed, arrested and taken to the Tower while the blaze was brought under control. The next day he apologized and was freed. There were other misfortunes too. The crush at the gate by Buckingham House (which would become Buckingham Palace) was so bad that people were injured. A man fell to his death from the machine and a boy tumbled from a tree to a similar fate, while another man fell into a pond and drowned. A wayward rocket set a girl's clothes on fire, and, according to the writer Horace Walpole, she was saved only because someone had 'the presence of mind to strip her clothes off immediately to her stays and petticoats'. Over the Thames, reported a newspaper, 'the populace pressed so hard' to get into a boat 'that some were obliged to be thrown overboard to cool their zeal'.[60] The fireworks went on until midnight, but many were not used, perhaps including some of the damp ones, and it seems the Duke of Richmond bought them for a private show three weeks later, run by Desaguliers. Walpole thought this was 'the prettiest entertainment in the world', though he had been less keen on the official display, complaining: 'The machine itself was very beautiful and that was all that was worth seeing.'[61] As for the fireworks, they 'by no means answered the expense, the length of preparation, and the expectation that had been raised' and many 'were pitiful and ill conducted with no change of coloured fires and shapes'.[62] Newspapers and pamphlets also gave the performance a thumbs-down, with one calling it 'The Grand Whim for Posterity to Laugh at', and only Handel's music seems to have won general approval.[63] The government was compelled to release a rather defensive statement: 'To destroy all groundless reports concerning the extraordinary expenses of the fireworks in the Green Park, we are assured from good authority that the bills delivered to His Majesty's Board of Works amount to no more than £14,500 [something like £3.2 million today].'[64]

If peace was absent behind the scenes at the London celebrations, in Paris things were even worse. Again there was a falling-out between home-grown experts and those imported from Italy, with a contemporary newspaper reporting: 'there were forty killed and nearly 300 wounded by a dispute between the French and the Italians, who quarrelling for precedence in lighting the fires, both lighted at once and blew up the whole.'[65] In Britain, local pyrotechnists would start bemoaning what they saw as the favouritism shown to overseas practitioners. In his *Artificial Fire-Works, Improved to the Modern Practice* (1766), Lt Robert

Jones declared his 'chagrin' that whenever major firework displays were put on, 'we have almost always had recourse to foreigners to execute them. If this had been owing to the ignorance of our own people on this subject', he would not mind, but in fact, it resulted from 'that prevailing fondness we entertain for everything foreign'.[66]

Official displays in the second half of the eighteenth century seem to have been on a smaller scale, though they often featured large numbers of troops as extras. During the Seven Years War of 1756–63, sometimes described as the first world war because it saw fighting on five continents, the French tried to use pyrotechnics to stir up patriotic fervour. In 1756 there was a big show at Lyon to celebrate the taking of the island of Minorca from the British. (The British admiral John Byng was executed for failing to raise the French siege.) In Britain the Golden Jubilee of George III in 1809 (George had become king in 1760, and the event was held to mark the beginning of the fiftieth year of his reign) was said to be the first occasion celebrated with fireworks displays across the country. Manchester, Hull, Edinburgh, Dublin and thirty other places all participated, though Warwick refused. Did they remember how the show for Elizabeth I had turned out more than two centuries before? The king and queen invited 'every family in Windsor' to a display which prompted a local newspaper to write: 'A more striking spectacle was never witnessed.'[67]

In 1814 the sniping over cost that had been a feature of the peace celebrations of 1749 reared its head again with a display to mark the centenary of the Hanoverians' coming to the throne. The authorities warned people 'not to listen to those who would poison their minds – to those who are the constant enemies of public Joy'.[68] Perhaps they were thinking of *The Times*, which castigated it as having been 'of insufferable length, in consequence of the wearisome repetition of the same fireworks'.[69] Still, the writer Charles Lamb enjoyed it, telling Wordsworth: 'the fireworks were splendid – the Rockets in clusters, in trees and all shapes, spreading about like young stars in the making, floundering about in Space (like unbroke horses).'[70] Col. Sir William Congreve, who would play an important role in the development of military rockets, was the director. In 1821 the fireworks at the coronation of George IV were dismissed as 'very insignificant', even though the coronation itself was one of the most spectacular, and expensive, in British history, and those for George's successor, William IV, in 1831 were also considered below par.

Private Enterprise: Pleasure Gardens

The Vauxhall Pleasure Gardens that had staged Handel's rehearsal were one example of a new business sector that would play a crucial role in the history of fireworks. Spring Gardens was the first one to appear, in the 1630s, though it did not offer much more than bowls, but by 1700 others were beginning to spring up all over London. Vauxhall and Ranelagh at Chelsea were the biggest. They provided a suburban retreat where jaded townies could entertain family and friends, admire paintings and sculpture, and eat, drink and listen to music. Hogarth contributed ideas, designs and paintings at Vauxhall, but perhaps the biggest attraction for a patron was the other patrons – to admire, poke fun at, flirt with. Some pleasure gardens had no admission charge while Marylebone cost sixpence (around £5 in today's money). Vauxhall charged twice as much, a shilling, to get in, while Ranelagh was the priciest at two and sixpence. In the less reputable gardens, patrons risked being robbed by pickpockets and footpads. In the more fashionable, the admission price and the notoriously expensive food and drink was supposed to restrict the presence of undesirables. Even so there was some mingling of high and low life in an apparently safe environment, though with a frisson of risk – a place to expect the unexpected. Jenny's Whim in Pimlico was famous for its 'amusing deceptions' – hideous figures triggered by springs that would leap out at patrons. Most pleasure gardens had well-lit main *allées* and more secluded 'dark walks', frequented by courting couples and predatory men. There was a convention that what happened in the gardens stayed in the gardens, and acquaintances that were forged inside, in defiance of social standing, might not survive the cold light of day outside. A little louche they may have been, but the gardens became one of London's biggest attractions. The eighteenth-century French travel writer Pierre-Jean Grosley thought Vauxhall and Ranelagh were 'finer in appearance than the Houses of Parliament, Courts of Justice, or the King's Palace'.[71]

There is some evidence that by the 1820s the elite had withdrawn their custom. In spite of the attempt to exclude riff-raff, prostitutes plied their trade, and in 1828 *The Mirror of Literature, Amusement and Instruction* complained that Vauxhall had gone to the dogs and turned into 'a hot, glittering, and noisy compound of all that is inferior in theatrical representations, shows, and vulgar nonsense'. As for the clientele, it was 'now much lowered', comprising 'Low varlets, from the desk, the counter, and the shop-board, staring most impudently in the face of every woman.'[72] Chelsea's Cremorne gardens had an annual battle to get its licence renewed because of complaints over rowdiness.

Fireworks made their first appearances in the least reputable establishments which offered delights such as bull-baiting, dog-fighting and cudgel fights. In 1710 the Bear Gardens, Hockley-in-the-Hole, promised 'a bull to be turned loose, with fire-works all over him'.[73] A few miles away in 1717, the Boarded House in Soho was presenting 'a mad bull, and a bear, both covered with fire-works'.[74] By the following year, pyrotechnics had infiltrated the more respectable establishments, appearing at Marylebone to celebrate George I's birthday, though they would not became a regular feature there for another thirty years. Fireworks made their debut at Cuper's in the 1740s, and soon there were signs that competition was hotting up. In 1742 the proprietor of the Mulberry Gardens, sited on what is today part of Buckingham Palace's grounds, claimed its pyrotechnics had been so popular that a 'splenetic, envious temper' had prompted competitors to 'attempt the like amusements', and a couple of years later he promised 'the most curious fire-works' seen so far in England, while the Sir John Oldcastle gardens boasted that their display included some 'never exhibited before in any garden'.[75] But even as late as 1750, pyrotechnics may have been encountering some consumer resistance, with the Marylebone management feeling it necessary to reassure

Fireworks at Vauxhall, 1845.

patrons: 'The playing of the fireworks will not incommode the ladies.'[76] Pyrotechnics had particular significance at the Cremorne gardens, where the ten o'clock display was generally regarded as the starting gun for prostitutes to begin selling their wares.

Pleasure gardens copied some elements from official displays. In 1749 Cuper's presented miniature versions of the machines used to celebrate the Treaty of Aix-la-Chapelle. They also mounted their own celebrations of national events. From 1826 Vauxhall put on spectacular displays involving actors and sometimes foot soldiers and even cavalry. That year they featured the Battle of Waterloo, and repeated it on a number of occasions, though *The Mirror of Literature, Amusement and Instruction* was underwhelmed bv their effort in 1828, complaining that 'the footmen had walked here and there for about half an hour, and the horsemen had cantered up and down through the ten or a dozen trees and back again for as long a space of wasted time' while the fireworks consisted of 'squibs thrown, and at last a rocket or a Chinese candle'.[77]

Vauxhall's performances of the Battle of Waterloo happened well after the event, but in 1854 the Surrey Gardens showed they could be more topical. With Britain and France taking on Russia in the Crimean War, the gardens offered a fine jingoistic spectacle: 'an entirely new and brilliant pyrotechnic display! representing the British lion and Gallic cock trampling on the Russian eagle!'[78] Two years later, shortly after the war ended, the Surrey staged the Siege of Sevastapol, one of its main episodes. The gardens also put on more timeless displays: Vauxhall featured Venice 'with imitation water', while in 1741 Cuper's offered a burning gorgon's head, the like of which 'was never known' before in England. In 1769 the Grotto Gardens featured a combination of water and fireworks that formed 'a beautiful rainbow, in its proper colours, delightful to behold'.[79] For those who might find such things rather tame, stunts were enlisted to brighten them up. In 1813 the Vauxhall drafted in the celebrated French tightrope walker Mme Saqui, who descended a rope 100 metres long from the top of a 20-metre mast to one of the main walkways with fireworks exploding all around her, earning a mention in Thackeray's famous novel *Vanity Fair* (1848), while both the Ranelagh and the New Globe Tavern let off pyrotechnics from a hot-air balloon. Sometimes there was a trade descriptions issue. In 1788 Philip Astley, regarded by many as the inventor of the modern circus, started enhancing the equestrian performances at his Amphitheatre with new 'Philosophical Fire-Works'. Said to be from Paris, they were supposed to operate 'without smell, smoke or detonation'.[80] In fact, they were probably not fireworks at all, but just gas jets, some of which revolved.

Not surprisingly, there was fierce competition for the best pyrotechnic brains, and one of the hottest properties was a Frenchman, Morel Torré, who had established his reputation with a spectacular display at Versailles in 1751 to celebrate the birth of Louis xv's grandson. He put on shows such as 'Hercules delivering Theseus from Hell' at Marylebone, while Ranelagh was graced with his 'Mount Etna' spectacle. Another of his Marylebone epics is described glowingly in Fanny Burney's novel *Evelina* (1778): 'The firework was really beautiful, and told, with wonderful ingenuity, the story of Orpheus and Euridyce: but at the moment of the fatal look, which separated them for ever, there was such an explosion of fire, and so horrible a noise, that we all, as of one accord, jumped hastily from the form, and ran away.'[81] Less impressed with fireworks was the famous critic and dictionary compiler Dr Samuel Johnson, who wrote scathingly about the 'vast sums' spent on them for the *Gentleman's Magazine* in 1749. To what purpose, he asked? Do we end up with a fine building, a bridge, perhaps a work of art that might be 'the model of beauty'? No. 'Nothing more is projected than a crowd, a shout, and a blaze.' How many roads might be repaired, how many poor widows and orphans given relief 'by the expense which is about to evaporate in smoke, and to be scattered in rockets?'[82]

A quarter of a century later, Johnson dropped in to see one of Torré's extravaganzas at Marylebone. The weather was showery, the crowd was sparse and the organizers announced that 'the conductors to the wheels, suns, stars, &c., were so thoroughly water-soaked, that it was impossible any part of the exhibition should be made.' Furious, Johnson thundered: 'This is a mere excuse to save their crackers for a more profitable company. Let us but hold up our sticks, and threaten to break those coloured lamps that surround the Orchestra [the area where an orchestra would play], and we shall soon have our wishes gratified.' Johnson claimed 'the core of the fireworks' were not damaged and it must be perfectly possible to light them. His outburst produced action: 'Some young men who overheard him, immediately began the violence he had recommended, and an attempt was speedily made to fire some of the wheels which appeared to have received the smallest damage; but to little purpose were they lighted, for most of them completely failed.'[83] Experts!

At Ranelagh, Torré worked with Thomas Brock, a scion of that great fireworks family, who also served the Surrey and other gardens. His ancestor, John Brock, had set up a fireworks factory in London in the last years of the seventeenth century, but in 1720 he was killed in an accident there. The firm was taken over by his son, and continued to prosper, so by the 1770s they were probably Britain's top pyrotechnic family. They may also have worked on spectaculars at Versailles, such as the marriage in 1770 of the future and ill-fated Louis XVI and Marie Antoinette. In 1812 the Mermaid Gardens in Hackney announced 'the greatest feast for the eye ever exhibited . . . by that unparalleled artist, Mr Brock, Engineer'.[84] That was William Brock, great-great-great-grandson of the firm's founder. Among the other places where he strutted his stuff was the Ben Jonson Tea Gardens in Stepney. Brock was obviously attuned to the importance of young people as a market for fireworks, promising that a show at Highbury House would finish by nine in the evening so 'families and schools may be gratified with so novel a spectacle.' He also claimed the show would demonstrate 'his superiority in the art'.[85] The Brock family gave a new phrase to the English language: 'Brock's Benefit', used to describe any loud, thunderous event. This might be fairly literal, as when a British soldier in the First World War recounted: 'The shells burst right over us – thousands of them every hour. Talk about Brock's Benefit!'[86] It gave its name to a key artillery observation post at the Somme, and even found its way into one of Edmund Blunden's poems. Or the phrase might be used more metaphorically, with the *Daily*

Crystal Palace: Brock's Benefit crowd.

Herald writing that one of the speeches by firebrand Irish unionist Sir Edward Carson denouncing Home Rule was 'like a Brock's Benefit'.[87]

It had its origins in the charity events that became an important feature at pleasure gardens. Ranelagh put on fireworks for the first time in 1761 at a display 'for the benefit of the Middlesex Hospital', and by 1766 benefits had become a regular attraction there. In 1814 Vauxhall held a show to raise money for veterans of the Peninsular War against Napoleon in Spain and Portugal. The admission charge was a pretty steep one guinea (one pound and one shilling). The Eagle in the City Road, the one the narrator goes in and out of in the nursery rhyme 'Pop Goes the Weasel', put on a whole series of benefits. Some were for conventional good causes, such as 'clothing the children of the needy', but others were more exotic, helping, for example, 'Decayed Druids and their wives and orphans'.[88] Thomas Brock put on the first recorded Brock's Benefit at the Eagle in 1826. It was for his own benefit following a factory explosion the previous year, which had 'nearly annihilated his prospects of providing for a numerous family'.[89] The proceeds from the show were enough to save the business, and the Eagle would put on other such events for the Brocks in the years to come, but it would be at the Crystal Palace in the second half of the nineteenth century that Brock's Benefits would become an institution.

Although the most famous pleasure gardens were in London, they also surfaced in other places such as Norwich, Shrewsbury and Tunbridge Wells. In 1828 Hull's Brazil Gardens put on a firework display by Mr H. D. Mortram 'of the Royal Gardens, Vauxhall, London'. It was advertised as featuring 31 attractions, including 'A grand Horizontal Wheel, discharging Rattle Snakes, red-hot Shots, Bombs &c. finishing with a grand Fountain of Italian Fire'. The audience was assured that the show would be 'of unparalleled magnificence, superior to any ever exhibited in this country. No danger need be apprehended from the Fire.'[90]

Attempts were also made to export the pleasure gardens concept. Torré opened a number around Paris, including 'Torré's Vauxhall' in 1769. In languages such as Dutch, German and Swedish, 'Vauxhall' became the word to describe a pleasure garden. A Russian 'Vauxhall Gardens' was built near St Petersburg in the 1830s. They also appeared in the United States in places as diverse as New York, Charleston and Butte, Montana. New Orleans had fourteen. By then, some of the London gardens were already falling by the wayside, as the bricks and mortar of the capital advanced relentlessly. (During the nineteenth century, London's population increased from 1 million to more than 6 million.) As early as 1755 Cuper's gave up fireworks, while Marylebone shut in 1776 (for its last few years, it had faced constant battles with local residents who tried to get its pyrotechnic displays stopped); Ranelagh in 1803. When Vauxhall closed its doors in 1859, the final show featured the message 'Farewell For Ever' in letters of fire. Cremorne packed up in 1877, but by then the Crystal Palace's firework displays would be setting a new standard.

The Path to Real Colour

With no cameras to record them, we cannot be sure, but it is a fair bet that the fireworks of this era would have been pretty unimpressive to a modern audience. Still, new special effects were beginning to appear. In 1735 another Jesuit specialist on China, Jean-Baptiste Du Halde, described seeing 'Chinese Fire': a brilliant 'shower of fire . . . the light of which was like silver, and which in a moment turned night into day'.[91] By the 1750s the Ruggieris were using it in Europe, having bought the secret recipe from an 'artificer who for a long time exercised his art in China'.[92] Its active ingredient was powdered cast iron, which became known as 'iron sand', and gave out very attractive sparks when added to a firework mixture. It was made by putting broken-up old pots and pans in a fire until they were red hot, then throwing them into a trough of water, and leaving them to cool. Rust fell off in scales and was ground down to 'iron sand'. Later versions of 'Chinese fire' used iron filings instead. John Bate had suggested something similar: 'iron scales' designed to achieve an effect like sparks flying from a blacksmith's anvil. Other writers proposed other additives – brass and copper filings, sawdust or even ground pottery, though it is doubtful whether the effects were very different.

The mainstay of the modern firework display is the shell, which can contain hundreds of stars, and back in the seventeenth century John Babington had published instructions for making a fairly primitive version from a hollow canvas sphere containing a slow-burning composition and stars, though it is not clear whether he had ever set one off. Unlike a rocket, which provides its own motive power, a shell had to be fired from a mortar using a lifting charge. At around the same time, John Bate described what he called a 'balloon', which was more cylindrical, with a fuse made from a 'little cane' which faced downwards in the mortar and was lit by the lifting charge. A century later, Amédée-François Frézier wrote about a 'ballon' made of linen, wood or papier-mâché that could be spherical or cylindrical. Its 'principal beauty' was that as it ascended, it had only 'a small stream of fire', which changed 'suddenly into a great number of others at the moment of its highest elevation'.[93] It could include effects like 'a waterfall or a head of hair', made from thin tubes or canes filled with a slow-burning composition, or serpents, stars and shapes made on small wire frames covered with composition. The Frenchman also writes about 'double and triple ballons', putting smaller shells inside the bigger one.[94] As the bigger one bursts, it lights a short time-fuse in the smaller one, which falls for a while before bursting itself. These would develop into 'multi-break shells', sometimes known as 'bouquet shells', containing a number of smaller shells. The initial explosion scatters them across the sky, then each shell bursts.

The Ruggieris must have been pretty apprehensive after the French Revolution of 1789 that swept away the Bourbon monarchs who had been such good customers and had heaped honours and riches on them, but their family motto was 'I burn without getting burned' and they showed they had political as well as pyrotechnic skills by surviving and serving Emperor Napoleon I. (When he was overthrown in 1815, they successfully turned their coats again and worked for the restored Bourbon king Louis XVIII.) In 1812 Claude-Fortuné Ruggieri was the first pyrotechnician to write about putting the lifting charge inside the shell in one unit, which eventually became standard practice. A variation of the shell is the comet, a spherical case fitted with an enlarged time fuse which left a spectacular tail following the firework as it rose in the sky. A favourite technique in a display was to fire a couple from opposite sides, producing an arch in the sky, then having them explode just after they had passed each other.

But it was in the field of colour that the biggest changes would come. Various tricks had been tried to give more vivid hues, such as putting coloured glass screens in front of the fireworks, but none really worked. In the early seventeenth century Jean Appier Hanzelet, who also worked as an artist, was ahead of his time in suggesting that fireworks could be made to look green by using verdigris (usually copper carbonate, but sometimes another copper compound such as copper acetate), which occurs naturally on copper or brass exposed to the air. It may be that he also added antimony to give a hint of yellow. As we saw, perhaps as early as the fifth century the Chinese were able to generate coloured smoke, and there were also claims that they had created coloured fireworks, but Frézier probably put it most honestly when he wrote about 'tints' that were 'reddish' or 'yellowish'. It was claimed that in 1710 Peter the Great invented 'beautiful light blue and green' fireworks, but some are not convinced. Green was an important colour in Russia. It symbolized a garden state, nurtured by the tsar, in which trees, plants, flowers and all manner of vegetation flourished. In 1737, a dozen years after Peter's death, a Russian display was said to have boasted 'palm trees made with white and green fire'.[95] (The palm would become a feature of pyrotechnic displays, meaning a shell containing a few big comet stars arranged so they burst with tendrils falling downwards like a palm tree. The most elaborate also feature a thick rising tail as the shell goes up, creating the effect of the trunk.)

In the 1750s the Italian Sarti was outshining Mikhail Danilov and another Russian pyrotechnist, Matvei Martynov, who had 'difficulty in making fires and sparks similar to his, which by their great size appeared excellent'. So they strained every sinew to produce real 'green fire', which they said 'had never been found in all the world'. Finally, with 'Venetian iar', a kind of verdigris used to make green pigments in painting, they got a mixture that 'burned with a very green flame'. Their recipe seems to have been regarded by contemporaries as superior to the 1737 green, and in 1755 one of their competitors, Mikhail Lomonosov, founder of the chemical laboratory of the Imperial Academy of Sciences, tried to build on it by making 'high-reaching green stars', but this initiative appears to have failed.[96] Again, without photographs, it is hard to reach definitive conclusions, but Jacob Stählin, the Academy's professor of rhetoric and poetry and for a time its leading designer of fireworks scenery, claimed that in the first half of the eighteenth century Russia had brightly coloured fireworks, including some that had a 'gold brilliance'. In his *Elémens de pyrotechnie* (1801), Claude-Fortuné Ruggieri, drawing on reports of friends who had seen it, paid tribute to Russian green fire, 'whose colour rivals that of nature'.[97] The name 'Russian fire' stuck to green-coloured fireworks.

It is also unclear how far the Chinese had progressed with colour by this time. Europeans were still seeking out Chinese recipes, especially for pyrotechnic 'trees' that were said to be created from coloured fireworks. In 1744 Joseph de la Porte, abbé of Fontenai, recounted seeing in Canton 'entire trees, covered with leaves and fruits; grapes, apples, oranges, with their particular colour . . . This is something our French artificers have not yet been able to do.'[98] In 1753 the Chinese physician Zhao Xuemin gave recipes for tinting fire as well as smoke, using verdigris for green and arsenical sulphide for yellow. A number of them did not include gunpowder. He mentions sulphur with copper sulphate for intense blue light, and saltpetre alone or with other combustible chemicals for violet, but it is not clear how successful the mixtures were. Still, the geographer Sir John Barrow, after spending two years in China in the 1790s, said 'diversity of colours' was one of the 'chief merits' of its fireworks, while in 1823 the American chemist James Cutbush opined: 'The Chinese have long been in possession of a method of rendering fire brilliant, and variegated in its colours.'[99] In 1801 Claude-Fortuné Ruggieri had seemed to take a similar view, saying it was possible the Chinese were 'superior' to the French and Italians, but by 1821 he was declaring the Europeans were now ahead. Into the twentieth century, incidentally, a class system was said to have governed who was allowed to set off which fireworks in China; yellow ones were reserved for the aristocracy, green for those connected with the law and red for the general public.

In the early years of the nineteenth century, Ruggieri tried adding sal-ammoniac (ammonium chloride) to pyrotechnic mixtures. This made the metal salts that provide colour more volatile, and the hues with which they burned more intense, but the chemical's drawback was that it tended to absorb moisture from the air, and it was superseded by another ingredient, potassium chlorate. In Alan Brock's view, this chemical kicked off the modern era of pyrotechnics.[100] It had been discovered by accident in 1786 by the French chemist Claude Louis Berthollet while he was researching the use of chlorine to bleach cloth. Like saltpetre, potassium chlorate supplies oxygen to a mixture, but while nitrates give up only a third of their oxygen, chlorates release all of theirs, leading to a stronger reaction. Berthollet reported that it could be used to make a more powerful form of gunpowder. The French authorities gave it a go. The following year, two people were killed in an explosion at a gunpowder mill making the experimental mixture, and after seven years, the quest was abandoned. It is not clear when pyrotechnists cottoned on to the fact that the chemical could make firework colours more vivid, and it may be that some who did were coy about publicizing a discovery which could then be adopted by competitors. But by the 1820s it was plain that the effect had been discovered, because when James Cutbush wrote about using potassium chlorate with strontium nitrate to give a flame of 'the most brilliant red', he did not claim this was a new idea, though he said it had not been used on an 'extensive scale'.[101] In his treatise *A System of Pyrotechny* (1825), published shortly after his death, he also explained how potassium chlorate could be used to make Russian-style green fire. Two years later, William Brock, who had been keeping abreast of developments, declared he had come up with 'a variety of colours, the result of chemical research, amongst which will be produced (a recent discovery of Mr Brock's), an Emerald Green Flame'.[102] Twenty years after that, Ruggieri published a pamphlet of colour recipes, including ingredients still in use today. A notable omission was blue, which was proving the toughest nut to crack – partly because the night sky against which fireworks perform is itself blue. Pure sulphur or a mixture of saltpetre, sulphur and antimony sulphide, known as 'blue light', was a stopgap, though what it actually gave was a white flame with a bluish tint. Eventually pyrotechnists discovered that if they burned other copper salts with potassium chlorate, it produced blue, instead of the green they got with verdigris. From then on, green was made with barium salts, with calcium salts for orange, sodium for yellow and strontium for red, while iron could create a gold effect. More recently, lithium compounds have been used for pink, caesium salts for indigo and rubidium for violet, while titanium gives silver sparks. Secondary colours are made from mixing the ingredients for primary colours, so purple comes from combining copper salts and strontium salts.

3
From the Coming of Colour to Electrical Firing

When William Brock's son Charles first approached the Crystal Palace board in 1865 with a proposal to put on firework displays, they were not keen. In the directors' minds, fireworks meant pleasure gardens, and pleasure gardens meant prostitution. They had even banned firework makers from a Crystal Palace trade exhibition in 1862. The palace was one of the wonders of the world, a giant exhibition hall built from glass and iron, more than 560 metres long and 125 metres wide. Queen Victoria considered it 'incredibly gorgeous, really like fairyland'.[1] It had been erected in Hyde Park for the Great Exhibition of 1851; when the event closed, it was shifted, cast-iron frame, 300,000 panes of glass and all, to Sydenham Hill, one of the highest points in south London.

Crystal Palace and the Brocks

Charles Brock, who was still in his twenties, had become the driving force of the family firm. A tall imposing man with a big, black Victorian beard, his avowed ambition was to take fireworks 'to a level never before dreamed of'. His nephew Alan would write that he had 'a curiously impulsive temperament, fruitful of ideas, he planned on an heroic scale. Everything he undertook must be not only the best, but the biggest.'[2] He believed 'sound chemical knowledge' had to replace 'existing clumsy guesswork'.[3] From the age of nineteen, Charles had been cutting his teeth on displays, including what may have been Britain's first fireworks competition in 1863 at Rye House near Hoddesdon in Hertfordshire. In addition to the pyrotechnics, he had booked acrobats from France and arranged special trains to ferry in the audience. Brocks would put on displays in many places – South Shields, Leeds, Bristol, Whitstable, Belfast, Rothesay – but Charles considered the Crystal Palace the ideal setting for fireworks extravaganzas: 'Its terrace, fountains, and foliage offered unrivalled advantages for the display of grand effects.' So he would not take no for an answer. He pointed out to the directors that the 1862 trade exhibition had included 'almost every other branch of manufactures', and argued that 'fireworks were really not of an immoral tendency.' Brock assured them that if his display was not a success 'either financially or from a social point of view', he would not suggest another, but he was confident there would be 'a large attendance of the better classes' and that the board would want more shows. The directors sat on the proposal for many months before finally agreeing.[4] It seems like a good decision. Over the next three decades, Crystal Palace firework displays would attract, according to one estimate, up to 40 million spectators.

What the directors agreed to was another fireworks contest – a 'Grand Competition of Pyrotechnists', to be held on 12 July 1865 with a £25 prize and judged by 'Gentlemen . . . free to give their decision unbiased by interest and unprejudiced by favour'.[5] Each competitor was to be paid £30 expenses, and received very strict instructions on what the display was to include, for example: '12 rockets of ½ lb calibre . . . 200 rockets of ¼ lb calibre, 50 of which shall contain Bright Stars, 50 Tailed Stars; and 100 with Coloured Stars'.[6] Other exhibits included one set-piece (these are wooden frames, often very big, that stand on the ground and are studded with lances, sometimes thousands of them), three tourbillions (rockets with a hole at each end that spin in the sky, derived from the French word for whirlwind) and twelve 5-inch shells. The £25 was won by Charles's father, but he got a more important prize. 'The public response,' Charles wrote, 'far exceeded my most sanguine expectations.'[7] More than 20,000 people turned out to watch, prompting the Crystal Palace to put on another five displays that season, taking the total number of spectators to more than 200,000. Fireworks were firmly established at the venue, leading Charles Brock to believe that he was on the road to a 'new era in pyrotechny'. The Prince of Wales, later King Edward VII, became a great fan, and in 1867 he brought the Sultan of Turkey to Crystal Palace to see what *The Times* described as 'probably the grandest display of fireworks ever witnessed in Europe', put on in his honour.[8] The potentate was so impressed that he asked Brock to set up a pyrotechnics factory near Constantinople, but the project came to grief when fireworks about to be fired by local trainees from a raft on the Bosphorus went up in a huge explosion.

The Turkish ruler was only one of the foreign royals who were feted at Crystal Palace. In 1873 the Shah of Persia, Nasr-el-Din, came to watch the fireworks with the British royal family, and liked it so much that the following day he turned up incognito, and paid at the gate with the rest of the punters. Rumour of his attendance reached the manager and he tracked the shah down, to be told by the ruler that it was the most enjoyable night he had spent since he arrived in Europe, and that 'fireworks back home are not in the same street as Brock's.'[9] When the Sultan of Zanzibar was a guest at a display in 1875, it was seen by some as his reward for his rather reluctant help in suppressing the slave trade in his dominions. He liked it so much that he ordered a display complete with operators to be sent out to the island to welcome him home on his return. Not that the British royal family was neglected. In 1872 the Crystal Palace had put on its biggest display to date to celebrate the Prince of Wales's recovery from a serious bout of typhoid, attracting a crowd of 60,000. Charles Brock made it possible by buying from Woolwich Arsenal all eight hundred mortars that had been used at the official fireworks celebrations of victory in the Crimean War a decade and a half earlier.

The 1870s saw Charles Brock putting on ever more ambitious shows, partly financed by a big military contract for cartridges and fuses for Napoleon III, Emperor of France, who was going to war with Prussia. For Crystal Palace displays, Brock would have up to 70 men working on site for a month, while on the night, 200 would be toiling away, firing off, say, 2,000 rockets, 120 shells, 600 Roman candles and 400 'coloured lights' fireworks. A maroon would be detonated to announce the show was about to start, and the first item would be a flight of hundreds of rockets. Because Sydenham Hill was so high, the spectacle would be seen for miles around, and if the night was still, the fireworks could be heard in Trafalgar Square. At the end of the show, 'Good night' would appear in letters of fire. *Punch* wrote that Brock seemed 'fired by a noble sky aspiring ambition constantly to surpass himself', so there were frequent innovations such as 10-metre-wide silver firewheels and 'whistling rockets'.[10] (The whistling is sometimes created by mechanical means, attaching a conventional whistle to the rocket so the air rush creates the sound. The effect has also been generated by using chemicals such as potassium picrate, which appeared in the nineteenth century, and more recently sodium salicylate.)

In 1888 *The Times* sang the praises of Brocks' 'first aquatic firework fete' at Crystal Palace. Spanned by a model of Tower Bridge, outlined in lights, the venue's lake 'was a glare of coloured fires' for half an hour as the display featured 'rockets with prismatic tints, helix fountains, revolving rocket fountains and whales and dolphins', among other wonders.[11] There were about eighteen shows a year, usually accompanied by the Crystal Palace band. In those pre-cinema days, pyrotechnics presented an unrivalled spectacle. A contemporary newspaper proclaimed: 'There is no form of entertainment which pleases so many persons far and near at so small a cost as Fireworks,' while London writer Frederick Willis recalled: 'The audience never applauded in the usual way. All they could do was emit a long-drawn "Ooooo!" of admiration.'[12] Brocks, always masters of publicity, came up with the slogan: 'Parents bring your children! Children bring your parents!'[13]

Crystal Palace's 'Brock's Benefits' began in 1869, with the directors giving Charles the gate receipts from one display a year in recognition of his success. By 1889 the events were said to be attracting nearly 64,000 spectators. In 1897 the *Daily Graphic* declared they were a national institution, and that any Londoner who had not felt impelled to go along to Crystal Palace to witness one was 'almost as rare as the man who is not moved at the sight of his native land', because 'one thing we do manage better in England than anywhere else, is our fireworks. Brock is almost a pillar of our constitution.'[14]

For all that, the Crystal Palace sometimes lapsed into the fake exotic. In 1875 the venue launched the 'Descent of Jove', featuring a 'Signor Geregorini' who would slide down a wire from the top of one of the water towers during the firework display, clad in a skin-tight suit of reflecting mirrors. After painstaking calculations to determine how tense the line should be, a rehearsal apparently went well, but on the night, 'Signor Geregorini' got stuck halfway down, and his loud complaints revealed that he was very much an Englishman named not 'Signor Geregorini', but Bill Gregory. The famous French tightrope walker Charles Blondin proved a more successful human enhancement for Brocks' pyrotechnics, performing his act amid the bangs and flashes. In *The Rise and Progress of the British Explosives Industry* (1909), the Scottish physicist and gunnery expert Sir Andrew Noble wrote that the amount of fireworks let off in a year at Brocks' Crystal Palace displays 'probably exceeds ... the whole of the other private and public displays in the United Kingdom'.[15] But the firm was also active elsewhere. Whether it was commemorating the defeat of the Spanish Armada at Hastings or Charter Day celebrations at Richmond Park, *The Times*'s refrain would often be: 'the celebration wound up with a grand display of fireworks by Brock.'[16]

The Best of the Rest

The Crystal Palace might be pre-eminent, but there were important displays in other parts of the country too. Belle Vue Gardens in Manchester put on what is believed to be a record 87 consecutive years of themed firework displays, from the 'Bombardment of Algiers' in 1852 to 'Clive in India' in 1939. Staged in front of huge canvas backdrops on an island in the middle of what became known as Firework Lake, they involved plenty of extras, and went on right through the First World War, although rockets were banned for the duration of that conflict. In the early years, until his death in 1881, the backdrops were painted by the artist George Danson, who provided scenery for London theatres and also worked at the Surrey Pleasure Gardens. Alan Brock considered Belle Vue 'the most outstanding' pyrotechnics venue outside London. Until 1926 it even made its own fireworks before Brocks started supplying them. After the Second World War, a steel rail track was laid to the display site from huge wooden sheds in which lancework set-pieces could be protected from the Manchester weather. Here they were made and stored before being rolled out shortly before the show. The last of Belle Vue's dramatic story-led displays was 'Robin Hood and His Merrie Men' in 1956, though more conventional firework shows continued for another thirteen years. Scarborough Spa also put on prestigious displays for seventy years, and other important out-of-London centres included Clifton Zoo in Bristol and Rosherville Gardens at Gravesend.

New Chemical Developments

The arrival of potassium chlorate in pyrotechnics has been compared to Technicolor's impact in the movies, as it produced vivid colours by generating a very hot flame that vaporized metal salts. The trouble was that when it was combined in recipes with sulphur, it also produced a spate of accidents. In a report on fireworks safety in 1872, Charles Brock wrote that coloured stars made with sulphur and potassium chlorate were 'dangerous, a little friction will fire them'. By that time he said, all the sulphur in Brocks' shells and rockets had been replaced by powdered shellac, a fuel made from a naturally occurring resin, and soon manufacturers were finding other gums and resins. In 1894 the use of potassium chlorate alongside sulphur was banned by law in Britain, and as the chemical industry grew, alternatives to the chemical emerged.

While potassium chlorate may have revolutionized what fireworks looked like when they were set off, until you lit them they appeared much the same – packed in thin cylindrical paper cases that were designed to burn away. Apart from being more colourful, rockets and shells functioned as before, as did the small heaps of 'coloured fire' still burned as part of a show. Then in the 1860s another new key ingredient, magnesium, first became available in commercial quantities. It burns very brightly and made fireworks much more brilliant, greatly enhancing, for example, the royal family portrait at Crystal Palace for Queen Victoria's Golden Jubilee in 1887. For a time, aluminium appears to have been used as a substitute in America, because it was cheaper, but as the price of magnesium came down, it was employed on both sides of the Atlantic. Besides burning brilliantly, magnesium and aluminium can both generate sparks, which allowed firework makers to dispense with spark-making ingredients such as copper, brass and zinc, though iron and steel filings remained in use. Mixing aluminium powder with saltpetre also produced a much louder bang. As modern chemistry supplanted alchemy, so firework makers started to adopt a more disciplined approach to their recipes, eliminating 'clumsy guesswork' just as Charles Brock had hoped, though colour compositions still had more ingredients than nowadays.

Official Displays Flourish and the Aristocracy Adopts Pyrotechnics

After the rather lacklustre displays for the coronations of George IV and William IV, at Queen Victoria's in 1838, pyrotechnics had made a comeback, with fireworks 'provided on the most liberal scale'.[17] The display was also innovative, replacing the machines of canvas and plaster with a set-piece. By the middle of the century, the machine was on the wane as the fireworks themselves became the stars of the show, although scenic locations such as the Crystal Palace or, later, the Palais de Chaillot in Paris were often used as a background. For Britain, the nineteenth century had been much more peaceful than the eighteenth, and after the Battle of Waterloo, there was no major European conflict until the Crimean War nearly forty years later. Britain failed to score a decisive victory, but the war did dent Russia's expansionary ambitions, and that was enough for the government to mark its end in 1856 with four official displays in London, in addition to the ones put on by the pleasure gardens.

By the 1850s pictures of firework displays were beginning to feature more frequently in weekly illustrated newspapers such as the *Illustrated London News* and the *News of the World*, and a history of the Crimean War published the year after it ended gave a glowing account of the official celebrations, featuring two hours of 'every conceivable design of elegant and dazzling pyrotechnic art'. Half a dozen flights of rockets comprising 10,000 in all, 'revolving wheels, suns, stars, golden streamers, and fiery serpents chasing each other through the air', were among the delights: 'It was strange to believe that so fierce and ungovernable an element as fire could be rendered so delicately obedient to the will of man.' The climax was 'the last grand attack upon Sebastapol – the blowing up of the magazines and works, and general conflagration'. A set-piece proclaimed 'God Save the Queen', and in the writer's view, 'It was such a spectacle as a man could not reasonably expect to witness more than once in his life.'[18] Building on the experience of Victoria's coronation, it was the first show on this scale to be put on without giving the fireworks a helping hand in the form of scenery, buildings or transparencies. Celebration displays were held in other cities all over the country: Edinburgh, Glasgow, Dublin, Liverpool, Bristol, Manchester, Brighton, Portsmouth, Plymouth.

Britain's ally France was also carrying pyrotechnics to new levels. Emperor Napoleon had been very keen, mounting displays to celebrate his victories and his wedding in 1810, and even taking a copy of Frézier's *Traité* with him on his campaigns. By the 1850s his nephew Napoleon III was emperor, and always trying to emulate the *gloire* of his uncle, without ever quite getting there. Like the first Napoleon, he enlisted the services of the Ruggieris as he commissioned spectacular annual firework fetes, an approach the *Illustrated London News* dismissed as 'government by shows'.[19] When Queen Victoria visited France during the Crimean War, the emperor decided to use Versailles as the backdrop for a display 'to surpass anything achieved by Louis XIV'.[20] An illustration by Gustave Doré, no less, recorded a miniature Windsor Castle disgorging thousands of rockets to light up the sky. The emperor's 1869 display was his biggest, celebrating as it did the centenary of his uncle's birth. It was also the last. The following year came the Franco-Prussian War, which he lost

The display put on by Napoleon III for Queen Victoria, Versailles, 1855.

in spite of all those Brock fuses, and he was then deposed. Charles Brock tried to sell the Prussians a firework display to celebrate their victory, but, perhaps not surprisingly, got nowhere.

Possibly helped by the Prince of Wales's enthusiasm, in the second half of the nineteenth century fireworks became fashionable at private parties in polite society. In the summer of 1872 Brocks put on displays for at least ten aristocrats, including the Duke of Bedford, but some of the nobility were not content just to watch. In 1851 the Earl of Rosse mounted the 'most magnificent display of fireworks ever witnessed in Ireland' at Parsonstown (now Birr). More than 20,000 turned out to applaud rockets, tourbillions, firewheels, shells and Roman candles manufactured at the earl's seat of Birr Castle. The *Illustrated London News* said they were all wonderful, 'but we cannot help expressing our admiration of the rockets – their brilliancy, force and the remarkable height they rose to, and then their burst into different-coloured lights and graceful fall were perfect.' The fireworks lit the castle as bright as the 'noon-day sun'. The paper noted that Rosse set all of them off himself, and that it was 'gratifying to think that no accident occurred'.[21] Mind you, the earl was no run-of-the-mill aristocrat: he was also President of the Royal Society, and owned what was for a time the biggest telescope in the UK.

British Fireworks Go Global

The nineteenth century saw fireworks rolled out across the British Empire. In 1858 India staged its biggest show yet, in Calcutta, to mark the subcontinent passing from the East India Company to the British Crown. Eighteen years later came another big date in British imperial history when Queen Victoria was named Empress of India. Charles Brock's younger brother, Arthur, then aged only eighteen, went to the subcontinent as one of the Brocks team who put on what were said to be the first truly modern European displays ever seen there, as the Prince of Wales toured the country for seventeen weeks in a prelude to the empress's proclamation. Arthur was delayed on the outward journey and found himself in a race against time to set up the first display at the famous Elephanta Caves on an island off Mumbai. He managed flights of rockets and coloured fireworks that lit up some of the smaller caves. A display put on by local pyrotechnists reassured one of his operators that 'they hadn't much to beat', and on 1 January 1876 the team decided to light the Taj Mahal with coloured fireworks. One contemporary account claimed they had given it 'an inconceivable beauty,' while another declared that compared with the more traditional moonlight illumination, Brocks' effort was 'almost like desecration'.[22] After India, it was on to Sri Lanka, where one display was so triumphant that the *Ceylon Observer* quoted a local pyrotechnist declaring they might as well give up and buy all their fireworks from England in future. When they had finished on the subcontinent, two of the Brocks team travelled to Thailand to spread the word there.

By the mid-1870s Charles Brock was confident enough to publish advertisements proclaiming: 'Displays undertaken in any part of the world'.[23] The company put on shows in much of Europe – France, Germany, Belgium, the Netherlands, Portugal, Spain and Italy – as well as more faraway places like the African kingdom of Dahomey. For some rulers, a firework display was a way of demonstrating their modernity credentials – something that inspired the young Sultan of Morocco, Abdul-Aziz IV, to put on a show at Rabat in 1899. An idea of the range of fireworks that Brocks had developed by this time comes from an account of the celebration of Queen Victoria's Diamond Jubilee at Kendal in Cumbria in 1897. (The jubilee was celebrated with pyrotechnic displays in almost every town and city.) The company provided no fewer than 62 varieties as the fireworks lit up and resounded around the Lake

District town for an hour. There was a Shower of Cowslips, Will o'the Wisp, Writhing Cobras, Fairy Glow-Worms, Aerial Treasures of Sinbad's Palace, Roman candles and spectacular set-pieces such as the Niagara of Fire and the Grove of Jewelled Palms. There were special Diamond Jubilee rockets, and one of the most spectacular moments came when a shell burst low over the castle ruins. The climax was a 9-metre-high fire portrait of the queen, the flags of her nations and the dates of her reign, encircled by the motto 'God Bless Her'. The crowds, said the local newspaper, were 'spellbound'.[24]

Fireworks continued to be an important way of overawing people not in on their scientific secrets. When Tāwhiao, King of the Maoris, saw a Crystal Palace display in 1884, he exclaimed: 'Such things cannot be!'[25] But now pyrotechnics also became a way of demonstrating British expertise, discipline and organization. Sometimes this called for exploits of imperial derring-do. Victoria's Diamond Jubilee in 1897 brought celebrations on an unprecedented scale in the huge tracts of the globe marked pink, and Brocks did not have enough operators to go round, so sometimes they sent out a complete display plus instructions for local people. Blantyre in what was then the British Central Africa Protectorate (now Malawi) was particularly inaccessible. The precious pyrotechnic cargo, including a giant lancework head of the queen, had to be carried 300 miles through swamp and jungle from the mouth of the Zambezi, sometimes by canoe, sometimes by cart and sometimes on the heads of porters. It got there in time to be fired on the appointed day before a huge crowd. Brocks had opened a factory in Adelaide in 1885, and for Victoria's Diamond Jubilee the firm put on displays in Sydney, Melbourne and Adelaide. Rival British manufacturer Pains also moved in, and Brocks fans would write to the newspapers decrying their efforts with excruciating puns, such as a 'pain-ful exhibition'.[26]

Getting on for a couple of centuries after Pains allegedly sold gunpowder to Guy Fawkes, they had started working with Italian masters on firework displays in England in the late eighteenth century, and then began putting on their own events. In the 1860s James Pain started manufacturing in south London, close to the Surrey Pleasure Gardens, with the help of his uncle, a member of the Mortram family, who had worked on pyrotechnic displays at the Vauxhall Gardens. In 1862 James had put on a display for Cowes Week regatta, a job the firm kept into the present century, and in the 1870s he mounted shows at Alexandra Palace, which had been designed as north London's answer to the Crystal

Palace, but which was bedevilled by building delays and then by being burned down two weeks after it opened in 1873. After two years it reopened, but in fireworks at least, it never threatened the pre-eminence of its south London rival, though *The Times* would report in September 1907 that more than 60,000 people turned up there to a 'Pain's Benefit' featuring acrobats, contortionists, a high dive from 20 metres high into 60 centimetres of water, and a balloon ascent, in addition to the fireworks. It began with a daylight display in which 'many toys showered' from rockets on to the watching children. The evening event included humorous set-pieces such as squabbling cats, but the 'sensation' was a rail crash followed by 'explosions and flames, with the entire destruction of the engines and coaches'.[27]

The rivalry between Brocks and Pains was fierce. In 1902 Brocks sent a senior representative, James Sharpe, to travel across India for six months and win contracts for the widespread displays being put on to celebrate the accession of Victoria's son as Edward VII. In Calcutta, he discovered he had competition from a man named Schoenberg, representing Pains. Sharpe befriended him, and one night they had a game of billiards. At eleven o'clock, they decided to call it a day and resume at half past ten the next morning, but Sharpe stood his opponent up. By six he was on a boat to Rangoon, getting there a full week before Schoenberg, who was then unlucky enough to catch typhoid and die without clinching a single display. The show that Brocks would put on in Delhi featured fireworks set off from gas balloons thousands of feet in the air that could be seen from 50 miles away. In 1910, the Crystal Palace sacked Brocks and gave the contract to Pains, but the venue went bankrupt the following year, ending firework displays there until after the First World War. After Pains won the Crystal Palace gig, the rivalry ended up in court, with Brocks seeking an injunction to stop Pains using the brand name 'Pains Crystal Palace Fireworks'. Brocks had been selling their wares as 'Crystal Palace Fireworks' for decades, and they claimed Pains were infringing their trademark. Brocks won.

America

Brocks also played an important role in America's love affair with fireworks. In 1876 Charles put on four displays at the Philadelphia Centennial Exposition. According to *Frank Leslie's Illustrated Newspaper*, this 'far surpassed anything of the kind seen in this country'.[28] The climax was a barrage of 2,000 large rockets, and the spectacle was of such 'peerless grandure [*sic*]. . . that the stars above paled'.[29] The Fourth of July display attracted more than a quarter of a million people. Three years later, Charles tried to cash in on his success by opening a factory near New York's Coney Island amusement park, but the venture failed to thrive. Still, they had better luck at the city's Brooklyn Bridge, which became a favourite site for big displays. One marked its opening in 1883; nine years later came the celebration of the four hundredth anniversary of Columbus's discovery of America. Brocks' display for that occasion was said to have been watched by more than a million people, and the highlight was another 'Niagara of fire'. The *New York Times* described how 'there began to fall from the entire span between the two towers a great stream of fire, so dense that it could not be seen through. It fell steadily as if it were water' for three or four minutes, and the effect was 'superb'.[30] That same year, Brocks again demonstrated its trailblazing credentials when it was said to be the first manufacturing company in the world to advertise with a flashing electric sign on Broadway.

But, as in Australia, Brocks found itself locked in battle with other fireworks companies – not just Pains, but also the Consolidated Fireworks Company of America, who put on a display at the Brooklyn Bridge the night after Brocks' memorable effort. By the late nineteenth century, America also had other big firework players such as the Unexcelled Manufacturing Company of Staten Island, but it was dominated by smaller outfits. And there was plenty of demand, with St Louis, Chicago, Cincinnati, Louisville and other cities mounting spectaculars like 'Rome under Nero'.

Pains opened a factory on Long Island in New York State while the company became famous for its three-decade residence at Manhattan Beach on Coney Island, which started in 1879 with James being helped by his son Henry until James returned to England five years later, leaving Henry in sole charge. They designed their own amphitheatre, holding 12,000 people, with a huge stage and an artificial lagoon, sited as far as possible from any wooden structures at the resort. Unlike Brocks, Pains were still focused on story-led productions using actors, but the pyrotechnics were spectacular too. Their first show at Manhattan Beach featured a 15-metre firewheel, and a 12-metre-high Fairy Fountain with gold and silver jets pouring out.

There followed a whole series of 'pyrodramas' depicting international events such as the Great Fire of London, the Burning of Moscow during

One of Pains' 'pyrodramas' at Manhattan Beach, 1891.

the French invasion of 1812 and the Siege of Sevastopol. But Henry Pain had also studied the American market and came up with home-grown winners like the Storming of Vicksburg in 1893, marking the thirtieth anniversary of a major engagement in the American Civil War. The performance required five hundred infantry, two cavalry squadrons, two artillery batteries and gunboats on the lagoon. Pain's greatest hit, which he reprised several times, was 'The Last Days of Pompeii', telling the story of the Roman city destroyed by the eruption of Vesuvius in AD 79. It made its debut in 1882, when it became the most ambitious of the company's shows so far, featuring music from Manhattan Beach's resident band. A poster from the early years of the twentieth century offered: 'Pompeii! The Ancient City will be destroyed again tonight. Weird, pyrotechnical effects! Gorgeous scenery! The Greatest, Most Sublime Spectacle on Earth! . . . New Features Every Night! Never Twice Alike!'[31]

Once everyone was sitting comfortably, the stadium lights were turned off and the lights on the set turned on, revealing a square with the city and Vesuvius in the background. Amid authentic reproductions of historic buildings, children played while adults watched a festival complete with singing, dancing, clowns and jugglers, all of them oblivious to a tiny wisp of smoke emerging from the volcano. It got bigger and bigger. Then there was a rumble and flame burst out from the crater.

As panic spread, fires started in the background and lava seemed to flow down the mountain, engulfing the city. To spare the audience too much distress, the children and some of the adults were allowed to escape across the lagoon, which was playing the part of the Bay of Naples. Then came Pains' spectacular firework show, lasting up to an hour. 'The Last Days of Pompeii' made the firm famous, and offers flooded in. In 1886 Pains provided the fireworks for the opening of the Statue of Liberty, and in 1893 it won the contract for the Chicago World's Fair. In Europe the company scored a major coup five years later by being chosen to provide fireworks in Lisbon to celebrate the four hundredth anniversary of the Portuguese explorer Vasco da Gama's historic voyage to India. In 1892 Pain had been tempted away from Manhattan Beach by a bigger fee to do the fireworks for neighbouring West Brighton, where he put on a spectacular based on the Venice Carnival. Manhattan Beach hired Brocks to plug the gap, but it seems they failed to outshine Pains, because the following year Henry was back, exhibiting an ability to turn his shows into a kind of pyrotechnic newsreel. So in 1905, while the Russo-Japanese war was still raging, Pain staged one of its key battles, the siege of Port Arthur. The pyrotechnician put on his last Manhattan Beach show in 1911, but carried on with his pyrodramas at other venues until 1914 when he turned to making munitions for the First World War.

Asia

In their original home of China, fireworks continued to be a pervasive feature of life, marking big domestic events such as births, weddings, funerals and even the settlement of quarrels as well as religious ceremonies, and other public occasions like the eclipse of the moon and New Year. Governor of Hong Kong Sir John Francis Davis wrote in 1836 that so many fireworks were let off at New Year in Canton, over the Chinese border, that the authorities there had tried in vain to put a stop to them 'on the ground of undue wastefulness'. Sir John was not overly impressed with Chinese fireworks, declaring them 'inferior to our own', but he was very taken by one known as 'the Drum' which he thought 'the best thing of its kind'.[32] A traveller in early nineteenth-century China described it as a 'chest, five foot square' that was hoisted 18 metres in the air by a pulley. At this point the bottom and then the sides fell out, allowing strings of lanterns to fall from it, each with 'a beautifully coloured flame', possibly created by tinted glass. Then came a 'general explosion and discharge of suns and stars, squibs, crackers, rockets and grenades, which involved the gardens for an hour in a cloud of intolerable smoke'.[33]

By the end of the century, some believed China was falling behind the West. In 1896 the emperor's viceroy, Li Hung Chang, came to a Brocks display at Crystal Palace, and was allowed to electrically fire a set-piece of Chinese characters wishing him long life and happiness. Li told the *Daily Telegraph* that Brocks' display was 'much superior' to what he could see in his native land, adding that he had also seen firework displays in Germany, but that they were not 'half as good' as Crystal Palace.[34] The Chinese were still sourcing their charcoal from interesting materials – bamboo knots, grasshoppers and snakeskin – and still trying to soothe the soul of the gunpowder by banning loud talk. It is easy to poke fun at these apparent eccentricities, but whatever the viceroy's opinion, in the middle of the nineteenth century America was still importing plenty of Chinese firecrackers because they were considered better than anything home producers could manage, while by the 1890s Brocks was bringing in 100 tons of crackers a year from China, as well as buying shells from Japan.

As in China, some religious festivals in Thailand were marked by setting off rockets, often very big ones. A traveller writing at the end of the nineteenth century said the case could be 2.5 to 3 metres long and contain up to 13 kilograms of 'coarse native powder', while the bamboo stick to which it was attached might be as much as 12 metres long, decorated with coloured paper and tinsel and fitted with whistles. The rockets were fired from rough scaffolds and could rise very high, though accidents, it was said, were frequent.

Lancework, Set-Pieces and Other Innovations

At the Crystal Palace, the Brocks appear to have taken lancework to a new level. A setting on such a grand scale demanded displays of similar size, so the management installed a 60-metre-long permanent gantry that could be extended to 75 metres and support set-pieces 21 metres high. The biggest needed 35,000 lances and getting on for 3 miles of quick-match fuse. The venue cut its teeth on pyrotechnic representations of major buildings – Salisbury Cathedral, the Arc de Triomphe, even the Crystal Palace itself – but sea battles soon became great favourites: the Defeat of the Spanish Armada, the Battle of Trafalgar. From 1879 the Palace started using the technique for huge portraits of famous people.

Charles Brock died two years later when he was only 37. He had arguably made Britain the world leader in fireworks. Arthur, then aged 23, took over the firm. In 1886 we have possibly the first example of using an electric current to set off fireworks – by Princess Alexandra, the Princess of Wales, from the Royal Box. A contemporary journalist put it this way: 'The Princess touched an electric cord communicating with a set device, which instantly burst ablaze, depicting in the brightest hues and tints of fire the national emblems of the rose, shamrock and thistle, presently changing into fire portraits of the Prince and Princess of Wales.'[35] (However, the following year, the *Daily Telegraph* reported that the princess had 'for the first time' become a 'pyrotechnist' when she pushed the electric button that started the display for Queen Victoria's Golden Jubilee.[36]) Foreign royalty were also portrayed, including the Maori king Tawhiao, who, in addition to expressing his wonder at the fireworks, was also astonished by the size of the crowd, telling Charles Brock he had not realized there were that many people in the world. That great royal fireworks fan the Shah of Persia got his portrait done in 1892. The band struck up some Persian music, but were drowned out by the audience breaking into a popular music hall song of the time: 'Have you

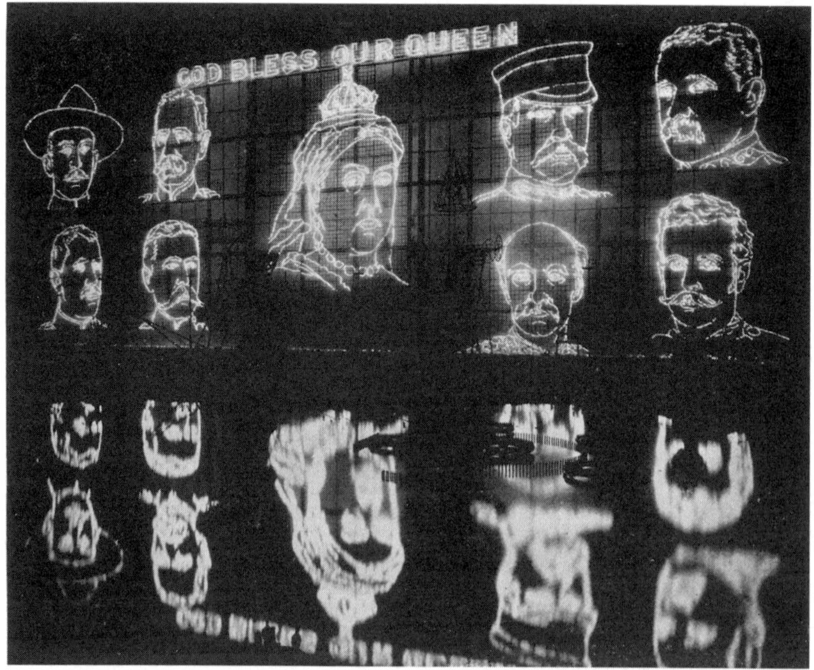

Crystal Palace set-piece portraits from the time of the Boer War, *c.* 1900.

seen the Shah?' which contained lines like: 'with five-pound notes, he lines his coats.'[37] The occupant of the peacock throne was thrilled. There was the occasional technical hitch, as with a giant portrait of Queen Victoria whose right eye kept winking suggestively, and when Arthur suggested giving the Prince of Wales his own pyrotechnic portrait, the future king replied: 'Don't go giving me a green nose or a blue ear.'[38] In America, too, firework portraits were popular, with huge likenesses of presidents putting in an appearance on the Fourth of July.

Like Pains, Brocks went in for pyrotechnic newsreels, and the biggest ever Crystal Palace set-piece was the one put on in 1898 showing the destruction of the Spanish fleet in Manila Bay during the Spanish–American war, which was then raging. It was 215 metres long, covered 5,500 square metres and was based on photographs and sketches of the action. The piece was commended for its accuracy, and Brocks commented: 'the artist is not permitted to rely upon his imaginative faculty.'[39] Imagination might be out, but resourcefulness was in. When war broke out between China and Japan in 1894, it was clear there would be a decisive battle, probably at the naval base of Port Arthur, so Brock gathered every photograph he could find and set to work constructing the backdrop. Then word came through that what would turn out to be the biggest naval battle of the war had happened, but at the Yalu River. Arthur did a quick rejig and just ten days after the event, a 180-metre version of the 'Battle of the Yalu River' appeared. A local newspaper once commented: 'anything happening in the world is very shortly afterwards to be seen reproduced in fireworks at the Crystal Palace.'[40] Like Pains, Brocks also created set-pieces of the Russo-Japanese War in which Port Arthur was again a flashpoint. A flavour of one of these martial set-pieces comes in *The Times*'s description of 'A Sortie from Port Arthur' in September 1904: 'Ten battleships in motion were depicted throwing shells here, there, and everywhere. During the action one of these vessels struck a mine, and was immediately blown to pieces, and some excitement was aroused by a race between two torpedo-boats, which were eventually destroyed by shell. While this was going on the guns at the fortress were active.'[41] In 1905 sharp-eyed observers noted that the portrayal of the naval battle of the Tsushima Strait between Russia and Japan bore a remarkable similarity to the earlier Battle of Manila Bay. Brock also seems to have diversified into prophecy. In 1909 he put on a display depicting the airship bombing raids Britain would suffer during the First World War.

One of the Crystal Palace's favourite set-pieces was 'The Avalanche', featuring the Alps with their peaks outlined in fire. A train ran along the base until suddenly a huge mass of 'snow', made from white smoke, thundered down and swept away a chalet at the bottom, narrowly missing the train. Some were more light-hearted, like the donkey that reared back and kicked the cart it was pulling, knocking over its contents and the driver, or music-hall star Lottie Collins performing 'Ta-ra-ra-boom-de-ay' with a spirited kick of her leg on 'boom'. There were more tranquil set-pieces too, such as a 'Trio of Peacocks' in 1904, in which the tail of the biggest bird had a diameter of 22 metres. The 'gold and purple plumage of the birds' made 'a pretty sight'. More 'rich combinations of colour' were seen in 'rotofonts', which changed from 'vertical suns to revolving fountains of molten coloured fire', while prismatic wheels displayed 'many attractive geometrical designs in many colours', and fireworks lit two fountains in the grounds in a feature known as 'The Temples of Light'.[42]

Arthur Brock's motto was: 'Not to progress is to retrogress,' so innovations kept appearing.[43] A refinement of the giant portrait was the 'transformation', in which an emblem changed into a portrait, such as the one fired by Princess Alexandra in 1886. The effect was achieved by using longer fireworks for the second design and embodying it in the first. The shorter lances expired more quickly, leaving the longer ones burning to display the second picture. The effects got more ambitious and in 1889 the Crystal Palace put on a 'Four Seasons' display, morphing from spring to summer to autumn to winter. Then there was the famous Niagara of fire, which covered an area of 2,300 square metres and burned a ton of iron filings.

In 1888 Arthur introduced 'living fireworks' – matchstick figures performing different routines. The first was a boxing match, and it continued to be one of the most popular. He patented the method and stayed tight-lipped about it, so some people thought they were watching elaborate automata. In fact, the effect was achieved by performers dressed in asbestos overalls, with the side facing the audience attached to a light wooden frame carrying a lancework design of the characters they were playing. Kaiser Wilhelm II got 'unbounded delight' from the boxers, while the Shah of Persia was 'particularly amused' by the fighting cocks. Other favourites included firemen struggling with a blazing house, and a bullfight, in which the bull actually was an automaton, known as a 'mechanical' – a cut-out profile, parts of which could be moved by wheels or cords. Mechanicals also portrayed hansom cabs, bicycles, or, more ambitiously, tableaux of greyhound races, Derby Day and even a procession of animals into Noah's Ark. In 1891 *The Times* noted that Brocks had been putting on their shows at Crystal Palace for more than a quarter of a century, and that 'like good wine they may safely be said to have improved with age.'[44]

Firework Manufacturing Takes Off in the UK and the USA

By the 1880s Brocks were making the biggest shells the world had yet seen, in south London. Weighing more than 110 kilograms and 63 centimetres in diameter, they were designed to climb up to 300 metres, creating a canopy of stars half a mile wide, and scattering debris over a similar area. (Collateral damage from fireworks could be an issue. In 1888 a woman was granted 25 shillings for burns to her dress and jacket caused by sparks at a Crystal Palace display.) They had to be fired from a mortar 2 metres high that needed a horse or mule to pull it into position. A couple of the shells were ordered by the king of Portugal, who had been very impressed by a Crystal Palace display in 1885. The first was set off in Lisbon the following year as part of a major display involving thirteen ships and 580 mortars to celebrate the marriage of the crown prince of Portugal, and the second at the same place in 1888 to mark a visit by the king and queen of Sweden. A similar shell was fired to celebrate the opening of Devon's Lynton & Barnstaple Railway in 1898.

His success at Crystal Palace had led Charles Brock to open a big new factory in southeast London in 1868, and begin 'manufacturing on a scale never previously dreamt of in the trade', making shells, he said, a hundred times bigger than those of his early days.[45] (The factory's presence is commemorated to this day by a pub called the Pyrotechnists Arms.) By the 1890s Brocks claimed they had the biggest fireworks factory in the world. The writer and illustrator John Corbett Anderson was very impressed by its safety precautions. Work went on in small sheds, connected by tramways but set well apart in case there was an explosion. The only artificial light came from gas jets outside the windows, storage jars were made from papier-mâché instead of glass, and the 'most scrupulous cleanliness' was observed 'so as to avoid grit'.[46] If a worker needed anything, he would hang out a red flag to attract the attention of an attendant. To reduce stockpiling at the factory, explosive materials were stored on hulks 20 miles downriver from London Bridge near Gravesend. When extra temporary workers had to be taken on in the autumn to gear up for 5 November, a big Newfoundland dog would sniff each one as they came in each day to weed out any impostors. For all that, the company was fined in 1886 for seven offences against the Explosives Act, including not properly sweeping up explosive debris from shed floors. In 1902 Brocks moved to an even bigger site at Sutton in Surrey, with 160 buildings connected by 3 miles of tramways. One of the factory's first tasks was to create a firework portrait of King Edward VII for his coronation.

When Brocks opened a shop in central London close to St Paul's Cathedral in the 1880s, selling everything from halfpenny squibs to ten-guinea shells, it was said to be one of the first in the country to have a telephone. The company shifted 2 million squibs every year, along with the same number of penny crackers and a million Catherine wheels. Having been pioneers in advertising in America, Brocks also spent heavily on publicity in Britain, with Arthur once entertaining a hundred journalists to dinner at the Crystal Palace. Like his elder brother, he always wanted to try something new, so in the 1890s he did a deal with the organizers of the Boat Race to let off maroons at the finish at Mortlake, so those spectators still strung out somewhere along the course from Putney would hear them and know who had won. Two maroons meant it was Cambridge, five signified Oxford. In 1901 he used coloured rockets to give news of the America's Cup yacht race. But it was not just sporting results that were announced by firework. For the 1906 general election, a Brocks team set off rockets from Crystal Palace and the Thames embankment whenever a seat changed hands – red for a Liberal gain, blue for a Tory – while Pains fired them from three other places in London. The blue rockets ended up being surplus to requirements as the Conservatives failed to gain a single seat.

A nephew of William Pain named Joseph Wells had set up Wells Fireworks in 1837. As a lighterman on the Thames, he had been used to handling explosives, and he had also worked as a 'public decorator', providing flags, bunting, lanterns and such for streets and houses as people celebrated births, weddings, religious festivals and the visits of royalty and dignitaries. The company made fireworks in a succession of places in south London, and put on regular displays at the Cremorne and North Woolwich Gardens. In 1875 it won the prize for the best Roman candles at an Alexandra Palace international competition. Soon after, a tightening of the law by the 1875 Explosives Act meant it had to move to new premises (Pains had to do the same). From its new factory at Honor Oak, it acquired the reputation of being the Rolls-Royce of the fireworks business, building up a huge trade across the British Empire while putting on regular displays in Europe and establishing an American manufacturing company in Boston. By the time the First World War came, Wells was the third biggest manufacturer in Britain, behind Brocks and Pains.

In the North, Huddersfield emerged as a hotbed of firework manufacturing. Allen Jessop, who lived in the suburb of Lepton in the 1840s, had learned about explosives when he was working in the coal mines and started making squibs in his cellar as a hobby. Then he and his wife went from door to door selling them from a basket. Business boomed and by 1873 he was employing fifteen 'girls', but he was fined for illegally storing explosives. As the law got tighter, Jessop went formal in 1876, setting up the business of Allen Jessop & Sons with his four sons. The workforce more than doubled, though a lot of tasks were still done by female outworkers.

After Allen died in 1880, rivalry between his sons spawned other fireworks firms. One took over the original business, which would sell out to Standard Fireworks in the 1930s, as would a company set up by another son. This younger Jessop drew into the business his nephew Harry Kilner, who would found the Yorkshire Firework Company in 1906. Two other sons started a business that would eventually be absorbed into Globe Fireworks. Harry Kilner's mother, Mary Ann, later described what working conditions were like in those days. As a girl of eight, she said she toiled from six in the morning until ten at night, standing on a stool filling fireworks while the adult workers perched on barrels of gunpowder. During the First World War, some of the Huddersfield factories won contracts from the government to fill hand grenades with explosive.

Standard Fireworks also originated in Huddersfield. Wholesale draper William Greenhalgh had supplemented his income by selling fireworks in the run-up to Bonfire Night. His son James started working with him, and eventually took over the pyrotechnics, leaving drapery to his father. In 1891 James set up Standard, importing some products from China, getting others made by outworkers, often local coal miners earning a bit of extra cash, and buying the rest from other local firework makers, who agreed at first to put Standard labels on them. After a while, they went cold on this idea, and James and his son Edward opened their own factory in 1910, taking over an old quarry that was big enough to allow the production sheds to be spread out, and which already had purpose-built gunpowder stores. A few miles from Huddersfield, at Ossett in 1844, Michael Riley founded Riley's Fireworks. The company continued to grow until the First World War, and became one of the biggest pyrotechnics firms in the country, supplying hundreds of varieties and putting on displays across the north of England, sometimes regular events at resorts such as Bridlington, sometimes for special occasions like the coronation of George v. During the First World War, they apparently filled more than 9 million grenades for the military, but in 1927 a huge explosion completely destroyed their factory, killing the then proprietor, Michael Riley's grandson, Arthur, and two workers. That was the end of the business.

Across the Atlantic, the Du Pont family became probably the first American manufacturers of fireworks for pleasure. In 1802, they had begun producing gunpowder near Wilmington, Delaware, and by 1809 they were making fireworks to let off at family occasions as well as handing them out to their workers. DuPont grew into a major chemicals company but kept making fireworks up to the 1940s. The family had originated in France, but it was fiercely competitive Italian immigrants who dominated aerial fireworks in America through family businesses such as Grucci and Zambelli, often making their name via competitions. The Zambellis came to Pennsylvania in 1893 from a village near Naples with a little black book of the family's recipes, which in 2020 was still locked securely in the company safe. The Rozzis also came from the Naples area, and initially tried their luck in Pennsylvania, but by 1930 they had moved to Cincinnati, Ohio, where in 1935 they put on a display for the first ever Major League Baseball night match, beginning a long relationship with the Cincinnati Reds. Ohio was also home to American Fireworks, set up in 1902 by another Italian immigrant, Vincenzo Sorgi, who came from central Italy. He had three generations of pyrotechnics experience behind him when he arrived in 1899 but he had to do a variety of jobs, including laying railway tracks, before founding American Fireworks. The firm prospered and is still run by the Sorgi family to this day. The patriarchs of these fireworks families would guard their recipes jealously. If they were written down at all, it was usually with the wrong ingredients or the wrong percentages in case competitors got hold of them. They would reminisce about the good old days when the wives patrolled their mortars with shotguns to scare off rivals who might try to tamper with them.

The Gruccis came from Bari to Long Island in 1870, eventually settling near the village of Bellport. A woman in the family was supposed to have won a prize from the king of Italy for mounting a firework display

Greek fire being deployed in a naval battle, illuminated manuscript, 12th century.

The Battle of Legnica, illuminated manuscript, 1353.

Madame Saqui, surrounded by fireworks, about to descend the rope, print, 1822.

Jacob Philipp Hackert, *Fireworks over Castel Sant'Angelo in Rome*, 1775, gouache.

Utagawa Hiroshige, *Enjoying the Fireworks and the Cool of the Evening at Ryogoku Bridge*, *c.* 1847, woodcut print.

Utagawa Hiroshige, *Fireworks over Ryogoku Bridge*, 1858, woodblock colour print on paper.

James Ensor, *Fireworks*, 1887, oil on canvas.

Joseph Wright, *The Annual Girandola at the Castel Sant'Angelo, Rome*, 1775–6, oil on canvas.

James McNeill Whistler, *Nocturne in Black and Gold: The Falling Rocket*, 1875, oil on panel.

Edward Middleton Manigault, *The Rocket*, 1909, oil on canvas.

J.M.W. Turner, *The Campanile of San Marco, Venice, from the Hotel Europa (Palazzo Giustinian) at Night, with Fireworks over the Molo*, 1840, watercolour, bodycolour and chalk on paper.

from a balloon. There was also a story that they had had to leave the old country because neighbours complained that bangs from their fireworks were stopping hens laying eggs. The company's founder had been a barber as well as a pyrotechnician, and kept the hairdressing sideline going after crossing the Atlantic. When they first set up in Long Island, the Gruccis did all their firework making outside. Their first customers were Italians who wanted pyrotechnics for their religious festivals, and it was not until the 1920s that they were able to put all their eggs in the fireworks basket. Then along came the Great Depression. Phil Grucci, the great-great-grandson of the founder, who would run the company in the twenty-first century, said: 'During the Depression, there wasn't much fireworks. There were no celebrations happening.'[47] To make ends meet, his grandfather Felix Sr, who was then in charge, started playing drums with a band, as well as making explosion simulators for the military. As the economy took off again, the Gruccis' business grew, but those Italian saints' days remained a crucial market. They would start with the saint's effigy being paraded through the neighbourhood while people pinned money to it to pay for the festivities, and would climax with a fireworks show, while the audience sat at long tables and banged them to demand more noise. Over the decades, the Grucci company's name evolved, from Suffolk Novelty Fireworks to New York Pyrotechnic Products to International Pyrotechnics. In 1954 Felix was credited with a major technological innovation – the stringless shell. When traditional twine-wrapped shells exploded, burning fragments came down to earth. With the stringless shell, all you got were tiny harmless pieces of confetti.

There were also home-grown companies, such as Standard Fireworks (no relation to the British firm), also based on Long Island. Founded in 1828, by the 1880s it employed 75 people, manufacturing and importing fireworks. The company claimed to be guided by a 'perfect knowledge of chemistry'. It said it had the 'most extensive and finest assorted stock of colored fireworks in the world', and traded with 'South America, Canada and other foreign countries'. For its new range in 1888 the highlight was an 'entirely new' product range of 'Chinese Animalettes' which threw off 'a profusion of various-colored fires, which form into shapes of flies, reptiles, etc., burning from two to ten minutes, and making a very attractive fireworks toy'.[48]

In nineteenth-century America, committees were springing up everywhere to plan Fourth of July celebrations, but fireworks were also becoming more and more popular as the climax for all kinds of events, and long queues would form outside places selling them. In 1866 it was reported that two firms in Washington, DC, had each sold about $250,000 worth. This was in spite of restrictions introduced in places such as New York City, where in 1886 a law threatened anyone letting off a firework with a $5 fine. In 1898 a reporter wrote: 'the American Fourth of July is the greatest event the maker of firecrackers knows,' and claimed that of all countries in the world, the USA 'spends the most upon fireworks'. To keep the market growing, companies had to constantly come up with new products. 'Startling' in 1897 was the 'Devil among Tailors'. You hurled it into the air and when it burst, it threw out 'a number of life-like figures, one larger than the others, supposed to represent the ruler of the infernal regions'. Then there was a big rocket that could 'ascend as high as, or higher than, the Washington Monument [the tallest building in the world, at 170 metres when it was erected]'. A comet-like stream of sparks trailed behind, and an explosion generated 'balloons and golden chains'. Making its debut at a price of ten cents was the 'buzz saw' – two wheels revolving in opposite directions, 'the sparks resembling the jagged edges of two saws in rapid motion'.

Still, fireworks were tame compared with other ways of celebrating Independence Day, such as setting off dynamite. This was popular in the West, where it was readily available in mining camps. In 1901 the mayor of Colorado Springs banned the explosion of all dynamite within the city limits, but as late as 1951 there were reports of sticks being thrown in Utah to celebrate the great day.[49]

The Ups and Downs of Bonfire Night

While pyrotechnics manufacturing grew, some people complained their big day in Britain was not what it used to be, as places introduced restrictions on fireworks and 5 November celebrations. In 1822 a firework maker named James Barlow produced a spoof 'proclamation' from King George IV noting that 'many of our loving Subjects' used to like to mark 5 November as the anniversary of the foiling of the 'wicked, profane, malicious and detestable conspiracy' against James I and that letting off fireworks had 'very essentially contributed to the pleasure' of the occasion. King George, it said, was saddened that demand for fireworks made by these 'loving subjects' was declining, to their 'great injury'. He wished to restore the trade to its former 'vigour and prosperity', and was therefore appointing Barlow as one of a group of 'Royal Commissioners' to gather 'charitable contributions' for these impoverished firework makers.[50] Then, in *The Every-Day Book and Table Book* (1826), the radical journalist and campaigner for press freedom William Hone complained that Bonfire Night 'scuffles' had become rare. When he was young, he said, rival bands would stage a tug of war, with the winners taking the losers' Guy, while those who had been too poor or too lazy to make their own Guy would set out like knights of old to 'smug', or steal, one by '"force of arms," fists, and sticks, from its rightful owners'. On Bonfire Night itself, butchers in the capital would thrash each other 'with the strongest sinews of slaughtered bulls', and 'by ten o'clock, London was so lit up by bonfires and fireworks, that from the suburbs it looked in one red heat. Many were the overthrows of horsemen and carriages, from the discharge of hand-rockets, and the pressure of moving mobs inflamed to violence by drink.' But by the 1820s 'This fiery zeal has gradually decreased.'[51]

In 1834 *The Times* lamented that children trying to get pennies for their Guy appeared ignorant about the notorious historical figure he was supposed to represent. Even a magistrate who had to deal with a Bonfire Night affray five years later 'thought the day was almost forgotten'.[52] In 1859, 5 November was removed from the official calendar of the Church of England as a date that should be observed, and five years later the Scottish writer Robert Chambers looked back nostalgically in his *Book of Days* to a time in London when Guy Fawkes Night had meant 'a most important and portentous ceremony'. The bonfire at Lincoln's Inn Fields, he said, was once 'magnificent', with two hundred cartloads of fuel burned and more than thirty Guys hanged from gibbets before being consumed by the flames. 'The uproar, throughout the town,' he declared, 'can but faintly be imagined by an individual of the present day.'[53] In 1884 *The Times* said that observance of the day in the capital 'was gradually dying out'.[54]

But perhaps these Jeremiahs were looking at the past through smoke-tinted glasses. Hone also noted that before each 5 November the authorities still found it necessary to deliver a letter to every house in the City of London notifying inhabitants of their duty 'to prevent any tumults and riots'. In 1825 Beadle C. Puckeridge warned: 'you are required to charge all your servants and lodgers not to make fireworks or throw them in the street' or face prosecution. Hone also tells a colourful tale from 'a year or two ago' of 'a poor hard-working man' who was tied to a chair and whose kidnappers painted his face, 'put a wig and paper cap on his head, fastened a dark lantern in one of his hands, and

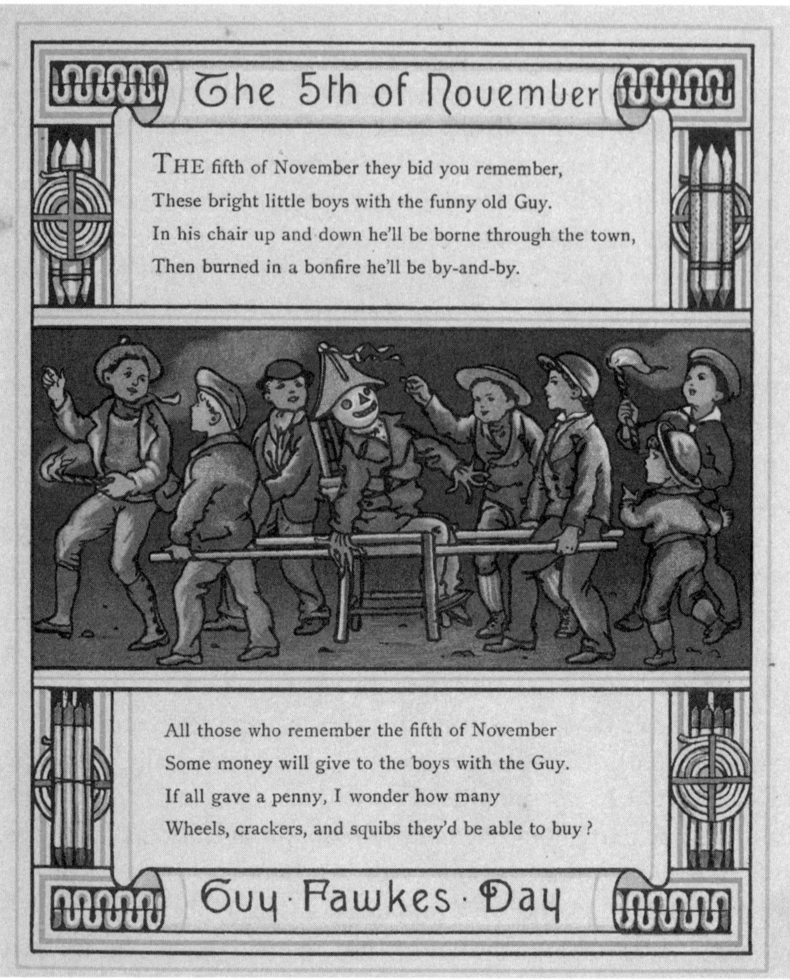

'Guy Fawkes Day' poem, London, 1887.

a bundle of matches in the other, and carried him about all day, with shouts of laughter and huzzas, begging for their "Guy"'.[55] And there are plenty of other reports of 'ruffianism, theft and riotous conduct' from nineteenth-century bonfire nights, indicating that some regarded 5 November as a night when normal rules and restraints did not apply. Certainly, it looked as though Lewes had lost none of its boisterous reputation. In 1806 eighteen people had been arrested and police had to put out fires all around the town. In 1829 there was a near riot when a magistrate tried to lay down the law, and three years later the authorities attempted to ban the festivities, but locals took no notice. In 1847 a resident complained that 'the grossest riots and excesses' took over the town every year, as 'ruffians' and 'bonfire boys' in masks and 'fantastical dress', armed with bats and bludgeons, rolled lighted tar barrels through the streets.[56] The authorities had to bring in extra police whom the bonfire boys engaged in skirmishes, but while some local tradespeople barricaded their premises, others supported the revellers. In 1851 Sussex historian and anti-Catholic propagandist Mark Antony Lower republished *Foxe's Book of Martyrs*, reviving the cult of the Sussex martyrs burned by Bloody Mary, though Lower is said to have been no fan of the bonfire boys. The conversion of the Anglican archdeacon of Chichester to Roman Catholicism in the same year further fanned Protestant resentment.

In Guildford, too, wild times continued with peaceful folk barring their doors as gangs of men disguised by blackened faces and outlandish outfits, calling themselves Guys, took over the town during their 5 November 'lark'. They would let off enormous fireworks that would sometimes fly into people's houses, and if the bonfire looked as though it might go out, the mob would rip down a fence or two to keep it going. Sometimes the revellers would hold a collection to pay for damage they had caused. According to the memoir of a former mayor of Guildford, Henry Peak, disorder got worse after 1850, and Guys drawn from the

'Guy' on its money-making way, southeast London, 1877.

'rougher parts of the population' would use 5 November to make life a misery for people they disliked. Of four arrested in 1865, two were painters, one a cooper and the other a labourer, though there is evidence that some Guys were sons of better-off tradesmen, and P. W. Jacob, the mayor who eventually put down the riots, said that even some people 'of wealth and influence' were willing 'to connive at – a certain amount of riot, mischief and damage to property'. In 1852 a boy had been killed playing with fireworks and the then mayor admitted special constables had been 'overpowered by the mob'. Even when miscreants were prosecuted, they either got off scot-free, or local people clubbed together to pay their fines. The following year three hundred special constables were sworn in, with the result that 'perfect order was maintained.' But two years later, some local notables had their windows smashed and the Riot Act had to be read. In 1856 there were clashes with police, and the next year rioters and police fought a pitched battle in which one person died. Perhaps because of this, for the next few years the police took a more softly, softly approach, but that seemed only to embolden the rioters. A contemporary wrote that the troubles became 'more riotous, the tumult more tumultuous, the attacks on individuals more violent and mischievous', with fireworks being hurled through the windows of unpopular people.[57] In 1863 the crowd threw a policeman on the bonfire, nearly killing him, and attacked the homes of a magistrate and a former mayor. Jacob now took over, and armed the police with cutlasses. The authorities recruited 160 special constables, as well as sending in fifty dragoons, 150 soldiers and two corps of local rifle volunteers. Some 'bands of roughs' tried to cause trouble, but the mayor read the Riot Act and constables cleared the streets.[58] The last serious riot in the town happened not on 5 November, but on Boxing Day 1865. Three of the rioters were sent for twelve months' hard labour and that put an end to the troubles.

In other places 5 November commotions coalesced with local grievances. So in 1867 there was unrest in Exeter over rising food prices, as in Kettering a century before, and on 4 November people rampaged through the streets smashing windows and looting bakers' shops. In response, the local council banned the traditional 5 November bonfire. Incensed, thousands rioted in defence of 'our rights and usage which has not been interfered with for centuries', stoning butchers' and bakers' shops and shouting: 'Bread!'[59] The police were overwhelmed, and the authorities had to bring in soldiers to clear the streets at bayonet point.

At Oxford and Cambridge, Guy Fawkes Night had traditionally been a time of friction between town and gown, but by 1876 it was said that 'the utmost decorum prevailed at Oxford.'[60] (Although as an undergraduate there in the 1960s, this author recalls dire warnings about the dangers of wandering after dark on 5 November, something he never did.) Indeed, by the end of the nineteenth century the authorities in many parts of the country were trying to regulate, and sometimes ban, the sale of fireworks, while the middle classes made determined efforts to tame the occasion, setting up committees to run organized events. Landowners chipped in by providing fields for the festivities to try to keep rowdy elements away from town centres. At Dorchester, Lord Aldington, the local MP, and other donors stumped up £50 for a procession of Guys, music from the town band and a firework display. In north London, the Hampstead Bonfire Club tried to draw together previously diverse events, while south of the river the Lewisham Bonfire Society did the same. The night's traditional rowdiness found itself caught in a pincer movement, with the authorities trying not only to take control of large-scale events, but to encourage people who wanted to let off their own fireworks to do it at home.

In Lewes, too, 5 November celebrations were taken under the wing of four recognized bonfire societies, one of which – the Cliffe, founded in 1853 – is sometimes claimed to be the oldest in the world. But this did not seem to calm the Sussex town, and Bonfire Nights still had a strong whiff of anti-Catholicism. In the 1890s the Northern Ireland Protestant Orange Order formed a local lodge in the town, and in 1893 a Lewes clergyman started holding Thanksgiving Services on the Sunday before 5 November, attended by 'crowded and reverent congregations' in which he warned against the perils of popery.[61] At first, women were banned from attending. Then in 1906 the local authorities tried to prevent burning tar barrels being dragged through the streets, provoking a near riot as bonfire boys marched on the police station. Home-made fireworks called 'Lewes Rousers' had supposedly been prohibited by the authorities in 1904, but continued to appear. About 15 centimetres long and as thick as a marker pen, they would shoot along the ground in unpredictable directions before finally going bang. Alan Brock, damning with faint praise, noted that accidents at Lewes were 'less frequent than might perhaps be expected'.[62]

In 1919 Lewes's first Bonfire Night after the First World War did not include burning the pope's effigy, because this was still forbidden by

DORA, the wartime Defence of the Realm Act. The following year, a local Presbyterian minister expressed his hope that 'the celebration had lost its religious significance.' It was high time, he added, that this 'was relegated to oblivion and forgotten'. The Cliffe Society disagreed, and in 1921 they marked DORA's repeal by burning the effigy of Paul V, pope at the time of the Gunpowder Plot, to the accompaniment of a virulently anti-Catholic speech. A speaker from the Protestant Truth Society had already denounced those as he saw as Enemies of the Bonfire: 'Let them remember the martyr fires that burned in Lewes and other places.' In 1925 a High Church Anglican clergyman who had just moved to the area expressed his horror at rhetoric of this kind, declaring: 'This sort of Protestantism is incompatible with the religion of Christ.'[63] For that year's Bonfire Night, the Cliffe Society put together a tableau – 'The Road to Rome' – attacking High Church Anglicans, whom they considered little better than Catholics. In 1933 the mayor of Lewes asked the Cliffe to drop the pope-burning and their 'No Popery' banners, but the society refused.

The Second World War's blackouts brought another pause to Bonfire Nights. For the first one of the post-war era on 5 November 1946, *Life* magazine went to Lewes, and reported on the burning of an effigy of the pope filled with firecrackers that 'blew up in a tremendous staccato of explosion', though the magazine said it was just an 'ancient jest'.[64] *Life* may have thought it was all good clean fun, but a leading member of the Cliffe Society pitched in to attack 'the attitude of the Vatican during the war'.[65] In the 1950s the other bonfire societies excluded the Cliffe from their United Grand Procession because it insisted on keeping its 'No Popery' banners. To this day, it continues to march on its own.

Sussex was a focal point for 5 November activity, and the Battel Bonfire Boyes, from the town of Battle, would certainly contest the Cliffe's claim to be the oldest bonfire society in the world. They claim lineage back to at least 1830 and more tenuously all the way to 1646, when St Mary's Church allocated two shillings and sixpence for 'gunpowder treason rejoicing'.[66] The Boyes have tried to put on a bonfire every 5 November, although they were stymied by a crackdown in 1906 when Sussex County Council slapped a ban on fires within 25 yards (23 metres) of main roads, by the Second World War (for its duration, the Bonfire Boyes were allowed to put just a single candle in the place where the bonfire was normally lit) and in 2020 by COVID-19. As long ago as

1543, gunpowder was being manufactured at Battle, probably illicitly, and in 1676 a gunpowder mill was given an official licence. It was said, in all likelihood wrongly, that Guy Fawkes had sourced some of his gunpowder from the town, but the rumour raised its profile. In the 1720s, in his *A Tour Thro' the Whole Island of Great Britain*, the author of *Robinson Crusoe*, Daniel Defoe, wrote that Battle was known 'for making the finest gun-powder, and the best perhaps in Europe'.[67] It supplied the Royal Navy, among others, but after a series of accidents the gunpowder mill was stripped of its licence in the nineteenth century.

Home-made fireworks were a traditional feature of Battle's bonfires. The most fearsome was probably the town's own 'Rouser', which would screech along at ground level for about 100 metres, giving out white sparks, and then explode. It is said to have been invented in the 1880s by a hairdresser and firework maker named William Longley. From a collection of wooden sheds, he supplied hundreds each year for Battle's bonfire celebrations. His activities led to a fine of a shilling in 1891. In 1937 one of his descendants was injured in an explosion that killed a man, but it was not until 1951 that the Rouser was banned. In one important respect, the Battle bonfire festivities broke with tradition. They did not burn their Guy, which is perhaps understandable when you realize that its carved wooden head dates back to around 1795. Until about the 1940s it was accompanied by a body that was burned every year. Since then, body and head have lived in the local museum, being let out only for the Bonfire Night parade as the 'oldest Guy in the world', and kept well away from the fire.

With the Guy's head sacrosanct, an opportunity opened for other effigies to be burned at Battle. The first appears to have been of John Jones, the 'Denham murderer', who bludgeoned to death a family of seven in the Buckinghamshire town in 1870. Bonfire Night's versatility has meant a likeness of whichever hate figure was in vogue could be put on top of the fire. During the Crimean War, Tsar Nicholas I of Russia was selected. At that time, the Ottoman Sultan of Turkey was Britain's ally, but as the Wheel of Fortune turned, he too got his turn on the flames, as did Kaiser Wilhelm II, Hitler, Margaret Thatcher and Saddam Hussein. One official of the Battel Bonfire Boyes was sceptical about whether Fawkes was actually the first effigy to be burned, asking: 'Can that really be Guy Fawkes we're putting on the bonfire, when Guy Fawkes wasn't burnt but hung, drawn and quartered?'[68] He pointed to the possibility that Bonfire Night had much earlier origins, perhaps in the ancient Gaelic autumn festival of Samhain, 'summer's end', which also featured bonfires, and was first mentioned in Irish literature in the ninth century.

During the run-up to the First World War, the pyrotechnics industry wanted to rebrand 5 November as 'Firework Night' as they stepped up production. Brocks sold 30 million fireworks in 1908, while Pains shifted nearly 500 tons. Brocks started selling life-size figures packed with pyrotechnics, and in 1909 you could buy a toy dreadnought that exploded 'with a fiery display' (the dreadnought was a kind of super-battleship which featured prominently in the arms race between Britain and Germany). In 1910 demand for fireworks was said to be up by 25–30 per cent on the previous year, but the shift to enjoying them in the privacy of your own home or garden was well underway, especially among the better off, at least according to *The Times*, which reported: 'firework parties are becoming quite an institution in the suburban districts.' The Great War, understandably, was rather a wet blanket, but enthusiasm revived when it ended, as 5 November became more of a children's event, with a suggestion in 1930 that it should be turned into 'children's play day'. Across Britain, children became the leading pleaders for 'a penny for the Guy'.[69]

The Ends of World Wars and Other Official Celebrations

As far as public displays were concerned, the twentieth century carried on where the nineteenth had left off in Britain and its empire. Arthur Brock's son, Frank, mounted a major event on New Year's Day 1903 for the Delhi Durbar to proclaim Edward VII emperor of India. Two years later, Frank was putting on a show from 58 ships at Spithead, near Portsmouth, to celebrate the Entente Cordiale with France. *The Times* reported it was 'scarcely possible to convey by description any adequate idea of the scene presented . . . The epithets "magnificent", "brilliant", "imposing", "effective", "successful", are all summed up in one word, "unprecedented".'[70] The *Morning Leader* declared: 'Messrs Brock out-Brocked Brock!'[71]

In 1906 the royal family showed it too could enjoy fireworks at home, with a daylight display on the Buckingham Palace lawn to celebrate the birthday of one of Edward VII's daughters. Two years later, London hosted the Olympic Games and a firework display at the White City illustrated one of the drawbacks of pyrotechnics in a stadium: smoke lingered and impaired the view because there was no wind to blow it away.

Some said the best Olympic fireworks display was at a private party at a grand house at Bourne End in Buckinghamshire featuring 'living fireworks', depicting Olympic sports such as running, rowing, boxing and wrestling. The host was the American wine importer George Kessler, known as the 'Champagne King', who would survive the sinking of the *Lusitania*.

The Delhi Durbar for Edward VII's successor, George V, in 1911 was billed as the most spectacular ceremony in the history of the British Empire. Attended by four hundred Indian princes, rajas and maharajas, it was the only Durbar at which the reigning monarch was present. During the run-up, a big cache of fireworks blew up, destroying the building in which they were stored. It was never established whether this was sabotage by independence fighters, but after the Durbar, official shows started to fall away as international tensions rose. The last public display of 1914 was at Scarborough a week after the First World War started. Four months later, the town was bombarded by German warships, and seventeen local people were killed. Within days of Britain entering the war, the Defence of the Realm Act banned the lighting of bonfires or fireworks, and most firework manufacturers turned their attentions to the war effort.

Firework displays may have been understandably muted during the First World War, but the end of that dreadful conflict made up for it. The Treaty of Versailles was signed on 28 June 1919, and the following week the government gave the order for the 'National Peace Display' on 19 July in Hyde Park, leaving the organizers just a fortnight to prepare for what was then the most ambitious show in British history. They must

First World War victory celebration, London, 1919.

have been relieved that elaborate machines were no longer in vogue, but they still had to supply fire portraits of the king and queen and of war heroes, as well as the greatest concentration of aerial fireworks ever assembled. There were shells of up to 40 centimetres calibre fired in salvoes of as many as fifty at a time, Roman candles in batteries of two hundred, a cascade 300 metres long, and rockets to be set off in flights of one hundred, with a finale of 2,000 all going at once. By five in the evening, everything was set for the nine o'clock start when the heavens opened. But even this downpour did not stop the *Daily News* declaring the show 'vastly more marvellous than anything of the kind seen in this country before'.[72] According to some estimates, it was witnessed by more spectators than any previous display. The king and queen watched from a platform erected on the roof of Buckingham Palace, while virtually every city in the country put on its own display, and tons of fireworks were shipped out to the colonies and dominions. The spectacle in Bombay was said to have attracted the biggest crowd ever assembled in the city.

During the 1920s Brocks' expertise continued to be in demand across the world. In 1924 the company staged what was then the biggest display ever seen in Scandinavia to celebrate the three-hundredth anniversary of the founding of the Norwegian capital, Kristiania, and its renaming as Oslo. The following year, the company mounted a series of events across South Africa for a royal tour by the Prince of Wales, later King Edward VIII, while 1929 saw probably the most poignant battle tableau ever staged by Arthur Brock as he used Douglas Harbour in the Isle of Man for a reconstruction of the Royal Navy's raid on Zeebrugge in Belgium in 1918 in which his son Frank was killed.

By the time that display was put on, the Great Depression was stalking the world, but pyrotechnics seemed to escape at least some of its effects as what were said to be the biggest crowds ever seen in Finland gathered in Helsinki in 1933 to watch the fireworks for 'British week'. There were no official fireworks in London for the Silver Jubilee of George V in 1935, but Crystal Palace put on a display of its own, and there were three hundred others across the country, as well as many throughout the empire, including 76 in Africa. George would die early the next year, and elaborate firework shows were planned to mark the coronation of his son, Edward VIII, in May 1937, but he abdicated, leaving his younger brother George VI to take the throne. The coronation and fireworks went ahead as planned – 'same day, different king,' as the saying went. Perhaps the most impressive part of the celebrations was the simultaneous firing of 100,000 of the biggest available from the fleet at Spithead.

The Treaty of Versailles may have brought Britain's then biggest ever firework celebration, as it closed the First World War, the 'war to end all wars'. But as the spoof history of Britain *1066 and All That* notes, the Treaty of Versailles turned out to be the 'peace to end peace'.[73] Twenty years after it was signed, the world was fighting again, and in 1946 Britain put on another huge firework jamboree to mark victory in the Second World War. This time, the site chosen was the same stretch of the Thames used for the celebration of James I's daughter's marriage back in 1613. St Thomas's Hospital had been severely damaged in the Blitz, and it was from its roof that Alan Brock directed what was then the biggest aerial pyrotechnic show ever seen. As the royal family watched, the fireworks went on for an hour and a half, with 750 shells being fired, along with 3,000 aquatic fireworks, while two dazzling cascades of fire spanned the entire width of the river, falling into the water from a height of 15 metres. The author A. P. Herbert wrote in the *News of the World*: 'The Thames burned – and bravely. Her muddy waters turn red, turn silver and gold and green.'[74] He also described how the 'Big Bomb', claimed to be the biggest firework shell ever seen, filled the sky 'with golden rain'.

Britain's Fireworks Industry Revives after the First World War

After the First World War, Brocks' shows at the Crystal Palace resumed in 1920. The following year, *The Times* remarked that visiting families sometimes could not agree on which were the venue's most appealing attractions, but there was 'one feature about which there will be no difference of opinion' – the fireworks.[75] In 1929 more than 62,000 people attended a daylight firework display at Whitsun (which happened roughly at the same time as the late spring Bank Holiday) 'during which toys were showered on them from the bursting rockets'.[76] The shows continued until the Crystal Palace was burned down in a spectacular fire in 1936. The cause of the blaze was never conclusively established, but it had nothing to do with fireworks. Meanwhile Brocks' rivals Pains were also busy putting on a series of events at the new Wembley Stadium for the British Empire Exhibition in 1924, but two years later the Pains family line ran out, and two nephews started running the company.

In 1932 *The Times* reported that Brocks were making 96,000 fireworks a day, plus 200,000 sparklers, using nearly 20 miles of wire. (A sparkler's basic ingredients are an oxidizer, aluminium or some other metal powder to create the sparks, plus a fuel and a binder. Sometimes an ingredient such as sugar or starch is used to do both jobs. The mixture is made into a slurry that is used to coat a length of wire. Sparklers come in outdoor and indoor versions; the indoor give out less smoke.) The following year, the company moved to a new factory at Hemel Hempstead in Hertfordshire, then said to be the biggest fireworks complex in the world, with two hundred buildings spread over more than 200 acres (80 hectares). Up in Huddersfield, Harry Kilner's Yorkshire Fireworks Company adopted the Lion brand in 1936, with its famous logo of a lion leaping through the letter 'O'. Two years later, Wells' Fireworks established its headquarters at Dartford in Kent, which the Home Office was said to have considered the best-laid-out fireworks factory in Europe. Under its 'Crown Brand', Wells displayed its wares at the Cowes and Henley Regattas, and at coronations and royal jubilees. Its displays would also penetrate America – the Los Angeles Olympics of 1932, the Squaw Valley Winter Olympics of 1960, the Rose Bowl American football game and Disneyland in Florida. During the Second World War, the Dartford site was hit by a German bomb, and it was inundated in the great floods of 1953, when Wells lost almost all its stock, but competitors rallied round to provide it with enough fireworks to meet its Bonfire Night orders. John Bennett, editor of *Fireworks* magazine, would comment in 2019 that this chivalrous action was 'something which would never happen today'.[77]

The end of the Second World War saw a spate of new fireworks companies in the UK. Wessex Fireworks, based near Salisbury, emerged from the Wessex Aircraft Engineering Co. (WAECO), which made signalling equipment for aircraft and wind direction smoke generators, and would produce the fuel pack for the Olympic torch at the London games in 1948. In 1961 the company was taken over by matchmakers Bryant & May, which had bought Pains the previous year. It merged the two companies as Pains Wessex, and later moved all production to Wiltshire. There would be another move in the 1970s to the old Wells site at Dartford. Lion Fireworks prospered, often using female outworkers to fill the cardboard cases with powder, put glue on the labels and add the blue touchpaper. (Touchpaper is paper impregnated with saltpetre to make it burn slowly.) Meanwhile, two Jewish refugees founded Astra Fireworks near Sandwich in Kent in 1946. They began by making sparklers, then graduated to bigger fireworks. Rainbow Fireworks, who were noted for their high-quality artwork on products and publicity material, started in 1948. Seven years later there was an explosion at their factory at Finchampstead in Berkshire that killed two workers. Another company to start up around this time was Benwell Fireworks, founded in 1949 by Benjamin Weller of the Haley & Weller firm of toy manufacturers, which specialized in dartboards. With its headquarters at Draycott in Derbyshire, by 1959 Benwell's was producing more than 20 million fireworks a year. All this time, Standard Fireworks continued to grow until it was said to be the biggest manufacturer in Europe, employing more than six hundred people. Although it put on some big displays, the mainstay of its business was the fireworks it sold in its shops. It was renowned for making everything from sparklers to the biggest shells for public displays, and for its unmistakeable delivery vans, each with a giant rocket on top. Having supplied munitions to the government during both world wars, in 1959 Standard would become the only fireworks manufacturer to be listed on the London stock market.

That year, *The Times* reported that there were 'some 10 or more' British manufacturers, employing more than 3,000 people, that depended on 5 November for up to 90 per cent of their business, and that they were expecting record sales. It added that most were also working on bird-scarers, film effects and government contracts for the military. They tended to do good export business, with Pains reckoning a quarter of its fireworks were sold overseas. Business might be booming, but *The Times* concluded that, except for a few space-age 'gimmicks', such as a 'sputnik' rocket that carried a small plastic dog in a mini-container, and a banger branded an 'atom-smasher', 'fireworks are still basically the same as they always have been.'[78]

By the 1950s, wrote the Revd Ron Lancaster, firework displays might be 'exciting and spectacular' for the crowds, but to the manufacturers 'they were often more useful as means of publicity' than for generating income, with profits coming from shop sales.[79] Lancaster, who was a chemistry teacher and school chaplain at the private Kimbolton School in Cambridgeshire, founded Kimbolton Fireworks in 1964. As a young boy in Huddersfield during the Second World War, he and his friends would go up on the moors to watch Standard testing their parachute flares by the hundred. Each one drifted down on a square yard of silk, and Lancaster was very popular with his mother when he salvaged a

The Revd Ron Lancaster.

few to take home. The boys also collected flares that had not gone off, and soon they could make their own fireworks 'quite easily', thanks to the advice of more knowledgeable people. After being a curate in the West Riding, Lancaster went to Kimbolton School in 1963 to teach chemistry and divinity, and persuaded them to let him put up a couple of sheds in his back garden as a firework laboratory. After he had done some consultancy research for Pains, the operation eventually evolved into Kimbolton Fireworks. Lancaster started putting on displays at local fetes, then graduated to events such as Henley Regatta before becoming an adviser on the Queen's Silver Jubilee celebrations in 1977. His manufacturing methods were traditional: 'I have a small hydraulic compressor but a lot of the powder is just knocked in with a stick.'[80]

American Favourites: Flashcrackas, Fire Engines and Cherry Bombs

In the early years of the twentieth century, Chinese firecrackers were not very popular in the United States, with Americans preferring 'cannon crackers', up to 35 centimetres long, which would be banned in 1966. In comparison, the 'mandarin crackers', sold in plain wrapping without branding, from the original home of pyrotechnics seemed very tame. Then in 1916 the Hitt Fireworks Co. of Seattle made a breakthrough.

The company had been established in the early 1900s by Thomas Hitt, who had left England after studying chemistry and getting into hot water for making fireworks and storing them under his bed. He made the firm one of America's leading firework manufacturers, putting on set-pieces such as that old favourite, 'The Last Days of Pompeii', as well as Fourth of July shows. The reputation he won brought Hollywood calling and the company provided pyrotechnic effects for films such as *All Quiet on the Western Front* (1930) as well as the famous burning-of-Atlanta sequence in *Gone With the Wind* (1939). But Hitt's bread and butter came from selling small fireworks to ordinary folk – Roman candles, sparklers and 'Flashcrackas', small firecrackers. While the Chinese used gunpowder in their crackers, Flashcrackas were fired by photographic flash powder made from powdered magnesium or aluminium with an oxidizer. These 'flashlight crackers' made a much louder bang than gunpowder crackers. (They would be used from 1936 to 1960 to brighten up the annual Firecracker Golf Tournament at Spokane in Washington State, where the normal hushed tones that accompanied golfers' shots were replaced by a cacophony of crackers.) Hitt shared his formula with the Chinese, and they began mass-producing Flashcrackas. The company survived the Great Depression: 'People needed entertainment,' said one of the family, and 'fireworks didn't cost much.'[81] At its peak, the business employed two hundred workers, but as local authorities put more and more stringent restrictions on manufacturing (a woman worker had been killed in an accident in 1921), Hitt's gradually moved production to China and the Philippines, until the American factory closed in the late 1960s. The Chinese started using the Hitt formula to produce crackers of their own, branded as 'silverfish salutes' or 'thunder firecrackers', which combined a brilliant silver flash with a loud bang. They also switched over to bright wrappings, often carrying pretty pictures of beautiful birds or flower maidens, and brand names they thought would appeal to American consumers such as Lone Eagle or Yan Kee Boy.

Between the wars, die-cut cardboard novelty fireworks became a popular genre in the USA, featuring elephants that shot sparks from their trunks, fire engines that raced around giving off smoke and so on. In each case, the climax of the little performance was the object blowing itself up in a shower of paper shards. A special for the Fourth of July was the so-called 'SOS Ship', a 12-centimetre cardboard ocean liner that was quite elaborately decorated, with people depicted standing on the deck looking out to sea, while down below faces peered out of portholes. It had a single funnel with a fuse sticking out of the top, and could be launched on a pond or swimming pool. When it was lit, you were promised 'a shrill siren whistle followed by several loud reports ending in complete destruction of the ship'.[82]

A catalogue of 'harmless indoor fireworks' from 1932 offers for 10 cents a 'Joke Bottle Cork', which looked like the real thing, but when you put it in a bottle, it would 'throw out numerous sparks, snake, snow, electric light, and other harmless fireworks'. Top of the range was a 'Miniature Vesuvius' at 50 cents, promoted as 'a great joke novelty and perfectly harmless'. Outdoor fireworks promised more formidable delights: the 'Tom, Dick, and Harry' featured a 'powerful Flash Bomb', a shell that delivered a 'terrific shower of beautiful stars', plus a 'whistling aerial bomb'. In 1935 five dollars spent with the American Fireworks Distributing Co. of Chicago would buy you a 'Children's Assortment' of more than fifty items, including sparklers, firecrackers, 'Python Black Snakes', Roman candles and a Catherine wheel. American author and fireworks enthusiast George Plimpton records how instructions such as 'Lay on Ground – Light Fuse – Get Away' brought a frisson of excitement to the Fourth of July firework parties that were often the 'first community gatherings one experienced in childhood'.[83]

Fireworks, and especially rockets, remained risky right up to the 1950s, according to Orville Carlisle, owner of what was claimed to be the world's only firecracker museum, in Norfolk, Nebraska. A self-taught expert, considered by some to be 'the father of modern model rocketry', he said that amateur 'rocketeers routinely lost fingers and hands due to crude rocket construction.'[84] His interest in fireworks began when his father, a travelling sweets salesman, would bring firecrackers home from his journeys. On the Fourth of July, he and his two brothers set them off from four in the morning until midnight. Decades later, in the 1980s, he would put on spectacular displays, including a firecracker stunt called 'Norfolk Avenue on Saturday Night', an evocation in bangs, squeals and flashes of the town's main street on the busiest night of the week.

One of the most disturbing American favourites was the cherry bomb. About an inch in diameter, it was usually coloured red, hence the name. It had a core of flash powder or black powder surrounded by sawdust hardened with a mild adhesive in a stiff paper cover, with a fuse like a stalk reaching into the explosive mixture. It was said to be twenty times more powerful than today's firecrackers, and after you lit the fuse, you got three or four seconds before the cherry bomb exploded. Keith Moon, aka 'Moon the Loon', drummer of the rock group The Who, discovered them when the group were on tour in the USA in 1968. Fellow band member Pete Townshend described how he went into Moon's hotel room in New York City and found the toilet had been blown away, leaving only the piping. The drummer's story was: 'Well this cherry bomb was about to go off in my hand and I threw it down the toilet.'[85] Moon thought they were 'incredible', and he also liked to fling them out of his hotel window. Antics of this kind resulted in the band being banned from a number of hotels. The U.S. government officially prohibited cherry bombs in 1966, but as recently as 2021 the state of New Hampshire, for example, was having to sternly declare: 'These devices and others of like construction are federally banned explosive devices and never should be referred to as fireworks. If you find someone in possession of, and/or selling illegal explosive devices IMMEDIATELY notify the New Hampshire State Police.'[86] But some authorities have admitted defeat. In the run-up to the Fourth of July celebrations of 2020, the mayor of Washington, DC, admitted: 'It is unlikely, and let me just be perfectly candid, that the police can chase down every cherry bomb that pops in the District of Columbia.'[87]

Japan Claims a Record

In the early twentieth century, according to Alan Brock, Japanese firework displays were notable for shells that burst with 'patterns of the most astonishing symmetry and beauty'. He credited this to the 'painstaking care and exactitude' with which they were made – 'a lengthy process that Western rates of pay render prohibitive'.[88] To celebrate the emperor's enthronement in 1928, Aoki Gisaku, known as the 'god of fireworks', devised a chrysanthemum, with the centre of the flower in red, the inner petals blue, and amber round the edge.[89] (If the stars that burst from a shell leave trails in the sky, it is called a chrysanthemum. If the stars have no trails, it is a peony. The peony is now the most widely used shell in displays.) He believed three layers was the most that could be achieved, but his son Tamon managed to add a fourth, and other *hanabishi* would take the chrysanthemum even further. The Land of the Rising Sun also specialized in shells for daylight displays, which, instead of creating effects with fire, released human or animal paper figures. Other effects included paper streamers or rows of flags drifting down from parachutes. The story goes that at a big event for Hitler, Germany's leading pyrotechnic company brought in a consignment of shells from Japan. Swastikas were supposed to pop out of them, but rising suns appeared instead, to the Führer's fury.

In 1956 the Japanese took over the record for the world's biggest firework from Britain's 'Big Bomb'. The 'Bouquet of Chrysanthemums' rose 900 metres above Tokyo Bay, before bursting in a typical oriental pattern. Weighing more than 90 kilograms, and carrying a price tag of about $8,500, it had taken the Marutamaya Ogatsu Fireworks Co. four months to make, and it was fired from a mortar a metre wide. A Grucci worker named Bernie Wells remarked on how little noise mega-shells of this kind made as they emerged from a mortar – a 'small *harrumph*, a sort of clearing of the throat. But then the launching site ... *trembles*.'[90] Some pyrotechnicians can be dismissive, suggesting that equally spectacular effects can be achieved much more cheaply by using, say, a dozen smaller shells and setting them off at the same time, but breaking records certainly generates publicity, and the Ogatsu company became a major supplier of shells to the U.S. market.

The company had started in the eighteenth century by providing fireworks for feudal lords. Toshio Ogatsu, the twelfth-generation boss, came to America just after the Second World War to promote its products, and caused a stir by calling himself an 'artist', talking about how he was inspired by the aesthetics of waterfalls, fish and birds, and naming one of his aerial spectaculars 'Tropical Pool'. He would paint a design on canvas and then try to emulate it with fireworks. Ogatsu became celebrated across the world, but in the Soviet Union he made the mistake of completely outclassing the local pyrotechnic efforts with a dramatic portrayal of a fiery Mount Fuji, and he was not asked back. In the USA, he made his name with displays in New York City in the 1950s and '60s, notably the Fourth of July show sponsored by Macy's famous department store and fired from a string of barges in the Hudson River, which attracted more than a million spectators. John Serpico, owner of a small firework manufacturing company in New Jersey, used to fire displays for Ogatsu, and said that before each one the Japanese pyrotechnician would pray. For the 1953 show, unusually, Ogatsu was not on the barges. Halfway through, a big shell burst prematurely when it was just a few metres out of its mortar, setting fire to a whole deck-load of fireworks. A lot of spectators on the shore applauded, thinking it was all part of the show, but two of Serpico's men were thrown into the water and drowned.

National Days and Special Occasions

By the nineteenth century, pyrotechnics were being used across the world to celebrate important national occasions. Ten days after America's Fourth of July comes France's Bastille Day, when perhaps 70 per cent of all the fireworks consumed by the country in a year are set off. According to some historians, fireworks marked the first anniversary of the storming of the Bastille in 1790, though others say the pyrotechnics came a few days later. Some revolutionaries were hostile to fireworks, because of the way they had been used by French kings to overawe the populace. Expense had been no object. Indeed, France's new revolutionary government found itself saddled with paying off the firework bills the royals had run up. But America demonstrated that pyrotechnics were compatible with a republican government, and in 1880 Bastille Day was made an official holiday, with the French government instructing it should be 'celebrated with all the brilliance that local resources allow' in every town and village, while Paris put on a spectacular pyrotechnic display.[91]

The French capital boasted one of the greatest of all launchpads, the Eiffel Tower. In 1897, during its construction, fireworks were set off from the partially built structure. Just a couple of months after it opened in 1899,

Worker in pyrotechnics factory, France, 1906.

the Ruggieris used it for a display. In 1950 they were there again with a twelve-button electrical panel which they used to set off a couple of thousand fireworks, generating, according to one writer, 'an apotheosis ... in showers, balls, streamers, rockets, and what looked like silver and gold clouds of burning snowflakes'.[92] Another spectacular setting in France is Carcassonne, a UNESCO World Heritage Site, which started its displays in 1898. Alluding to the city's turbulent past – conquered by the Muslims and the Franks, being at the centre of the Cathar rebellion – it uses the magnificently preserved medieval ramparts as its set, concluding by turning the sky red as if the city was ablaze. In 2016 tragedy would strike at a 14 July fireworks display in Nice. About ten minutes after it finished, an Islamic State terrorist deliberately drove a lorry into the crowds who had been enjoying the spectacle, killing more than eighty people.

Pyrotechnicians have long been keen to exploit water reflections to enhance their shows. So where better than Lake Annecy in the French Alps, regarded as the cleanest lake in Europe? The display held there on the first Saturday in August is part of a festival first put on to honour Napoleon III's visit to the medieval city of Annecy in 1860. Mirrored in the crystal-clear waters of the lake against a backdrop of mountains, the fireworks display is longer than usual, going on for well over an hour. Fireworks are set off from more than fifty positions, many of them on the lake itself. One spectator in 2013 said they had never seen anything like it: 'the sky was permanently alight with a mix of beautifully choreographed fireworks, lasers and 10-metre high water jets.'[93]

Fireworks also mark Switzerland's national day on 1 August, but more idiosyncratic is the *Sechseläuten*, the 'six o'clock ringing', held in Zurich every spring. It began in the sixteenth century, with a bell in the Grossmünster church pealing at six o'clock in the evening on the first Monday after the spring equinox. This signalled that until the dark evenings returned, the working day would by law end at that time, allowing people to enjoy what was left of the daylight. In 1952 the date of the festival was shifted to the third Monday in April, but there was no tampering with its spectacular climax – the burning of the *Böögg*. The *Böögg*, a kind of bogeyman, is a 3-metre-high figure that looks like a snowman and has a head packed with firecrackers. Its destruction marks the end of winter. At first, local youths in different parts of the city would make a number of *bööggs*, which they would jeer at as they trundled them round the streets on wagons before setting fire to them. Only at the end of the nineteenth century did the occasion focus on a single *Böögg*.

Tradition has it the effigy, set on a 10-metre-high bonfire, can deliver a long-range weather forecast. If its head explodes shortly after the wood is lit, that means it will be a good summer, but if it takes a long time, the weather will be miserable. The fastest time was set in 2003, five minutes and 42 seconds, and that was followed by a blisteringly hot summer. But the *Böögg* does not seem infallible. The slowest time was recorded in 2016, when the head survived for more than 43 minutes, but that year's summer was one of the hottest ten on record, while two years earlier the head blew up in a brisk 7 minutes 23 seconds, but summer was poor. After the effigy has met its end, local people barbecue their sausages on the embers.

Over the years, the *Böögg* has faced various enemies. In 1921 a young man, allegedly put up to it by communists, set it on fire four hours before the official ceremony. Eighty-five years later, leftist revolutionaries kidnapped it from the workshop where it had been made and replaced it with a chocolate Easter bunny and a hammer and sickle. They later paraded the stolen figure at their May Day festivities, but the *Böögg* burning had gone ahead as planned, using a substitute effigy. In between these two events, there were other mishaps. Four times, the *Böögg* fell off the bonfire before its head exploded, and once it toppled into Lake Zurich. Coronavirus stopped the ceremony altogether in 2020, and the following year, for the first time, the *Böögg* was burned outside the city to discourage crowds.

Fake snowmen may be all very well, but the combination of real snow and ice with fireworks can also be seductive. Certainly it seemed to be so for President Charles de Gaulle of France, who is supposed to have had the train on which he was travelling halted so he could watch a pyrotechnic display for the Winter Olympics at Grenoble in 1968 against its snowy alpine backdrop. Another spectacular winter setting is provided by the Harbin International Ice and Snow Festival, said to be the biggest of its kind in the world, held every January and February in China. The fireworks burst over huge, full-size ice sculptures of palaces, castles, pagodas, the Colosseum, you name it – all lit up in bright colours. The festival began in 1963, but was halted by the Cultural Revolution and got into its swing again only in 1985. Winter temperatures in Harbin can go as low as −25°C, but perhaps global warming took a hand in 2019, when the festival had to pack up ten days early because it got so mild the sculptures started to melt. In Japan, they go one better at the Lake Akan Ice Festival on the island of Hokkaido, letting off fireworks from the frozen surface of the water. It happens in a national park, and the absence of the light pollution you get in big cities is supposed to make the show especially striking. At another spectacular winter festival in Japan, near Nara on the country's main island, Honshu, the firework display is the starting gun for the incineration of a mountain. 'Wakakusa Yamayaki' means 'burning Mount Wakakusa', and on the evening of the fourth Saturday of every January, as the pyrotechnics die away, monks dressed as warriors light torches at a sacred shrine, and then set fire to the dead grass on the mountain. Flames leap up to 12 metres in the air and the blaze goes on for an hour, with the fire brigade standing by to make sure it does not get out of hand. The festival's origins go back to the Middle Ages. Some say it was first held to celebrate the resolution of a territorial dispute between rival temples, while others maintain the fire was meant to stop spirits getting out of a tomb on the top of the mountain and frightening people.

In 2016 UNESCO designated one of Spain's great firework festivals an important part of the 'intangible cultural heritage of humanity'. Las Fallas in Valencia, which runs from 15 to 19 March every year, reaches its climax on the feast of St Joseph, the carpenter who was Jesus's earthly father, and attracts up to 2 million people. Some historians believe the event dates back as far as the fifteenth century, and that it celebrates the end of winter, when carpenters gave their workshops a spring clean, throwing away old bits of wood and candles they no longer needed as daylight hours lengthened. Neighbours would then get together to make bonfires in the streets from the rubbish in honour of St Joseph. Nowadays Las Fallas is like an endless street party with fireworks, music and processions.

One unusual feature is the *mascletà* in Valencia's main square, the Plaza del Ayuntamiento. While other firework festivals may be about beauty in the sky, the *mascletà* is about noise. It is supposed to have been inspired by the gun salutes used for civic or religious celebrations. Because it happens in broad daylight, it is not a setting for stunning visual effects. The renowned theatre critic Kenneth Tynan published an account of his visit to the event in 1975. 'Since even a Valencian,' he wrote, 'might balk at attempting to outshine the sun, the emphasis by day is on unaccompanied sound: if they cannot dazzle you, by God they will deafen you . . . conversation ceases, windows shake.'[94] In those days, strings of firecrackers ran above streets leading to the main square, but these were banned soon after, because of the damage they could do.

Waiters were often seen dousing the awnings of restaurants with water to stop them catching fire.

The *mascletàs* start well before the festival, and on each day of Las Fallas they become louder and louder, reaching a climax on the last. They are supplemented by the bangers set off day and night by local people, so sleep can be a scarce commodity. (Valencians' love affair with fireworks is not limited to Las Fallas. They are liable to let them off all through the year – on public holidays, at weddings and street parties, or for no particular reason.) That seasoned television traveller Michael Palin was in Valencia for Las Fallas in 1999 and relates how the official proceedings began just after eight in the morning. He describes being woken by a band followed by a procession of elderly men. One was pushing a supermarket trolley full of firecrackers, which his two 'lugubrious' companions would light with their cigars, then throw across the street. But that was nothing compared with the *mascletà* itself that erupts at two in the afternoon. Palin was able to watch the proceedings from a balcony above the square, while two or three thousand people thronged below. Above the crowd was a network of wires from which hung thousands of small packets of explosive. Palin's host gave him what appears to be standard advice for the *mascletà* audience: don't wear earplugs, and keep your mouth open to 'let the blast pass through'.[95]

Three shells were fired high into the air. Then the fun began, with 'a thunderous wall of sound which rolls towards us, the speed of the explosions carefully orchestrated to vary the pace whilst building up a counterpoint of overlapping echoes. One huge report follows another, the blasts hurling shock waves across the square.' It was enough to set Palin's jacket flapping. Then the pace accelerated: 'as the fire sprints along the wires of thunderflashes, sending up a ripping, shattering din and when you think you can take no more, the big mortars start to blow with such force that you can only hang on and let it thrill and terrify.' Finally 'thunderous explosions on the ground and soaring shell-bursts in the air, build to a relentless ear-splitting cacophony, an unbelievable tremendous roar, which, with one last mighty salvo, stops as suddenly as it began.' This climax is known locally as the *terremoto*, earthquake. The whole thing lasted just over five minutes. Then after a 'fragment' of complete silence, 'a great cry' went up and people spilled through the barriers that had held them back, racing across the square to salute the pyrotechnic teams 'who emerge like mythological heroes from the shroud of white smoke they have created'.[96] Rivalry between these different pyrotechnic teams probably eggs them on to going the extra mile. Ron Lancaster's son Mark, who was a director of the family firm before becoming a Conservative government minister, wrote that the *mascletà* 'makes our Guy Fawkes day appear like a public safety demonstration'.[97]

At midnight every night, there are also conventional firework displays, with the most colourful and spectacular known as the *Nit del Foc*, or 'night of fire', held on 19 March. Kenneth Tynan was very taken with it, calling it 'one of the greatest free entertainments on earth; a prolonged spasm of organised fire animating the night sky in streaks and splashes ... illuminating the whole townscape'. There were rockets in

> regiments ... rushing upward to re-enact in multiple form the big-bang theory of cosmology – initial flash, bright centrifugal spray, and final decline into darkness ... You realize that an art superficially childish can be emotionally overwhelming, touching some very resonant chords indeed. Thanksgiving by fire, the element that warms us and cooks our food, must be one of the oldest and most appropriate means of human celebration.

If it had been a good show, people's eyes would be shining. 'So are your own,' wrote Tynan, 'and strangers look at you in recognition. You have shared with them a glittering, shimmering, shattering, zooming-every-which-way experience.' Spectators walked home through the smell of

Mortars lined up for Valencia's *Nit del Foc*, 2014.

Las Fallas festival, Valencia, 2023.

cordite along avenues strewn with rocket sticks, feeling 'a momentary glow of communal bliss'.[98]

The whole event gets its name from the giant *Fallas* – witty tableaux of grotesque figures up to 25 metres high, made of wood, papier-mâché, cardboard and polystyrene foam, often designed to poke fun at the powerful and famous, and exhibited all over the city. They were said to have been made originally from those old bits of wood discarded by carpenters, with gloves and masks added to make them look a bit more convincing, but by the early twentieth century hands and faces were being sculpted in wax. Nowadays the figures are elaborately made by specialist artists who congregate in a particular area of Valencia, dubbed Falla City, and commissioned by local groups who raise the necessary money and compete to create the best. There are 750 of these groups, with a total membership equivalent to more than a quarter of Valencia's population. At midnight on the last night of the festival comes the *cremà*, when these impressive creations are all burned, with the help of fireworks that have been put inside them, though each year the best one is saved and exhibited in a special museum. As in so many places, politicians are a favourite target for the effigy-makers, so in 1996, for example, the winner featured them in a work entitled 'Outlaws', and used Desperate Dan, cowboys, a pig and a vulture to get its message across. It was said to have cost £70,000.

Along the coast from Valencia, in Barcelona, there is another festival featuring fireworks but it marks the end of spring and summer rather than the beginning. The Fiesta de la Mercè started in 1902, after Pope Pius IX declared the Virgin Mary the patron saint of the city. The big night is 24 September, when 'devils' and 'dragons', actually locals in fancy dress, chase around the streets in the *Correfoc*, or 'fire-run', carrying powerful sparklers and spraying the crowds with sparks. Would-be spectators are warned this is not for the faint-hearted and that they should be well covered in hats, protective glasses and non-inflammable clothing. A gentler version for children happens earlier in the evening. Up north in the Basque city of Pamplona, fireworks feature in the famous, or should that be notorious, nine-day festival when bulls rampage half a mile through the streets, occasionally goring or trampling those brave or foolish enough to run with them. It is said that back in the seventeenth century, rockets were attached to the bulls to make it that bit more exciting. These days there is a children's run, in which a man carries a wood-and-papier-mâché figure of a bull adorned with firecrackers and colourful fireworks as he gently pursues a crowd of youngsters. As with the festivals in Valencia and Barcelona, this one too honours the city's patron saint, St Fermin, though there was a bit of chicanery with dates. The saint's day was 25 September, but in 1592 the celebrations were shifted to July. Pyrotechnics are supposed to have featured in the event ever since the sixteenth century, and each night there is a fireworks competition. The festival became known for riotous behaviour, though the authorities have tried to calm things down in recent years. George Plimpton writes about fireworks flying wildly around the streets, including a rocket that soared into the open window of a third-floor apartment. He says the only response was the window being closed angrily.

Papier-mâché bulls adorned with fireworks and spewing out sparks also feature in festivals in Mexico. Known as *toritos*, or 'little bulls', some are small enough for a man to carry above his head, while others are life-size monsters that have to be pushed around on wheels by a squad of helpers. They put in an appearance on the Day of the Dead on 1 November, but they get a starring role on 8 March at the feast of St John of God, patron saint of firework makers and firefighters. A sixteenth-century Portuguese, he won his title by running into a burning hospital, rescuing those inside and emerging unscathed. In the *pamplonada*, named after Pamplona, 250 *toritos* take over the streets of Tultepec, Mexico's fireworks capital, flinging out sparks in all directions at the 100,000 spectators, the boldest of whom get as close as they dare. In 2018 one spectator using a shield improvised from a cardboard box told a reporter it was frightening, 'but the adrenaline one feels seeing the show and how the people get is marvellous'.[99] That year, more than five hundred people were injured, mercifully most of them not seriously, and in 2020 *Fodor's Travel Guide* selected the festival as one of the 'nine most dangerous on the planet'.

It is estimated that pyrotechnics grace more than 3,000 festivals every year in Mexico, and among the most distinctive elements of the country's fireworks tradition are *Castillos*, reminiscent of the 'machines' of old. A competition to choose the best is a feature of the National Pyrotechnics Festival. Around since at least the eighteenth century and towering up to 30 metres high, they are built of wood with lots of moving parts. The home-made fireworks attached to them can take up to half an hour to go through their routine. Traditionally they were transported to the site of the display, but then some bigger communities started putting up more permanent aluminium structures. According to one description: 'Like a sculpture before lit, it is a fantasy of moving colour when exploded. All these movable parts – gyrating wheels, swirling fans, or pivoting petals which unfold; the teetering squares and reeling rectangles; wheels within wheels and circles within squares.'[100] The wheels can be up to 12 metres in diameter, and the various moving parts rejoice in traditional names such as 'the burning sun', 'the column of wheels' and 'the ball of fire'. The wheels are works of art in themselves, burning spectacularly for minutes on end, and sometimes using similar techniques to 'transformation' set-pieces, where one image changes into another.

Another Mexican tradition is the burning of 3.5-metre-high papier-mâché figures of Judas the day before Easter Sunday. They are destroyed by lighting the fireworks attached to them. Sometimes Judas bears a remarkable resemblance to some current political figure, and while Maximilian was emperor of Mexico in the 1860s, they were banned because they were thought to look too much like him. (Maximilian was deposed and executed by firing squad in 1867.) There are various theories about how the tradition began. Was it started by Christian missionaries to give a bit of oomph to their proselytizing, or did it arise from the grass roots as a way of mocking the Inquisition's persecution of heretics? In some villages, it was said to be the custom to bring saints' statues out of the churches during firework displays so they could 'watch'.

Also listed in Fodor's 'nine most dangerous on the planet' is Taiwan's Yanshui Beehive Rocket Festival. Hardly surprising, when its centrepiece is a barrage of rockets fired not vertically into the air, but mainly horizontally at spectators! It happens every year in the city of Tainan on the fifteenth day of the lunar New Year, and some say it got its name because the rush of the multiple rockets sounded like a swarm of angry bees. It began around 1885 when cholera was raging through the Yanshui district of the city. Doctors had no answer to the disease, so local people prayed to Guan Di, the god of war. He ordered them to have his statue paraded around in a litter from evening till dawn while they walked behind letting off firecrackers, and afterwards the epidemic died away.

Today statues of Guan Di and other gods are still paraded. Along the route, they are set in front of wooden racks, 'beehives' or 'gun-walls', about the size of a minivan, holding hundreds of bottle rockets, which are unleashed on the statues and any daredevils who congregate around them. This 'baptism of fireworks' allegedly washes away troubles, and if you are struck by a rocket, it is said to bring you a year's good luck. Indeed, the more often you are struck, the luckier you will be. Fortune may favour the brave, but the (relatively) sensible wear protective helmets, thick fireproof clothing, scarves and gloves, though these do not always prevent burns, temporary deafness and injuries from the rockets or flying shrapnel. In 2019 a Canadian journalist found himself 'surrounded by excited people wearing motorcycle helmets and heavy jackets. Their hands are covered with protective gloves and their faces are wrapped in towels, and some are carrying plexi-glass shields.' His guide assures him it is all perfectly safe and then recalls the huge bruises he has suffered when rockets have hit him and the time his clothes caught fire. As a giant statue of the god of war looks down, and the rockets start flying, 'hardcore' spectators stand at point-blank range. Wearing a heavy fireman's jacket and a motorcycle helmet with the visor down, the reporter relates how he was hit by bits of shrapnel. Those landing on the jacket he does not feel, but it is a different story with the ones that strike his legs, then: 'One rocket explodes inches from my eye in a blinding flash and my head jerks back.' Mercifully, 'the barrage lasts for only a few minutes, but at its height, it's a crazy scene of red and orange streaks whizzing in all directions.' After the first barrage dies away, he decides to stick around for a second, understanding 'why people get an adrenaline high from it and risk getting closer and closer to the rockets'.[101] There have been calls to ban the festivities, but in 2021, while other events fell victim to coronavirus restrictions, the Beehive Festival went ahead in a scaled-down version, 'to show respect to the gods', as the city council put it.[102] After all, it had apparently seen off cholera, so, asked the Guan Di temple's secretary, why could it not do the same with COVID-19?

One of Italy's most famous pyrotechnic festivals is Venice's Festa del Redentore, 'Feast of the Redeemer', which opens at the Redeemer church, with its imposing dome across the water from St Mark's Square. On the third Sunday in July, the city commemorates its deliverance from the plague of 1576 that killed 50,000 people, nearly one in three of the population. Decorated boats take to St Mark's Basin, while the shorelines are strung with coloured lanterns and long banqueting tables set up beneath them. Local people liked the festival because it was not really on the tourist beat. Pyrotechnics had featured occasionally from as far back as the 1860s, but in 1978 the local council decided to round off the evening every year with a midnight firework display, and each one seemed to be bigger than the one before. Soon the tourists began arriving. Locals complained the noise would dislodge tiles from historic roofs and that the smoke would corrode the marble. Then there was the 'tide of garbage' and the visitors who would sleep rough or make trouble in the discos on the Lido. In 1998 there were petitions and protests when the residents found their view blocked because the authorities had allowed the biggest cruise ship in the world, nearly 300 metres long and 60 metres high, to tie up for the evening so its passengers could watch the display. But the Redentore fireworks survived, with St Mark's basin being seen as one of the world's greatest settings, and when Italy won the football World Cup in 2006, it was celebrated there with fireworks in the colours of the national flag.

They say that the further south you go in Italy, the louder the fireworks get, and one of the country's most spectacular displays is at Ravello above the Amalfi Coast, nearly 500 miles south of Venice. It is part of another religious festival, for Our Lady of Sorrows, but it also celebrates a military victory. In 1135 the Pisans tried to sack the town but were beaten off by the courageous defenders of the hamlet of Torello, which lies below Ravello. Now every year on the third Sunday of September, the houses of Torello are outlined in lights while a firework display, which crowds watch from Ravello, recalls the battle as the 'fires of Torello'. Incidentally, the invaders returned a couple of years later and captured Ravello. But as with Valencia, the pyrotechnic enthusiasm of ordinary people seems at least as impressive as the big display. A couple of travel writers noted that the locals 'set off firecrackers and fireworks to celebrate *everything* ... A christening, firecrackers; little Maria gets an A in math, firecrackers; the Torello family buys a new *colabrodo* to strain their pasta, firecrackers; Christmas Eve, Christmas Day, New Year's Eve, firecrackers *and* fireworks.'[103]

Hard Times Hit the UK Fireworks Industry

From the 1960s in the UK, safety concerns began to hit sales of fireworks for home use, and then in the 1970s came a double whammy from tightening regulations and general economic woes. There had been a dramatic fall in the number of accidents around Bonfire Night, from more than 3,000 in 1962 to 685 fourteen years later, but that was still agreed to be too many, and a lot of injuries were caused by people throwing fireworks. By 1970 firework manufacturers had reacted by forming a new trade association, the Firework Makers' Guild, to lobby the government and the media against what they saw as 'sensationalist campaigning' by those who wanted to restrict firework sales. Its president, Richard Greenhalgh, the latest family member to head up Standard, announced that the industry was conducting its biggest ever safety campaign, working with the Royal Society for the Prevention of Accidents, the Home Office and others, but it was not enough. Government pressure continued, and in 1976 the Guild did a deal with the politicians called the Firework Code. Manufacturers would make fewer bangers (46 million had been produced in 1974) and those they made would be less powerful. Flying fireworks, such as 'flying saucers', would be banned, as would jumping fireworks like Jumping Jacks. (Alan Brock believes these were a British invention, noting that back in 1635, Bate had written that 'every boy can make these.' Safety instructions on Standard's Flying Imps, one of the genre from the 1950s, had the reassuring advice: 'Stand clear when you have lit the touchpaper as they fly in any direction.'[104]) Fireworks would be on sale for only three weeks leading up to 5 November, instead of six, and the age at which youngsters could buy them would go up from thirteen to sixteen. At the same time, the maximum fine for letting off fireworks in the street was raised from £20 to £200. Increasingly, smaller fireworks could be bought only as part of a boxed set, and any individual ones that were available, such as mini-shells, were likely to cost £5 or more and be beyond the pockets of most youngsters. Another challenge for the industry was that by the 1970s British firework makers were suffering from what some described as the 'American juggernaut' of Halloween, pushed hard by supermarkets, and coming less than a week before Bonfire Night. Although fireworks sometimes figured in Halloween celebrations, they were much less central, with family budgets consumed instead by scary outfits and novelty food and drinks.

To try to perk up sales, fireworks were given more violent names reflecting the greater firepower of weapons in the real world, such as Space Bomb, Atomic Bomb and Polaris Missile, but it did not help. Firms had to start reducing their ranges. While Pains had once produced thirty types of banger, by the mid-1960s that had been reduced to just four. Then came the closures. Wizard Fireworks had opened in 1949 at the former RAF station at Chedburgh in Suffolk, to exploit an apparent gap in the market for cheap bangers. The company became known for items like the 1d Whizz Bang, and then graduated to making a full range of fireworks. It also produced distress flares and its special effects featured in films such as *Bridge on the River Kwai* (1957) and *Cleopatra* (1963), but Wizard ran into financial problems and ceased production in 1963, though the name would later be used by other firework companies. In 1974 Benwells moved to its old site at Chedburgh. Globe Fireworks also seems to have disappeared in the 1960s. The Wells brand bowed out in 1971, though the Dartford site continued to make fireworks under other labels. Some believed Wells made products that were simply too good for the price they were charging. The editor of *Fireworks* magazine, John Bennett, said it was always his favourite firm: 'They put so much into the quality of their fireworks compared to other companies.'[105] In 1972 Rainbow Fireworks ended production, with Astra taking over the brand name. The following year Lion shut down, while Pains Wessex stopped making items for the shops in 1976, as its parent company concentrated on military and marine products.

4
Bigger, Brighter, Louder: Electricity, Electronics and Computers

Electricity and electronics brought a revolution in the way firework displays were mounted and enjoyed, as events grew more and more elaborate and were watched by billions on television. The Revd Ron Lancaster's colleague Roy Butler wrote in his *History of Fireworks* (1998) that at one time

> a new chemical composition might produce an original star colour or noise effect, or a new shell burst or set-piece pattern might be achieved. Today, progress is measured mainly in terms of the spectacle that can be accomplished with the use of vast quantities of fireworks, sophisticated electronic firing devices and the enhancement that musical accompaniment and lasers can give to a show.[1]

But while this revolution was happening, British fireworks manufacturing was going through a familiar story of decline.

UK: Death of a Manufacturing Industry, Growth of a Service Industry

After the troubles of the 1970s, there was some good news at the start of the 1980s, with the number of firework injuries in the UK falling to 555, the lowest total recorded up to that time. *The Times* reported that there were 20,000 shops in Britain selling fireworks, and out of the 100 million made each year in the UK, 90 million were said to be used on or around Bonfire Night. The first year of the decade saw Standard achieve record sales in shops – up by more than a quarter. In 1981 the company's managing director (and president of the British Pyrotechnists' Association, which replaced the Firework Makers' Guild) Derrick Worthington announced there would be no lay-offs at Standard after Bonfire Night, and that the next morning, its 550 employees would be working on export orders for New Year's Eve celebrations in countries such as the Netherlands, Norway and Denmark, as well as building up stocks for the following year's 5 November.

But problems were mounting. A third of Standard's business derived from what Worthington called 'non-entertainment' products, notably pyrotechnics for the army, such as thunderflashes for making exercises more realistic. Worthington conceded that these had been hit by public spending cuts, with stories that the pyrotechnics had been replaced by the cheaper alternative of getting soldiers to shout 'Bang!' In the fireworks-for-fun sector, there was a drift away from back-garden parties towards organized displays, which resulted in fewer accidents. In 1969 there had been 701 at private parties compared with 211 at organized events. Professional pyrotechnicians estimated in 1985 that big displays cost £1,000 a minute, and that year Greater Manchester Council announced it was spending £250,000 on half a dozen events, while nine years later the UK's *Independent* newspaper would list 37 organized Bonfire Night displays in Greater London alone.

Another difficulty for grass-roots fireworks was that they were getting expensive. In 1985 the *New Scientist* reported that a high-end professional set of 250 or more from Brocks cost £2,380 (about £8,300 at today's prices), but even a more middle-of-the-road selection of 29, which would last about ten minutes, would set you back £65 (more than £225 today). Families were having to club together and hold joint bonfire parties. The magazine also noted how little automation firework manufacturers had introduced. Astra had been bought out by its management in 1981, and the best it could do was to install some wooden machinery that allowed a worker to put charges in six rockets at once. Companies complained the UK market was too small, with Astra's technical manager, Martin Guest, telling the reporter: 'You can't get your money back on the machinery.'[2] Some also grumbled that safety regulations allowing them to hold only 25 pounds (11 kg) of explosive powder at each production point made it difficult to establish a streamlined manufacturing process, as did having to make fireworks in small, isolated huts. A worker who had started at Astra in 1983 said: 'The place was built in the mid/late 1940s and little had changed when I got there, it really was a living museum. The work practices, tooling, firework designs (down to the labels) and buildings were . . . just as they had been when the place had been set up.'[3]

Among the leading companies, Pains gave up making shop fireworks in 1976, having become something of a corporate football after it was taken over by Bryant & May and merged with Wessex. It had changed owners again in 1973 when Bryant & May joined up with razor-blade specialists Wilkinson Sword, to form Wilkinson Match. When Wilkinson Match was acquired by an American conglomerate in 1980, pyrotechnics enthusiast John Deeker bought Pains for £1 because, he said, he 'just loved' fireworks. Deeker's father had been the company's auditor, and John had caught the pyrotechnics bug on his first visit to the factory as a five-year-old. When he qualified as an accountant in 1959, he was invited to join the firm by the Milholland brothers, nephews of the Pains, and the last family members to own it. Deeker agreed to do the accounts, but only if he could spend nine months of the year working in the factory. Apart from making fireworks, he also helped put on displays at events such as Brixham Regatta. When the Milhollands retired in 1961, he had become managing director of the Pains Wessex group. Deeker believed the pyrotechnics operation had suffered through being part of a bigger organization: 'It was neither here nor there to the group whether the fireworks business lived or died.'[4] He thought it would do better as an independent firm in the display business, and in 1981 he was put in charge of pyrotechnics for the wedding of Prince Charles and Princess Diana. Deeker would die in 2012, but in 2023, Pains was still around and claiming to be the oldest fireworks display company in the UK and Ireland.

Brocks had closed its Hemel Hempstead factory in the early 1970s, and concentrated production at new facilities at Swaffham in Norfolk and Sanquhar in Dumfries and Galloway. The *New Scientist*'s assessment a decade later was that they were the company that had invested most in mechanization, with, for example, a machine that could make Roman candles ten times as fast as working by hand, as well as producing more consistent results. But by 1983 Brocks had closed Swaffham and employed just 120 mostly seasonal workers in Scotland. By then, two-thirds of its business came from military products such as flares or simulated machine-gun fire. Its main new consumer product that year was a mini-shell to be fired from a cardboard tube as if from a mortar, but the *Financial Times* complained about a lack of innovation across the industry, saying many fireworks had names that had been around for generations, such as 'Devil among Thieves' and 'Mine of Serpents'. The FT also reported UK companies were having kittens over a new rocket that was made from plastic instead of cardboard and gave a 'breath-taking performance', which German competitors were manufacturing by machine.[5]

There were still some good times. In 1983 it was estimated that Britain's firework companies sold about £20 million worth of pyrotechnics for Bonfire Night, with around 2,000 people working in the industry. In 1985 the owners of Benwell, now named MY Holdings, reported a doubling of turnover in its pyrotechnics business, and a loss turned to a small profit, while in 1989 Astra, which had been getting half of its turnover from the military and industrial markets, increased its profits by half. Then a serious fire brought an end to the company's manufacturing. For another eight years, they sold Chinese imports until the firm collapsed in 1997.

By 1987 Brocks was losing money, and was taken over by Standard for a mere £55,000. The previous year, the founding Greenhalgh family had sold Standard to a mini-conglomerate, Scottish Heritable Trust, with businesses ranging from oriental carpets to housebuilding. The new company was named Standard Brock, and all firework production was transferred to Yorkshire, although the Brocks brand name was kept going. Standard's new management thought there were big opportunities in the British fireworks industry. Brocks had had a research staff of ten against Standard's three. The company planned major improvements in, for example, how they made Catherine wheels and in powering rockets with liquid resin rather than the traditional powder, making it easier to automate the manufacturing process. It would need plenty of investment, but they thought it was justified by the chance to increase UK sales for events other than Bonfire Night, especially if they could reduce their prices, and for increasing export sales for 14 July displays in France and New Year's Eve in the Scandinavian countries.

For Benwell, the good news did not last. In 1987 it had plenty of orders but was unable to meet them because of production problems, and started losing money again. Its parent company was better known for dartboards and packaging, and being part of a bigger organization did not seem to work any better for Benwell than it had for Pains. While pyrotechnics struggled, the rest of MY's business had been doing well, and the following year it pulled out of fireworks, selling the Benwell name to a German competitor, Feistel, which sold pyrotechnics for a time under the Feistel & Benwell label. By 1990 Standard was the only major fireworks manufacturer left in Britain, controlling up to 85 per cent of the retail market, but its ambitions were dented when its parent company ran into trouble, and in 1992 SHT sold Standard to the people running it in a management buyout. That put Mel Barker, another lifelong fireworks enthusiast, in charge: 'I'm still addicted to fireworks,' he said. 'There's something about them that just gets into your blood.' Standard made some fireworks for displays, with a price tag of up to £70, but Barker reckoned the average person spent only about £7 a year on pyrotechnics, and the mainstay of the business was the 26.5 million sparklers and 8 million or more rockets they sold to the home and back-garden market. And by 1995 he was finding it a struggle, saying he would 'manufacture as long as the market place allows', but conceding 'it is far more profitable to import.'[6] Meanwhile, the first firm to make sparklers in the UK, Bristol matchmakers Octavius Hunt, had given up in 1992 to concentrate on other lines such as smoke generators, ending a sixty-year tradition.

As the end of the century approached, the year-round market for display fireworks was growing – with, for example, half a dozen shows in the summer of 1991 at Hampstead Heath to accompany outdoor concerts, and a big event over Buckingham Palace to mark the end of that year's G7 summit in London – but Bonfire Night still accounted for most sales. Meanwhile Ron Lancaster blamed regulation for the decline in firework manufacturing in the UK, claiming that the British Standard rules for fireworks, updated in 1988, were almost impossible to comply with: 'They're all made by bureaucrats who know nothing. They try to enforce scientific criteria on things which are impossible to regulate,'[7] such as how long a touchpaper should burn. On a damp night, Lancaster argued, it might well need longer. For more than a decade he had been complaining that Britain had become 'over-protective'. (The iconic blue touchpaper has now largely disappeared, replaced by fuses that have a predictable burning time, made from a black powder core coated to keep it waterproof.) The sixty-page standard codified things like the minimum height at which a rocket can explode and the height by which debris must have stopped burning, and ordered that a Catherine wheel should not spray sparks more than 3 metres. *The Times* reported in 1991 that rather than spend money developing a wheel that met the requirement, UK manufacturers simply gave up making them, and instead they were being imported from Germany. John Woodhead of the British

Pyrotechnics Association said the new rules had put up costs because every consignment now had to be tested. According to one estimate the standard increased the price of fireworks by about 10 per cent. Woodhead also argued: 'The explosive nature of the product means you can't use sophisticated machinery,' adding: 'You need lots of people and if you look at wage levels in China and the UK, it's obviously cheaper to make things over there.'[8] Still, no one in the industry denied regulations were necessary, and some maintained that higher standards had actually increased demand for domestic fireworks by making customers more confident they were safe.

Indeed some insiders believed the industry was partly to blame for its problems. In 1994 Andy Hubble, a fireworks expert who advised the UK government and would go on to chair the British Pyrotechnists Association, complained British companies were producing poor-quality, overpriced goods in selection boxes that were strong on presentation and weak on content: 'Some companies pile on extra packaging and think they can get away with selling inferior fireworks inside.'[9] Chinese fireworks, he said, often offered better value. This seemed to be at least partly confirmed by a consumer test conducted by *The Independent* in the run-up to Bonfire Night 1995, with an expert panel from events company Fantastic Fireworks. It examined one box by Standard/Brocks, one by Astra and two by the Chinese firm Black Cat, all satisfying the British Standard. The Standard/Brocks 'International Selection' was the most expensive at £26.25 for twenty fireworks. The panel thought it had a good balance of 'pretty' and 'loud' fireworks, but that it was overpriced. The Astra Box at £20 for 24 fireworks got a unanimous thumbs-down, with complaints that they were 'poor and very hard to light' and 'produced less interesting sparkles and crasser colours than the others'. The cheaper Black Cat selection cost £10.50 for fifteen fireworks. Despite its low price, the panel felt it had the biggest wow factor.[10]

In the first half of the 1990s firework sales in the UK increased by about 20 per cent, but UK manufacturers suffered a blow in 1993 when the government relaxed restrictions on firework imports. In 1997 the age at which you were allowed to buy fireworks went up again, from sixteen to eighteen. To make things worse, Halloween seemed to go from strength to strength, with Hamleys famous toy store in Regent Street saying it had sold more costumes and other monstrous paraphernalia than ever before. Standard's Ron Rapley lamented: 'In my young days we didn't even have Hallowe'en.'[11] In 1998 the company was sold to Black

Cat, said to be the biggest firework maker in the world. That was the end of Standard's manufacturing operation in the UK, though the new owners kept the brand name alive and retained the Huddersfield site as its sales, marketing and distribution centre.

The Independent's headline said it all: 'British fireworks industry fizzles out.' All that was left was Ron Lancaster's Kimbolton. Even they could no longer afford to make fireworks to sell in shops, but they were the only remaining British company left producing a full range of display fireworks, though a couple of others made special effects pyrotechnics for the theatre. Lancaster said: 'It's a tragedy that there are no other British firms, but Chinese fireworks are easily available and cheaper than we could ever make them.'[12] He had retired from teaching in 1988, but continued to supervise Kimbolton's production, building a new factory with upgraded machinery and a bigger workforce. Lancaster was awarded an MBE in 1993 for his services to the industry, as the company mounted many successful displays, taking the silver Jupiter at the Montreal International Competition in 1993, putting on events for the fiftieth anniversary of VJ Day in London in 1995 and helping mark the handover of Hong Kong to China in 1997. But by 2013 Lancaster was bemoaning the fact that their hand-made three-break shells were getting too expensive to make, and in 2019 Kimbolton announced it had experienced 'a sharp fall in sales over the last year along with rising costs' and that 'after 55 years in the fireworks industry . . . we have had to take the very difficult decision to close the company.'[13] The Kent display firm Phoenix Fireworks kept the Kimbolton name alive, buying it from the administrator, and using it for its retail sales operation.

Another Lancaster-style firework boffin was Malcolm Armstrong. With 45 years in the industry behind him, he lectured at schools and universities while also owning Theatrical Pyrotechnics of Ramsgate. Their speciality was special effects for films such as *Alien* (1979) and the James Bond franchise, but he also made fireworks to sell. His favourite was the Armstrong Comet, for professional displays only, with four effects – 'one in purple, one in magnesium, one in orange and then finally there is a bang in the form of a whistle, a hummer or a machine gun'.[14] Armstrong's son, James, was killed in an accident while he was working at the factory in 1987, but the business carried on until 2016. His local MP, Roger Gale, paid tribute to his courage in Parliament, saying: 'He did not give in; he continued to manufacture superb displays that gave pleasure to thousands of people.'[15] Wells also found a refuge in the entertainment industry after the company stopped manufacturing for shops in the 1970s, as some of the employees moved to Sussex and kept the brand alive. In 2003 it was acquired by special effects firm Pyrojunkies, who retained the Wells name. They worked on concerts by artists such as Westlife and the Pussycat Dolls, and television shows like *The X Factor* and *Strictly Come Dancing*. Later Pyrojunkies would expand the manufacturing plant in Sussex, selling gerbs, comets, waterfalls and other pyrotechnics to professionals and amateurs in the UK and abroad. Still, home-made fireworks remained a tiny part of a UK market that saw just short of £500 million spent on fireworks for Bonfire Night in 2017.

Fireworks' shift from the manufacturing to the services sector should not have been a surprise. The whole British economy was going that way, with some commentators describing the UK as the world's first post-industrial society. In 1951 more than 30 per cent of workers in England and Wales had been employed in manufacturing. By 2011 that had fallen to 9 per cent. Former *Daily Mail* sub-editor John Culverhouse was part of this flourishing new service sector. His enthusiasm for pyrotechnics went back to the Bonfire Nights of the early 1960s when, he recalled, 'fireworks were very much a once-a-year occasion and there was always a great sense of excitement when they appeared in the shops.'[16] Then came school chemistry lessons and discovering the formula for gunpowder in the *Encyclopaedia Britannica*, which stimulated him to make his own

Modern organized Bonfire Night display, Tiverton, 2012.

fireworks, spiced up with ingredients like strontium nitrate from the chemist's to provide red colouring. Further inspiration came from space exploration. When the Russians sent up a dog, he says he fired a mouse 60 metres up in a plastic capsule secreted in the nose of the biggest available Standard rocket, and brought the animal back safely to earth. At university in the 1970s, he bought commercial fireworks to put on displays at summer balls. After graduating, he started selling them as a sideline to journalism, until the business grew so big that he quit Fleet Street in the 1980s and founded Fantastic Fireworks. Then he found people wanted to hire him for shows at weddings and parties, and in 1986 Culverhouse got his first big commission – from the Torbay Tourist Board, to celebrate the wedding of Prince Andrew and Sarah Ferguson, for which he built a 'huge' lancework set-piece of the couple. Running Fantastic with two full-time employees from a tiny office suite in the Hertfordshire village of Redbourn, he managed to turn over £300,000 in 1989. All his fireworks were imported, from China, Japan, Taiwan, West Germany, Italy and Spain. Working with a team of freelancers, he created wedding displays for £1,000, while selling do-it-yourself packs starting at £60 and rising to £2,000 for the top-of-the-range 'Meltdown'. Culverhouse said one of his biggest costs was insurance, at £30,000 a year. Not many insurers wanted to take on the risk, even though he said no claim had ever been made against him: 'Fireworks are inherently dangerous. We do all we can to minimise danger.'[17] Fantastic's biggest ever display was a celebration of Liverpool's eight-hundredth birthday in 2007, fired from the roofs of its two cathedrals, the waterfront and a barge on the Mersey, at a cost of £250,000.

Britain was not the only European country where fireworks manufacturing was running into trouble. In Sweden, Tomer's, who had started in Stockholm in 1880, closed in 1972. C. R. Hansson, who had been making fireworks in Gothenburg since 1888, gave up in 1983, while Hammargrens, who had begun manufacturing in the same city in 1920, ended production in 1992. Meanwhile in France, the Ruggieri company was taken over by its main rival, the Etienne Lacroix group. Founded in 1848, Lacroix had won gold medals in international competitions in Paris and Amsterdam. Fifteen years after the takeover, it would revive the famous Ruggieri name and, under it, put on major national displays.

China Rules OK?

Hong Kong harbour is one of the world's great pyrotechnics display settings, but as Red Guards rampaged through China and riots spread to the colony in 1967, the British authorities banned fireworks because they provided material for home-made bombs. The ban was lifted in 1975. Seven years later, the giant Jardine Matheson conglomerate put on a huge show at the harbour for Chinese New Year to celebrate its 150th birthday. According to some estimates, it was seen live by more than 5 million people, perhaps the biggest ever attendance for a firework display. Until the 1970s China used to put on big displays in Beijing's Tiananmen Square, but in the uncertain times that followed Mao Zedong's death in 1976, these came to an end, though people still bought small fireworks for private celebrations such as weddings and birthdays. Around the time of America's bicentennial celebrations, also in 1976, demand for fireworks began to outstrip supply, and companies like Sorgi's American Fireworks started to import from Italy and Mexico, but most of all from China. Immigrants had probably brought in the first Chinese fireworks, but in 1948 the flow was interrupted as the new Communist regime stopped all trade. Still, Chinese pyrotechnics managed to get in via Hong Kong, Macau and Taiwan. In 1972 President Nixon made his historic visit to see Chairman Mao, trade resumed and the Chinese never looked back.

Meanwhile, the Italian presence in America had remained strong. In the first decade of the twenty-first century, Nancy Rozzi, great-granddaughter of the founder, was still running Rozzi Fireworks. In 2019, having teamed up with the Italian company Panzera, they won the Jury Prize at Cannes' international fireworks festival. The Zambelli dynasty was also still busy putting on displays – eight hundred across the country around 4 July 2019. (Chairman George Zambelli Jr's day job was as an ophthalmologist and, wearing that hat, he saw plenty of firework injuries. He advised those involved with pyrotechnics to wear goggles.) The total value of the U.S. market that year, the last before COVID, was estimated at $945 million. Despite the fact that they were restricted in some states and even banned in Massachusetts, sales of domestic fireworks had increased by more than 230 per cent by value over the previous twenty years, while those for displays had gone up 155 per cent.

As for the Gruccis, in November 1983 they suffered a terrible blow when an explosion flattened their Bellport factory, killing Jimmy Grucci, the company's CEO and son of Felix Sr, who had run the business for decades, and also Felix's nineteen-year-old niece. Even so, just a few weeks later, the company managed to put on a New Year's Eve display in New York City, and they mounted a show at the closing ceremony of the Los Angeles Olympics the following summer. Rebuilding in a more remote part of Long Island, the Gruccis continued to be a major force in pyrotechnics, putting on displays for the centenary of the Statue of Liberty in 1986, three more Olympic Games and seven presidential inaugurations, as well as other major events. When Felix died in 1993, *Time* magazine called him the 'patriarch of pyrotechnics', adding that during his time in charge, Grucci's 'productions rose to world class, with visual choreography worthy of Broadway'.[18] In 2021 the *Wall Street Journal* still described them as 'the country's best-known fireworks show operator'.[19]

In 2009 Grucci's vice-president Phil Butler said their success came from always looking for something new: 'No matter what kind of entertainment it is, without variety it becomes repetitious.' They still made their own shells, which, after a century and a half in America, they continued to describe as 'Italian-style', adding that these were 'generally the ones that make the most noise, especially in the grand finale. Italians are loud.' But the company also used imported fireworks, scouring the world for the best. It helped that many manufacturers came chasing them, 'because they know their inventory might be displayed at the next Olympics or the next presidential inauguration'.[20] As the company became known primarily for displays, they changed their name to Fireworks by Grucci, so they sounded more like a designer fashion house.

By 2018, according to Julie Heckman, executive director of the American Pyrotechnics Association, China completely dominated the U.S. market, supplying 90 per cent of backyard fireworks and 70 per cent of display pyrotechnics. The sleeping giant had truly awoken. Echoing comments made in the UK, Heckman said: 'Manufacturing fireworks is very labour-intensive. As the regulations got tighter people really aren't interested in making things by hand, and it made sense to rely more on China.'[21] As in the UK, American fireworks companies shifted from manufacturing to service, with some, like the Sorgis, taking on more workers in the process. American firework displays became bigger and bigger business. According to the APA, Thunder Over Louisville, the firework display that kicks off the Kentucky Derby Festival, generates more than $56 million for the local economy.

Across the globe, China went way out in front as the leading exporter of fireworks as of so many other things. According to the Statista business data organization, in 2019 China was responsible for an astonishing 28.7 per cent of all the world's manufacturing output. In 2020 it was calculated that it accounted for no less than 84 per cent of global firework exports, selling eighteen times more than the next most successful country, the Netherlands, which was followed by Germany. The United States was in seventh place, with one-time giant Italy down in eleventh. Neither the UK nor France appeared in the top fifteen. Worldwide sales were badly hit by COVID that year, down more than 20 per cent on 2019, but the league table of exporters was not much different in that last pre-pandemic year, with China still dominant with more than 80 per cent of sales. According to the Observatory of Economic Complexity, by far the biggest importer of fireworks in 2021 was the United States, with Germany second, Italy third and the UK fourth.

For all China's domination, its fireworks industry remained something of a mystery. In 2018 two Reuters reporters got a glimpse of its centre, Liuyang, now home to 1.3 million people, describing 'concrete bunkers carved into the hillside, where workers gingerly handle piles of explosive black powder'. Each employee was in their own individual bunker, with metre-thick blast-proof concrete walls, watched over by surveillance cameras that transmitted live feeds to the local police, as required by new safety regulations. The previous year, the Chinese government had introduced curbs on fireworks in nearly 450 cities to try to combat pollution, hitting Liuyang's livelihood. At the fireworks wholesale market, 'business was slow, with shopowners and staff mostly idle ... Numerous shopfronts were shuttered.' One trader claimed sales were down 60 per cent: 'there isn't a single customer on the street, not even a ghost.' Others said that while demand was still strong in villages and smaller towns for occasions such as weddings and funerals, it was waning in the big cities, partly because of government curbs, but also because of fears about safety and a feeling that fireworks were old-fashioned. According to official figures, the number of firework makers in Liuyang had fallen from 946 in 2015 to 558 three years later, though the city was still reckoned to produce two-thirds of China's pyrotechnics. A local businessman who had worked his way up from making rockets on an assembly line to employing 120 people complained the government did not care about the industry, because it was only a 'drop in the ocean' in the context of China's huge economy.[22] Difficulties in the domestic market had led to even more stress on exports, with Liuyang Standard Fireworks (no relation to the British company), for example, now selling 90 per cent of its products abroad.

Electric Shock

As we have seen, electricity was setting off fireworks at the Crystal Palace by the late nineteenth century. In 1950 Maître Ruggieri was directing the Bastille Day show in Paris with a twelve-button electrical panel, and by 1976 the electrical firing revolution was really underway, with a car battery powering the mortar that would send up what was then world's biggest firework. Car batteries, which could be attached to a switchboard from which hundreds or thousands of individual wires each ran to a firework, became the usual power source. George Plimpton wrote that before the electrical revolution, 'a fireworks man would reach in the bomb box, drop a shell into the mortar, light it, and then often would be just as surprised at what blossomed in the sky above him as the spectators.'[23] That was surely unfair to many pre-electrical displays, but there is no doubt that electricity, electronics and the digital revolution have enabled pyrotechnic choreography of unprecedented sophistication.

By the 1980s displays in America were being plotted on paper beforehand. Shells would be put in mortars and wires connected to squibs, which would send them soaring into the sky at the flick of a switch. This was also the decade when computers started to play a role. John Conkling, technical director of the APA, said: 'The biggest impact was on choreography – the ability to precisely time shows and to use multiple firing sites linked to a main system,' meaning you could 'co-ordinate the whole visual experience'.[24] In the early 1990s an engineer-turned-radio station boss named Dan Barker took over the Great American Fourth of July Fireworks Festival at State College, Pennsylvania, and decided to turn it into a world-class event. He got together with some engineer friends to create a system that could set off fireworks to music with split-second timing. With 8,000 shells and a $200,000 production budget, Barker boasted he was letting off twice as many fireworks as nationally televised shows. He and his friends formed a company and devised FireOne, which used a Windows-based software package that allowed users to import music and choreograph a sequence of fireworks. They could then put this on to a laptop, which would be connected to a box wired to small firing modules for the individual fireworks, meaning each was now controlled by the laptop program. By the end of the decade, they had two hundred customers across the world, including Disney. Competing companies entered the field, but at the end of the twentieth century Barker said that still only about 15 to 20 per cent of American displays were being run by computers, because of the cost. A system for a relatively small show of 1,000 fireworks would set you back $14,000.

The revolution was also coming to the UK. In 1992, a *Times* reporter joined Andrew Jolliffe of display company Fox Fireworks on a London rooftop 60 metres up to fire a display set to Vivaldi's *Four Seasons* from a £35,000 computer, but electricity did not destroy the age-old sensations of fireworks. First off were two Chinese crackers, 'each producing a thousand detonations in the space of a minute'. The air was filled 'with a layer of dust, grit, and fragments of paper so dense that breathing them is like swallowing emery boards'. They gasped for oxygen as 'the first shells whoosh into the air, and a dozen flares along the parapet erupt into fountains of sparks 20 feet high.' The mortars made the roof shake, and the noise was 'terrifying'. In five minutes, they got through £2,500 worth of fireworks, and the show was over. But not all pyrotechnicians had been won over. 'Everyone in the profession has a story about a display sabotaged by a power failure, or a faulty connection setting off the entire show at the same moment,' wrote the journalist. Others, like Ron Lancaster, queried the expense: 'Electricity is useful if you want to fire a lot in a short time, or from several places at once, or you want symmetry, but if it's a small show, why pay much more when you can do it just as well by hand?'[25]

But by then the pyrotechnic new wave looked unstoppable. In 1999 a reporter from *The Independent* gained access to the working partnership between Standard Fireworks' Display Designer, Graham Wilkinson, and Sally Smith, a former pianist. The journalist saw them take pieces such as the *William Tell* overture and Ravel's *Boléro* and break them down into 'time passages' – picking out quiet moments for 'pretties' and loud sections for showers. Wilkinson would say something like: 'What we need here is a blue to crackling gold aerial shellburst.' He revealed that they tried to avoid rockets 'because the fusing can be erratic'. They preferred shells, but their electric firing was still a bit primitive. For the performance, Smith would stand by the side of the stage, watching the conductor, and then shout: 'Fire!' into a walkie-talkie, up to fourteen times in one piece. She pointed out that the firing board could be quite a way from the fireworks, so she had to try to take account of the delay.

'It's terribly complicated . . . I can't tell you how dreadful it is when it goes wrong. When there's one that . . . staggers up two minutes after the piece has finished. Awful, awful.'[26] Still, fireworks started to be in much demand for outdoor classical music concerts on summer evenings, often at stately homes, when a display might accompany the closing piece.

By 2017 things had moved on a lot. In a Cambridgeshire office, Tom Smith, a chemistry graduate whose grandfather had worked for Brocks, showed an *i-news* reporter a 12,000-line list on his computer – each line referring to one of the fireworks that would combine to form the coming London New Year display lasting just ten minutes. Their colours and sounds, the angle they would be fired at and the height they would reach had all been planned months before, but on the night, all sorts of factors then unknown would intrude – weather, air pressure, the Thames tide. Smith, who had put on major displays all over the world, had developed a computer program that could predict the impact of all these variables to ensure none of the fireworks went off where it should not, sparing the audience from being showered by debris. One effect of the electronic revolution had been to make displays shorter. 'Shows used to last 40 or 50 minutes because everything had to be reloaded by hand,' said Smith.[27] They were also safer because those putting them on could now keep their distance from where the firing was happening. Electronic firing even reached back-garden firework parties. In the UK by 2022 there were systems with four cues available for around £20, while £100 might get you a dozen cues, and to each cue you could link two or three fireworks. Instead of using a portfire or a blowtorch to light them, you just attached an electric wire to the fuse, which could then be fired at the push of a button. You could also get a remote control operated by wireless, while in 2021 a new system arrived from America which, for about £180, allowed you to control your system via a mobile phone or tablet app.

Back in the 1980s George Plimpton had maintained that the electrical revolution would allow the creation of 'extraordinary patterns and effects in the sky', so fireworks would become the 'eighth art' alongside architecture, sculpture, painting, literature, music, performing and film.[28] While marvelling at the technological changes, Grucci's chief executive Phil Grucci, Felix Sr's grandson, said it was crucial to make sure the technology served the art and not the other way round, but others had stronger reservations. Mark Lancaster wrote in 1998 that big international displays were getting too similar. He said that over three months he saw 'One by Kimbolton Fireworks, one by an Australian company and one by an American company. Whilst different in detail, they were the same in style.' Globalization, he believed, had been a mixed blessing. He recognized that the exchange of know-how at events such as international competitions had helped improve safety, but he was worried that the rules were reducing diversity, with 'national characteristics' being sacrificed to 'a more generic approach . . . I doubt, for instance, if the site or the audience at La Ronde in Montreal would really allow the intricacies of a Mexican Castillo to shine.'[29]

Another factor pushing pyrotechnics towards uniformity in Lancaster's view was the closure of many, particularly smaller, factories across the world and 'an over-reliance on Chinese material . . . a Chinese 3″ Peony Shell is going to look the same wherever it is fired in the world.' Driving in the same direction, he argued, was the growing importance of corporate clients. While traditional events such as Bonfire Night remained important, 'the volume of business is dwarfed by the demand over the summer for corporate product launches, balls, pyromusicals and other such events.' National styles had grown up around traditional occasions, but increasingly it was commercial companies who paid the pyrotechnician and called the tune, and they tended to want essentially the same thing: 'an all aerial display of relatively short duration where it can be difficult to impress the audience with anything less than a massive array of colour and noise'.[30] Two decades later in *Gunpowder and Glory* (2020), their biography of Frank Brock, Harry Smee and Henry Macrory came to a similar conclusion: 'Today's displays, partly because of the size of the audience, are mainly aerial in nature and can be repetitive if of a high standard.'[31]

But some traditional religious festivals survived globalization. Take the annual Easter event at Vrontados on the Greek island of Chios, during which two local churches bombard each other with up to 100,000 home-made rockets while Mass is celebrated inside, in what is known as the *Rouketopolemos*, or 'rocket war'. The Orthodox churches of St Mark and the Virgin Mary Erethianis stand on hilltops 350 metres apart, and the winner of the 'war' is the one to score the most hits on the other's bell with its rockets, though often both teams claim victory. Some say the event goes back to the era when Greece was part of the Turkish Ottoman Empire and Chios was the scene of a notorious massacre in which tens of thousands died. Others argue that it celebrates how the serenity of the Mass survives any turmoil in the world outside. In 2015 a documentary on the event praised the dedication of the amateur rocket makers, which demonstrated 'a sense of devotion that feels lost in the modern world . . . We're all after something we can give our lives to.'[32]

Firework Competitions

International firework competitions first appeared in the nineteenth century, but easier travel globalized them. In 1998 the Czech Republic's second city, Brno, launched one around its reservoir, enabling participants to make use of water reflections. Some events clustered around a bigger expanse of water, the Mediterranean. Tarragona in Spain holds an international contest for six companies every year in July, with the winner getting to put on a display for the town's biggest annual festival, Santa Tecla. Cannes' Festival d'Art Pyrotechnique, which started in 1967 sees half a dozen companies compete every July and August. The fireworks are set off from barges in the bay and are judged on 'music, stage synchronisation, rhythm, sequence and colours'.[33] In 2019 the contestants came from France, Germany, Austria, Italy, Sweden and the USA, but perhaps the most prestigious of all the European competitions is the one held in Monte Carlo since 1966, which was renamed Art en Ciel in 2018. It features five competitors, who each get one night to put on their display. One of the things that make it special is the setting, a natural arena where steep hills surround the little harbour with its narrow entrance, making the sound of the fireworks echo and reverberate. In 1979 the Gruccis were invited to take part.

The boss, Felix, then aged 75, was nervous. In the past American companies had failed to set Monaco alight, as it were, but his two sons were more confident. They had heard the Europeans were still lighting their shells with flares, while the Americans had moved on to electrical firing so their show could be choreographed beforehand with split-second precision, and they thought its climax, which they had christened 'Grucci in the Sky with Diamonds', would blow the judges away. They spent six months preparing to have shells arching over the harbour and matching Niagara Falls cascading down each breakwater at the harbour entrance, while the Gruccis' trademark 'split comet' shells danced overhead. Each contained sixty comets and Phil Butler, who worked on the display that day, explained: 'when the shell breaks, they leave a golden trail. Halfway through the burn there's a small charge, which breaks up the comets into dozens of pieces. It creates a golden Milky Way effect.'[34]

The finale, or 'bouquet' as the French call it, would feature more than 2,000 shells. But the best laid plans, and all that. A third of the fireworks, including all the split comets, were delayed en route. Then there was another problem. If the mortars were fired electronically, they could not be reloaded, meaning each could be fired only once. The organizers could not provide enough, so it was panic stations on the day of the show as the Gruccis had to modify every shell to allow it to be fired manually, eliminating one of their trump cards. Worse, the European mortars were the wrong size for American shells. The Gruccis rounded up all the Vaseline they could find and used it to help squeeze some shells into mortars that were really too narrow, while others had to be put in mortars that were too big and ended up bursting too low. Phil Butler said that every time he did a show, he swore it would be his last – 'You get pushed around by the concussions, buffeted. It's like being roughed up by four or five muggers pushing you from one to the other' – but this was 'the most chaotic' he had ever been involved with.[35] Still, the audience seemed to like it, with the split comets drawing plenty of applause.

For the finale, the Gruccis managed to let off 1,500 shells in five minutes. George Plimpton, who was with them, said that because of the setting, the explosions 'were gathered by the surrounding hills and flung back over the dark harbour as if from the throat of a vast horn'. Then, 'just as the last thundering echoes of their finale died away', a pair of shells went up from each breakwater, producing 'a slowly descending cluster of fluttery stars . . . a shift of pyrotechnical effect from concussion to beauty'.[36] Everywhere car horns hooted approval. Ships at sea radioed in to ask if Monte Carlo was on fire, and gamblers even left the tables in the casino to rush out and take a look. Despite tough competition from France, Italy, Spain and Denmark, the Gruccis won, leading the New York press corps to dub them 'the first family of fireworks' for winning 'the Super Bowl, the Olympics of all fireworks competitions'.[37] Felix commented: 'I still love to see six months' work go up in smoke in five minutes.'[38]

In the United States, Pyrotechnics Guild International puts on more specialized contests. Founded in 1969, in 2021 it had 1,600 members. The PGI holds separate competitions for commercial fireworks and those made by members, and for different categories such as aerial shells, rockets and ground fireworks. But for many, Montreal's International des Feux Loto-Québec is the most prestigious competition in North America. Launched in 1985 and sponsored by the government of Quebec's lottery corporation, it too has a spectacular location, on an island in the St Lawrence River, where up to nine companies compete for its gold, silver and bronze Jupiter trophies, sometimes considered the Oscars of pyrotechnics. The twentieth competition in 2004 featured eight previous gold medal winners who fought it out for a special platinum Jupiter. The German company WECO, based in Eitorf, not far from Bonn, came out on top.

In 2018 Montreal's international competition was won by a company from the Philippines, and the globalization of pyrotechnics was emphasized the following year when Joho Pyro Professional Fireworks AB of Finland were victorious at the Da Nang International Fireworks Festival in Vietnam. Their display, using 10,000 fireworks coordinated by a hundred computers, was apparently inspired by the lives of Vietnamese fishermen. The Philippines have a major competition of their own, which began as the World Pyro Olympics before toning its name down to Philippine International Pyromusical Competition. Since it started in 2005, the UK has been the most successful country, providing six winners, including three victories for Pyrotex Fireworx, based at Burton upon Trent in Staffordshire. No other country has won more than twice. Pyrotex have also triumphed in Monte Carlo, as well as twice taking the prize at the British Musical Firework Championships in Southport and winning competitions in Belgium, Italy, Malta and Poland. Taking a leaf out of the Gruccis' creed, the company says: 'We cherry pick the very best fireworks from the very best suppliers.' It also sells fireworks and puts on displays for Diwali, Bonfire Night, New Year's Eve, birthdays and weddings, 'or even if you're just having a few friends around'.[39]

Another major British competition is the British Firework Championships, held annually on Plymouth Hoe since 1997. The deputy council leader, Pete Smith, described it in 2021 as the jewel in the crown of Plymouth events, attracting about 100,000 spectators from all over the country.[40] The first winner was Fantastic Fireworks. In 2015 they battled high winds and torrential rain to win again. One of the most unusual British firework competitions is Firework Champions. Organized by MLE Pyrotechnics of Daventry, winner of the British Fireworks Championships in 2005 and 2011, it involves competing teams putting on displays each summer at a series of stately homes, such as Ragley Hall and Belvoir Castle. Illusion Fireworks, set up by a husband-and-wife team in 2014, won at Stanford Hall in 2018, and also took the British Firework Championships and the British Musical Firework Championships that year.

The World's Biggest Fireworks

There is no prize for the world's biggest firework except a certificate from and a mention in *Guinness World Records*, but there is still plenty of competition for the title. As we saw, the Japanese Ogatsu company got into the book in 1956 for its 'Bouquet of Chrysanthemums' that weighed more than 200 pounds, and had to be fired from a mortar nearly 40 inches wide. Nobody showed much interest in beating its record until 1976 when Harvard University's undergraduate humour magazine, *Harvard Lampoon*, decided that setting off the world's biggest firework would be a good way to celebrate its centenary, and turned to former editor and pyrotechnic enthusiast George Plimpton. He hired the Gruccis, who began referring to their outsize firework as 'Fat Man' – the nickname of the atomic bomb dropped on Nagasaki. As with the Monte Carlo competition, Felix Grucci was not that keen, but his two sons were, and the firm got to work. As usual with East Asian shells, the Japanese record breaker had been shaped like a ball, but the Gruccis decided to follow the customary American cylindrical approach. To beat Ogatsu, they went for a diameter of 40½ inches, 1 inch more, but, 'somewhat arbitrarily', according to Plimpton, they decided on a length of 3 feet (90 centimetres), which meant its estimated weight would be well over 320 kilograms, more than three times that of the Ogatsu shell.[41]

For propellant, they would use coarse-grained black powder, but there was a good deal of argument about how much. A rule of thumb said that for big shells the propellant should be about a tenth of the weight of the shell, but that would mean more than 30 kilograms, and the Gruccis were worried it might blow the mortar and the shell to bits. Again rather arbitrarily, they decided to go with 34 pounds (15 kg). There was talk about resolving the dilemma by dropping the shell from an aircraft, but Plimpton went off to seek advice from the U.S. Army instead. They explained that their biggest shell weighed in at a mere 200 pounds (90 kg), and were astonished that the Gruccis were going to use a mortar more than 40 inches wide. That was 4 inches more than anything that had ever appeared in the U.S. Army's inventory. Delving into the history books, Plimpton discovered the Turks had used a 42-inch artillery piece when laying siege to Constantinople in 1453. It had an 8-metre-long barrel and needed sixty oxen and two hundred men to get it into position.

In an arithmetical bombshell, army experts declared the monster firework should require only 4 pounds of propellant. The Gruccis were sceptical, prepared a block of wood the same size and weight as Fat Man and put it in a 3-metre-long mortar, buried almost up to its lip in sand, near their Long Island headquarters. Plimpton thought the propellant charge looked puny, and when they fired it electrically from about 275 metres away, all they heard was a 'mild thump'. Then to the writer's amazement, the formidable lump of wood emerged from the mortar 'quite slowly, but it kept rising inexorably, almost as if it were being drawn up into the sky by an invisible fishing line'.[42] The army experts reckoned it had risen 995 feet, near enough to the 1,000 the Gruccis had planned for their shell to reach before it exploded. They had got it right!

The next step was to fire a test shell, Fat Man I, which like the real thing, now known as Fat Man II, included 180 kilograms of magnesium stars, 4.5 kilograms of flitter stars and 45 kilograms of black powder at its centre to blast it apart at the highest point of its flight and ignite the contents. If everything went according to plan, the magnesium stars would arch across the sky like a great umbrella of silver, while the flitter would hang as a golden cloud of dust. This time when they fired the charge, all they got was a faint plume of white smoke. The fuse for the propellant had not lit, only the fuse for the bursting charge, designed to blow the shell apart after about ten seconds when it had reached 300 metres. And explode it did, right there in the mortar, sending great metal shards flying through the air, and leaving a huge crater in the ground. A quarter of a mile away, the shock wave knocked a man off his sofa and crockery was dashed to the floor in distant houses. Harvard's local fire commissioner got wind of what had happened, and banned the firing of Fat Man II at the *Lampoon*'s centenary celebrations, so all the Gruccis could do was to put on a conventional display. The firm's embarrassment at the failure of Fat Man I was heightened when *Guinness World Records* included it in its latest edition as the world's 'lowest' firework, but the company was about to be thrown a lifeline.

With a slowdown in NASA's space programme, Florida's Cape Canaveral and its vicinity had suffered a steep decline in tourism, and a car dealer named Remar 'Bubba' Sutton had persuaded the local authorities he could help. His idea was to use the area to put on a collection of assaults on world records during what he called 'Guinness Record Week' in the autumn of 1977. While a whippet was trying to set a new mark for the longest ever jump by a dog, and a man tried to beat the world record for opening oysters, the Gruccis drove Fat Man II down to Florida. Sutton was hoping to get the Space Center to host its firing, but they were worried about how much damage it might cause if something went wrong again, and Fat Man II was packed off to a small sandbank in the middle of a river. This time, instead of firing electrically, the Gruccis lit the fuse manually. It was designed to burn for five minutes, giving the team plenty of time to get away in their motorboat. The craft sped off until they were a couple of miles away. Then they cut the engine and turned to watch lift-off. As the five-minute mark passed . . . nothing happened. One Grucci murmured: 'Oh God!' as they thought they were going to have to go back and investigate why the monster shell had not stirred. But suddenly an orange fireball appeared as if a gas tank had exploded. Almost immediately, it vanished. Next a shock wave reached them, then 'a thundering blast of sound'. The shock wave would set off fifty burglar alarms in the nearest town and blow out the window of a furniture store. Stars from the shell 'soared helter-skelter over the water – like a huge flock of outraged birds', as one witness put it. This was not the harmonious visual effect the world's biggest firework was meant to create, because the shell had burst prematurely when it had risen perhaps only 15 metres out of the mortar. Still, it was enough to set a new world record. The Ogatsu company were presumably not impressed. In 1980 they sent up a much bigger version of their 'Bouquet of Chrysanthemums', weighing in at 256 kilograms, saying it performed perfectly, forming a starry umbrella 610 metres in circumference, and noted: 'height of ascent and size are matters of secondary importance. No matter how large a flower may open, if its shape is warped or disintegrating, that flower is valueless. If one of a thousand stars fails to appear, one missing star is a shame to the "fire-flower master."'[43] But it was Fat Man II that got into the *Guinness World Records*.

Ogatsu may have thought size did not matter, but other Japanese pyrotechnicians took a different view. In 1985 Zenji Honda brought the world record back to the Land of the Rising Sun with a shell weighing 420 kilograms at the Katakai Fireworks Festival. Katakai, part of the city of Ojiya, has a great pyrotechnic tradition going back four centuries, and in 2014 the Katakai Fireworks Co. went one better with its 'Yonshakudama' shell, which was 1.2 metres in diameter, weighed 460 kilograms, about the same as a male polar bear, and cost around £1,150. The shell was set off at a fireworks festival at Konosu, about 30 miles from Tokyo, exploding into a huge ball of orange light half a mile wide, the top of which was nearly 900 metres from the ground.

Three years later, petrodollars entered the contest. To celebrate New Year's Eve 2017, one of the United Arab Emirates, Ras Al Khaimah, decided to challenge the record on the man-made island of Al Marjan. The pyrotechnic team they hired were our old friends the Gruccis. More than 100,000 people showed up to see a shell weighing more than a ton, more than twice the size of the Japanese record holder. Fired from a mortar 7 metres long, 4 metres of which were buried in sand, the shell, which had been two months in the making at the Gruccis' factories, climbed in the sky to more than 1,120 metres before it exploded. Phil Grucci said: 'It's been a dream of mine to attempt to bring this record back into our family.'[44]

But even as the Gruccis' mega-firework was ascending, a group of Americans from the ski resort of Steamboat Springs in Colorado had been working for four years on their own record attempt. Calling themselves Steamboat Fireworks, they included Jim Widmann, a former Gruccis apprentice, who had founded his own displays company. Widmann said that when he was a boy, his favourite day was 5 July, when he could go around picking up any dud fireworks lying around, and 'cobble them into something that went boom!'[45] He had worked on Dubai's show for New Year 2014, which set a record as the world's biggest ever display, and also on the record-breaking UAE shell of 31 December 2017. Steamboat Fireworks was headed up by a local banker named Tim Borden, who had done motorcycle treks across Australia, New Zealand and North Africa, and competed in international bobsleigh competitions. He had also been involved with fireworks for twenty years. Another team member, Eric Krug, was a professional product design engineer, who had worked on pyrotechnics for nearly forty years. At the age of 54, he had covered more than 50 metres on a skateboard while doing a handstand.

Their approach was to build a series of fireworks, each one bigger than the last. They started with a 24-inch shell. Then in 2017, they launched one of 48 inches, at the time the biggest ever seen in North America. By 2019 they had progressed to a 62-inch shell weighing more than 2,500 pounds (1,100 kg), but, like Fat Man 1 it came to grief, exploding prematurely without getting out of the mortar. They decided the lifting charge needed to burn slightly slower, so they changed the formula, and they made the shell 3 inches thicker by using a specially made machine to wrap it in more than 50 miles of sticky tape, which took a month. It weighed nearly 2,800 pounds (1,270 kg), about the same as a

Toyota Corolla car, and contained 380 comet fireworks. They also strengthened the 8-metre mortar. Firing the redesigned shell was to be the climax of Steamboat Springs' Winter Carnival on 8 February 2020. The mortar would be sunk into the ground on Emerald Mountain overlooking the site. Widmann was a stickler for safety and Borden met the local fire chief and other officials to agree on road closures to protect people and vehicles from fallout. The banker said he had spent a 'small fortune' on the project.[46] Even his wife did not know how much. Someone allowed to see the shell in the mortar, waiting to be fired, remarked that it was like looking down the barrel of the biggest gun in the world.

There was a late hitch. A storm dumped 60 centimetres of snow, which then had to be cleared, but the moment finally came when Borden hit the button that sent a wireless signal to fire the shell. A few bright sparks flew from the mortar. Then nothing. Was it going to be a repeat of the previous year's failure? The team waited nervously, but after a few seconds more, the shell flew out and rose nearly a mile into the sky. The 15,000 spectators, along with many more watching over the Internet, saw quite a small streak of light climbing, then dwindling to a glowing dot before it exploded in a great ball of red light. Almost immediately, the snow started to fall again, coming down quite heavily. Steamboat Fireworks had got into the record books by the skin of their teeth.

Other World Records

In Japan, the Church of Perfect Liberty became famous for its August fireworks displays, which were claimed in 1980 to be the biggest in the world. George Plimpton went to see the show that year at a golf course at the organization's headquarters near Osaka, where a million people watched $1 million's worth of fireworks. That was between six and seven times the cost of a major event of that era in America, such as the Brooklyn Bridge Centennial celebrations of 1983. The religious order had been founded in 1924 by a priest who wanted to promote peace. It declares that 'when we express our true selves in everything we do, we will be able to express our full human potential,' which would allow 'the dream of true World Peace' to become a reality.[47] The founder's last words were said to have been: 'fire *hanabi* for peace!'[48] Fireworks became the emblem of the organization, celebrating the idea of using explosives to bring goodwill and harmony instead of destruction.

The proceedings began with a daylight display. Plimpton was particularly impressed by the 'Dragon Shells' that seemed to unwind in the sky like paper streamers in red, green, blue, purple and black. By nightfall, a 'huge, respectful crowd' had arrived, and an upward sweep of the arms by the order's high priest got the show on the road. There was no electrical firing. The shells, 4,400 of them just in the first barrage, were dropped into mortar pipes, each of which had a red-hot coil at the base. Each coil lasted about two minutes, long enough to send up around thirty shells. Then the firemaster would reach down the pipe using a stick with a hook on the end, fish out the coil and replace it with a new one that was white-hot. Next to each mortar was a rattan shield, behind which the igniter could shelter. Among the favourite shells was a chrysanthemum that changed eight times. Each shell contained hundreds of stars built around a husk, usually a rice seed, that was rolled in eight different chemical mixtures to achieve the constant changes. Perhaps the most spectacular item of all was a Niagara of coloured fire a kilometre long suspended between two cranes. There were also star mines with tails like 'a great curtain rising into the sky'.[49] (Star mines are similar to shells and often used in finales. They are connected with quick match and so go off all at once rather than one after another, like shells.) At one point the heavens were filled with *kamuro* shells, named after the Japanese word for a boy's haircut, a type of willow shell containing stars that burn long enough to produce an effect like a weeping willow with tendrils of gold fire reaching almost to the ground. As other shells burst, they displayed the names of leaders of the religious order, and the finale was a great wall of gleaming white magnesium resembling a towering glacier, accompanied by a terrifying shriek, which for twelve seconds lit up the golf course like bright moonlight. Plimpton says this one stunning effect would have cost about $200,000, more than had ever been paid for an entire display at that time in the United States. By the end, the golf course was burning in places. (As time went on, magnesium was often replaced by magnalium, an alloy made with aluminium, which was less prone to corrosion and easier to grind into powder.)

Perfect Liberty's kilometre-long Niagara may have been impressive, but in 2008 another Japanese event, the Ariake Seas Fireworks Festival at Fukuoka on the island of Kyushu, surpassed that mark with one that stretched more than 3.5 kilometres. Then at the celebrations for the New Year of 2020, Fireworks by Grucci set another world record for Ras Al Khaimah's artificial island of Al Marjan. As part of a spectacular thirteen-minute display, the company put on a Niagara nearly 3.8 kilometres long. A spokesperson explained it was designed 'to position the emirate as one of the world's first choices for New Year's Eve celebrations'.[50] A further example of the taste for pyrotechnic record-breaking acquired by the oil-rich countries of the Middle East was set in Kuwait in 2012 for the biggest ever firework display, with more than 77,000 fired in an hour at a reported cost of $15 million during celebrations to mark the fiftieth anniversary of the country's constitution. That record had belonged to Madeira ever since the moment when 2006 had turned to 2007. New Year's Eve is particularly special on the island, because legend has it that long ago on the last day of the year, the Virgin Mary was looking down from heaven and felt sad, thinking about the lost continent of Atlantis, which had been sunk by the Lord as a punishment for its people's wickedness. A tear seemed to fall from her eye, but really it was a pearl. It fell where Atlantis had been, and there Madeira, the 'Pearl of the Atlantic', was born. It was said that in ancient times, every New Year's Eve, as the clock struck twelve, a fantastic vision of light and colours would appear in the skies over the island. As the years went by, it seems the visions faded, but then, in a sense, pyrotechnics brought them back. In the eighteenth century English expats started firing a rocket to mark the New Year. Later a local banker took up the idea; well-heeled families began competing with each other, and soon rockets were going off all over the capital, Funchal. Nowadays one of the most famous pyrotechnic displays in the world takes advantage of the natural arena provided by Funchal Bay, with fireworks being let off from nearly forty different places, while cruise liners anchor offshore to join the thousands of spectators on land.

Seeing in the New Year of 2014, Dubai in the United Arab Emirates broke Kuwait's record in the first minute of a display that saw nearly 480,000 fireworks fired in six minutes. This display still holds the record for the most set off in a single minute, at just short of 80,000. They were fired from four hundred places, and the event took ten months to plan. Talal Omar from Guinness World Records said the old record had been 'broken on a phenomenal scale'.[51] The show was designed by Phil Grucci, whose father had been killed in the 1983 accident and who now headed up the family business. After winning the Monte Carlo competition, the Gruccis had put on shows at every presidential inauguration from Ronald Reagan to George W. Bush and at four Olympic Games, as well as up to seventy shows on each Fourth of July. Two hundred people worked for the company, which mounted displays costing anything from $3,500 to more than $10 million. The year after breaking the record in Dubai, Phil said that in spite of all the technological changes the business had seen, they were still performing some of the same shows his grandfather had devised: proof, as he saw it, of the universal appeal of fireworks: 'Look at a seven-year-old child watching a fireworks show and look at an 80-year-old person watching a fireworks show. Short of the wrinkles on the face of the older person, the expression is almost always the same.'[52]

Dubai's record was beaten in turn by a Norwegian display in November 2014 that featured more than 540,000 fireworks. Then, as 2016 dawned, Norway's mark was shattered by a religious movement in the Philippines. The Iglesia ni Cristo, 'Church of Christ', had been founded in 1914 by Félix Ysagun Manalo. Raised as a Roman Catholic, he decided humanity needed to return to what he saw as the original church established by Christ himself. He attracted so many followers his church became a formidable political force, and the date of its foundation was made a national holiday. So in spite of pouring rain, about 100,000 people turned out to watch nearly 811,000 fireworks set off to celebrate New Year at the Philippine Arena Complex, north of Manila, which is owned by the Church of Christ. The event also set a new record for the highest number of sparklers lit at the same time in a single venue, with a total of 1,070. And speaking of sparklers, a 28-year-old Ukrainian named Yuriy Yaniv set off the biggest of all time in 2016. In a stunt that would definitely fall into the 'don't try this at home' category, he made his record breaker by packing 10,000 individual sparklers tightly into a metal bin. This contraption weighed 50 kilograms, and if the sparklers had been set off one by one, the show would have lasted for two days. Yaniv commented: 'we had to be extremely careful when we were setting up – one wrong move and it could have gone off.' He put the giant sparkler in the middle of an open field and had 'a couple of fire extinguishers' on hand just in case.[53] The first attempt had to be abandoned because the wind was too strong, but the second time Yaniv lit the fuse, it created a spectacular tower of flame.

Another pyrotechnic record that sounds pretty risky is 'Most fireworks launched from a pyrotechnics suit', set at 642 by Frenchman Laurent Nat in Grenoble in 2014. A pyrotechnics artist and performer for ten years, Nat based his 'suit' on a firefighter's uniform, and stood on stilts to maximize the number of firing sites. It took him eight months to get in shape: 'I had to build up a lot of muscle to be able to cope with the weight and the pressure of the fireworks.'[54] One record proudly held by a Briton for a time was 'most rockets launched in 30 seconds'. In 2006 Roy Lowry, an explosives expert and university lecturer, decided to target the then record of 39,210 set in Jersey in 1997. Black Cat provided 56,649 rockets, which were loaded on to fifteen specially built frames and fused by Fantastic Fireworks. The rockets were ignited electronically at Plymouth's National Fireworks Championships, and Lowry found himself recognized by Guinness World Records. Fantastic Fireworks' John Culverhouse had a crack at the record himself in 2009 at Dorset Festival in Bournemouth. He had 110,000 rockets mounted on a barge at sea, and when they were fired, he was convinced they had broken the record. Then he and his team got 'a somewhat hostile reception from the audience'. It transpired that the first rockets launched had set fire to the rest, which had then gone up in a great explosion. 'The only crumb of comfort I could take', said Culverhouse, 'was that in the *Daily Mirror*'s Top 10 Disappointments of 2009 we came top.'[55] The following year, the world record went to the Philippines when Pyroworks International set off nearly 126,000 rockets in seventeen seconds.

New Year Fireworks: Australia Leads the Way

Australia played a crucial role in giving fireworks a mass television audience. Across the world, the turn of the year is marked with pyrotechnics, but international time differences mean Sydney's New Year show is one of the first major displays to be seen, arriving eleven hours before London's, for example. According to some estimates, it is the most watched New Year celebration in the world, with more than a billion viewers across the globe, while a million watch it live at Sydney Harbour. But it was not always so. The city used to have what some considered a rather clunky event in January known as the Waratah Festival. A columnist for the *Sydney Morning Herald* dismissed it as 'lethally dull', adding: 'It was breathtakingly parochial and uninspired. Everyone who had something to sell – from a new Toyota Corolla to whatever – put it in the parade and it was alternated with the odd band and marching girls. It was like some hick town in the mid-West.'[56] In 1977 the city fathers decided to revamp it as the Sydney Festival, to be launched by pyrotechnics on New Year's Eve.

The Harbour Bridge became the centrepiece of the show, inspired, it was said, by the way New York had used the Brooklyn Bridge, though fireworks also go off from the Opera House and from barges in the harbour. Sydney's shows were based on big themes – a dove of peace in 2001 after the 9/11 attacks; in 2015 a celebration of the First Nations with a display echoing the black, red and yellow of the Australian Aboriginal flag, while two years later it was rainbow-coloured pyrotechnics to mark the legalization of gay marriage. Sometimes, as in 2015, the display featured audacious stunts, like getting jet-skiers to release fireworks. The display of 2017 also featured an unusual kind of pyrotechnic competition, with children invited to draw their ideal firework exploding and the event organizers, Foti International Fireworks, given the task of designing the pyrotechnic device that would produce the imagined effect. Appropriately, the prize went to an entry called Rainbow Kiss, and featured a multicoloured umbrella with a silver palm-tree centre. The winner also got to come to Sydney to push the button that set the whole show going. Foti was still a family business, started in Italy in 1793. Fortunato was its seventh-generation maestro, and seven other family members were on the staff. Its fireworks came from China.

On New Year's Eve 2018, a hitch led to revellers being welcomed to the year 2018 instead of 2019, but, nothing daunted, the following year's show was to be the 'most choreographed to date', featuring 36,000 fireworks: 23,000 of them going off the bridge, and the remainder from 27 other firing positions.[57] One of the trademarks of Sydney's show has been a pyrotechnic 'waterfall', created by dropping fireworks from the Harbour Bridge into the water. The effect was said to have been invented in 1986 for the 75th anniversary of the Royal Australian Navy by Syd Howard, grandson and namesake of the founder of another Australian pyrotechnic dynasty.

A dozen people worked full-time on the New Year show for about three months, and fifty for the final twelve days to set up the firing positions and 60 kilometres of wiring. The launching of individual fireworks could be computer-controlled to an accuracy of one hundredth of a second, but Fortunato Foti was nostalgic: 'When I first started, all the fireworks were generally hand-lit – so they've sort of taken the fun out of it really, haven't they?'[58] According to one calculation, the celebrations generate about £85 million's worth of spending in the city, while by 2020 the cost was estimated at £3.4 million. As Sydney prepared to welcome 2020, an almost equally splendid show was happening in Melbourne 500 miles to the south, with a team of 85 pyrotechnicians setting off 14 tonnes of fireworks from the tops of 22 skyscrapers. The company in charge was the Howard & Sons fireworks dynasty, founded in 1922 when the original Syd Howard got fed up of buying fireworks from England because they never seemed to work. 'By the time they got to Australia, after travelling on boats and getting wet,' said his great-grandson Andrew, a director of the family firm, 'a lot of them were duds.'[59] So Syd decided to make them himself in Eastwood, New South Wales. His son Harry soon joined the business, and they turned out Roman candles, fountains, aerial shells and mines. (Mines are high-impact, short-duration fireworks that stay on the ground and fire a single burst into the air. Sometimes they start with a small fountain, then come stars, bangs and glitter. In the UK, all the effects used to be held in a single cylinder, rather like a shell minus the lifting charge, but in recent years, there has tended to be a switch to multiple smaller tubes all fired at the same time, though often still contained in a bigger cylinder.) Harry's son, the younger Syd, said his grandfather was 'slightly eccentric, very clever and not like any Australian today – he wouldn't go out the front gate without a suit, a hat and a tie on'.[60] In the 1930s granddad Syd had his left hand blown off in a firework accident, said to have happened because a supplier had mislabelled chemicals, and a decade later, Harry lost his right hand during a mock battle scene. Syd the younger recalled working on a show with his father when he was eleven. Not long after, he was dispatched to Queensland after one of the Howards' agents fell ill just as he was due to mount a display. The client was rather taken aback when Syd turned up in short trousers, but by the time the show was over they were already booking him for the next.

Howard & Sons' big breakthrough was winning the contract for the display to celebrate the opening of Sydney Harbour Bridge in 1932. Other highlights included the Coronation in 1953 and the opening of Sydney Opera House in 1973. By the early 1980s the company was being run by Harry, Syd, and Syd's younger brother Les, Andrew's father. It had become one of the most successful pyrotechnic companies in Australia, supplying Disneyland and Disney World in the United States, but it would break up in a bitter family feud. In 1985 Harry and Les bought out Syd, who created a new business, Syd Howard Fireworks International, bringing in pyrotechnics from China and Japan for his displays before he started manufacturing himself. The company produced shows for Australia's bicentenary celebrations in 1988, as well as masterminding some of Sydney's New Year's Eve events. Overseas, it won big contracts, such as the closing ceremony at the Atlanta Olympics in 1996, and the

British handover of Hong Kong to China the following year. In 2008 one of his colleagues told Australian Broadcasting Corporation television that Syd Howard was an artist: 'The only difference between a conventional artist and what he does is his canvas could be a 450-metre span of a harbour bridge.'[61]

Even without Syd, Howard & Sons remained a major force, surviving a devastating explosion at their plant in 2007, and putting on shows across the world, while they also worked within a rich tradition of fireworks at local Australian events – agricultural and country shows, carnivals, school fetes and proms, weddings, concerts, theatrical productions – as well as spicing up product launches and corporate events. Andrew Howard argued that pyrotechnics still brought people together because of 'a sense of magic and mystique about it all. Only a few select people know how it works.' He welcomed the precision computers had brought, allowing event organizers to create an exact video animation before the display, so clients would know precisely what they were getting. It could also be shared with a music composer. On the other hand, he argued the fundamentals remained the same: 'That basic mix of gunpowder hasn't changed at all.' The maker still had to get the amount right, the stars still had to be put in the right places inside the shell and the trajectory of the mortar had to be right: 'That's probably one of the elements that I love about it . . . it's not an exact science, there's always an element of risk.'[62]

London: A Wallflower No More

In terms of major displays in the UK, the 1980s started fairly dismally. The wedding of Charles and Diana was marked by what was meant to be a pastiche of the celebration of the Treaty of Aix-la-Chapelle in 1749, but the machine was criticized for being too small compared with the original and looking like a 'slab of cardboard'. The pastiche theme was carried as far as trying to reproduce the fire that destroyed most of the 1749 machine, and eighteenth-century fire engines were on hand to attack the flames, but the 1981 version stubbornly refused to catch light. The culmination of the show was a giant Catherine wheel like a sun that bore the monograms of the prince and princess, but purists complained that, instead of being turned by the power of pyrotechnics, it was actually rotated by a man with a crank handle who was clearly visible through the smoke. The *Evening Standard* critic scored the show:

'Wedding 6 Fireworks 0', although the marriage turned out not to be a great success either.[63]

Nowadays London's New Year's Eve fireworks are said to be the biggest annual display in Europe, but the UK capital was comparatively late to the scene. *The Independent* columnist Mary Dejevsky wrote that she had always been 'envious of continental cities' which put on pyrotechnic celebrations before 'London finally jumped on the bandwagon,' and even then the city had a rather stuttering start.[64] By the mid-1990s it had become the tradition for revellers in the capital, who might number as many as 80,000, to gather in Trafalgar Square to welcome the New Year, and concerns about safety were growing. In 1997 Fantastic Fireworks wrote to Sir Max Hastings, then editor of the *Evening Standard*, who they 'knew was a fireworks enthusiast', to ask if he would sponsor a New Year's Eve display on the Thames.[65] It was held downstream from Tower Bridge, well away from Trafalgar Square and London's main tourist highlights, and police told the crowds to stay away from the square as 'there was nothing for them to do there except to stand around and get cold.'[66] Fantastic say more than 100,000 people lined the river as, from a pontoon on the water, 5,000 fireworks were sent soaring 300 metres in the air. River barges tooted their horns and, on land, motorists joined in. The spectators, according to a Sky News reporter, were 'well impressed'. Fantastic's John Culverhouse considered it a 'great success' and wanted to repeat the event the following year, but the City of London police said they could not afford to police it, so for the beginning of the last year of the millennium, there was no firework display in central London.

It took a once-in-a-thousand-years celebration – the start of the new millennium on 1 January 2000 – to kickstart the next great central London display. As the home of Greenwich Mean Time, the city had the credentials to be the global centre of this jamboree. Fantastic Fireworks, to their great disappointment, were passed over. Tony Blair's Labour government brought in Bob Geldof's company Big Time to take charge of the event, and he hired none other than Syd Howard from Australia to organize the fireworks. As we saw, setting the Thames 'burning' was a feature of the celebrations for the end of the Second World War, and the 'Rhine in Flames' had been Germany's major pyrotechnic event since 1955, with displays along 17 kilometres of the river. Now publicists promised that a 60-metre-high 'curtain of flame' would race along the Thames at 650 mph, travelling from Tower Bridge to Vauxhall in just over ten seconds, and released computer-generated graphics of what it would look like.[67] What became dubbed the 'river of fire' was supposed to create the illusion that water was turning to flame thanks to fireworks on a string of barges 100 to 250 metres apart. A computer on shore would send radio cues to operators on each barge, who would then trigger the detonations at an average interval of about two-thirds of a second. Each signal would send hundreds of fireworks up in a fan shape. The organizers claimed this would achieve the desired effect. A million turned out to watch along the Thames, with another 2 million looking on from other vantage points around the capital, but many people were disappointed and assumed the effects had failed to go off as planned. One watching from Southwark Bridge complained the flames reached only 15 metres. A father watching with his two teenage sons 12 metres from the river said Big Time should have been prosecuted under the Trade Descriptions Act. Even one reasonably complimentary student in the crowd complained: 'There was supposed to be a wall of flame. That's what we came to see. The fireworks were amazing, but I could have seen them from my home.'[68] Matt Wells of *The Guardian* wrote that it looked 'just like what it was – a load of rockets being let off from a dozen or so barges'.[69] He said many of the spectators saw only the fireworks from the barge closest to where they stood and maybe a few from those on either side.

One of the British companies that had supplied the fireworks put the blame squarely on the organizers, saying they 'went over our heads and told the public about the event in terms that were simply never going to happen'. He claimed everything had, in fact, gone according to plan: 'It worked, it was impressive, but it wasn't what people expected so of course they were going to find it disappointing.' One of Syd Howard's directors was singing from the same hymn sheet, saying he was proud of the show: 'What we did was exactly what our contract said we were to do ... The concept got blown out of all proportion.'[70] Big Time was, if anything, even less repentant, but in his memoirs, *You Can't Say That* (2011), the controversial Ken Livingstone, then mayor of London, claimed the 'river of fire' never happened because civil servants, alarmed at the cost, slashed the budget by 90 per cent without informing the government ministers who were supposed to be in charge.

It was a shame the show had been over-hyped. For all his criticism, Matt Wells conceded the display was 'spectacular' and the biggest in British history. In twenty minutes, 39 tonnes of fireworks were fired from sixteen barges, and could be seen from 20 miles away. The 3 million packed into central London made it the biggest party in the capital since the Coronation, and an estimated 20 million watched on television in the UK, with perhaps a billion more across the globe. Some critics ruminated on whether the problem was that London lacked a real focal point, unlike Paris with the Eiffel Tower or Sydney with the Harbour Bridge, though, as we have seen, the Thames has been a venue for firework displays for centuries. Paris did put on a mind-blowing event designed by Yves Pépin, who created the opening ceremony for the 1998 World Cup. Climbers installed 20,000 fairy lights on the Eiffel Tower, and while they flashed, jets of fireworks, all producing a white flame, moved up the tower as midnight approached. Then at the striking of the hour, a great explosion at the base of the tower suggested the structure was a rocket about to take off. But despite the efforts of Sydney, Paris and other cities, CNN declared London's show to be the best in the world. Syd Howard was not there to see it, incidentally. He was back home in Sydney, believing New Year's Eve was jinxed because the accidents that cost his father and grandfather their hands had both happened on that night.

In his memoirs, Ken Livingstone says that the following year he was asked to take the event over, but disagreements with the Tube over what late services they would run prevented him reviving it until he was given control of London Underground in 2003. When the pyrotechnics did return, it was for a display lasting just three minutes at the London Eye. Potential spectators were told to stay at home and watch on television, but 100,000 still turned out. For the first few years the annual budget was just over £1 million, and the crowds grew each year, allowing Livingstone to enthuse in 2007 that London was 'the most exciting place in the world to bring in the New Year'.[71] By 2011, with future prime minister Boris Johnson now mayor, the budget was up to nearly £2 million, as London prepared to enter the year that would see it stage the Olympic Games. Johnson was in never-knowingly-understated mode as he declared: 'the sky will light up with a dazzling display of pyrotechnic magic. 2012 will open, not with a timid whimper, but a colourful bang, a noisy clarion call to herald one amazing year.'[72] A major coup was needed, and executive producer Jim Donald knew just the thing. He wanted to set off fireworks from Big Ben. 'No-one's ever fired anything off Parliament,' he said, 'the last one to attempt that was Guy Fawkes.' He got Johnson to write to the Speaker of the House, John Bercow – Brexit had not yet turned them into sworn enemies – and with less than a month to go, Bercow gave permission to let off fireworks from the iconic building as each bong of midnight rang out. The pyrotechnics also being fired from barges and from the London Eye all had to be synchronized to a musical soundtrack while they created the five Olympic rings, among other things. Donald enlisted GPS satellite technology – 'the most accurate clock you can use'.[73] The result was a three-hundred-page cue list, with 5,500 separate triggers for the fireworks.

For New Year's Eve 2013 London offered what was claimed to be 'the world's first multi-sensory firework display'.[74] Boris Johnson waxed boosterish as usual: 'A spectacular display of pyrotechnics that you can taste and even smell! Where else but London would you get such an experience?'[75] The organizers drafted in a company called Bompas & Parr, in its own words 'globally recognised as the leading expert in multi-sensory experience design'.[76] Of the quarter of a million people reckoned to have turned out on a rainy night, about 100,000 were given scratch 'n' sniff programmes and fruit-flavoured sweets that were supposed to coordinate with the fireworks. But the full experience was reserved for 50,000 people between Westminster Bridge and Hungerford Bridge. As 12,000 fireworks were set off from the London Eye, red pyrotechnics were matched with strawberry-flavoured mist. There was also firework-coordinated peach snow, edible banana confetti and 'floating oranges' – thousands of big bubbles filled with smoke tasting of Seville orange. Bompas & Parr said it was 'the first time in the history of mankind that specific flavours have been choreographed to match the pyrotechnics'.[77]

But by the end of 2014, Johnson had had to do something very unboosterish, turning the great free fireworks show into a ticketed event. The reason given was that now on a fine night, it could attract half a million people, and that this was too many, so Johnson decided to limit attendance to 100,000 who had bought tickets at £10 a time to ensure the event 'continues to be a safe, enjoyable and sustainable event for the long-term'.[78] Mary Dejevsky understood the safety concerns, but complained that Johnson's decision meant there was 'one less popular event in the capital that is truly open to all'.[79] The £2 million bill was also causing disquiet, but Johnson's chief of staff, Edward (later Lord) Lister, said it was a crucial investment to demonstrate that London was one of the world's top cities.

From 2003 the company in charge of London's celebrations was Jack Morton Worldwide, a 'brand experience agency' that had started out in the 1930s in America by booking technicians for cinemas and bands for college dances.[80] By the twenty-first century, the firm was producing opening and closing ceremonies for the Athens Olympics in 2004. For London's New Year's Eve celebrations, it brought in pyrotechnic experts Titanium Fireworks, a Northamptonshire company formed by four close friends who were still offering shows for weddings and parties but whose track record included Hogmanay celebrations in Edinburgh, the Commonwealth Games, the fiftieth anniversary of the Forth Road Bridge and the opening celebration for Hull City of Culture. They also put on what was claimed to be the 'world's smallest firework display' for Legoland's Miniland at Windsor. In Miniland, the London Eye is just 2.7 metres tall – one-fiftieth the height of the real thing – so instead of soaring hundreds of metres into the sky, Titanium had to use small precision fireworks that would ignite only 3 metres off the ground. Director Darryl Fleming said it was 'an operation of military accuracy' and that they 'needed to get the positioning just right to ensure the end result was as spectacular as any full-scale display and exactly the right amount of powder and explosive was used'.[81]

Perhaps Titanium's highest-profile firing was at the acclaimed opening ceremony of the London Olympics of 2012 – 'terrific, spectacular, moving, wonderful', wrote one critic.[82] Although the event was being televised all over the world, the artistic director, Danny Boyle, told Titanium that television would 'look after itself'. He wanted something that would be a great experience for the people inside the stadium. The millennium's 'river of fire' might have proved a damp squib, but Boyle's 'ceiling of fire' would be a triumph, soaring over the heads of 80,000 spectators, 4,500 performers and 2,500 athletes.[83] It meant setting off fireworks from the inner gantry, an effect Titanium say 'had not been done before on this scale', but although the stadium provided the centrepiece of the display, there were more than two hundred firing positions.[84]

Pyrotechnics needed to pitch in at three key moments in the ceremony: just after the athletes started to parade; then after the queen declared the games open; and last, the finale. The fireworks fired over the stadium had to be guaranteed debris-free, what with the queen, other heads of state and 90,000 people below. Fleming, who was running the show, said the pyrotechnics lasted a total of two and a half minutes, and within that time he 'created a red, white and blue crown of fireworks for the Queen and had the colours of the Olympic Rings chasing each other along the river and wrapping themselves around the stadium'. He worked for 36 hours without a break setting up the positions, 'fervently hoping none of the police marksmen would mistake the guy crawling around the roof for a terrorist'. Then at the last minute he had to change some of the fireworks because they had got damp in heavy rain.

Fleming says pyrotechnics 'are a unique medium. You can see them, hear them, smell them and feel them.' He had caught the bug in school chemistry lessons, and after qualifying as a chartered surveyor he went into the fireworks business. When he started, they were still hand-firing from mortars. 'Did we really do that?' he asked. 'The noise and the recoil was amazing.' Modern technology meant he was now often a kilometre away from the fireworks. If he was as close as 50 metres, 'my crew wants to know what's wrong.'[85] But the digital revolution also had its drawbacks. Once as he was about to fire a display, 'my computer suddenly died and the screen went blank, my face dropped and I turned to see what had happened. The client had unplugged my desk-top to charge up his phone.' Some displays might involve 150 firework cues in a single second. When Fleming is preparing a major show, he says: 'the anxiety and stress levels can be off the scale, but with it comes immense satisfaction and euphoria,' as soon as the first shell is fired.[86] (Mortars were changing too. A reporter at America's PGI Annual Convention in 2020 said they were increasingly made of PVC rather than metal.)

Among Fleming's other credits are hurling a gigantic rugby ball of light around the top of Twickenham, and putting thirty seconds of pyrotechnic effects to Adele's song 'Set Fire to the Rain' at Wembley. This called for 32 firing positions on the great arch, which took four days to set up and two to dismantle. In 2021 he declared the highlight of his career had been pushing the button for the fireworks as the queen declared the London Olympics open. As for the tensest, that was London's New Year's Eve display. By 2018 he had done eight of them, all centred on the London Eye. He started choreographing the show in September when the soundtrack – 'a mash-up of the year's big tunes' – was finished: 'The music dictates what fireworks we use. If it's something erratic, I'll go for Scrabbly Comets, or if it's slow and evocative I'll go for something more ethereal.'[87] In 2017 he had to rig 32 positions on the inner rim of the London Eye and another sixteen on the central spindle. Then there were three barges and fifteen pontoons along 250 metres of the Thames. In all a crew of 36 technicians was enlisted to fire 12,000 fireworks of perhaps four hundred different types, and they could not start work on the Eye until after it closed to paying customers at six o'clock: 'It's so stressful that I have to turn my back on the control panel when the testing starts.

I can't bear to watch . . . until you test it you don't know if you are going to get all the London Eye, half the Eye or none of the Eye going off.'[88] It is all controlled by GPS, and at midnight, a satellite sends a signal to the system to start firing.

In 2016 Labour's Sadiq Khan took over from Boris Johnson as mayor of London, and the UK had voted to leave the European Union against the wishes of London, where almost 60 per cent had backed Remain. Soon New Year fireworks were mired in political controversy. On New Year's Eve 2018 Khan was criticized for lighting up the London Eye in the yellow and blue colours of the EU flag and for making the theme of the show 'London is Open', while complaining that Westminster politicians were 'giving the impression we're insular, inward looking, not welcoming to Europeans'.[89] Right-wing blood pressure rose still higher two years later during the lockdown of 2020, with Thames bridges coloured blue and yellow, and drones overhead forming the fist that was the symbol of the Black Lives Matter movement alongside the NHS logo as fireworks exploded over Tower Bridge. Conservatives complained it was 'a disgusting waste of money'.[90]

Traditions Survive: Bonfire Night and Others

Ron Lancaster aired a heretical suggestion for Bonfire Night, saying the date should be moved: 'it's a terrible time to fire fireworks. It's usually damp and cold. Much better in the summer.'[91] Still, 5 November it has remained. At Lewes in Sussex, the anti-Catholic feeling that had been such a feature of the night seemed to have become more muted from the 1950s, and usually flared up only when someone had the temerity to complain about antics like pope-burning. In 1980 a Catholic priest wrote to the local newspaper criticizing the Cliffe Bonfire Society, saying that keeping alive 'anti-Catholic sentiments, even if they are not meant seriously, is both shocking and offensive to many people'.[92] On Bonfire Night 1981 he was burned in effigy. That year, the outspoken Northern Irish Protestant leader the Revd Ian Paisley turned up at the festivities and handed out anti-Catholic pamphlets. But the following year, Paisley's effigy was burned. Margaret Thatcher would receive the same treatment, suggesting a drift away from anti-Catholicism to broader 'anti-elite' feelings. In 1989 BBC Television's 5 November edition of *Songs of Praise*, which came from Lewes and included a firework display, was devoted to the theme of religious toleration. But seven years later, a thanksgiving service for bonfire supporters on the Sunday before 5 November saw a preacher wearing an Orange Order sash and warning that 'ecumenicalism would lead to one unified church with the pope as leader,' while a newly appointed Roman Catholic priest in the town said the burning of crosses and effigies at that year's Guy Fawkes celebrations reminded him of the Nazis.[93]

The event at Lewes, sometimes dubbed the 'bonfire capital of the world', continued to be spectacular, with the number of spectators claimed to reach 80,000 (in a town with a population of fewer than 20,000), as local bonfire societies still vied with each other to put on the best bonfire and firework display. Hundreds of people dressed as smugglers or Vikings or in other exotic outfits bore blazing torches, while some carried placards with the names of the Protestants martyred in 1557. 'Bonfire Boyes and Belles', often in hooped Guernseys, let off ear-splitting agricultural bird-scarers called 'Rookies' and drove flaming tar barrels through the streets. The burning of effigies of topical figures such as George W. Bush, Angela Merkel and even disgraced American cyclist Lance Armstrong continued, but a correspondent in 2019 reported that representations of the pope were still common.[94] Accidents might be

Bonfire Night, Lewes, 2017.

less frequent than expected, as Alan Brock had put it, but the Lewes festivities of 2010 saw a member of one of the bonfire societies seriously injured when he was hit in the chest by a stray rocket. The following year police appealed to people not to bring their own fireworks, and for the first time, plain clothes officers operated among the crowds and confiscated a number. Still, 22 people were taken to hospital and another 150 were treated for lesser injuries. Though some were the result of mishaps such as falls, fireworks were responsible for others. In 2019 there were nine arrests and 55 injuries, mainly minor. Police warned the event was unsuitable for children.

Other parts of Sussex continued their rowdy Bonfire Nights, even if they were less anti-Catholic. In the 1980s the Robertsbridge society even adopted a Cistercian monk's habit as their principal uniform because in medieval times the village had been famous for its monastery. The outfits got a bit of booing on their first appearance, but it was said to be good-natured. As we saw, at Battle, the 'Battle Rouser' home-made firework was banned in the 1950s, but that did not mean calm pervaded. In 1984 some Battel Bonfire Boyes wore convict uniforms as a protest against what they saw as over-zealous policing of the previous year's event, and in 2010 the society's publicity officer had to take to the local newspaper's letters page to apologize that some people had experienced 'upset' at that year's event, adding that anyone 'caught throwing fireworks into the crowd . . . would be dealt with severely'. He concluded with a warning that the event was 'not suitable for young children or those with a nervous disposition', although he had taken along his 'nieces and nephew, who are all under six'.[95] In 2018 the distinction of being burned in effigy was bestowed on then prime minister Theresa May, who was depicted astride a barrel of gunpowder with the slogan 'Gunpowder, Theresa and Plot', while a figure of Boris Johnson with fireworks shooting out of its bottom lit the fuse and exploded her.

Sussex bonfire nights were not confined to 5 November. A plethora of local societies put on events throughout the autumn from September to December – 35 of them in 2013, for example. This flexibility on dates allowed societies to support their neighbours' festivities, swelling turnouts. As at Lewes, they wore a variety of costumes – smugglers, convicts, pearly kings and queens. These may have been used originally for disguise, along with the blacking of faces, with participants not wanting to be recognized by the authorities, or neighbours or employers. They might collect money for good causes, but the bonfire events often involved unruliness, cocking a snook at authority or the settling of scores, and even the more innocent-sounding pranks would certainly have annoyed some people – secreting fireworks in prize marrows or in pub chimneys to dislodge a mountain of soot. Then there was the practice of setting off bangers in an oil drum, creating a fearful noise. Another troublesome firework genre was 'Drop-Down' bangers, which were thrown into the crowd. In 2011 a woman from the Seaford society suffered a serious eye injury when one exploded at her feet. A ban on them led some of the Hastings society to start a drumming band because they thought the event had got too quiet. When a policeman told them to dial the noise back a bit, they refused and he gave them a caution under Section 5 of the Public Order Act. The band then adopted the name Section 5.

Hair-raising bonfire customs also survived in two Devon towns. On the Saturday nearest to 5 November, Hatherleigh has teams of men dragging flaming barrels on a sled at breakneck speed through its streets, with some of the more intrepid spectators running behind them. At Ottery St Mary, men run with flaming tar barrels on their backs. Each barrel is bigger than the last, until the biggest of all appears at midnight. Although it happens on Bonfire Night, it is thought this may reflect an even earlier tradition of setting tar barrels on fire to warn of danger, such as at the time of the Spanish Armada in 1588. In 2009 up to a dozen people needed hospital treatment for burns after someone threw a metal aerosol can into one of the blazing barrels, causing an explosion that sent tar flying into the crowd.

Somerset's Bridgwater Carnival has its very own pyrotechnic, the 'Bridgwater Squib', a big, long-lasting firework that gives out showers of white sparks. The town was a Protestant stronghold, so Guy Fawkes's failure was no doubt celebrated with enthusiasm. Early records are sparse, but we do know that a man and his two children were killed in an explosion at their home in November 1716. Were they making Bridgwater squibs? By the mid-nineteenth century the town's festivities included the usual burning of effigies of Fawkes, the pope and other hate figures by masked revellers to the accompaniment of squibs, but the 1880 event turned into a riot. By one in the morning, about three hundred people were still making merry. The local authority ordered the newly formed fire brigade to put the bonfire out, but the revellers turned the fire hoses on the firemen and generally created mayhem. Officialdom's response was to try to turn the event into a more organized carnival, but the squibs survived. In 1892 the government tried to ban them, but without success, and in 1929, more than 2,000 were let off. The biggest were monsters 60 centimetres long, with a 5-centimetre bore. Television brought a slump in the carnival's popularity in the 1950s, but by the 1990s it was claimed that the event attracted more than 100,000 visitors a year. By then, the squibs were being attached to the end of poles and held aloft by a hundred 'carnivalites' as the night's proceedings culminated in the 'squibbing', which filled the high street to rooftop levels with huge eruptions of sparks.

In Northern Ireland, Derry or Londonderry is a divided city. People cannot even agree on what to call it, with Catholics referring to it as Derry while Protestants plump for Londonderry. A stronghold of Irish nationalism, it is not surprising that Guy Fawkes Night celebrations have been pretty muted there. Instead, spectacular fireworks from the banks of the River Foyle grace Halloween, making the city, according to USA *Today* in 2015, the 'best Halloween destination in the world'. Some argue that Halloween is actually an Irish invention, morphing from that ancient Celtic festival of Samhain. Derry/Londonderry's modern celebrations date back to the 1980s. It was the time of the Troubles, and the story goes that some patrons of a pub had put on fancy dress for Halloween, and that there was a bomb scare, so they moved on to another pub. Perhaps those who saw them en route in costume were inspired, because the next year half the population turned out in home-made outfits, and the city council got in on the act by mounting a big pyrotechnic display. Local people were not allowed to buy fireworks, so this was quite an attraction. Each year the event seemed to grow. In 2013 it was one of the highlights of Derry/Londonderry's year as UK City of Culture. Shirt-making had been one of its key industries, and this skill has possibly stimulated the widening variety of costumes that promenade around the walled city – nuns, nurses, pirates, priests, zombies, film stars, mermaids, witches, Donald Trumps. Shop-bought outfits are frowned on. In 2016 the city council estimated that 80,000 people attended the four days of festivities.

While some worried that organized Bonfire Night celebrations seemed little better than controlled hooliganism, fireworks continued to feature in uncontrolled hooliganism. In 1997, at Sale in Greater Manchester, they were thrown into postboxes, while a few miles away at Trafford Park they were used to set fire to industrial units. Meanwhile, about 30 miles north in Accrington, youths attacked police and firefighters who were trying to put out a bonfire that had been lit directly under power lines. Even worse was the incident the same year at the village of Beddau in South Wales where a firework started a blaze that burned down a school. And the turning of a new millennium did not seem to make much difference. In 2021 Greater Manchester Police reported 'large groups of people throwing fireworks and other missiles' at officers. In Yorkshire, police officers in Bradford and a fire crew at Shipley were attacked, while police and firefighters were also targeted in Scotland. Nor was trouble of this kind confined to Bonfire Night. In May 2023 rioters threw fireworks at police in Cardiff.

Disney: The Biggest Customer

As we saw, one of the feathers in Howard & Sons' cap was its sales to Disney, which was said to be the biggest buyer of fireworks in the world, and the second biggest buyer of explosive devices after the U.S. Department of Defense, spending more than $18 million in 2016. Disneyland opened in 1955 at Anaheim, California, and Walt Disney introduced the regular pyrotechnic shows three years later as a way of getting people to stay in the theme park for longer. The first was *Fantasy in the Sky*, which used the backdrop of Sleeping Beauty's Castle. It would have looked pretty tame to modern eyes, with Disney staff lighting the fuses with flares, and it lasted just five minutes, but over the years, the display got more elaborate and it ran at Disneyland until 2000, then made a number of brief reappearances from 2015 onwards. *Fantasy* has also featured at Disney, Florida, Tokyo and Paris. The organization has put on a whole series of events featuring fireworks, and in later years added a wide range of visual techniques such as searchlights and lasers. Independence Day would see the patriotic *Disney's Celebrate America*; the autumn brought *Mickey's Not-so-Scary Halloween Party*, while the Christmas season had *Believe in Holiday Magic*. In 2021 Disney sparked an international row when it changed the greeting on its firework displays from 'Ladies and gentlemen, boys and girls!' to 'Dreamers of all ages!' in an effort to be less gender-specific.[96] Some social media users went apoplectic – 'I hate that!', 'utter garbage', 'stupid asses' – and Disney was accused of the dreadful, if poorly defined, crime of being 'woke'.[97]

As you might expect from an organization investing so much in pyrotechnics, Disney has been an innovator. In 2004 it began using compressed air to launch some of its fireworks instead of gunpowder, reducing noise, smoke, fumes and pollution. In a conventional shell, the explosion that flings it into the air also lights the time fuse that will cause it to burst at the right moment. For the compressed-air launch, Disney developed a cutting-edge computer chip that carried the charge for igniting the shell with a timer, which was much more accurate than a conventional explosive mechanism. The downside was that it needed a much more elaborate set-up than a conventional mortar, with air tanks, a compressor, a power supply and a computer, and was much more expensive.

Pyrotechnic Hotbed: India

India's first fireworks factory is said to have opened in Kolkata during the nineteenth century, but while the subcontinent was part of the British Empire, sophisticated fireworks were the preserve of the rich, though primitive 'sand-crackers' or 'dashing-crackers' enjoyed wider circulation. The European versions of these were made by mixing a small amount of the explosive mercury fulminate with grit, then twisting it into a piece of tissue paper. When you threw it on to a hard surface, you got a sharp bang. In India, a mixture of potassium chlorate and arsenic trisulphide was used instead, often in bigger quantities. This led to a lot of injured firework makers, and there was talk about banning the formulation, but it was only after coconut shells filled with the mixture began to be a favourite weapon of independence fighters that it was finally outlawed in 1910. After independence in 1947, import restrictions and the growing prosperity of the middle class helped the fireworks industry to flourish.

India is said to be the world's second biggest producer of fireworks, £225 million's worth in 2012, almost all of them for home consumption. Sivakasi in Tamil Nadu is the industry's centre. It is home to more than 1,000 registered firecracker manufacturing companies, making about 90 per cent of India's firecrackers, and creating 300,000 jobs directly as well as supporting another half million indirectly, thanks to two brothers who left the town in the 1920s to look for work in Kolkata. After learning how to make safety matches, they returned home and started manufacturing them, eventually diversifying into firecrackers. As well as featuring at weddings, fireworks are also let off at funerals. During the coronavirus lockdown in 2020, there was a political storm when two hundred people defied restrictions to give a pyrotechnic send-off to a bull that had become a star turn at festivals where villagers had to try and hold on to him as he ran. One of the subcontinent's most impressive displays happens every year at the Thrissur Pooram festival in the Vadakkumnathan Temple in the Keralan city of Thrissur. People come from miles around to see four major shows, including one that runs from midnight to dawn.

Pyrotechnic Hotbed: Japan – Practice and Theory

As well as being great practitioners, Japanese pyrotechnicians are also enthusiastic theorizers. In *Fireworks: The Art, Science and Technique* (1981), Dr Takeo Shimizu, director of a Tokyo fireworks company, wrote about the feelings produced by different shells and combinations. Referring to fireworks choreographers as 'drama directors', he argued that perfect chrysanthemums, especially those with flashes at the end of the petals, generate tension, while flower shells with 'rounded shoulders' promote relaxation, as do willows. A combination of red and yellow colours 'sometimes succeeds', while red and green 'looks dirty'. The circle made by a bursting shell must be perfect and filled with enough stars to be aesthetically pleasing: 'If it is too large, the density of the stars is low and the flower feels lonely.' Should these rules be broken, the display will become 'unstable and can give unpleasant feelings'. Toshio Ogatsu of the Ogatsu company was similarly exacting, warning that if one star fails to perform properly in a chrysanthemum or a peony, it is 'as if one petal of a flower is missing or has been eaten by a caterpillar'.[98]

Echoing Alan Brock, Plimpton considered Japan the 'most enlightened and enterprising nation when it comes to fireworks', saying it manufactured pyrotechnics 'of exceptional distinction, quality and beauty'.[99] After nearly three hundred years, the Sumida River display in Tokyo on the last Saturday in July remains a major event, featuring a competition between rival manufacturers that sees 20,000 fireworks set off over 90 minutes and attracts about a million spectators. Every year there are more than 1,000 displays across the country, mainly in July and August. The Nagaoka Fireworks Festival commemorates nearly 1,500 people killed in an air raid on the city in the last days of the Second World War. The finale spans 2 kilometres of the Shinano River. One of the most unnerving events is held every October at the Tominaga Shrine festival in Shinshiro City, featuring huge hand-held *tedsutsu*, fountains that spew sparks out everywhere.

Pyrotechnic Hotbed: Mexico

The papier-mâché bulls known as *toritos* are said to have featured on St John of God's day in Mexico since the nineteenth century, but in 1989 the event was amalgamated into Tultepec's new week-long National Pyrotechnics Festival. Mexico's self-proclaimed 'fireworks capital' produces between half and three-quarters of the country's pyrotechnics, and, according to some estimates, nearly two-thirds of its population are involved directly or indirectly in the industry. After a firework seller's booth exploded in a Mexico City market in 1988, killing more than fifty people, the authorities tightened up regulations around the manufacture and storage of pyrotechnics, so the new festival was something of a sweetener for Tultepec, designed to draw in visitors. But with most of the city's fireworks made in small workshops, often with the whole family pitching in, it is not clear how much effect the crackdown had. According to Tultepec's director of artisanal development and pyrotechnics in 2018, there were more illegal establishments than legal ones. The risks are no secret, with a mural in the city depicting townspeople with hands missing, cavorting among fireworks. One local said a stigma was attached to Tultepec after an explosion killed four people in 2017, but he did not care: 'the show must go on.'[100] In 2018 a journalist reported there was a smell of sulphur all over the city as he met Luis Enrique Urban Gomez, aged twenty, who had been injured with seven other people when a fireworks store blew up a couple of months before – one of three explosions within a month. His cousin had lost a leg and Urban's body was covered in scars and bandages, but he wanted to get back to work as soon as possible: 'In spite of it all, it is a pleasure. It is a job with tradition . . . something we decided to do when we were young. When people talk about fireworks in Mexico they talk about Tultepec, and that's something that fills you with pride.'[101] Across the country, it is reckoned that perhaps 50,000 families are involved in making fireworks, often working illegally in their own homes.

We have seen how fireworks and religion came together in Japan and the Philippines, but in Mexico in 2017 the Catholic Church expressed concern about how dominant pyrotechnics had become in the celebration of holy festivals. Father Hugo Valdemar Romero, from the Archdiocese of Mexico City, recognized they were 'a way of expressing the joy of the fiesta . . . It's a very old tradition,' but said the amount spent on pyrotechnics was excessive. Then there were the accidents. But a pastor for an Indigenous community in Chiapas state maintained fireworks were 'deeply rooted in the popular religious culture'. He told how he had performed a baptism in a church lit by candles while the congregation filled fireworks with gunpowder so they could let them off during the service. They believed this 'amplified' their prayers.[102]

Pyrotechnic Hotbed: Malta – Small Island, Big Fireworks and Another Record

There was a saying that any man on the island of Malta who did not cut himself shaving in the morning would fire a rocket to celebrate. When a Maltese won the Monte Carlo international fireworks competition in 1980, the year after the Gruccis, he was carried shoulder high from the airport on his return. Alan Brock wrote of the island that 'almost every anniversary in the Church calendar' was marked by a firework display.[103] Every village has at least one patron saint, and some have two. Each saint is celebrated at a *festa*, organized by the local brass band club, with food, drink, decorations, marching bands and fireworks. There is nothing like competition for keeping up standards, and there is fierce rivalry between the adherents of different saints at the island's sixty annual *festas*. Across Malta, there are 35 pyrotechnics factories, with 2,000 or more people working in them, all unpaid volunteers. Josef Camilleri, president of the Malta Pyrotechnics Association, started making fireworks when he was twelve. Half a century later, he said: 'I've never stopped working with fireworks. The fireworks factory is our second home after the family.' They made 'huge sacrifices . . . Many volunteers come in every day at 4pm after work and stay on till midnight, and sometimes even work through the night.' A typical display would cost £50,000, so the factories also sell fireworks to raise money. Camilleri believed the standard was getting better and better, with the 'pyrotechnicians of today true artists. They are painters of the sky.'[104] After a display they take just two weeks off before they start planning for next year.

Mark Lancaster wrote that in Malta, except for a no-holds-barred finale, shells were fired singly, with an interval after each one, so it could 'be appreciated without its beauty being marred by an infringement of colour by another firework'. Almost as beautiful as the pyrotechnics, he said, were 'the amazing snaking lines of mortars' winding their way 'up the hillside forming a continuous stream of fire'.[105] Camilleri ran the St Mary's Fireworks Factory in the village of Mqabba. Its displays are renowned, and feature the 'tower of light', a 50-metre-high structure packed with fireworks, which are set off by a computerized system synchronized with music and make shapes like stars, dolphins and Maltese crosses in the sky. The village also boasts a world record. Malta is famous for its Catherine wheels, and on the day of the feast of Our Lady of the Lilies in June 2011, Mqabba's Our Lady of the Lilies fireworks factory decided to try to build the world's biggest. The record was held by the Newick Bonfire Society, who had fired a 26-metre wheel in the East Sussex village in 1999. One Maltese attempt to break the record in 2010 had to be called off when strong winds damaged the wheel. At another festival that year, a woman was injured by a piece of burning wood that flew off a wheel in the village of Għaxaq. Still, the following year, the Our Lady of the Lilies team built a 32-metre-diameter wheel that was, according to the *Times of Malta,* 'slender for its size and elegantly designed'. As a safety measure, it was mounted on a tower crane and spectators were kept more than 30 metres away. To break the record, it needed to make at least one turn powered by the rockets attached to each of its six points. In fact, it managed four without mishap, and the *Times of Malta* rejoiced that 'Mqabba has set itself on the world map.'[106]

Let Them Burn Cakes

By 2000 in the UK, indoor fireworks meant sparklers, and a new genre – 'neon' sparklers – appeared on the scene. They were supposed to give out coloured sparks and a coloured flame, but some complained the tints could be anaemic. Other indoor fireworks had been taken off the UK market towards the end of the twentieth century because of safety worries, but in the new millennium they made a comeback, and Warren Thomas, boss of Norwich-based Trafalgar Group Trading, became the country's biggest importer. In the millennium's first decade, customers started approaching him about indoor fireworks 'they remembered from the old days'. At the time, there was 'very little on the market', but sensing an opportunity, he bought stock from one of the few suppliers available. After 'just a tiny advert in a tabloid newspaper' they were 'deluged' with orders. Thomas worried that the fireworks might look feeble compared with what people had become used to seeing outdoors, but they 'had phone call after phone call where customers would ask whether indoor fireworks were just as naff as the old days'. When they answered yes, 'the reply was invariably "That's great, I'll take a couple of packs."'[107]

Encouraged, Thomas contacted a factory in China and got them to start manufacturing for him, as he set up Indoor Fireworks Ltd. He survived threats of legal action over copyright infringement after branding one firework Flash Gordon; he changed the name to Flash Harry.

By 2022, one of the most ambitious indoor fireworks was the 7.2-centimetre Pyrogiochi Vulcano Moon, which sent sparks up into the air for about half a minute. A reviewer who tested it on his kitchen table said there was hardly any smoke and no hot fallout, nor was there any damage to his ceiling. The same reviewer ran the rule over one of Trafalgar's indoor fireworks sets. Some were just little things you set light to on an old plate or tin lid, such as Sizzling Strobes and Disco Inferno, and which provided assorted flames, flashes and crackles. Then there were Blazing Bengals – free-standing flares giving out coloured light. Most unusual was Snakes Alive, a flame from which emerges an ever-lengthening coil of gooey black stuff. Another old favourite that got a revival around this time was the 'fun snap' – a bit of explosive material wrapped in tissue paper that detonates when thrown on the floor, and which can be secreted for a practical joke under a doormat. It also became fashionable to use sparklers to decorate cakes or drinks, but there was concern about traces of aluminium, iron or titanium falling on to food. So new specialist food-friendly pyrotechnics called ice fountains or cake fountains appeared. Some played tunes, like 'Happy Birthday'. They burned for half a minute or so, usually giving off a coloured flame or silver sparks, while causing little smoke and no hot fallout.

Apart from selling indoor fireworks, Warren Thomas diversified into 'cakes' – a whole new genre. Cakes contain multiple shots, each sitting in its own tube. There can be just a handful or in the biggest, there can be hundreds. Called cakes simply because they looked like big solid lumps, they also went under aliases such as barrages or repeaters or the official term, a 'battery of shot tubes'. Effectively providing the non-professional with an entire mini-display comprising a range of different effects, they had made their UK debut in 1985. Some are quite quiet, others very noisy. Dump cakes are fused for all the shots to fire at once, while fan cakes have angled tubes so the shots fan out across the sky. Sometimes a number of cakes are fused together to make a compound or link cake. The beauty of the cake, especially on a winter's night, is that you light just one fuse for a whole set of pyrotechnic effects.

Thomas bought them in from China and gave them lurid English labels such as ASBO and 19th Nervous Breakdown. It was the names that did it, according to Thomas: 'one of our weaker cakes was called Severe PMT and on performance alone it wouldn't have sold. But with that name it was one of our best sellers.'[108]

When cakes first appeared, some of the remaining UK firework manufacturers, such as Standard, tried to get in on the act, and Kimbolton produced Gold Bees, featuring nineteen shots in a 'sedate, relaxing, and colourful piece'.[109] By the 1990s Black Cat had taken over Standard, and was making a big impact with cakes such as Crackling Golden Palms and low-noise Silver Spirals. As millennium celebrations approached at the end of the decade, the cake's convenience enabled it to grab a major slice of the fireworks market. Then in the twenty-first century, along with cakes that continued the artistic tradition such as Rainbow in the Dark and High Art, came more blood-curdling offerings like Devastation Nation, Tornado Warning and Disaster Master. In 2022 the cheapest cost about £10 for up to sixteen shots, and lasted for twenty seconds or so, with the biggest having a duration of a few minutes and costing up to £200, while compound cakes might cost £500 or more.

Also becoming available to ordinary folk was lancework of the kind that had graced the Crystal Palace. Words could be spelled out in various colours by small fireworks attached to a wooden frame, which was then mounted on a post. 'Goodnight', or just 'Bye' for the budget-conscious, was a favourite for the climax of a show. Then there were more specific messages such as 'Will you marry me?' In 2022 'Bye' was selling at about £100 or over and 'Goodnight' started at £200, while for customized missives, the price was about £30 to £50 a letter.

Onwards and Upwards

Some pyrotechnicians may be unimpressed by what they see as the sameness of modern displays, but that does not mean innovation has come to a stop. Perhaps it is just happening away from mega events. The Chinese artist Cai Guo-Qiang, now based in America and winner of the prestigious Golden Lion at the Venice Biennale, created *Sky Ladder*, a glittering 500-metre ladder of fire climbing slowly to the heavens, which he ignited from a helium balloon floating above it. It took him 21 years to complete the project, but he said its inspiration went back even further, to Apollo XI's voyage to the moon in 1969. It was 'a clear childhood dream of mine. Despite all life's twists and turns, I have always been determined to realize it ... *Sky Ladder* ... touches my heart deeply. It carries affection for my home town, my relatives and my friends.'[110] His first attempt in Bath in 1994 had to be called off because it was raining. He was going to try again in Shanghai in 2001, but the authorities withdrew permission in the aftermath of 9/11. A third go in Los Angeles in 2012 was cancelled because of the threat of wildfires. His wife complained that each abortive attempt felt like burning banknotes, and it was only in 2015 that Cai was finally able to pull it off in his home Chinese province of Fujian, and in the nick of time. He had dedicated the ladder to his 100-year-old grandmother, and she died a month later. When Cai was a boy during the Cultural Revolution, she had saved their house from disaster after one of his early experiments with gunpowder had started a fire. The artist fired his ladder not at night, but at five in the morning in the half-light of dawn, seeing it as a symbol of hope. Among Cai's other pyrotechnic works was the black rainbow he generated over Edinburgh Castle in 2005. Three years later, he was appointed Director of Visual and Special Effects for the Beijing Olympic Games opening and closing ceremonies, during which he sent giant pyrotechnic footprints marching across the sky. Then in 2018, inspired by Botticelli's painting *Spring*, he used fireworks to create the impression of giant flowers in the daylight sky above Florence. He relished the inherent risks of pyrotechnics: 'I always chase after uncertainty or the unstable factor, the troublemaker that sparks the surprising element I do not anticipate.'[111]

Every year the creative pyrotechnic envelope was being pushed, according to Michael Tockstein, founder of the American company Pyrotechnic Innovations, which trains pyrotechnicians. One shover was Florida photographer Calder Wilson, who captured extraordinary images of the abstract patterns in the sky made by fireworks strapped to drones. The American feminist Judy Chicago first flirted with pyrotechnics in the 1970s, then abandoned them, only to take them up again half a century later when she was in her eighties. For one of her pieces, she set fireworks off in front of the Santa Barbara Museum in California, making it look as though the building was on fire. Then in 2021 she created a 'smoke sculpture' outside the De Young Museum in San Francisco, erecting a huge pyramid of scaffolding to hold the canisters that would release smoke of many colours into the air. One critic was not won over, writing that 'a murky gray mass of smoke swept down from the scaffolding and engulfed us. It stunk . . . The crowd's anxiety was palpable.' The writer also claimed that noises from the fireworks that accompanied the smoke had terrified the wildlife in Golden Gate Park as well as parents and children: 'In official museum photos of the event, the billowing colors look cool, but if you look closer, you can see the smoke swooping to the ground. Wherever that smoke touched down, inside it there were frantic beings.' Judy Chicago responded that the smoke and pigments had been 'extensively tested' and did 'not present any danger'. She said she had created more than fifty 'colored pyrotechnical performances' which were 'intended to bring joy and beauty to viewers while also addressing important issues', such as climate change, a hot topic thanks to the wildfires that had devastated the San Francisco Bay area that year.[112]

Other innovations fell outside what you might call high art but were still exciting. Two German breakdancers saw in the New Year of 2015 in the Frankfurt snow by strapping fireworks to their feet as they went into their spectacular routine. Around the same time, another even more spine-chilling fad was appearing: pyrotechnic skydiving, which saw teams activating fireworks strapped to their legs as they fell through the air. In 2021 'Skydive Dubai', a group of twenty, set a world record for the highest ever 'altitude skydiving fireworks display', jumping from 4.5 kilometres up and letting off pyrotechnics as they descended.[113] An Australian company, Skylighter Fireworx, has specialized in water displays involving fireworks carried on jet skis, water skis and flyboards, while that serial record breaker Ras Al Khaimah, perhaps inspired by Calder Wilson, set a new mark during the 2021 New Year celebrations for the most fireworks launched simultaneously by drones.

Howard & Sons exploited the vogue for corporate team-building exercises by offering a package based on mounting a firework display, because firms were 'looking for wackier and increasingly out-of-the-box experiences'. While competing teams planned and then put on their shows, the Australian pyrotechnic firm promised there would never be 'a moment when the concept of fun and enjoyment is ignored', but that safety regulations would be 'followed to the letter'.[114] Howard & Sons were also one of the companies pioneering pyrotechnic funerals – 'for the person or pet . . . you literally want to go out with a bang'.[115] The loved one's ashes are inserted in a shell and fired over some favourite location so they scatter as the firework explodes. In the UK, an organization called Heavenly Stars offered something similar, 'incorporating cremation ash' into fireworks that could be supplied for a 'self-fired tribute' or set off in a professional display: 'The whole process has been respectfully developed to be caring, tasteful, discreet and professional.'[116] In 2020 the ashes of an 83-year-old Falmouth woman named Barbara Sisson were pyrotechnically scattered by Heavenly Stars above Pendennis Point, just as she had requested after seeing the company's advertisement.

5
Accidents, Disasters, Rules and Regulations

You can be killed or injured making pyrotechnics, setting them off, watching them or even doing none of these things, like the couple in Warwick who were asleep in bed when a stray firework from a display for Queen Elizabeth I set fire to their house. In his *The Great Art of Artillery* (1650), Kazimierz Siemienowicz warned everyone using gunpowder to keep a 'continual eye upon Heaven . . . For the accidental shock of two stones, the hasty attrition of two strings, nay the very impetuous rubbing together of two straws, may be the death of you.'[1]

Early Mishaps

The death of the couple at Warwick may be the first fireworks accident to have a decent historical record, but by the second half of the seventeenth century, casualties were coming to notice more regularly. A squib was involved in a death in London in late October 1674, and in 1696 someone died of injuries caused 'by squibs' in the capital, while in November 1697 a man and a woman were 'killed by a rocket stick'. In 1730 a soldier was seriously injured when he tried to remove a 'serpent' a boy had thrown at a small cannon being used in a military display. It is not clear how often incidents of this kind happened, but they were frequent enough for the City of London authorities to ban the making and throwing of fireworks, described as a 'great mischief', on six occasions between 1673 and 1714.[2] The fact they did it so often suggests the orders were not very effective, and in January 1715 up to fifty people were killed by an explosion and fire, one of the most devastating of the century, at a 'little Gun-powder shop' in a house by the Thames. 'Mr Walker' was upstairs 'with a light; and making rockets and squibs' when he 'unwarily set fire' to some gunpowder, 'upon which the house blew up'. A strong wind spread the flames and, according to contemporary reports, about 120 houses were 'burnt or blown up'. Trinity House was also destroyed, as were many 'rich goods' in the warehouses that lined the river.[3]

Five years later, on 5 November 1720, an accident claimed the life of John Brock, founder of the great firework dynasty. An eccentric character who dressed like Guy Fawkes in a broad-brimmed hat, Brock had set up a factory in Islington a couple of decades before, when he was in his early twenties. Little is known about the accident except that it also caused fatal injuries to his daughter. John Brock's descendant Alan Brock speculated that perhaps he had been examining a firework that had failed to go off. Two years later, just a couple of miles away, came the death of another firework maker after 'the Gunpowder took fire and blew him up', setting his house on fire and also damaging the one next door.[4] Because, since the Great Fire, firework making in London was officially illegal, it was impossible to have any regulations to reduce its dangers, so unsafe practices were rife. Gunpowder was kept in open containers, candles were used on workbenches and fireworks were left to dry by open fires, sometimes overnight while the family who had made them slept. It may be that methods in China and Japan at this time were safer, with work usually done on the floor where components and tools were spread out, meaning implements could not fall off a table and cause a spark.

Another well-known firework man was Benjamin Clitherow, who put on displays at pleasure gardens such as Marylebone and Ranelagh. When he died, his widow took over his London shop, which boasted an 'extensive' range of fireworks sold, he claimed, 'by none else in England', and including 'vertical wheels', 'brilliant fountains' and 'gold flower pots to fire in rooms', all of which he offered to deliver anywhere in the country. On 2 November 1791 she was killed making fireworks for Bonfire Night along with three of her children and seven other people. The explosion demolished the two adjoining houses and set two more on fire. The tragedy moved an anonymous versifier to adapt the famous 5 November rhyme, declaring:

None knows how this mischance befell.
They are all blown up who best could tell.

After each of the seven stanzas came the melancholy chorus:
Let all in future with care remember,
Fire-works for the fifth of November.[5]

Around this time, misuse of fireworks played an important role in British legal history in what became known as the 'flying squib case'. On the evening of 28 October 1770 someone named Shepherd threw a lighted squib from the street into the covered market at Milborne Port in Somerset, where a 'large concourse of people were assembled'. It landed on a gingerbread stall and a bystander threw it across the market 'to prevent injury to himself' and the wares on the stall.[6] The squib landed on another stall operated by a man called Ryal, who threw it on again. This time it hit a man named Scott in the face. At this point the squib exploded and put out one of his eyes. Scott sued Shepherd and won £100 damages. The case was important because of the number of other people who had been involved between the action of the defendant, Shepherd, and the injury to the plaintiff, Scott. The defendant argued that he was not responsible for the injury because other people had also thrown the squib before it hit the victim, but the court ruled the injury was the direct result of the unlawful act of throwing the squib because the intermediaries were not 'free agents . . . but acting under a compulsive necessity for their own safety and self-preservation'.[7]

Sometimes it was not the explosives in fireworks that caused accidents, but their popularity. On 4 June 1763 a big display was mounted on London's Tower Hill to mark George III's birthday. Unfortunately, 'the populace repaired thither in such shoals, and crowded so fast on each other, that the rails which surrounded a well' gave way, and people fell about 9 metres. Six were killed outright and another fourteen fatally injured, while many others were 'most dreadfully bruised'.[8] According to a contemporary writer, by 1801 official firework displays for the king's birthday in London had been 'discontinued for several years' following a petition from people objecting to 'the inconveniences' they caused, though some of the pleasure gardens put on their own events.[9] The *Gentleman's Magazine* described what may have been an example of these 'inconveniences'. After a fracas when 'a Jew robbed a sailor' in the crowd, the alleged thief was chased to a house where the inhabitants tried to protect him. The building was left in 'the most ruinous condition' and three sick children were thrown on to the street.[10] Celebrations in Edinburgh carried on until 1810, though there was plenty of disorder there too.

Other countries were also having pyrotechnic accidents. At Regensburg in Germany on 4 January 1673, Dr Carl Bernoju, a 'famous surgeon' or a 'quack-doctor' depending on who you want to believe, put on 'a display of recreational pyrotechnics as artistic as it was wanton', effectively turning himself into a human firework, with 'many firecrackers and small rockets tied to his body and limbs, and even on all his fingers'. Then, a bit like the dove in Florence's Scoppio del Carro, he set off down a 90-metre rope from the top of a tower to the ground. Perhaps the least surprising thing is that it did not end well. On the way down, Dr Bernoju was consumed by fire, 'looking more like a burning devil than a man', then fell from a great height. A contemporary pamphlet relating the disaster ended with a homily in verse:

> Another Icarus wished to fly into the air
> But like the other one had to fall earthward
> With the only difference that this one burned.[11]

A ban on stunts of this kind followed.

In his diaries, John Evelyn has a rather tantalizing entry for 23 July 1699 – 'The city of Moscow burnt by the throwing of squibs' – though in 1825 the Scottish surgeon and Russia watcher Robert Lyall, who had studied medicine in the country, rather dismissed the fire as 'one of those accidental conflagrations to which that city has always been subject'.[12] A better-documented blaze took place in 1757 at the laboratory in St Petersburg where the Russian pyrotechnist Mikhail Danilov worked. He describes 'a great number of people', including bombardiers from the military, toiling in a room 20 metres square, some making background scenery, some filling fireworks. The fire, said Danilov, was caused by carelessness. The flames were accompanied by 'mercurial smoke', and people made 'a headlong rush for the single door. One after the other was crushed' while 'many were seized by the smoke and stopped breathing.'[13] Fortunately, the premises were located away from the centre of the city.

Another city prone to fires was Edo, now Tokyo, with its tightly packed houses mostly built of paper and wood with thatched roofs, so from the seventeenth century onwards the authorities kept trying to control fireworks. In 1843 one of Japan's best-known firework makers, Tamaya Ichibeh, would be expelled from the city after a fire in his shop near the Ryogoku Bridge burned down a whole neighbourhood. By 1706 firework manufacturing had been banned from the city of Paris, while in America too regulation began in the eighteenth century. Rhode Island would be the first of the American colonies to renounce allegiance to the British Crown, so was it a sign of general bolshiness in the population that in 1731 the authorities there had to outlaw the use of fireworks for 'mischievous ends' after a spate of pranks?

What was perhaps the deadliest firework-related accident in history was caused, like the one on Tower Hill, by their popularity. In May 1770 Paris was celebrating the marriage of the future king Louis XVI of France to Marie Antoinette. (Both would end up being guillotined.) Huge crowds gathered to see a firework display by the Ruggieris at what is now the Place de la Concorde when a sudden gust of wind blew rockets into 'the midst of thousands of excited and closely-packed spectators'. This caused 'terrible confusion' as people trying to get away ran into crowds still trying to enter the area: 'women fainted, fell and were trampled to death.' In the panic 'some desperate men drew their swords' and tried to cut their way out.[14] Some estimates put the number killed at 3,000, though most modern commentators think 800 to 1,000 is more realistic.

Nineteenth-Century Britain: The Perils of Manufacturing

Whatever the law might have said about firework manufacturing, London's pleasure gardens had a voracious appetite, and what was essentially a cottage industry grew up to satisfy it, especially in Lambeth just south of the Thames. As we saw, the Mortram family was heavily involved in displays at the Vauxhall Gardens. In 1814 there was an explosion at their business in Westminster Bridge Road because of spontaneous combustion while they were mixing composition, and three people suffered severe burns. The Mortrams then moved to other premises in the area, but in 1818 sparks from a tool set off two explosions that completely destroyed the building while 'thousands of people ran with terror' to find out what was happening. The only casualty was a monkey 'chained on the roof'. No doubt to the delight of the inhabitants of Westminster Bridge Road, the Mortrams moved back there, and in 1821 one of their 'boys' working on composition stars set one on fire. The result was another explosion. Locals were terrified that it might start a chain reaction by spreading to the nearby 'extensive workshops' of Mme Hengler (she was really just plain 'Mrs', the 'Mme' was to add a touch of the exotic), 'celebrated pyrotechnic to His Majesty'.[15] But workmen with buckets of water rushed in and 'happily' prevented any further damage. Three years earlier, an accident at Mme Hengler's had killed two men.

Married to a circus performer, she had begun by providing fireworks to spice up circus acts, performing herself on the tightrope 'amidst a shower of fire' before moving on to supplying pleasure gardens including Ranelagh and Vauxhall.[16] Charles Dickens and the poet Thomas Hood both wrote about her. Most of her manufacturing was done nearby at Kennington, but she had fireworks finished and stored at her home, a three-storey house on the south side of Westminster Bridge. When they had started up there in 1795, the area was largely undeveloped, but over the next couple of decades it became much more densely populated and Mme Hengler's activities caused more concern. On 9 October 1845, when she was about eighty years old, the house was full of men, women and children hard at work when an oil lamp showered sparks onto some fireworks, triggering an explosion. Soon Mme Hengler's room was on fire. Although she was disabled, she managed to get to the window. Outside, firemen and people with ladders were ready to help, but her figure was now too full for her to climb out, and she perished in the flames.

Then it was a case of: 'the Fireworks Queen is dead! Long Live the Fireworks Queen!', as 'Mme Coton' (her 'Mme' was just for show too) took over Mme Hengler's mantle. She also lived in a big three-storey house in Lambeth, and by 1854 she was the Vauxhall Gardens' new 'fireworks artist'. On the evening of 6 March Mr Coton had gone up to the top floor with a boy to paper fireworks, leaving Mme Coton, her sister and two children in the basement. A few minutes later, the house was rocked by a fierce explosion that was felt a quarter of a mile away. As the building collapsed, Mme Coton managed to run into the street and scream for help, while inside there was a series of blasts as stores of pyrotechnics and explosive went up. A crowd gathered, even though people were being injured by fireworks flying out of the building, and firefighters managed to rescue everyone apart from Mr Coton and the boy working with him.

By 1858 Mme Coton had a rebuilt house and a new husband, a mild-mannered soul named William Bennett, and she was back in business in a big way, with contracts for the Vauxhall and Cremorne gardens. Now the more hazardous work was meant to be done at a house in Peckham, with just some filling in Lambeth, a task for which boys aged ten to thirteen were paid the pittance of three shillings a week. According to her foreman, Mme Coton wore the trousers, while her husband's role was mainly confined to fetching and carrying between the two premises and the pleasure gardens. On 7 July Mr Bennett had departed on one of his errands, leaving Mme Coton, her mother-in-law and a few child workers in the house. As two boys were filling cases with a 'coloured fire' mixture, it suddenly caught light. Explosions started going off, but the boys managed to shout a warning and escape into the street with minor burns. An eyewitness said that soon after, Mme Coton emerged, 'enveloped in flames', and ran into a nearby shop. The obligatory crowd gathered, and 'several persons, who were tipsy, insisted upon getting into the house, but afterwards came out again.'[17] This was probably wise. By now fireworks were flying in all directions. One stray rocket set fire to another firework maker's house across the road, fomenting a fresh barrage. An eleven-year-old girl was hurled across the road, her clothes on fire. She died on the way to hospital. A young woman ran for her life and was hit by a rocket that set her garments alight. Then she was trampled by a terrified horse. She too would die from her injuries. The house was destroyed, as was the other firework maker's, and Mme Coton died

The explosion at Mme Coton's house, London, 1858.

from her burns a few days later. Overall, at least five people were killed, more than three hundred were said to have been injured and eleven buildings were seriously damaged. There was an outcry, with an influential group of local ratepayers writing to the government to demand action. The only available scapegoat was William Bennett, who had the book thrown at him. He was convicted of manslaughter under the old seventeenth-century anti-fireworks law, but many felt he had been unfairly treated in view of the resolutely blind eye the authorities had turned to the industry for so long.

It was not only the Mortrams, Henglers and Cotons whose establishments saw multiple accidents. The Clitherows' run of bad luck, or bad management, continued with three people badly burned at their Bethnal Green factory in 1813, and in 1850 their premises at Spitalfields were razed to the ground. John Clitherow and a workman were blasted into the street, but survived, while a bystander was killed by one of the fire engines rushing to the scene, and nearly forty houses were damaged. Then there was a Mr d'Ernst, who had provided fireworks for the coronations of William IV and Victoria. At midnight on 28 February 1842 the factory he had built in the backyard of his Lambeth house was 'levelled', leaving only an 'immense mass of ruins'. A contemporary account spoke of a noise like 'the discharge of artillery in rapid succession' as flames rose high into the sky, and d'Ernst, his sister-in-law and two workers were killed.[18]

As d'Ernst joined Hengler, Coton and Brock as big names who died in the cause of pyrotechnics, Queen Victoria gave £50 to a fund set up to help his family. Henry William Darby presented himself as the successor to d'Ernst. A lot of firework making was put out to homeworkers, and in 1846 Darby had sent a teenage worker home with an explosive mixture of sulphur, saltpetre and antimony to turn into stars. As the youngster was chatting with a group of friends, the mixture blew up. He and another youth were killed and four other people were badly burned. Eleven years later, an explosion at Darby's Lambeth home and factory destroyed all his stock. Then in 1860 two men were killed when 'coloured fires' being dried by his stove burst into flames and reached a nearby stack of explosives.

Meanwhile the Brock family had suffered further disasters. On 3 September 1825 William Brock and his workmen had popped out of their factory at Whitechapel for breakfast, leaving two boys, whom he had taken 'out of the poor-house' a few weeks before, ramming powder into sky rockets as they learned the trade of firework making. Brock and his companions had barely sat down to eat when they 'heard a sort of rumbling noise as if of distant thunder, and the next moment a tremendous and deafening explosion'. Then came 'continued reports'. Roofs were torn off Brocks' premises and the factory next door, while sixty houses were damaged, with their windows blown out and objects flying right, left and centre. *Bell's Weekly Messenger* reported that the explosion caused 'the greatest state of agitation', but the newspaper was full of praise for Brocks' safety precautions, noting that the fireworks and combustible materials were stored in a special building which held three magazines lined with lead and were 'perfectly secure from fire', concluding: 'Mr Brock was remarkable for the method he had taken to prevent any accident.' Although, in this case, obviously not remarkable enough. The two boys who were 'blown a considerable height and were much injured' said the explosion was caused by a spark, though Brock disputed this.[19] But if there was some mystery about this accident, others were plainly the result of time-honoured dangerous practices. An explosion at Bethnal Green in 1839 was blamed on 'the most miserable negligence', with a man making a squib by the fire with a lighted pipe in his mouth, while a pile of gunpowder lay loose on the table.[20] There were also blasts at more reputable premises. In 1814 four men were killed at Woolwich Arsenal as they were working on fireworks for official displays. Ten years later, two perished at a factory in West Ham making rockets for the military, when a worker generated a spark while he was nailing up a case.

And, of course, there were manufacturing accidents in other parts of the country. In Bath in 1810 a firework maker named Mrs Invetto and her assistant were both killed by an explosion which blew up her house and an adjoining property while they were producing rockets for part of George III's Golden Jubilee celebrations at the city's Sydney Gardens. Mrs Invetto was the second wife of the famous Italian pyrotechnist John Invetto, who moved to Bath around 1785 and put on spectacular displays at the Sydney gardens and others in the area. His first wife and his son had also been killed in firework-making accidents.

British Rules Are Tightened

As we have seen, the law was a mess. In 1825 people in the City of London got notes through their letterboxes telling them the current rules on firework making had 'not expired, as some ignorantly suppose'.

The authorities had created the worst of all possible worlds. There was no effective regulation of firework making because it was notionally illegal, but people were merrily turning them out under the radar in back-street factories. In 1860 the government tried to grasp the nettle with a new Explosives Act, which gave magistrates the job of licensing people who stored explosives or sold fireworks and limited the quantities they could hold. Buildings used for firework making had to be a minimum of 50 yards (45 metres) away from homes or workplaces not connected with the factory, and within the factory, buildings used for filling fireworks with explosive had to be at least 20 yards (18 metres) from other workshops. If it had been fully enforced, it would have effectively outlawed manufacturing in the inner city, and it did bring some companies out of the back streets. Brocks, then the biggest fireworks manufacturer in the country, moved out to a new factory at Nunhead in south London, but much of the trade just stayed underground.

Worries soon emerged over whether magistrates had the expertise they needed to carry out their duties, and faith in the new law was undermined as disasters continued. At Erith in Kent in 1864, gunpowder magazines blew up, killing at least a dozen people. Then in Lambeth in 1873 Darby had yet another accident and eight people died. In the same year, the factory of another Lambeth firework maker, Ralph Fenwick, went up in smoke, killing another eight people, including Fenwick and his wife. Fenwick had lost a worker in an explosion in 1843, and had carried on manufacturing illegally after the Explosives Act came in, but even when magistrates granted a licence, that was no guarantee of safety. A shopkeeper named Titheradge kept a big stock of fireworks in his London confectionery store, above which he and his family lived in tiny rooms. One night in October 1869 they were asleep when the fireworks blew up and the building was engulfed in flames. Out of the thirteen people inside, seven died.

Meanwhile, Charles Brock was helping tighten the law. In 1872 he produced a report for government explosives expert Col. Sir Vivian Majendie which listed ingredients he considered dangerous, and set out the basis of a safe factory. Brock also recommended that no boys under fourteen or girls under sixteen should be employed. Two years later, Majendie warned a parliamentary select committee that licensed manufacturers were being undercut by unlicensed: 'the November trade in fireworks is almost exclusively carried out in garrets, dwelling houses and other unauthorised places.'[21] Most of Brock's ideas found their way

Fireworks at Disney World, 2017.

Sydney Harbour fireworks, New Year 2019.

Dubai fireworks, New Year 2017.

Fireworks in Malta, 2021.

Roman candle.

Sparklers, London, 2017.

Castillos, Tultepec, Mexico.

London's New Year's Eve display, 2018.

Independence Day celebration, the Brooklyn Bridge, 2014.

The burning of the *Böögg*, 2011.

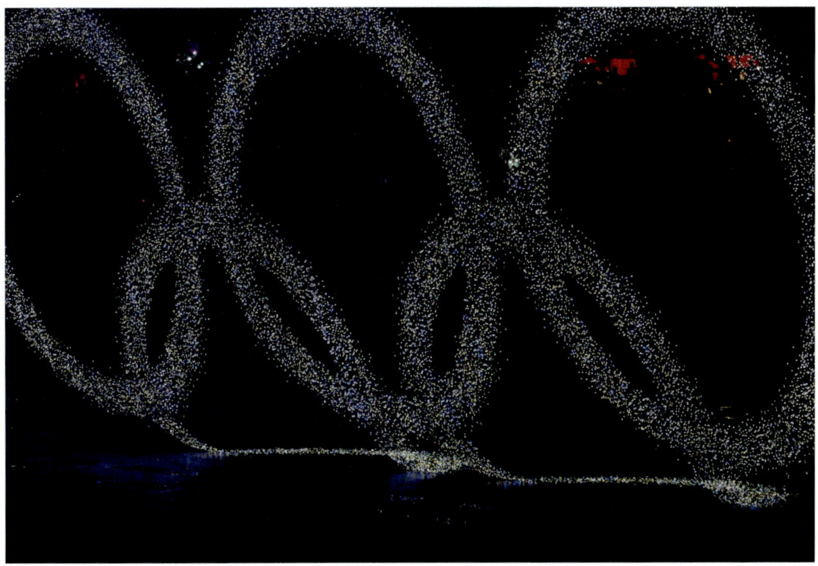

Pyrotechnic rings in the sky at the opening ceremony of the 2008 Olympics in Beijing.

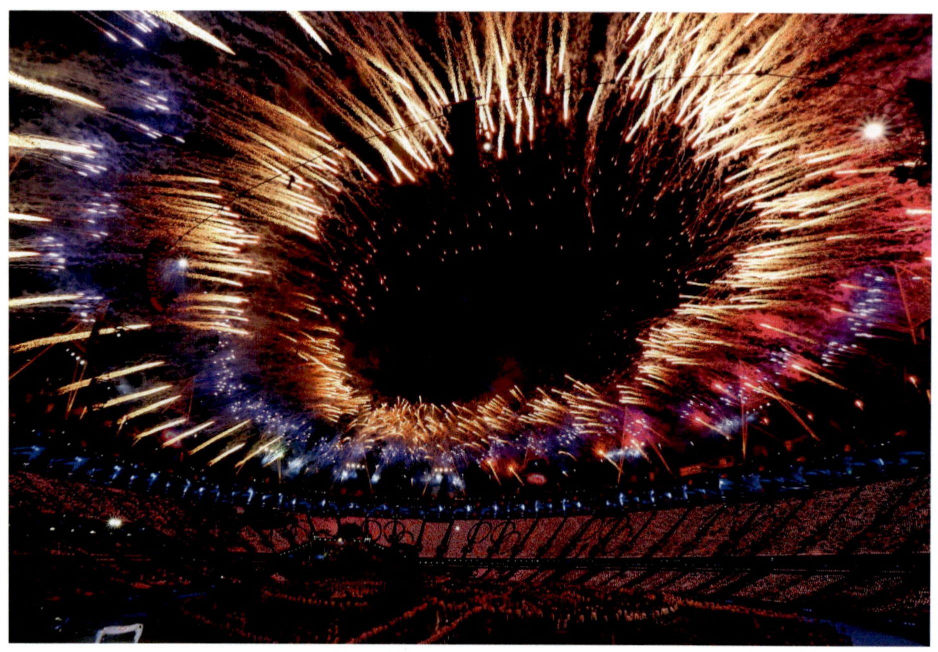

The London Olympics opening ceremony, 2012.

Stately home display, Leeds Castle, Kent, 2017.

into a new Explosives Act in 1875, which also made the government responsible for licensing rather than magistrates, though smaller firework manufacturers were allowed to apply to their local authorities. Other new measures included tighter rules on using metal tools, while workers were to be forbidden from smoking and would have to be searched for items such as matches, while adults would be required to supervise any under sixteen.

The Act had one immediate effect: Darby moved to the Channel Islands, where its writ did not run. But prosecutions soon began. In the Yorkshire fireworks capital of Huddersfield in 1878, George Newsome was fined for making fireworks without a licence. He then obtained one, but three years later, he and his son and partner were charged with seven offences under the Explosives Act, including making fireworks within 50 yards of a footpath, having grit on the floor, employing more workers than he was licensed for and not supplying them with protective clothing. He was fined, had all his materials confiscated and appears to have gone out of business.

The Act reduced accidents dramatically, but did not eliminate them. In 1886 a 67-year-old woman from the family that owned Huddersfield's Globe Fireworks, a licensed business, was drying some damp fireworks by her fire. A spark set them alight and she suffered fatal burns. Still, the law's defenders claimed that even when there were accidents, its provisions saved lives. So at a factory in Mitcham in south London in 1885, a workman was nailing a piece of wood to a tourbillion. Instead of hammering the nail into a section of clay, he drove it into the explosive composition and set the firework off. The contents of the building caught fire and tourbillions took flight, one of them entering a magazine that held more than a ton of fireworks, sending rockets flying in all directions. Ten buildings were destroyed, with three more seriously damaged, but casualties were limited to just two people, who were both slightly injured.

Unfortunately, the law had one glaring omission: it did not ban dangerous mixtures that combined sulphur with potassium chlorate. Sulphur by itself is not very reactive and is quite difficult to ignite, and potassium chlorate is also relatively stable at normal temperatures, but when they are mixed together, the combination is unstable and liable to ignite spontaneously or explode if subjected to the slightest friction. In his *Rudiments of Chemistry* (1811), the manufacturing chemist Samuel Parks said potassium chlorate had been involved in bad accidents, and that it was 'feared by chemists in general'.[22] Alan Brock also put later incidents down to the chlorate–sulphur combination, among them the d'Ernst disaster of 1842 and the Coton accident of 1858. In the two decades after the 1875 Act, there were 28 accidents and eleven deaths associated with the mixture. As we have seen, before it came into force, Brocks had already removed sulphur from some of their recipes that also contained potassium chlorate, though Charles Brock said it would be difficult to do this for all firework mixtures, and instead suggested special precautions when using them together. In 1893 came the last of those 28 accidents caused by sulphur–chlorate combination. It happened at Brocks' factory in South Norwood, while a worker was emptying a few crimson stars, the only ones still made with the mixture, on to a canvas tray from an earthenware jar. This caused enough friction to start a serious fire, in which two men died. The following year, the government banned the formulation. (Potassium chlorate continued to be used in other compositions until it was replaced in the 1970s by potassium perchlorate, which is safer, igniting at over 600°c compared with 350°c for potassium chlorate.)

Concerns remained that the law was too lenient. In 1895 Globe Fireworks was convicted of seven breaches. There was too much explosive, it was not being stored properly and the premises were filthy, with grit and spilt materials on the floor that could easily cause a blast. This was worrying not just for the workers, but also because there were houses nearby. Still, the company was fined only £7. It was inspected twice a year, and up to that point had been regarded as a model factory.

Brocks argued that firework factories should be based on the principle of 'dispersion', with a clear distinction between the 'green area' of offices, paper-cutting and so on, and the working section, where ingredients were mixed and poured into cases. This should be done in small, isolated sheds built of light materials, with no iron fittings and no iron nails exposed inside, and a door at each end to make it easier to get out. There should be a limit to the number of people in each shed at any time, and all workers should be required to wear non-inflammable clothing without pockets, and overshoes without nails to minimize the risk of igniting any explosive material that might have fallen on the floor. Partially finished fireworks should be stored away from working buildings, and explosives magazines should be kept away from everything. This approach was followed widely in Britain and other developed countries.

America: Accidents and New Rules

In America, not everyone was thrilled that Independence Day came to mean fireworks. A Pennsylvania man confided to his diary in 1866: '4 July is the most hateful day of the year, when the birth of democracy is celebrated by license and noise. All last night and all of today, the sound of guns and firecrackers around us never stopped.'[23] There were stories of fireworks being thrown at horses or put under milk bottles or flowerpots so the explosion flung out nasty shrapnel. Around the same time, in Pennsylvania's great city Philadelphia, it was said that 'as a general rule, 30 or 40 houses are set afire every 4 July.'[24] In 1865 the *New York Times* had complained about 'gangs of young men' roaming the streets and commented: 'That sundry of these reckless youth should have blown off their fingers and mutilated their hands was to be expected and perhaps pleasurably anticipated.' Injuries soon became the norm, with the *Cincinnati Daily Star* reporting in 1877: 'The usual amount of accidents and incidents which always accompany the celebration of the Nation's Birthday occurred.' In one, a boy had his hand blown off. Seven years later, it was reported that a group of Colorado miners flew into a rage because they did not receive the fireworks they had ordered, so they blew up the post office. It is not clear whether Pennsylvania was a particular black spot for firework accidents, but in 1891 the *Pittsburgh Dispatch* reported so many that a reporter wondered aloud whether it was worth celebrating 4 July 'with such violent explosives'. A 22-year-old man had his eyes burned and his face 'horribly' disfigured when someone threw a firecracker into his can of gunpowder! But people without cans of gunpowder were also victims. A man had his hand 'torn off by a cannon cracker', and a woman carrying a baby met a similar fate. In 1893 the *Omaha Bee* lamented the 'series of distressing accidents' that seemed to mark the Fourth of July, and injuries became so common that newspapers would celebrate a relatively accident-free Independence Day as 'contrary to the usual order of things'.[25]

Authorities in various parts of the country had tried to clamp down. Back in 1832 the national magazine *Niles' Weekly Register* complained that although there were laws to prevent abuse of fireworks, they were 'grossly violated', and said that people selling them should be sent to prison. In 1865 the mayor of Washington, DC, tried to put restrictions on firecrackers, but youngsters apparently treated his strictures with 'contempt'. Two years later, New York City banned people from letting off fireworks in Central Park but when they tried to extend the ban across the whole city in 1886, that may have been a step too far: a journalist wrote that on the Fourth of July that year, the noise from fireworks had gone on for 36 hours and 'Every adult who is able to do so flees from the city to escape them.' In 1895 the *New York Times* reported that the city's police commissioner had failed to enforce the rules and that the celebrations had become 'barbarous' and a 'municipal nuisance'.[26]

America also suffered manufacturing accidents. In 1887 Arthur Brock's brother-in-law George Ashby had crossed the Atlantic to investigate business opportunities for the family firm. He reported that there appeared to be no regulations governing how you made or stored fireworks. The city of Chester, Pennsylvania, suffered a huge explosion in a pyrotechnics factory in 1882, with victims being flung 45 metres through the air. Nineteen people lost their lives, including eleven firemen, and in 1894 an explosion at Charles Romaine's fireworks factory in Petersburg, Virginia, also 'burned to the ground' three neighbouring factories, killing a dozen people, including Romaine himself.[27]

The turn of the century made little difference. In June 1901 in Paterson, New Jersey, fireworks being stored at the bottom of a tenement building exploded and set off a fire that killed seventeen people. The following year, a display went badly wrong. Mortars were always a potential hazard; at a show in Philadelphia in 1876, for example, a technician was killed when a shell burst inside the tube, but the accident that happened in New York City in 1902 was on a different scale. By the early years of the twentieth century, fireworks were so popular in America that when he was running for Congress, the newspaper tycoon William Randolph Hearst, regarded as the model for Orson Welles's Citizen Kane, handed them out liberally to his audiences, though he had to stop when recipients started letting them off while he was still speaking. On 4 November Hearst decided to put on a huge display to celebrate his election. About 10,000 people flooded into Madison Square. When the first shells were detonated, one of the sixty mortars blew up, flinging out sparks and shrapnel, and causing explosions in some of the other mortars. Since they were free-standing, many toppled over and fired shells point blank into the crowd. Seventeen people were killed and many more injured. The next day, the *New York Times* reported that 'in an instant' the venue was turned into 'a scene of death and carnage which a battlefield could scarcely have surpassed in its horror'.[28] Hearst's newspapers buried the story, but he was sued in a series of lawsuits that were finally settled only in the 1930s.

On 4 July 1903, 466 people were killed in firework accidents and nearly 4,000 injured. It was said that over the years, nearly as many people had died celebrating America's independence as had been killed in the war that won it, so it became known as the 'Bloody Fourth'. The Playground Association of America noted: 'The killed and injured at the battle of Bunker Hill [one of the main engagements of the war] were only 1,474 as compared with 1,622 killed and injured while "celebrating" 4 July in 1909.' In 1903 a Pennsylvania lawyer named Charles Pennypacker had decided to do something about it, declaring: 'A spurious patriotism has brought a day of terror, misery, noise, destruction, and death.' He urged people to move to a 'quiet and sane' celebration, suggesting that rather than letting off fireworks, they should pass 'a quiet day under the trees' or bake a nice cake, and spend their money on 'sandwiches instead of squibs'. According to a local newspaper, young men in his area 'resented' his initiative, and at midnight on 3 July 1904 a 'large number' gathered outside his house with Roman candles and other fireworks and created merry hell for the next fifteen minutes.[29]

'Buy shoes, not firecrackers'. Postcard issued by a shoe manufacturer, Toledo, Ohio, 1910.

But across America, Pennypacker's ideas inspired the movement for a 'Safe and Sane Fourth', as the *New York Tribune* decried the 'carnage' of Independence Day. The year he spoke out, the mayor of Chicago banned the 'discharges of fireworks, firecrackers, gunpowder, or other explosives in any alley, back yard, or other confined space'. Cannon crackers got a complete ban, as did firearms, dynamite and putting explosives on the tracks of 'any street railway'.[30] On 3 July 1908 in a department store in Cleveland, Ohio, an assistant was demonstrating a sparkler to a four-year-old boy and his mother when a stray spark started a fire that set off other fireworks, and soon there was a major blaze. Seven people died, including the boy. Within days, the city council had banned the sale or possession of fireworks.

Other cities tried to provide wholesome alternatives to Fourth of July pyrotechnics. Kansas City hired thirteen bands to perform in parks across the city, while Santa Fe put on a beauty pageant, though Minneapolis provided every child with 'a lunch and firecrackers'. There was no national ban, but in 1909 President Taft wrote that he was 'heartily in sympathy' with those trying to get rid of 'distressing accidents' on the Fourth of July, and the next year he attended a 'Safe and Sane' Independence Day march in firecracker-free Boston, saying he hoped the movement would 'spread throughout the Union'.[31] The fireworks manufacturer Ray Hitt would complain: 'They've taken the independence out of Independence Day,'[32] and sometimes when restrictions were brought in, bootleg dealers sprang up to fill the gap, but deaths on the Fourth of July did fall: from 215 in 1909 to 131 the next year, 57 in 1911 and 41 in 1912. Factory accidents continued, however. In April 1904 seven women were killed in Priceburg, Pennsylvania, when a girl threw a squib into a stove 'for a joke'.[33] A month later in Camden, New Jersey, six people died in an explosion after a worker took potassium chlorate from a barrel with a scoop that had some sulphur on it, and in June twenty 'girls' were killed at a factory in Philadelphia.

Europe also had its share of accidents. In 1885 ten workers were killed in an explosion at a factory in Civitavecchia in Italy, while four years later in France, seven 'girls' perished in a blast in a room where potassium chlorate was being stored with red phosphorus. Soon other countries were adopting regulations like Britain's. In 1895 Sweden brought in rules that effectively stopped fireworks being made by casual workers in kitchens and sheds so that by the end of the century, there were just half a dozen firework factories in the country. France was said to have seen a 'steady decline' in accidents partly because of the adoption of the 'dispersion' method of factory design. When a 'violent explosion' ripped through the Ruggieri plant at Saint-Ouen, near Paris, in 1904, just one 'small hut' was destroyed, and the three men working in it escaped with slight burns, but Italy suffered eighteen deaths in three accidents in 1901, 21 in four in 1903 and 23 in five in 1907. Accidents happened with 'comparable frequency' in Spain and Portugal.[34]

Between the wars, Germany was thought to have a fairly good safety record, though during the First World War there appear to have been some serious accidents at factories working on military pyrotechnics. In southern Italy, on the other hand, *The Times* considered accidents 'not infrequent', as it reported on two in eight days in the summer of 1926. On 5 August, at Castelfranci, during a celebration for a local saint, there was a 'terrific explosion' that plunged the town into darkness and blew out 'most of the windows'. People believed there had been an earthquake and 'scenes of panic' followed.[35] Up to thirty were killed and nearly a hundred injured. The cause was a lighted candle falling into a pile of fireworks. Just eight days later, about fifteen people were killed in an explosion at a fireworks factory near Bari.

In Britain there was a steady stream of accidents. Three people, including the owner Arthur Riley, were killed at Riley's factory at Ossett, about 12 miles from Huddersfield, in 1927. Wells's suffered an accident at Colchester in 1931, in which two men were killed, and at Honor Oak in south London the following year when two women died. They had been filling 'Empire torches', designed to be held in the hand, which sold for a halfpenny each and 'would give off a flash and some sparks'.[36] Standard's factory at Huddersfield had fires in 1933 and 1937, during which young women had to carry water from the nearest hydrant 230 metres away to fight the flames. In between these two blazes, an explosion in 1935 killed a woman filling jumping crackers, while two women were killed at Kilner's factory in the town in 1937.

Across the Atlantic, in 1925 Michigan put restrictions on the size and contents of firecrackers, rockets and Roman candles. Alan Brock considered that during these years in the USA, accidents happened with 'monotonous regularity, if with less frequency'.[37] The following year, two men were fatally injured in Chicago, when the sun's rays are believed to have lit a fuse, while four died in an accident at an unlicensed factory in Bristol, Rhode Island, in which five hundred homes were damaged. Another explosion in 1926, at North Bergen, New Jersey, was blamed on rats gnawing on explosive material. Firefighters were delayed because of the crowds who had flocked to watch the unscheduled 'vivid fireworks display' that resulted.[38] There was no loss of life but police shut down the factory and two others in the neighbourhood. In 1929 four people were killed when a series of blasts wrecked the National Fireworks Company's plant at Hanover, Massachusetts, though the magazine *Fire Engineering* praised the orderly evacuation of the works that employed 350 people, noting: 'Employees who were trained for just such emergencies, quickly filed out to safer zones.'[39] The following year, up to fifteen people were killed in a series of explosions at Devon, Philadelphia, that shook 'fashionable suburbs'.[40] Two of the victims were little girls playing outside the plant, and passengers on a train were cut by flying glass. The cause was thought to be spontaneous ignition in a magazine where shells were stored. Perhaps not surprisingly, in the 1930s America saw more anti-fireworks campaigns. One of the most effective was launched by the *Ladies' Home Journal*, which printed dozens of pictures of maimed children. Individual states started to pass more laws, and federal rules banned the biggest firecrackers.

As we saw, Mme Hengler had started manufacturing in a fairly empty area of London before running into trouble when people began building houses around her, and a similar thing happened to Hitt Fireworks in Seattle. By the 1930s they were employing up to two hundred people, but their once sparsely populated district had become a residential suburb. After several fires and explosions, including one in 1921 that killed a woman worker, the city introduced increasingly stringent restrictions, so Hitt's moved more and more of their manufacturing out to China and the Philippines. It was said that Chinese families would work seventeen hours a day, seven days a week, for a few cents. Seattle would eventually close in 1977. Hitt's man W. E. Priestley, who had gone out to superintend the drive eastwards, wrote in 1931 that the Devil was often blamed for explosions in fireworks factories in East Asia, which may have been a relief to the owners. An explosion at one of Priestley's factories in Hong Kong killed thirty women workers. He was told that shortly before the blast, the Devil had been seen entering the building. After an accident, it was thought very important to conduct an exorcism, and Priestley describes a ceremony that involved slitting a dog's throat and using the blood to paint Chinese characters on the floor.

In Asia, according to Alan Brock, firework factory accidents were 'bewildering in their frequency'.[41] Details are often sparse, but we know that in 1928 more than twenty people were killed in an explosion at

Samarang in Indonesia. In Mumbai in 1935 sixteen perished in an unlicensed factory when an illegal mixture of potassium chlorate and arsenic sulphide exploded. Six months later, the same thing happened in another nearby factory, and nine more people died, including four children, while in April 1936, 39 were killed in an explosion in Andhra Pradesh. A month earlier, in China, 23 people died while making firecrackers near Macao, and in 1937 up to eighty lost their lives when a blast destroyed a Chinese fireworks factory at Manila in the Philippines.

From the Second World War to the Millennium: The UK

When the Second World War started, firework companies again switched to supplying the military, but there was a suspicion that the demands of the war machine led to corners being cut on safety. Kilner's factory made parachute flares for the Ministry of Aircraft Production, and in 1944 six women lost their lives there in a fire. Escape routes had been obstructed by boxes, and in 1946 the families of the dead and injured successfully sued the company even though a Home Office inspector said the factory was well run.

Thirteen years later, Bernard Weller, chairman and managing director of Benwell's, said of British fireworks: 'handled correctly they are as safe as a box of matches', adding that when the fire brigade was called out on 5 November, it was usually to deal with bonfires that had got out of hand, and rarely because of fireworks.[42] Well, up to a point. That same year, a woollen spinners in Bradford was seriously damaged after a firework was thrown into the building, and as we saw, in 1955 an explosion at Rainbow Fireworks at Finchampstead in Berkshire had killed two workers and injured another dozen people. One of the first ambulance teams on the scene said: 'The place looked as though a bomb had hit it.'[43] New restrictions in 1960 saw a ban on thunderflashes that contained flash powder, and three years later, firework manufacturers agreed to reduce the explosive content in bangers by 40 per cent. Meanwhile, the authorities ran safety campaigns. In 1968, for example, the Lancashire Home Safety Committee decked out a float under the banner 'Don't be a Gunpowder Clot!'[44] It reminded children not to throw fireworks or put them in pockets and to follow makers' instructions. The seven years from 1969 to 1976 saw a big reduction in accidents from more than 2,000 a year to 685, and the government's strategy for getting the total down further was a voluntary agreement, the Fireworks Code.

It seems to have done some good since Bonfire Night injuries fell to an all-time low of 555 in 1980, but by 1984 they had crept up again to 778, including 65 young children who were injured by sparklers. With the National Campaign for Firework Reform demanding that only trained people should be allowed to fire pyrotechnics, the new British Standard for consumer fireworks appeared in 1988, but in 1993 more than 1,000 people needed hospital treatment after firework injuries, the biggest total for two decades. That year the government had scrapped the requirement for companies importing fireworks to have a licence, prompting a big rise in the number coming in, so that by 1996 around 60 per cent of the UK's pyrotechnics came from abroad, mainly from China. Companies still had to be 'authorized', but critics like John Woodhead of Standard Fireworks said this was ineffective. The British Standard had graded fireworks into four categories: indoor fireworks; smaller outdoor fireworks; bigger outdoor fireworks – the biggest that should be sold to the public; with the fourth category of fireworks supposed to be only for professional displays. However, there was confusion over whether it would actually be illegal to sell them to non-professionals.

Newspapers were filled with horror stories about 'foreign fireworks powerful enough to kill' that were 'flooding' into the country, and being sold to children at car boot sales and from market stalls. In 1994 *The Times* reported on a Chinese Jumping Fish that cost £150 and sent 'a sheet of flame 100ft into the air'.[45] It was said that if it had been around at the time of the Battle of Trafalgar, it would have provided enough gunpowder to fire 22 cannonballs. The Jumping Fish was meant for professional displays but campaigners said it was being offered to ordinary consumers. Then there were German bangers, twenty times as powerful as British ones, jumping jacks, which had been banned for nearly twenty years, and other illicit products from overseas repackaged to look as though they were made in the UK and to UK standards. Two people were killed on Bonfire Night 1994, the first deaths since 1988, and 1,500 were hurt, a 50 per cent increase over the previous year. One accident in six involved sparklers, with toddlers being most at risk. The National Campaign for Firework Reform was on the warpath, demanding an increase in the minimum age for buying fireworks from sixteen to eighteen and a national training scheme for anyone putting on a display. The following year, Scotland's *Sunday Mail* newspaper sent out two girls aged twelve and thirteen as undercover reporters. Although no one under sixteen was supposed to be allowed to buy fireworks, the girls managed to purchase them in five shops, while only three turned them away.

In the run-up to Bonfire Night 1996, two people were killed in accidents involving big, powerful mortar shells: a headmaster at High Wycombe in Buckinghamshire and a City trader at Dartford in Kent. The trader was killed at a bonfire party in his garden in front of his two sons by a shell that had instructions only in Chinese. Trading standards officers said it was meant for professional displays. The headmaster died after a 3.5-kilogram shell exploded in his face. He had selected it as the star turn of a display for four hundred parents and pupils. Eyewitnesses said he leant over the firework, perhaps to relight it because he thought it had fizzled out, and it immediately flared up ferociously. The Royal Society for the Prevention of Accidents joined in the demands for tighter restrictions while the National Campaign for Firework Safety said that even when Chinese imports were marked with a British safety standard, this could not be trusted, and claimed there were fireworks on sale in the UK which would not be allowed in China. Trading standards officers in Liverpool had seized a huge batch of Chinese fireworks, branded 'Red Lion', which all had British safety standard labels even though hardly any complied, and the importing company gave a non-existent address. Some of the fireworks contained the sulphur-and-potassium-chlorate combination that had been banned in Britain since 1894. In 1997 shells and bangers were banned from public sale, and the minimum age at which people could buy any fireworks was raised from sixteen to eighteen, but because bangers remained legal in some other EU countries they could still turn up in the UK via the black market.

From the Second World War to the Millennium: The USA

As in the UK, in America fireworks companies played an important role in the war effort. The Unexcelled pyrotechnics plant on Staten Island was crucial in both world wars, and for the Second it made thousands of the incendiary bombs that wrought such havoc in Japan. While it was working around the clock on 28 March 1942, an explosion at the plant left five men dead. The Staten Island site closed with the end of hostilities in 1945. In November 1942 one man and eleven women, including one who had started at the plant only that day, died following an explosion at the Rochester Fireworks Company at Perinton, New York, which had turned to making flares for the military. Rochester would receive a commendation from an admiral for the part they played in the rescue of American pilots.

Peace did not end firework manufacturing accidents. In 1947 an explosion and fire ripped through a plant in Clinton, Missouri, killing a dozen workers. The part of the factory where the accident happened made 'buzz bombs', small flying fireworks. This appears to have been a new venture for a business used to turning out toy gliders and games. The inquest heard that workers were unable to escape from the fire because a big sliding door could not be opened. Six years later, in Houston, Texas, it was a warehouse which held more than 40,000 tons of fireworks that blew up, creating a blast local people compared to an atomic explosion as a mushroom cloud billowed thousands of metres into the air. The warehouse was destroyed and a number of other nearby buildings flattened. Four people died in a cottage next door to the warehouse. It had all been started by a spark while the general manager was nailing up a display case.

American fireworks legislation was being gradually tightened, and by 1953, 28 states had brought in restrictions. In 1966 a federal ban came in on cherry bombs along with M-80s, powerful firecrackers about 3 centimetres long that had originally been used by the U.S. military to simulate live fire in training exercises and contained as much as 50 grains (3.2 grams) of flashpowder. Also banned were silver salutes, sometimes known as M-100s, which were longer than M-80s but contained only about half as much flashpowder. Some states went further, banning sparklers and Roman candles too. By the 1980s the Consumer Product Safety Commission had laid down standards for all fireworks and limited the weight of powder in firecrackers, the main cause of accidents, to 2 grains, but bootleggers still sold offending items. The Bureau of Alcohol, Tobacco and Firearms (BATFE), who police firework laws, were arresting about a dozen people a year, with a typical haul of perhaps 50,000 M-80s and silver salutes.

Just as in the UK, expertise in pyrotechnics was no guarantee against accidents. On 24 November 1982, Thanksgiving Day, the secretary-treasurer of the PGI, Bill Hoyt, was blown up and killed along with his wife, also a fireworks enthusiast, in Pennsylvania. A year later, on the Saturday of the Thanksgiving weekend of 1983, as we saw, the great American fireworks dynasty of Grucci were the victims. Felix Grucci's son, Butch, said all firework makers had to live with danger, 'every day, sort of like knowing that nuclear weapons are pointed at you . . . you hear a sharp noise, like a window shade rattling up, or the slam of a door, or a car backfiring, and you think it's starting.' Their plant at Bellport on

Long Island had all the usual precautions – arranged in separate workshops each about 30 metres apart, with a copper plate people had to touch as they came in at each entrance, to ground themselves and eliminate the chance of a spark jumping to any explosive material. Women were banned from brushing their hair or wearing silk underwear. On the fateful day, Butch's brother Jimmy, the company CEO, and his cousin Donna, aged nineteen, had been working on some big shells. As they left the shed, they were hit by a shock wave and a fireball. Butch saw the explosion from his house nearby. The noise was terrifying, 'a ripping and tearing sound, high and piercing, almost a kind of shriek'.[46] The shock was felt for 20 miles, and nothing was left of the shed in which Jimmy and Donna had been working apart from a flight of stone steps that had led up to the door. Two dozen people were hurt and a hundred homes damaged. Felix, then aged 78, who was on the edge of the company's compound, suffered minor injuries. The cause remained a mystery.

With New Year's Eve approaching, the Gruccis had to decide whether they should try and fulfil their commitments. Jimmy's son Phil said they felt 'numb' but they scrounged and borrowed fireworks from friends in the industry, set up temporary premises and managed to put on the display they had agreed to do in New York's Central Park. Once the immediate crisis was out of the way, they held a family meeting and decided unanimously to try to rebuild the company. In the spring of 1984 they resolved to move to a more isolated location on Long Island, but each time they found a site, their neighbours-to-be objected. Eventually, the local authority suggested one that was shielded by 3-metre-high sand barriers and where the closest homes were nearly a mile away, and there they reopened in 1985.

In between the two Thanksgiving explosions came what was then America's worst ever fireworks manufacturing disaster. On 27 May 1983 eleven workers were killed in a blast that destroyed an unlicensed fireworks factory at a farm producing fishing bait in Benton, Tennessee. It is said the authorities knew nothing of its existence until the accident, even though it was the biggest illegal fireworks factory ever discovered, and is supposed to have manufactured more than 5 million M-80s and M-100s. Eventually 21 people were convicted, including the owner and a man said to be the mastermind of the operation, who had another conviction relating to an illegal fireworks factory in South Carolina. BATFE officials found cigarettes and a lighter, but they said the cause might also have been sparks from an electric drill or from a bare lightbulb.

Policeman examining the scene of the Aerlex Fireworks explosion, 1985.

Two years later, in May 1985, an explosion at another illegal fireworks factory in Ohio killed nine workers. A month after that, 21 people died in America's worst fireworks factory accident at Aerlex Fireworks, a legal establishment in Oklahoma, which was then the country's biggest fireworks factory. Investigators believed it was caused by friction. One man lost his brother, aunt, uncle and three cousins. The plant never reopened.

Hooliganism also continued. In 1996 someone threw a lighted cigarette on to a shelf crammed with fireworks at a store in Scottown, Ohio. In the resulting blaze, nine people died, including three children under ten. A 24-year-old man, who had suffered a serious head injury while skateboarding in his teens, was found mentally unfit to face trial.

From the Second World War to the Millennium: The Rest of the World

In France, the town of Monteux, not far from Avignon, was a traditional centre for pyrotechnics manufacture, and in the 1920s the Ruggieris moved in and bought up all the local workshops. By the 1970s they had three factories there employing about 150 people. In 1973 four Ruggieri workers were killed in an explosion, then on 12 April 1977 terrible blasts at the company's Bellerive plant shook the area. Inside the works, two people were killed and sixteen injured, but there were also a dozen injuries to children in nearby schools. Buildings had their roofs torn off, windows were shattered. As the town's mayor would put it on the thirtieth anniversary of the explosion: 'fireworks are synonymous with celebration, joy, jubilation. This time they brought misfortune and sadness, as a kind of tribute to pay for all the other festive moments.'[47] A grand plan emerged to shut the Ruggieri sites close to the centre of town and open Europe's biggest fireworks factory on the outskirts. But the scheme was overtaken by events as competition from East Asia hotted up and Ruggieri eased away from manufacturing to concentrate on displays. The great factory never saw the light of day and firework making in the town ended.

In pyrotechnics-mad Malta, back in the 1930s there had been a fabled man named Qonsru who specialized in huge set-piece wheels, 3 metres or more in diameter, which he would place one behind the other and set revolving in opposite directions to create the illusion of an eight-pointed flower of unrivalled beauty. He guarded the secrets of his formulae jealously, and it was said that once he had poured his coloured compositions into their cases, they would go off within 48 hours whether he fired them or not. One day in 1936 his factory in Mqabba blew up, killing three people, and over the years the island suffered a steady stream of accidents. On Maundy Thursday 1955, there was an explosion that flattened the St Philip Fireworks Factory in the village of Ħaż-Żebbuġ and killed four people. In 1980 two more firework makers were killed. One was a fourteen-year-old boy said to be an expert in multi-break shells. The story goes that the police commissioner slapped a ban on fireworks pending an investigation, but the fireworks lobby told him it would be too dangerous to leave stocks lying around. So he agreed to have them set off, as they would normally have been, at the fiestas that were so popular with tourists. The result was that the displays were the most spectacular Malta had ever seen, and the commissioner backed down.

But that did not mean the authorities gave up on regulation. After the 1955 accident, the St Philip Fireworks Factory had been rebuilt, but in 1982 it lost its permit and had to move to new premises, because too many new homes had been built nearby. Then in 1984 a naval vessel was given the task of dumping at sea illegal fireworks confiscated in the city of Żabbar. They exploded on deck, killing five crewmen and two police officers in what was the worst peacetime disaster ever suffered by the Maltese armed forces. The victims were dubbed the 'Magnificent Seven'. The cause was never established, though it could have been something as simple as a spark caused by closing a hatch. The co-pilot of one of the helicopters given the grim task of recovering bodies was Carmel Vassallo, who would later become commander of the Armed Forces of Malta. Thirty years later, he would complain that 'people still produce illegal fireworks, putting the lives of others at risk.'[48] Following another fatal accident at the St Philip Firework Factory in 1992, health and safety rules at the plant were tightened, and it stopped making any fireworks for sale, producing them only for the saint's festival.

Back in 1949 Alan Brock had said that Latin American firework accidents were 'almost too frequent, and fatalities too numerous, to list', and for the rest of the century nothing much seemed to change.[49] Brazil suffered a factory disaster on 23 June 1958, with ten killed at Feira de Santana. On the very same day at Santo Amaro, about 30 miles away, a fireworks booth exploded at a fair, killing more than sixty people who had crowded around it to buy pyrotechnics for a saint's day celebration. Six years later, more than forty died during a saint's day festival in the city of Atlatlahucan in Mexico. The blast happened when a pile of fireworks exploded next to two tanks of butane. In 1971 a fireworks explosion destroyed a school at Puebla, killing thirteen.

There were constant stories of the authorities in various countries trying to clamp down, but the accidents went on. On 12 December 1988 fireworks were being sold at the huge La Merced market in the centre of Mexico City to celebrate the day of the Virgin of Guadalupe. It seems that in an alley by the market, a butane gas cylinder being used by a street food vendor exploded and set fire to a box of rockets. This started a chain reaction, setting off more fireworks and sending the blaze through hundreds of market stalls to nearby buildings. Fires burned for most of the day and by the time they had been put out, more than sixty people were dead and nearly two hundred had been injured. The Spanish newspaper *El País* reported that there had been similar, though smaller, incidents over many years and that local people said they had constantly been complaining about the danger from firework stalls in the market. Vendors were supposed to need permits, but locals claimed that the officials responsible for enforcing the rules were corrupt. The local authorities promised 'drastic measures', while the festival went on regardless and the noise of fireworks 'resounded everywhere'.[50] Eleven years later, in the

Mexican city of Celaya, 63 people died on a busy Sunday lunchtime as a series of explosions ripped through illegal stockpiles of fireworks believed to have been left over from Independence Day celebrations a couple of weeks before. At the time, Mexico had restrictions on the storage of fireworks, but these were widely flouted. Brazil had another terrible accident in December 1998, as 38 women and a boy were killed when a fireworks warehouse exploded in Santo Antonio de Jesus. The city, a centre for legal and illegal firework making on low wages, suffered severe damage.

In Asia, Malaysia suffered its worst ever industrial accident at the Bright Sparklers fireworks factory in Sungai Buloh in 1991. It happened while the manager was testing a new product, and there appears to have been a spill of explosive chemicals. Witnesses said the scene was like a war zone, as the factory was demolished. The death toll was 26, and more than two hundred homes were damaged, with a woman describing 'stones flying into our house'.[51] The *New Straits Times* reported that some good came out of the tragedy, with a new health and safety law and the Fire and Rescue Department setting up a Hazardous Material Unit Team. Bright Sparklers went out of business soon afterwards. China's huge fireworks industry also had plenty of accidents. In 1996 it was estimated that 60,000 people a year were injured by pyrotechnics. That July, 36 workers and passers-by were killed in an explosion at Piya in the south-east of the country. The authorities had shut the factory down in April for safety reasons, but it reopened two months later.

India: Explosions, Fires and Child Labour

India's fireworks capital Sivakasi had a reputation for poor safety standards. In 2012 it was estimated that on average 20–25 workers died in accidents every year. As we have seen, it is often very poor people who end up making fireworks. A worker who had suffered severe burns told the BBC: 'We are scared, but what else do we do?'[52] In July 2009 four fires, including three in unregistered premises, had cost forty lives. The Fire and Rescue Service responded by ordering regular surprise inspections of firework factories, and by instructing them to have adequate water tanks and vehicle access, so firefighting units could easily reach them. The Firework Manufacturers' Association argued that most accidents happened in unregistered premises, but there were regular accidents in registered factories. In a typical story, in 2006 a forty-year-old widow with four children had been packing sheets with tiny round bulges containing an explosive mixture. The bulges would later form caps for children's toy guns at Diwali. She pressed down on the sheets too hard and the friction caused an explosion that killed four people. Some told the *Indian Express* that it was better to work illegally, except that they had to pay bribes to the police, and every now and then there would be a raid. They would be fined and have some of their stocks destroyed: 'We go through this ritual about two to three times every year.'[53]

Child labour was also a scourge, with an estimated 125,000 child workers in the area in the mid-1990s. In 2000 a *Sunday Mirror* investigation revealed a girl aged four rolling paper tubes for Catherine wheels 'under a baking sun for eight hours at a time without a break. Poisonous glue is smeared on her lips, mouth and hands and flies from the open sewer under her feet smother her face. Her reward is a bag of sweets from her mother and a few pence for her family.' The newspaper reported that children as young as three were being put to work, and it told the story of a ten-year-old boy, being paid 50p for an eight-hour day, who had two fingers cut off in a machine making cases for Roman candles. It said the chemicals the children were using could cause tuberculosis, cancer and brain damage. The plant supplied paper components to Standard Fireworks, then said to be the second biggest pyrotechnics company in the world with 24 factories. Standard had no connection with the Huddersfield company of the same name, but its products were sold in the UK under another label. All the four-year-old girl's family, including nine children, worked for the supplier company. Her mother said: 'It's a matter of survival. We would rather they play or learn but, if they don't work we can't feed them.' A foreman at another factory in the area said they needed to employ children to keep wages and costs down. 'We hide the children,' he said, 'when government inspectors visit.' As for 'surprise' inspections: 'The authorities tip us off beforehand.'[54] Bribes were handed out, and the *Mirror* found a corrupt medical records officer at the local hospital who was prepared to give false ages for child workers at a price.

Three months after the deadly fires of July 2009, a group of NGOs launched an inquiry. They concluded that all twenty years of campaigning had achieved was to drive child labour underground, with work generally done in people's homes. The Centre for Child Rights and Development said manufacturers avoided responsibility by contracting their work out to agents, who in turn sub-contracted it to families. Another NGO reported that many workers were paying off money they had borrowed from the agents. It was said that since 1986 there had been about 150,000 inspections but very few prosecutions. An official of the Petroleum and Explosives Safety Organisation complained there were four people to monitor 'over 1,000 factories and hundreds of other units. How do you do that?'[55] A particular Indian hazard was hot weather causing high temperatures in factories, which may have been the cause of a factory fire in 2012 that killed forty people, including some local villagers. Its licence had been revoked the day before for violating safety rules, and no work should have been going on. Instead, with the Diwali festival just a few weeks away, production appears to have been powering ahead. After the accident, a host of licences for other firework factories in the area were cancelled. The *Times of India* saw this as classic belated shutting of the stable door.

India has also had its share of accidents at displays. Kerala has a long tradition of using fireworks in religious celebrations, and in 2016 the state government listed sixteen fatal firework accidents over the previous half century, saying the main causes were 'Illegal storage, manufacturing, usage, unauthorized display agents, ignorance of safety measures'.[56] In 1952, 68 people were killed at the Sabarimala Hindu Temple when two firework sheds caught fire. Disaster struck twice at festivals at the Christian church of Kandashamkadavu. In 1984 a firecracker explosion claimed twenty lives, and five years later a dozen people died in another pyrotechnic accident. In between, in 1987, 27 people were run over by a train and killed as they sat on the track watching a display at the Jagannatha Temple in Thalassery, while twenty died at the Veloor Kootanmooli Temple, Thrissur, in 1988. But the worst accident came during a seven-day festival in 2016 when 15,000 pilgrims were visiting the Puttingal Hindu temple in the coastal town of Paravur, and a stray firecracker fell into a fireworks stockpile. Burning debris from the explosion then caused a major fire in a building storing more fireworks. Local residents spoke of 'huge pieces of concrete' flying through the air. One is said to have killed a biker a kilometre from the scene. Another 110 people died, and India's prime minister Narendra Modi described the accident as 'heart-rending and shocking beyond words'.[57] The local authorities said the temple was not permitted to store fireworks.

The Twenty-First Century: Nightclubs Bring New Dangers

In Europe, the twenty-first century picked up where the twentieth had left off, with a huge fireworks explosion at a warehouse in the Netherlands. It happened on 13 May 2000 in the town of Enschede and destroyed an entire city block. More than twenty people were killed, including four firefighters, and nearly 1,000 were injured. The business's two owners were found guilty of importing and selling illegal fireworks and breaking other safety rules. The judge was highly critical of the local authorities, saying they had failed to act even though they knew the law was being broken. Then in 2008, an illegal fireworks factory in Istanbul blew up, killing twenty people and injuring more than a hundred. The factory had been shut twice, but continued to operate amid allegations that officials had been bribed.

Just before Christmas 2016 came confirmation that Mexico had not solved its problems, as 42 people died when fireworks exploded at the San Pablito pyrotechnics market in the country's fireworks capital, Tultepec. The market had suffered blasts three times in a dozen years. In a familiar story, one initial explosion set off a deadly chain reaction, and the market was reduced to a 'scorched ruin'. Less than three months later, while it was still closed, Tultepec was echoing to bangs and crashes for Mexico's

Enschede fireworks warehouse explosion, Netherlands, 2000.

Devastation left by the explosion at the San Pablito fireworks market, Tultepec, Mexico, 2016.

National Pyrotechnics Fair. A local government official said it was a tribute to the victims: 'They're going to be paid homage to with fireworks because this is what we do in Tultepec.' San Pablito remained closed, but many small workshops were still turning out pyrotechnics. One firework maker told a *Guardian* reporter they had survived eight serious accidents: 'Mexican people have a special quality: we take the positive parts of a tragedy and turn it into a fiesta.'[58] The plan was to improve safety, then reopen the market, but in 2018 another Tultepec fireworks store exploded, killing 24 people. Meanwhile in Indonesia, Jakarta saw a fireworks factory hit by twin explosions three hours apart in 2017. Altogether, 49 people died. The UK, having effectively exported its fireworks manufacturing industry, had also exported most of the accidents associated with it, but in 2013 the owner of a fireworks shop in Stafford selling Chinese products was gaoled for ten years for manslaughter after an explosion there killed an employee and a customer.

But it was in nightclubs that some of the worst firework accidents of the early twenty-first century happened, beginning with the New Year celebrations for 2001 when 350 young people had packed into three cafés in a building in the picturesque Dutch fishing village of Volendam. As sparklers set fire to ceiling decorations that had not been treated with flame retardant, fourteen died. The Station Nightclub in the town of West Warwick, Rhode Island, was also packed in February 2003 – with fans of the rock band Great White, who had only just incorporated pyrotechnics into their act. Almost at once, the fireworks set light to highly inflammable foam used for soundproofing that lined the ceilings, walls and even an exit door. One of the brothers who owned the club grabbed a fire extinguisher, but was beaten back by the heat and flames. Within ninety seconds the venue was filled with thick black smoke. A Great White band member was among the 100 people killed. One of the club's owners was gaoled for involuntary manslaughter, as was the band's tour manager for using pyrotechnics without a permit. The dangers for performers of using pyrotechnics in stage acts were re-emphasized in 2019 when the Spanish pop performer Joana Sainz García was struck by a firework and killed while singing and dancing on stage in the town of Las Berlanas.

Still, being in the audience continued to be more risky. In 2004 Buenos Aires suffered a fireworks disaster eerily similar to the one in Rhode Island. On 30 December more than 4,000 people had packed into the Cromagnon Republic nightclub – a space intended for 1,500. It had a permit but no fire extinguishers, and emergency exits had been locked to stop people sneaking in without paying. As a rock band performed, someone let off a pyrotechnic flare that set fire to a foam ceiling, and 194 people were killed, mainly from inhaling poison gases, while 1,400 were injured. Witnesses claimed the band had encouraged the audience to set off flares. After protracted legal proceedings, the promoter, members of the band, its former manager, a police officer and a number of local inspectors received gaol terms. Nor was the story much different at Perm in Russia in 2009, where 156 people died at the Lame Horse club, some of them by being crushed to death. Once again fireworks ignited decorations, and the club had no fire exits. The owner was one of the people sent to prison.

The deadliest pyrotechnics nightclub fire happened at the Kiss club in Santa Maria, Brazil, in 2016. An estimated nine hundred students had squeezed in for a university party. In a depressingly predictable tale, the band let off a flare, which set fire to soundproofing foam on the ceiling, filling the building with toxic fumes. Police said the venue had no working fire extinguishers and only two emergency exits, which were poorly signposted. Most of the 242 victims died from inhaling smoke. The two club owners and two members of the band were sentenced to gaol terms of eighteen to 22 years, but in 2022 their sentences were quashed.

South America was also the scene of the worst ever modern fireworks disaster. The narrow streets of the Mesa Redonda shopping area in the middle of Peru's capital, Lima, were lined with wood-and-adobe buildings. On 29 December 2001 it was full of traders selling fireworks for the New Year celebrations. Witnesses said the blaze started while one was demonstrating his wares. The ground was covered with gunpowder that had fallen from fireworks being unloaded, and the flames spread fast, destroying five blocks in a few minutes despite the efforts of more than four hundred firefighters and forty fire engines. More than 290 people lost their lives, with a shopkeeper saying one reason was that many were trying 'to save their belongings'.[59]

Effigy of Mario Balotelli, Edenbridge, Kent, 2011.

From 2002 to 2016 in the United States, the Consumer Product Safety Commission received on average seven reports of firework-related deaths each year plus 11,000 to 13,000 injuries, two-thirds of them happening during the month around 4 July. More than a third of the causalties were children under fifteen, with burns to fingers, hands and arms the most common injury. Less than 1 per cent happened at public displays. In 2017 sparklers were the fireworks most commonly involved in Fourth of July injuries, figuring in 14 per cent. The American Pyrotechnics Association said most accidents resulted from fireworks being misused. From 2015 to 2019 in England, about 3,600 people attended hospital A&E departments with firework injuries in the months of Halloween and Bonfire Night.

Perhaps the oddest firework accident of the twenty-first century involved the Italian footballer Mario Balotelli. While playing for Manchester City in the English Premier League, he had appeared in a firework safety advertisement. Soon after, in October 2011, he decided it would be fun to set off some pyrotechnics in the bathroom of the house he was renting in a smart Cheshire village. Ten firefighters were needed to put out the blaze they started, and it did damage estimated at £400,000.

The Twenty-First Century: Rules Get Tighter, and Looser

In England and Wales in 2004, it became illegal to set off fireworks after eleven o'clock at night except on Bonfire Night, Diwali, New Year's Eve or Chinese New Year. On 5 November they could be fired until midnight, and for the other three occasions, 1 a.m. was the limit. Local authorities were permitted to put on displays outside these hours for special occasions. Except for specially licensed firework shops, retailers could sell fireworks only in the run-up to these named festivals. Selling them without a licence could result in a fine or even prison, and fireworks on sale to the public had a 120-decibel noise limit. You had to be over sixteen to buy sparklers, and over eighteen to buy anything else, with the most powerful pyrotechnics reserved for properly insured professional companies with licensed storage facilities. It was also an offence for anyone under eighteen to possess any other than category one fireworks in a public place. By this time, screech and mini-rockets were banned, and rockets had to be fired from specially supplied launch tubes, not the time-honoured milk bottles. Also forbidden were single-shot 'air bombs', which exploded with a loud bang and a bright white flash. You were allowed to let off fireworks only on your own land; firing them in the street or other public places was banned. Similar rules applied in Scotland until 2021, when an additional ban on letting off fireworks before six o'clock in the evening came in. The following year, the Scottish government announced plans to introduce much more stringent regulations, restricting fireworks to a few days in April and around Bonfire Night, New Year's Eve, Diwali and Chinese New Year, along with the creation of 'no firework' zones, and a requirement for people buying category two and three fireworks to have a licence.

During the Troubles, Northern Ireland had some of the strictest regulations in the world, with fireworks banned except at public displays. These were eased in 1996, but six years later tough new laws came in. Retailers had to be licensed and to keep a record of everyone who bought category two, three or four fireworks from them. Most buyers also had to have a licence, and while professionals could purchase category four fireworks, they had to get a permit for each display. As in other parts of the UK, some specific fireworks were outlawed, including bangers and jumping crackers. The Republic of Ireland also had strict rules. Ordinary folk could buy only small fireworks such as sparklers. Bigger items could be imported (Ireland had no firework makers of its own) but only by licensed professionals for organized displays.

In 2013 and 2014 the EU laid down basic regulations for member states, but they were allowed, as with the Irish Republic, to have additional rules. It divided fireworks into four categories, F1 to F4, similar to the UK's. Twelve was the minimum age at which F1 could be bought, the qualifying age for F2 was sixteen, and for F3 eighteen. F4 fireworks were reserved for professionals. Among other countries that had additional rules was Germany, where fireworks could not be let off near churches, hospitals, children's or retirement homes, and only licensed professionals could buy F3 and F4 fireworks. Finland insisted that all firework users must wear safety glasses. Apart from at New Year, emergency services had to be told about any firework event at least five days beforehand, and some local authorities banned them altogether. In Sweden, anyone wanting to set off a rocket had to do a training course and get a permit, while Spain allowed children as young as ten to have F2 fireworks so long as they were supervised by an adult and involved in 'well-established' cultural events.

America too has a patchwork of regulations, with the federal government laying down minimum standards, while individual states, counties and even municipalities can add to them. Fireworks were divided into two categories: 'consumer' and 'display'. The only state with a complete ban on consumer fireworks was Massachusetts. According to a survey by the Scottish government in 2019, thirty states permitted most kinds of consumer fireworks, though many had limited selling seasons, usually around the Fourth of July and Christmas and New Year. There were also minimum age limits, and sometimes permits were required. People wanting to buy display fireworks needed a federal licence.

American regulations have sometimes attracted derision. In 2017 a BBC correspondent reported from Delaware on 'the U.S. state that bans sparklers but not guns', noting that you did not need a licence to own a shotgun but that you could be fined $100 for possessing a sparkler if you did not have a permit. In 2016 seventeen people had been arrested for firework offences in the state. The reporter visited Patriotic Fireworks' store in Elkton, Maryland – 6 miles from the Delaware border. A sign on the door declared: 'Let freedom ring,' but this thirst for liberty did not extend to selling to customers from Maryland. The shop owner said the state's fireworks laws were so complex it was not worth the trouble, but they did sell to Delaware customers, so long as they signed a contract promising pyrotechnics would be used 'in accordance with all state and local laws'. Delaware's assistant state fire marshal was unrepentant about its strict rules, saying: 'fireworks are unsafe.' Sparklers, he declared, could burn at up to 980°C, and they acted as a 'gateway' to other fireworks. But across America, the wind of liberalization seemed to be blowing. Since 2000 nine states had legalized sparklers, and another seven had relaxed laws on other fireworks. The American Pyrotechnics Association argued that legalizing fireworks made them less risky, saying, 'where there was complete prohibition there was no safety message.'[60] The association maintained the number of firework injuries was the same as in 1976, even though the tonnage of fireworks being set off was getting on for ten times as high. According to the Scottish study, fireworks cause about 18,000 fires a year in the USA, with more reported to fire departments on the Fourth of July than on any other day of the year, but states with strict restrictions on sales are said to have fifty times fewer firework-related fires than those with minimal rules.

Australia may have a thriving firework events industry, but it banned unlicensed people from buying anything bigger than a sparkler everywhere except in Northern Territory and Tasmania, and even on that island you needed a permit and you had to notify the emergency services and anyone living within a kilometre of where they were going to be set off. In Northern Territory, fireworks could be used only on 1 July to celebrate Territory Day, and any left over had to be handed back. In New Zealand, fireworks could be sold to people aged eighteen and over in the days leading up to 5 November. Outside that time, retailers needed government permission, and it was given only if the fireworks formed a traditional part of a religious or cultural occasion. Despite these restrictions, they could be let off at any time of year, though many local councils had laws stopping people lighting them in public places. In 2007 restrictions were brought in on sparklers, which could now be bought only in packs together with at least three other fireworks. This was meant to stop people making Yuriy Yaniv-style 'sparkler bombs'.

The Challenging Future: Pets and Noise

The UK has an estimated 12 million pet owners. In 2016 one of them, Julie Doorne from Lincolnshire, started a petition to have fireworks banned except on the special occasions of Bonfire Night, New Year's Eve, Diwali and Chinese New Year. She said: 'The use of fireworks is getting out of control . . . celebrations are going on for weeks during autumn and winter. I have heard examples of pet owners having to put their pets in boarding and even some owners moving house to more rural areas to escape the noise.' Ms Doorne won support from the RSPCA, which ran its own 'Bang Out of Order' campaign, saying more than 60 per cent of dogs were scared by fireworks, as well as 54 per cent of cats and 55 per cent of horses. The British Horse Society reported twenty deaths and ten severe injuries in fireworks incidents over nine years but said 90 per cent of incidents were never reported to the society. In November 2020 the death of a baby zebra at a zoo near Bristol would be blamed on fireworks after she was alarmed by the noise from several local displays and crashed into the boundary of her enclosure. Doorne also demanded a reduction in the permitted noise level for fireworks, which was set at 120 decibels, 35 decibels above the level at which hearing damage can start, according to the Royal National Institute for Deaf People. The Scottish government's survey of 2019 found firework displays include peak sounds up to 137 decibels. Ms Doorne would be involved with half a dozen petitions, one of which passed a million signatures in 2022. But the government turned down any change in the law, saying it believed 'the majority of people who use fireworks do so at the appropriate times of year and have a sensible and responsible attitude towards them.'[61]

A woman from Wombwell in South Yorkshire also started a petition after her eighteen-week-old puppy died in November 2019 of 'fright caused by fireworks'.[62] Another horrifying case that year involved a horse that impaled itself on a fence near Holywell in Flintshire and later died. It was not just animals. In 2011, 5,000 blackbirds fell out of the sky in Beebe, Arizona, during New Year's Eve fireworks celebrations. It was thought the loud noises made them crash into buildings and trees. Research in the Netherlands, published in 2015, revealed that just before midnight on New Year's Eve, there were almost no birds in flight, but within a few minutes of fireworks celebrations starting, there were 'explosive' movements of wild birds – perhaps involving millions across the country. The panicked birds got up to altitudes of 500 metres and flew in dense flocks for 45 minutes, exposing them to the danger of crashing into power lines, buildings, trees and each other. In 2021 hundreds of dead birds, mainly starlings, were found lying outside Rome's Termini railway station after the New Year celebrations. The International Organization for Animal Protection said they had probably been literally scared to death. The city had banned people from setting off fireworks and had tried to impose a ten o'clock curfew to combat coronavirus, but both rules were widely ignored. This author kept a tally of the number of nights on which fireworks could be heard at his home in north London in the year from 1 February 2022 to 31 January 2023. The figure was 44, though this might underestimate the phenomenon slightly, as he was away for a few nights.

In 2018 Welsh Labour MP Susan Elan Jones expressed concern about the effect of fireworks on war veterans with post-traumatic stress disorder, while Julie Doorne would raise the plight of people with other conditions such as dementia or autism. According to the National Autistic Society, there were 700,000 people in the UK with autism for whom 'the unexpected nature of fireworks causes a lot of distress.'[63] After Bonfire Night 2019 several local councils began to take action. In January 2020 Bradford Council announced a wide-ranging inquiry into the apparent growing use of fireworks, as a poll by the local newspaper saw 94 per cent answer 'yes' to the question: 'Would you crack down on the use of fireworks in Bradford?'[64] At the same time, Cheshire West and Chester Council and Lincoln Council called for quieter fireworks, with one Lincoln councillor declaring: 'The thrill of fireworks is the way they light up the night sky, not the bangs that go with them.'[65] A Conwy councillor took a different view, maintaining that 'the noise is a big part of the enjoyment of public firework displays,' but he still wanted suppliers to offer quieter fireworks alongside their more traditional wares so people could choose to 'be more considerate [to] their neighbours'.[66]

The Italian town of Collecchio had decided in 2015 that exhortation was not enough, and banned loud fireworks, ordering people instead to use the so-called silent variety, though in reality these would be less noisy rather than actually silent. The city of Costa Mesa in California followed suit in 2017. American environmentalist Jane Desmond argued that 'silent fireworks' had featured in displays for a long time: 'the comet that shoots into the air with a long sparking tail, or the flying fish whose scattering sparkles swim out from a silent boom . . . actually display the most stunning colors, more so than big explosions.' But Julie Heckman, executive director of the American Pyrotechnics Association, maintained that 'silent fireworks' would be like watching pyrotechnics 'on a computer screen. It wouldn't be the real experience.'[67] British Fireworks Association chairman Steve Newham took a similar view, saying: 'There is no such thing as a quiet firework really unless you're talking about a sparkler.'[68] Companies working on low-noise fireworks in the UK included MLE Pyrotechnics and Flashpoint Fireworks, though, in Flashpoint's view, a silent display was impossible.[69] American companies like Phantom of Youngstown, Ohio, seemed to disagree, as they sold silent products such as Flying Stars as well as low-noise fireworks, and in 2019 Lee Smith, from Nottingham fireworks company First Galaxy, said he had been using 'quiet' fireworks for fifteen years, especially when putting on displays near livestock or at wildlife parks or where people did not want to annoy their neighbours.[70] Two years later, supermarket company Aldi said it had increased the number of low-noise fireworks it was offering in the UK, while in 2019 its rival Sainsbury's had gone a step further, ending the sale of fireworks in its stores altogether.

The Challenging Future: Pollution

Smog and smoke have long been associated with fireworks, especially when they get a helping hand from bonfires. On 5 November 1988 smog shut down Heathrow, Gatwick and other UK airports. According to the World Health Organization, chronic exposure to smoke can cause cardiovascular and respiratory diseases, as well as lung cancer, and by the 1990s smoke particles were thought to be causing 10,000 deaths a year in the UK. In 1995 the British government fought to win an exemption for Bonfire Night from new EU rules on clean air, which were designed to reduce the number of particles. On Bonfire Night 1994 they had reached four times the EU limit in Cardiff, Bristol, Leicester and Liverpool, and were six times higher in Leeds and Birmingham. Meanwhile, research by AEA Technology at Harwell revealed that levels of dioxins, thought to be among the world's most dangerous pollutants, soared fourfold at Guy Fawkes Night 1994, though most dioxin emissions were believed to come from bonfires rather than fireworks, and Bonfire Night smoke was found to contain 350 times the amount of benzopyrenes, which are suspected of causing cancer, as cigarette fumes. The UK's Environment Secretary John Gummer said he had 'always hated' Bonfire Night, and environmentalists had pressed for tighter limits to be applied all year long, but the government decided 5 November and other traditional firework nights, such as New Year's Eve, should be exempted.[71]

The twenty-first century brought further pollution worries, such as potassium perchlorate. As we saw, its introduction made firework mixtures safer, but now anxiety grew about its toxicity. Perchlorates dissolve easily and an American study in 2007 showed that following firework displays, levels of potassium and ammonium perchlorate were up to 1,000 times higher in a nearby lake than they were before the events. Perchlorates can disrupt the thyroid, causing memory or attention problems. In 2009 Zambelli announced it was working with its Chinese manufacturers to reduce the amount of perchlorate in its fireworks, and had managed to get it eliminated completely in some. It found silver and gold colours worked well without perchlorates but that blues, reds and greens were less intense. By 2021 six U.S. states had introduced regulations to limit perchlorates in drinking water, but the previous year the Environmental Protection Agency had decided not to set a national standard. Meanwhile a team from the U.S. Army's Pyrotechnics Technology and Prototyping Division had found that sodium and potassium periodate were safe and effective alternatives.

Then there were metals. A study on the effects of a firework festival at Girona in Spain in 2008 found ground levels of strontium had been raised by a factor of 86, potassium 26 and barium eleven, while quantities of lead, copper, magnesium and other metals were also significantly higher. Two years later, research in London on the effects of Bonfire Night and Diwali showed that as well as increased metal pollution, there were raised levels of sulphur dioxide and nitric oxide, which are harmful to humans and cause acid rain. A study of Valencia's Las Fallas festival, published in 2007, showed similar results, and four years later, investigations in Washington State revealed that metal particles could be carried 100 kilometres. Germany's Federal Environmental Agency has said that more than 2,000 tons of potentially harmful tiny particles are added to the atmosphere every year by fireworks, three-quarters of it generated on New Year's Eve. Defenders of pyrotechnics often say the pollution they cause is negligible compared with other sources, such as road transport, but the researchers in this study argued pyrotechnics were a special hazard because 'many of the elements released are both toxic and finely respirable,'[72] and because displays often take place in areas that are already polluted.

As we saw, in 2017 China tried a fireworks ban covering nearly 450 cities. The following year it was extended to more places, including Beijing. An examination of two cities where fireworks were forbidden indicated they had only a quarter to a sixth as much pollution as two where they were not. Once the Air Quality Index gets over 300, it starts to be damaging to health. During India's Diwali festival in 2019, it reached the worst possible score – 500 – in parts of Delhi. The following year the authorities in India's capital tried unsuccessfully to ban fireworks. In London, the New Year celebrations brought 2020's first air pollution incident, as lack of wind meant particles were not dispersed. It is not clear how long firework pollution remains in the air. The Scottish government survey of 2019 quoted American studies indicating it seemed to drop off within sixteen hours, but a review of international evidence for the *Journal of the Air and Waste Management Association* in 2016 concluded there was 'strong evidence' it could last for up to a month after major displays.

More prosaically, fireworks also contribute to pollution via plastic and paper debris. A German environmental group said 10,000 tons of plastic and hazardous waste was left by fireworks every New Year's Eve. The German town of Landshut brought in a fireworks ban, and became famous for its laser shows. Sydney, on the other hand, declared its display for New Year 2020 to be carbon neutral, with fireworks made from biodegradable paper and the city investing in carbon offsets for any emissions. There has also been innovation from firework manufacturers, like using wooden instead of metal sticks for sparklers. One reviewer was particularly impressed by a giant metre-long version that lasted four minutes, and remarked that it gave out a much brighter light with 'thicker sparks' because the stick burned too.[73] The downside was that hot ash dropped off and the packet carried a warning against using them over decking or anything that might scorch. The reviewer added that users should wear boots and trousers rather than flipflops and shorts!

6
Fireworks in the Arts

Some fireworks enthusiasts want them to be regarded as the 'eighth art', along with the seven more established disciplines, but how have those traditional arts portrayed pyrotechnics? One of the first mentions in literature comes in an Indian poem probably written in the second half of the sixteenth century by Sant Eknath, a Hindu saint and philosopher. In his *Rukmini Swayamvara* he describes the wedding of the goddess Rukmini to Krishna, who saved her from being married to a husband she did not want by carrying her off in his chariot. The festivities featured a range of fireworks from sparklers to rockets.

The Age of Shakespeare

Around the same time, pyrotechnics were being mentioned in Shakespeare's comedy *Love's Labour's Lost* (1598), in which 'a fantastical Spaniard' finds himself charged with impressing the princess of France, with whom King Ferdinand of Navarre has fallen in love, by 'some delightful ostentation, or show, or pageant, or antique, or firework'.[1] He seeks the help of a schoolmaster who he understands is an expert in such matters. Fireworks are also mentioned in one of the Bard's last plays, *Henry VIII* (1613), which he wrote with John Fletcher. This time they are denounced by a senior English politician as one of the fripperies of the French court that are having a bad influence on visiting English nobles, while in the anonymous comedy *The Maid's Metamorphosis* (1600), a witty repartee from one of the characters is compared to a squib.

By the late sixteenth century, pyrotechnic special effects had also become an ingredient of English drama. Robert Greene's comedy *Friar Bacon and Friar Bungay* (*c.* 1589) featured a dragon, while Ben Jonson's

Every Man in His Humour (1598) complained that firework effects were becoming too common, assuring his audience that in his work, there will be no 'nimble squib . . . to make afear'd the gentlewomen', unlike other plays in which such gimmicks had become one of 'the ill customs of the age'.[2] That did not put off Christopher Marlowe, whose *Doctor Faustus* (1604) featured all manner of pyrotechnic effects such as 'devils with squibs in the mouths' and 'a devil dressed like a woman with fireworks'.[3] Fireworks in plays of this era were often associated with the Devil and were frequently to be seen protruding from devils' orifices, while Shakespeare's *Julius Caesar* (1600) and *Macbeth* (1607) both included stage directions for thunder and lightning that would have needed fireworks effects.

Thomas Heywood used pyrotechnics in his *The Silver Age* and *The Brazen Age* (both 1613), part of a cycle of five plays described by one authority as 'the most ambitious theatrical undertaking of their time'. In one scene, a woman seduced by a disguised Jupiter, king of the Roman gods, demands he proves his identity, so Jupiter 'descends in his majesty, his thunderbolt burning . . . as he touches the bed, it fires', and she goes up in smoke. At another point, 'Medea with strange fiery works hangs above in the air.'[4] Across the Channel, the French dramatist Pierre Corneille gives fireworks a mention in his comedy *The Liar* (1642). The hero lies about pretty well everything: his part in a war, duels, marriages and the seduction of a beautiful woman on a boat on the Seine during a fireworks display.

One of the first English novels also refers to pyrotechnics. When he died, philosopher and statesman Sir Francis Bacon left behind an unfinished work, *The New Atlantis* (1626). It tells the story of a mythical utopian island that is found by accident by the crew of a ship lost in the Pacific. One of the many jewels of this land is its centre for scientific learning, the head of which shows the mariners various wonders including 'fireworks of all variety both for pleasure and use'.

Thackeray, Dickens and Nineteenth-Century Literature

That great English man of letters Dr Samuel Johnson had, as we know, been a rather delinquent spectator at a fireworks display by the celebrated pyrotechnician Torré at London's Marylebone pleasure gardens. Johnson, who had an acid pen, used the fireworks man as a putdown for the poet Thomas Gray, author of the famous *Elegy in a Country Churchyard* (1751), describing him as 'the very Torré of poetry, who played his corruscations so speciously that his steel dust is mistaken by many for a shower of gold'.[5] Another pleasure garden, the Vauxhall, plays a small but important role in W. M. Thackeray's satirical masterpiece *Vanity Fair* (1848). The heroine, Becky Sharp, who is no better than she should be, is trying to prise a marriage proposal out of rich Jos Sedley. When they go to Vauxhall, he calls her 'his soul's darling, four times', and she manages to throw herself into his arms when someone treads on her toe in the throng, but just as the crucial declaration was 'trembling on the timid lips of Mr. Sedley . . . oh, provoking! the bell rang for the fireworks'.[6] And that was as close as Becky ever got to becoming Mrs Sedley.

Vauxhall's reappearance in Thackeray's next novel, *Pendennis* (1850), illustrates how important the pleasure gardens had become in the lives of London's rich and poor. The eponymous hero, a gentleman who has been a bit of a wastrel, is now earning his living as a journalist. One night, feeling rather pleased after writing 'a brilliant leading article', he decides to 'regale himself with the fireworks and other amusements of Vauxhall'. There he comes to the rescue of a poor but pretty young woman, Fanny, who does not have the entrance fee. The girl is entranced by Pendennis and the fireworks: 'how she cried O, O, O, as the rockets soared into the air, and showered down in azure, and emerald, and vermilion!'[7] And Pendennis is very taken with her, but resolves he must not take advantage of her because of the difference in their social stations.

Thackeray's great contemporary Charles Dickens writes in *Sketches by Boz* (1839) about the disappointment of seeing Vauxhall by day, 'rudely and harshly disturbing that veil of mystery' that gilded night-time visits. Letting daylight in on magic meant the fireworks area generated only 'mortification and astonishment. *That* the Moorish tower—that wooden shed with a door in the centre, and daubs of crimson and yellow all round, like a gigantic watch-case!' Nor was it any more impressive at the spot where 'Madame Somebody (we forget even her name now) who nobly devoted her life to the manufacture of fireworks' – thought to be a reference to Mme Hengler – 'had so often been seen fluttering in the wind'.[8] In Dickens's third novel, *Nicholas Nickleby* (1839), Mr Crummles, the head of the theatrical troupe that Nicholas joins, confides to him that when he first beheld his wife, 'she stood upon her head on the butt-end of a spear, surrounded with blazing fireworks.' Later, when the hero leaves the troupe, Crummles suggests 'a brilliant display of fireworks' as the best way of generating the maximum audience for his final appearances. For eighteenpence, the troupe leader thinks they could place Nickleby with "'Farewell!" on a transparency behind and nine people at the wings with a squib in each hand – all the dozen and a half going off at once – it would be very grand – awful from the front, quite awful.'[9] But the idea is dropped. In one of Dickens's later novels, *Bleak House* (1853), a character recounts a series of industrial accidents of which he has been the victim, including 'being blowed out of winder case-filling at the firework business'.[10] Fireworks also crop up more metaphhorically in Dickens. So in *The Pickwick Papers* (1836), to his considerable irritation, Mr Pickwick is dubbed 'old Fireworks' on account of his periodic verbal explosions. In his novel of London's slums *The Nether World* (1889), George Gissing is very uncomplimentary about pyrotechnics and the delight the lower orders take in them. One August Bank Holiday, as a group of his characters head off to Crystal Palace for a day of drunkenness and violence, the author dismisses the famous firework display: 'Up shoot the rockets, and all the reeking multitude utters a huge "Oh" of idiot admiration.'[11]

Vauxhall also appeared in poetry. In 1839 it became the subject of a witty sonnet by Thomas Hood, perhaps best known for 'I Remember! I Remember!' It begins with an attack on the notorious priciness of Vauxhall's food. Next comes relief: 'hark the bell!' It is the fireworks queen's moment:

> Hengler! Madame! round whom all bright sparks lurk . . .
> All Noses are upturn'd! – Whish-ish! – On high
> The rocket rushes – trails – just steals in sight –
> Then droops and melts in bubbles of blue light –
> And Darkness reigns – Then balls flare up and die –
> Wheels whiz – smack crackers – serpents twist.[12]

Then it is time to go back to the overpriced food.

The same year, Hood produced a longer, tongue-in-cheek 'Ode to Madame Hengler', in which he describes her as a 'Starry Enchantress' and wonders whether, as a girl, she put fireworks in her mother's flower pots, gave the cook sausages full of gunpowder, or let off a firecracker as her sister was receiving a marriage proposal.

Pyrotechnics perform a more profound role in Robert Browning's novel in verse *The Ring and the Book* (1868–9). It tells the story of Count Guido Franceschini, an impoverished seventeenth-century Italian nobleman and jealous husband awaiting execution for the murder of his wife and her parents. The last of the twelve books begins with a description of the brilliant but ephemeral glory of a rocket as a metaphor for the transitory nature of all things human:

> Thus, lit and launched, up and up roared and soared
> A rocket, till the key o' the vault was reached.
> And wide heaven held, a breathless minute-space,
> In brilliant usurpature: thus caught spark,
> Rushed to the height, and hung at full of fame
> Over men's upturned faces, ghastly thence.

But soon the firework's brief moment of glory is done:

> The act, over and ended, falls and fades:
> What was once seen, grows what is now described.
> Then talked of, told about, a tinge the less
> In every fresh transmission; till it melts,
> Trickles in silent orange or wan grey
> Across our memory, dies and leaves all dark.[13]

The great German poet Johann Wolfgang von Goethe also wrote a number of novels. One of them, *Elective Affinities* (1809), in an echo of Corneille, uses fireworks as a tool of seduction. The title, incidentally, is borrowed from a chemical theory of the time. As an 'experiment', Baron Edward and his wife Charlotte decide to disrupt their idyllic rural life by inviting Edward's friend Captain Otto and Charlotte's beautiful niece Ottilie to visit. Affinities happen: Charlotte with the captain and Edward with Ottilie. Edward puts on a firework display for the lovely young woman. At first: 'Tenderly, timidly, he sat down at her side, without touching her.' Then 'rockets went hissing up – cannon thundered – Roman candles shot out their blazing balls – squibs flashed and darted – wheels spun round.' As the display got 'faster and faster . . . Edward, whose bosom was on fire, watched the blazing spectacle with eyes gleaming with delight', but Ottilie, 'in all this noise and fitful blazing and flashing, found more to distress her than to please. She leaned shrinking against Edward, and he, as she drew to him and clung to him, felt the delightful sense that she belonged entirely to him.'[14] The affair does not end happily, with Edward and Ottilie both eventually dying of remorse. A rocket features in the short story 'Easter Eve' (1886), in which the great Russian writer Anton Chekhov delivers a memorable pyrotechnic description: 'All at once, cleaving the darkness, a rocket zigzagged in a golden ribbon up the sky; it described an arc and, as though broken to pieces against the sky, was scattered crackling into sparks.'[15]

In these works, pyrotechnics are incidental, but they lie at the heart of an odd little fairy tale by Oscar Wilde, 'The Remarkable Rocket' (1888), which features a group of talking, if not particularly intellectual, fireworks, including a cracker, a 'little Squib', a 'big Roman Candle', a 'pensive Catharine Wheel' and 'a tall, supercilious-looking Rocket'. The fireworks are to be let off to celebrate the marriage of a prince and princess, and while all the others consider this a privilege, the rocket believes it is he who is doing the royal couple an honour. The king and father of the groom, incidentally, remarks of fireworks: 'I prefer them to stars myself, as you always know when they are going to appear.' To cut a short story even shorter, owing to a mishap, the rocket gets discarded and is found by a couple of boys, who put him on a fire they have lit to warm their kettle, hoping it will burn quicker. The rocket is elated as he catches light and flies upwards: 'I shall go on like this for ever. What a success I am!' he shouts. Then he gets a 'curious tingling sensation' and realizes he is about to explode: 'I shall set the whole world on fire, and make such a noise, that nobody will talk about anything else for a whole year.'[16] And explode he does, but no one sees or hears him, not even the two boys who have fallen asleep. The story became the basis of an opera performed during the lockdown of 2021 by Edinburgh Studio Opera, a student group performing online from their homes, with original lyrics set to old classic tunes.

Modern Literature

Ulysses (1922) by the Irish writer James Joyce is often regarded as the first modern novel. At great length, it tells the story of one day in the life of Dubliner Leopold Bloom. Once again, fireworks provide the accompaniment to a sexually charged episode. A young woman named Gerty MacDowell is by the sea with some friends when what seems like sheet lightning appears in the sky, but when it bursts 'blue and then green and purple', they realize it is fireworks. By then Gerty has spotted Bloom watching her, which 'set her pulses tingling'. She leans back to look at the pyrotechnics and 'revealed all her gracefully and beautifully shaped legs . . . and she seemed to hear the panting of his heart'. Excited by Bloom's excitement, 'she leaned back further revealing her blue garters.' As the sexual tension mounts, so do the fireworks, with one 'going up over the trees up, up and, in the tense hush, they were all breathless with excitement as it went higher and higher and she had to lean back more and more'. She blushes, and Bloom 'could see other things too', her fashionable knickers, 'the fabric that caresses the skin . . . and she let him and she saw that he saw and then it went so high it went out of sight a moment and she was trembling in every limb from being bent so far back he had a full view high up above her knee no-one ever not even on the swing' had seen this 'and she wasn't ashamed and he wasn't either to look in that immodest way like that because he couldn't resist'.[17]

Now it seemed Bloom was masturbating and this aroused Gerty even more, and the fireworks joined in their mounting mutual excitement: 'a rocket sprang and bang shot blind and O! then the Roman candle burst and it was like a sigh of O! and everyone cried O! O! in raptures and it gushed out of it a stream of rain gold hair threads.' Then the climax passed: 'all was silent.' Gerty looked at Bloom 'as she bent forward quickly' while 'he coloured like a girl . . . What a brute he had been!' But 'there was an infinite store of mercy in those eyes, for him too a word of pardon even though he had erred and sinned.' It was 'their secret, only theirs'.[18] Some commentators have suggested the episode happens only in Gerty's or in Bloom's imagination or perhaps in the imaginations of both.

Fireworks set the tone of what some critics consider the greatest ever novel about adolescence, *Le Grand Meaulnes* (1913), the only book published in his lifetime by the French writer Alain-Fournier, who would be killed in the First World War. Set in the 1890s, the story is told by a 'timid and forlorn' fifteen-year-old boy. One Sunday, Augustin Meaulnes, tall and a couple of years older, appears in the village where the narrator's parents run the school. He makes his entrance holding a couple of 'half-scorched fireworks' he has found dumped after the 14 July celebrations. Though he has never met the narrator or his mother before, the youth pipes up: 'See what I found in your attic. Didn't it ever occur to you to have a look in there?' Meaulnes sticks the fireworks in the ground and produces a box of matches, to the astonishment of the narrator, who is not allowed to handle such things. Then nonchalantly, 'as if this would do till something better turned up', Meaulnes lights the damaged fuses, and 'two great bouquets of red and white stars soar up from the ground with a hiss', while the narrator stands 'in a magical glow, holding the tall newcomer by the hand, and not flinching'.[19] His credentials thus established, Meaulnes bestrides the book like a colossus, quickly becoming the centre of attention for all the boys at the school though he says little, and experiencing a whole series of larger-than-life adventures – running away, chancing on a ball in a mysterious chateau, falling in love with a beautiful girl and so on.

Writing about the same time, the eccentric cigar-smoking American poet Amy Lowell, who was posthumously awarded the Pulitzer Prize for Poetry, used pyrotechnics as a metaphor for a stormy relationship in 'Fireworks' (1915):

> whenever I see you, I burst apart
> And scatter the sky with my bursting heart.
> It spits and sparkles in the stars and balls,
> Buds into roses – and flares and falls.

She ends with the lines:

> Such fireworks as we make, we two!
> Because you hate me and I hate you.[20]

In Ernest Hemingway's classic novel of the Spanish Civil War, *For Whom the Bell Tolls* (1941), one of the Republican guerrillas waxes nostalgic about Valencia – the food, the wine, the love making, and 'the smell of burned powder from the firecrackers . . . that ran through the streets exploding each noon during the *Feria* [festival]'. Firecrackers engulfed the whole city, 'the explosions running along on poles and wires of the tramways, exploding with great noise and a jumping from pole to pole with a sharpness and a cracking of explosions you could not believe'.[21] But fireworks get a bigger part in an earlier Hemingway novel, *Fiesta* [*The Sun Also Rises*] (1927), with much of the action set among a group of British and Americans during the bull-running festival in Pamplona. One morning while they wait for their sherry in a café, 'the rocket that announced the fiesta went up in the square', leaving 'a grey ball of smoke high up . . . in the sky like a shrapnel burst'. Then comes another and a crowd gathers. Loud music starts, men dance along the street, and 'all the time rockets were going up,' launching a week of partying.[22] Drink-fuelled tensions rose among the characters as they competed for the affections of an aristocratic Englishwoman. By the last night, the weather has turned wet and windy, and the 'firework king' in charge of the display is having a miserable time, as his creations 'exploded and chased about in the crowd', while the camaraderie of the protagonists dissolved into a series of fist fights.[23]

The most blameless and generous character in Iris Murdoch's first novel, *Under the Net* (1954), is firework maker Hugo Belfounder, who is 'extremely large, both stout and tall', with a 'huge head' but 'a very gentle pair of dark eyes', and said by some to be based on the philosopher Wittgenstein. 'Objective and detached' and 'highly intelligent', Belfounder has inherited a flourishing arms business from his parents, but, being a pacifist, he got rid of the warlike bits and concentrated on fireworks.[24] He is successful, 'somehow money always stuck to Hugo', but what he really loves is working as a craftsman in his factory: 'the contrasting appeal of explosion and colour, the blending of pyrotechnical styles, the methods for combining éclat with duration . . . Hugo treated the set piece as if it were a symphony.' He says pyrotechnics should not really be compared with any other art, but if you must, 'compare them to music.' While for Browning, the transitory nature of fireworks is a source of sadness, for Belfounder, the best thing about them is 'their impermanence . . . what an *honest* thing a firework was. It was so patently just an ephemeral spurt of beauty of which in a moment nothing more was left. "That's what all art is really," said Hugo, "only we don't like to admit it."'[25]

The Great Fireworks Novel?

Perhaps the most passionate fictional exploration of a pyrotechnician comes, appropriately, in a children's story, *The Firework-Maker's Daughter* (1995) by Philip Pullman, probably best known for the *His Dark Materials* trilogy (1995–2000). The opening words: 'A thousand miles ago', set a magical, alchemical feel for the tale. The firework-maker Lalchand and his daughter Lila live in a land beyond jungle and mountains. Lila's mother died when she was a child. She was a 'cross little thing', but cheered up when Lalchand made a cradle for her in the corner of his workshop where she could see 'the sparks play and listen to the fizz and crackle of the gunpowder'. As soon as Lila was old enough, she started to learn the art of firework-making with Leaping Monkeys and Golden Sneezes (rather than rushing for a database of firework types, it is best to see these as fun, made-up names). Soon Lila is coming up with pyrotechnics of her own such as Tumbling Demons that 'sprayed out wicked little sparks'. After a couple of triumphs at displays, she asks Lalchand:

'Am I a proper Firework-Maker now?' 'No!'[26] is his brisk reply, and he looks at his daughter with her eyebrows scorched, her fingers stained with chemicals, and wonders how she will ever get a husband. Lila continues to learn the tricks of the trade, but Lalchand refuses to reveal 'the final secret', and she discovers that to find it, she needs to run away to 'the Grotto of Razvani, the Fire-Fiend in the heart of Mount Merapi, and bring back some of the Royal Sulphur'.[27] (Mount Merapi is a real volcano in Indonesia.)

When he finds she has gone, Lalchand is overcome with remorse, wishing he had trusted Lila and told her everything. He asks her friend Chulak to get her some magic water from the Goddess of the Emerald Lake, or Lila will surely die in the Fire-Fiend's flames. To provide Chulak with transport, Lalchand helps free the king's much-prized White Elephant. Meanwhile, Lila has to overcome many dangers including a tiger she scares off with a string of fireworks called Crackle-Dragons, but when she finally sees Mount Merapi, she knows: 'I belong to that mountain, and it belongs to me!'[28] It is barren and empty, but the ground rumbles. Then a stone comes rolling down the slope, almost hitting her, and reveals a great hole. She goes in, of course, and encounters complete darkness, but soon little flames appear, then fire imps dancing to the clashing of hammers and anvils, until finally the rock walls melt and Razvani himself appears - his body a mass of flame, his face a scorching light. In a voice like a forest fire, he asks by what right she has come to his grotto. She replies she wants to be a firework-maker and asks him for Royal Sulphur. Razvani roars with laughter and shows her a procession of ghosts, each lamenting that they had not worked hard enough at the pyrotechnic craft. The Fire-Fiend says he will give her the Royal Sulphur, but first she must walk into his flames. Her feet blister and she fears she cannot go on in the dreadful heat, until she hears Chulak with the magic water. She drinks it, and the flames play up and down her body without harming her. 'When you reach the heart of the fire,' says Razvani, 'all your illusions vanish.' He tells her there is no such thing as Royal Sulphur. The whole world is an illusion: 'Everything that exists flickers like a flame for a moment and then vanishes.'[29] Then he disappears.

Chulak has some bad news. For helping the White Elephant to escape, Lalchand has been sentenced to death, but the beast is resourceful. Not only does it carry Lila and Chulak home, it also persuades the king to give Lalchand a chance. In a week's time, it will be the New Year fireworks competition. If the firework-maker wins, his life will be spared. In this ultimate pyrotechnics contest, the other competitors are Dr Puffenflasch from Heidelberg, who has invented a multi-stage rocket that explodes into the shape of a giant frankfurter sausage, Signor Scorcini from Naples, whose speciality is mock sea battles, and Col. Sam Sparkington from Chicago, with 'The Greatest Firework Show in the Galaxy'. Lalchand and Lila work flat out. The daughter devises a new fusing system to allow a hundred fireworks to be set off in one go, while Lalchand invents a fuse that will burn under water, and they come up with something so new they cannot find a name for it until they think of 'Foaming Moss'.

On the great day, Dr Puffenflasch has in tow a dozen pyrotechnicians in white overalls with clipboards. Scorcini has a great model galleon with a huge crew, while Col. Sparkington boasts an enormous red, white and blue rocket with a saddle on its back. The other competitors are unaware of the huge stakes for which Lalchand and Lila are playing. As they set up, they are polite enough, but it is clear they do not think much of the father-and-daughter show. The contest is to be decided on the duration of audience applause for each display. Puffenflasch goes first. The climax is a tribute to the king's favourite dish, with a giant prawn turning faster and faster until it dissolves into salmon-pink sparks. The crowd love it. Scorcini's galleon comes ablaze with sparklers and Catherine wheels. A giant octopus attacks and the sailors fight it off with Jumping Jacks until Neptune emerges from the waves to save the day. Sparkington kicks off with saucer-shaped fireworks that, unlike most pyrotechnics, travel down to earth instead of up from it. The climax sees the American jump aboard his giant rocket. A Cherokee chief fires a blazing arrow that ignites it and sends it soaring up to an artificial moon as Sparkington waves his hat. When it lands, a dozen craters fly open, and little moon people emerge, bow to the king and then depart on rockets of their own. The audience goes even wilder.

Follow that! Lalchand and Lila have no choice but to try. They start gently with 'little lotus flowers made of white fire' that suddenly 'open on the water with no hint of where the fire had come from', and the Foaming Moss, which spreads itself across the grass: 'a million million little points of light all so close together that they looked as soft as velvet'. Now a great 'Aaah' comes from the spectators. The next part will be the most difficult, inspired by Lila's visit to the Fire-Fiend's grotto, but all depending on the perfect performance of delayed-action fuses they had had no time to test. Everything is dark. Then a light 'shivered downwards, leaving a trail of red sparks . . . like a crack opening in the night'.

Drumbeats get louder and louder until out of that red crack, 'a great cascade of brilliant red, orange and yellow lava seemed to pour down and spread out like the carpet of fire in the Grotto.' Now their competitors are watching wide-eyed like children. 'When the lava carpet had flowed down almost to the edge of the lake . . . suddenly, dancing as he had in the Grotto, Razvani himself seemed to be there, whirling and stamping and laughing for joy in the play of the eternal fire.'[30]

Lalchand and Lila dance too. No matter what happens now, 'everything was worth it, for a moment of joy like this!'[31] Their fellow competitors lead the applause, which goes on and on. The king quietly sets Lalchand free, and the competitors chat, swapping bits of know-how, 'because there are no secrets among true artists'. Lalchand apologizes to Lila for failing to realize she would want to be a firework-maker. As for the Royal Sulphur, to Razvani it might be an illusion, 'but human beings call it wisdom.' And Lila understands: 'To make good fireworks you had to love them, every little sparkler or Crackle-Dragon.'[32] *The Firework-Maker's Daughter* was turned into an opera by the British composer David Bruce in 2013, using Indonesian gamelan instruments and puppetry. *Guardian* critic Alfred Hickling noted the firework effects were created with 'little more than marker pens and overhead projectors', but said the 'comically simple' approach elicited 'genuine oohs and aahs'.[33]

The Visual Arts: Early Depictions

Fireworks were appearing in art by the late sixteenth century. The oldest, reproduced by Alan Brock, is a print of a display at Nuremberg in 1570. Then we have two etchings by Franz Hogenberg, who specialized in depicting current events, showing celebrations for a duke's wedding on the Rhine at Dusseldorf in 1587: one portrays a mock naval battle while the other features 'firework machines in the form of sea monsters'.[34] Before the invention of photography, art had an important function that it has since largely lost – recording – and most of the pictures doing this job were perfectly workmanlike, but are not generally regarded as artistically distinguished, such as Jean Le Pautre's engraving of fireworks on the canal at Versailles (1676) and Jakob Wangner's portrayal of a display at Frankfurt in honour of Philip v of Spain (1741). Not that we can always be confident about the accuracy of these early representations. Often the artists did not attend the event, but relied on sketches by people who had. Indeed, sometimes the pictures were done before it

Anonymous 'before and after' depiction of fireworks display, Nuremberg, 1659, etching print.

happened. They might also exaggerate, because the point was to enhance the reputation of the powerful people who put displays on, and often more people saw the illustrations than the events.

During the seventeenth century, German artists sometimes took a 'before and after' approach, with the picture divided in half – one part showing the scene in daytime before the display was fired, the other the night-time spectacle as the fireworks went off. Meanwhile, more off-beat approaches emerged. Giovanni Ambrogio Brambilla's 1579 depiction of the girandola at the climax of the Castel Sant'Angelo display in Rome shows a blasé audience who seem to be chatting among themselves rather than admiring the show, but they are so small in the frame as to be almost a detail. By the eighteenth century, fireworks were also playing a more metaphorical role in pictures. William Hogarth's print *Before* (1736) features a man determinedly pulling a woman towards a bed. In the background a picture on the wall shows a cupid lighting a rocket.

Rome's girandola became a favourite subject for painters in the eighteenth century. In 1775 the German landscape painter Jacob Philipp Hackert portrayed the fireworks in dramatic style, very much as the 'wheatsheaf' described by Robert Adam. Hackert, incidentally, was a friend of Goethe, who wrote his biography. The best-known portrayal probably comes from the British artist Joseph Wright of Derby. The mid-eighteenth century saw the emergence of the theory of the 'sublime' in art – that it should concentrate on motivating the strongest feelings humans can experience. One exponent was Wright, who became celebrated for his dramatic depictions of industry and scientific experiments, but most of all for his expert use of light, particularly artificial light. So the Castel Sant' Angelo display was right up his street, and he painted it at least four times. The pictures make you think the real thing must

William Hogarth, *Before*, 1736, etching and engraving.

have been pretty intimidating. One bears a striking resemblance to a work Wright created of Vesuvius erupting, in which the volcano is placed at virtually the same place in the frame as the girandola. In 1776 Wright wrote of the two spectacles: 'the one is the greatest effect of Nature the other of Art that I suppose can be.'[35] This linking of fireworks and volcanoes was drawing on a well-established tradition. As long ago as 1637, for the visit to Rome of the Holy Roman Emperor, the Cardinal of Savoy had commissioned an elaborate fireworks machine simulating Mount Etna.

Early Asian pictures of fireworks often have a more intimate feel. While some Indian works feature large-scale events with distant pyrotechnics appearing in the background, as in *The Marriage Procession of Dara Shikoh* from the 1740s, more often they portray domestic scenes, like an eighteenth-century miniature from Rajasthan showing two women with sparklers merging their sparks to make a shape resembling a tree. Sometimes lovers are pictured, each holding a firework. In *Embracing Lovers with Sparklers* (*c.* 1775) the artist used reflective gold and silver paint for the sparks cascading to the ground, making them seem to flicker when viewed by candlelight.

In sixteenth-century Europe Brambilla may have poked a little fun at those watching fireworks, but the audience became a key component for Japanese artists, who often made the spectators more important than the pyrotechnics themselves. There were conventional pictures of big displays, such as *Fireworks over Ryogoku Bridge* (1858) by the great nineteenth-century landscape artist Utagawa Hiroshige, but in Utagawa Toyokuni's woodblock print of the same scene in the 1820s, the fireworks are virtually incidental and the artist is much more interested in the glamorous crowd in which wealthy business people rub shoulders with entertainers and sex workers. He picks out details such as a woman lifting the hem of her kimono to reveal she has used a red dye, forbidden under laws banning ostentatious clothes. And Hiroshige's own picture *Enjoying the Fireworks and the Cool of the Evening at Ryogoku Bridge* (*c.* 1847) concentrates on a couple of spectators rather than the event.

Western Art in the Nineteenth Century and the Great Whistler Controversy

J.M.W. Turner painted a number of watercolours of fireworks over Venice, such as *The Campanile of San Marco from the Hotel Europa at Night, with Fireworks over the Molo* (1840). By this time his preoccupation was exploring dramatic effects of light and shade, and these pyrotechnic pictures are quite abstract, with the artist using only a few colours: subdued blue, red and brown, with white for the flashes of the fireworks in the *Campanile* painting. If Turner is often regarded as Britain's greatest artist, another British, or at least British-based, painter is considered by some to have painted the greatest ever firework picture.

James McNeill Whistler was born in the United States but came to London when he was in his mid-twenties. He became interested in what he saw as the parallels between art and music, declaring: 'Nature contains the elements, in colour and form, of all pictures, as the keyboard contains the notes of all music. But the artist is born to pick, and choose, and group with science, these elements, that the result may be beautiful – as the musician gathers his notes, and forms his chords, until he bring forth from chaos glorious harmony.'[36] Whistler painted a series of *Nocturnes* – the title also of a set of piano works by Chopin. The painter lived just a short walk from London's Cremorne pleasure gardens, where fireworks were a major attraction, and three of his *Nocturnes* featured pyrotechnics. In *Nocturne in Blue and Gold: Old Battersea Bridge* (1872–5) they are very much in the background – the streak of a rising rocket and some golden stars falling into the river. *Nocturne: Black and Gold: The Fire Wheel* (*c.* 1872–7), a very dark picture, gives a bigger role to a huge blazing Catherine wheel, with sparks flying from its edge. Then there was *Nocturne in Black and Gold: The Falling Rocket* (1875). It is another dark picture, though the sky is speckled all over with golden pyrotechnic flecks of light. In the foreground is a small trio of ethereal, almost transparent spectators. Today many regard the picture as a masterpiece, but when it first appeared it stirred up a hornets' nest of controversy.

The Falling Rocket is almost abstract, and Whistler was anxious to evoke rather than to show, to break with the Pre-Raphaelite tradition of paintings that told a story, saying he wanted to divest 'the picture of any outside anecdotal interest which might have been otherwise attached to it. A nocturne is an arrangement of line, form and colour first.'[37] But his avant-garde approach attracted plenty of criticism. *Punch* summed up the view of its detractors: 'Above, all fog; below, all inky flood; For subject – it had none.' Even *The Times*'s art critic, who quite liked the picture, felt it was more like a study than a finished canvas, but the eminent critic John Ruskin launched a trenchant attack, accusing Whistler of flinging 'a pot of paint in the public's face' when he asked two hundred guineas for the work. Whistler sued him for libel. During the trial, the art critic William Michael Rossetti, brother of Dante Gabriel and Christina, doubted whether fireworks should be painted at all, opining: 'I have seen them represented before in pictures – but I do not think it is a good subject.' One of the most famous exchanges came when Whistler was asked how long the painting had taken him and he replied a couple of days. The Attorney-General was horrified: 'The labour of two days is that for which you ask two hundred guineas?' 'No,' replied the artist, 'I ask it for the knowledge I have gained in the work of a lifetime.'[38] Whistler won his case, but was awarded the deliberately derisory damages of a farthing. The legal fees bankrupted him.

Across the Channel in the later years of the nineteenth century, the French artist Ferdinand du Puigaudeau featured fireworks in some of his pictures. He was fascinated by traditional Breton festivals and by the effects of flickering light. These interests come together in his depiction of the 14 July celebrations, *Carnival at Night, St Pol de Léon* (*c.* 1894–8),

Winslow Homer, *Fire-Works on the Night of the Fourth of July*, 1868, wood engraving.

Félix Vallotton, *Fireworks, The World's Fair VI*, 1901, woodcut on tinted Japan paper.

with pyrotechnics in the background, while they play a bigger part in *Fireworks over the Port* (1890). Another French painter from that era, Gaston La Touche, also portrayed fireworks at big events, though the spectators in pictures such as *Dinner at the Casino* (*c.* 1903) and *The Joyous Festival* (*c.* 1906) tend to be drawn from higher society.

Regarded by many as the greatest American painter of the nineteenth century, Winslow Homer was another who put a pyrotechnics audience centre stage, in *Fire-Works on the Night of the Fourth of July*

(1868). As a large crowd watches, a falling rocket crashes into the top hat of a toff. Homer became better known for his paintings of American seascapes, and a dozen years later he produced a very different take on the Fourth of July festivities with a more conventional impressionistic night-time watercolour, *Sailboat and Fourth of July Fireworks* (1880). The Swiss artist Félix Vallotton, who settled in Paris, became known for his witty portrayals of bourgeois life. In a 1900 woodcut, he too featured a crowd watching fireworks, at the World's Fair in the French capital, showing faces, some rather apprehensive, gazing upwards from the bottom of the frame. Another painter more interested in the audience than in the fireworks was the Russian Konstantin Somov, though in *A Gallant Scene* (1918), it is not clear how interested the audience are in the display, as a harlequin tries to seduce a young woman while pyrotechnics grace the background.

Like Whistler, the Belgian artist James Ensor was a pioneer of the avant-garde. Regarded as a forerunner of Expressionism and Surrealism, he often painted apocalyptic scenes in apparently mundane settings. So his *Fireworks* (1887) features a catastrophic explosion of red, orange and yellow in the background, while in the foreground a host of small figures are strolling around quite unconcerned.

As mainstream art veered increasingly towards the abstract, fireworks seemed a natural subject. The Canadian-born modernist Edward Middleton Manigault depicted a display over the River Hudson in *The Rocket* (1909). If a single rocket is responsible for the dazzling white, orange, yellow, red and blue colours that burst in the sky, it must have been quite a firework. Manigault's bold, vibrant colours are similar to those being used by the Fauve ('wild beasts') school active at that time in Europe.

Modern Art

The Dutch artist of the impossible M. C. Escher, creator of staircases or flocks of birds that defy all laws of nature or geometry, turned his attention to pyrotechnics in his lithograph *Fireworks* (1933). It is actually a fairly conventional black-and-white portrayal of a rocket exploding in a parachute-like shape of perhaps forty falling trails of light over a circle of spectators. Also in the 1930s, the English painter Eric Ravilious, lost presumed killed in 1942 while working as a war artist and probably best known for his landscapes, painted a number of fireworks scenes. He also produced a book of shopfronts entitled *High Street* (1938) which included the print *Fireworks*. This depicts a newsagent's, leading outlets for pyrotechnics in those days, whose window is dominated by a stylized rocket.

Another modern painter who found good material in pyrotechnics was the idiosyncratic Spanish surrealist Joan Miró. As he entered his eighties, he produced a *Fireworks Triptych* (1974) with splashes and flicks of black and grey paint on a white canvas, plus the odd smudge or dot of bright colour. The result is like a negative of the usual firework effect of bright lights against a black sky. Five years later, he tackled pyrotechnics again, using rather mysteriously shaped coloured squiggles, perhaps more typical of his work, against a background of smoky grey. Pyrotechnics also proved an inspiration for the American Abstract Expressionists. Perhaps the best known, Jackson Pollock, used his technique of dripping paint on to the canvas to create *Number 17, Fireworks* (1950) – splashes of colour against black. Another, Sam Francis, used the drip technique to apply bright colours to a white surface, making his *Fireworks* (1963) a brighter and more vibrant work. Yet another, Helen Frankenthaler, applied a method known as 'colour field', covering the whole canvas in similar hues. In *Royal Fireworks* (1975) the predominant colour was orange. In 2000 she painted *Grey Fireworks,* which does what it says in the title. Is the work an evocation of the grey smoke that often envelops firework displays, especially when bonfires are lit?

The Swiss kinetic sculptor Jean Tinguely produced a lithograph entitled *Fireworks*, a miscellany of bright colours, children's imagery and text against a black background, but more significant is the role fireworks played in his theory of art. In 1960 he used flywheels, bicycles, bits of old machinery and other discarded items to build an 8-metre-high structure in the sculpture garden of New York's Museum of Modern Art which he called *Homage to New York*. It was meant to self-destruct. Tinguely said he wanted to 'liberate' himself, and 'the best way to do this was to make it self-destroying, like Chinese fireworks,' adding that they were 'a very powerful art'. Before it could completely self-destruct, *Homage to New York* caught fire, and firemen rushed up and hacked it to pieces with their axes, but the artist said what mattered to him was that there was nothing left 'except what remained in the minds of a few people'. Echoing Iris Murdoch's Hugo Belfounder, he declared that, like a fireworks display, it was 'ephemeral . . . the opposite of the cathedrals'.[39]

Some of Tinguely's absurdism was evident in the output of American conceptual artist Dennis Oppenheim, whose works sometimes featured pyrotechnics. *Launching Structure #3* (1982) was described by one writer as 'myriad glass tubes, reminiscent of a chemistry laboratory . . . Some of the tubes are loaded with fireworks, others remain empty.' It was an 'enormous and preposterous creation'. The writer believed 'Oppenheim's flares and fireworks – shooting out at all angles and at heady speeds' were a symbol of 'the unpredictability and mayhem' of a creative mind.[40] Fireworks featured in yet another genre with the Japanese artist Kiyoshi Yamashita, who had suffered neurological damage as a result of a childhood illness. It is said that at one point his IQ was measured at 68, but he became one of the country's best-loved artists and was dubbed the 'Van Gogh of Japan'. He produced several naive pictures of colourful firework events before his death aged 49 in 1971.

Fireworks in Films

Fireworks started appearing in films soon after films themselves appeared in 1895. During their first decade, a three-minute French silent comic short *Unexpected Fireworks* (1905) told the tale of a pyrotechnic prank. It was one of more than four hundred films made by Georges Méliès, a professional magician and theatre manager who was said to be the first person to hire actors to make films that told genuine stories. The short begins outside a closed fireworks shop where an unkempt drunkard attempts to proposition a woman who gives him short shrift. He then passes out. A group of slightly demonic youngsters appear, break into the shop and emerge with a selection of fireworks, with which they surround the unconscious figure. Once the mischief-makers set them off, he wakes and starts running round in alarm before disappearing in a cloud of smoke, to the delight of his tormentors.

The humorous possibilities of pyrotechnics have remained part of the movies' staple diet. In the madcap musical *Thoroughly Modern Millie* (1967), Twenties flapper Millie Dillmount, played by Julie Andrews, carelessly discards a cigarette through the window of a fireworks factory, setting off a series of explosions which enable her to dash in and release the man she loves and a group of girls who are about to disappear into the white slave trade. A chase in a Hong Kong fireworks warehouse provides the climax for *Revenge of the Pink Panther* (1978), the last of Peter Sellers's Inspector Clouseau comedy thrillers. An assortment of villains pursue the bungling detective to no avail as fireworks go off all over the place, and one of the baddies ends up with firecrackers attached to his bottom. Another police comedy, *The Naked Gun* (1988), centres on accident-prone Lieutenant Frank Drebin, played by Leslie Nielsen. In a car chase, he pursues a would-be assassin who crashes into a petrol tanker, then a ballistic missile and finally a fireworks factory. As an impromptu pyrotechnics extravaganza bursts out behind him, attracting a crowd, Drebin keeps shouting: 'Please disperse! Nothing to see here!'

One of the most acclaimed feature films in which fireworks make an appearance is also one of the earliest, *Sunrise*, which came out right at the end of the silent era in 1927. Directed in Hollywood by the German F. W. Murnau, who also made the pioneering vampire film *Nosferatu* (1922), its opening caption proclaims the film is a story 'of no place and every place'. In 2012 the British Film Institute's *Sight and Sound* critics' poll named *Sunrise* the fifth best film of all time, with its inventive cinematography, dreamlike atmosphere and dramatic expressionist lighting. There is not much to the plot. A farmer is tempted by a 'woman from the city', who is plainly very different from his virtuous wife, played by Janet Gaynor who won the first ever best actress Oscar for her roles in *Sunrise* and other films. The city woman tries to persuade the hero to drown his wife, sell his farm and go off with her. So the man rows his wife out in a boat, ostensibly on a trip to the city, but cannot bring himself to do the dastardly deed. When the couple get to the metropolis, they have a passionate, romantic reconciliation. While they are enjoying themselves in an amusement park, fireworks burst into the sky briefly but spectacularly. In the end, virtue triumphs and the man stays with his wife.

Some of the scenes in *Sunrise* might in later years have fallen foul of the Hays Code. This appeared in 1934 and barred assorted smut from the movie screen, such as 'excessive and lustful kissing'. So film director Alfred Hitchcock took a leaf out of Hogarth's book and used pyrotechnics as a metaphor for seduction in *To Catch a Thief* (1955). Set on the French Riviera, it is a typical witty Hitchcockian thriller with everyone double-crossing everyone else. The main characters are a possibly retired jewel thief, played by Cary Grant, and the daughter of a wealthy widow, portrayed by Grace Kelly. They flirt in an elegant room while pyrotechnics light the sky outside the window. She says: 'If you really want to see fireworks, it's better with the lights out,' and darkens the room. Then she adds: 'Tonight you're going to see one of the Riviera's most fascinating sights,' and, after a suggestive pause: 'I was talking about the fireworks.' She teases him about whether he is a thief and whether he is staring at the opulent necklace nestling just above her breasts. As the couple finally embrace, the director cuts to the spectacular fireworks. In *Adventureland* (2009), pyrotechnics actually lead to romance. James, freshly graduated from college, takes a job at an Adventureland amusement park to make some money. There he meets another worker, Emily, and while they are watching a spectacular display together, they realize their mutual attraction and go off to make love.

A sadder romantic use of fireworks comes in *Forrest Gump* (1994) when the simple but wise hero sits outside with Jenny, the girl he loves, watching a display reflected in the waters of a lake. The pair then go inside to watch more pyrotechnics on television, in what Gump says in voiceover was the happiest time of his life. It becomes the prelude to a marriage proposal, but Jenny turns him down. At the end of the film, the couple do finally wed, but Jenny dies soon after.

Fireworks also play a bittersweet romantic role in the BAFTA-winning *The Theory of Everything* (2014). As a young man, the great theoretical physicist Professor Stephen Hawking goes to a Cambridge ball with Jane, who will become his wife. Hawking politely but adamantly refuses to dance with her, and instead starts talking about stars and how they are born and die, just as the fireworks begin. They watch the display, laugh a lot, ride a carousel and then go out to look at the stars. He takes her hand and asks her to dance, and they share a first kiss, but the scene is tinged with sadness because we know their marriage will break up and that Hawking will be paralysed by motor neurone disease.

Not surprisingly, fireworks often feature in children's films. In Walt Disney's *Mary Poppins* (1964), Mary and the two little ones she looks after as a nanny are doing a song and dance routine on the rooftops of Edwardian London with a group of chimney sweeps when an eccentric neighbour and naval officer, Admiral Boom, announces: 'We're being attacked by Hottentots.' He orders his 'first mate' Mr Binnacle to fire a volley of fireworks, which scatters the sweeps, who rush down the chimney into the children's house, still singing and dancing. *G-Force* (2009) features a team of small furry animals – hamsters, guinea pigs and such – getting together to save the world from an evil billionaire. In a thrilling chase scene, the animals speed along in individual plastic balls that can go 65 miles an hour. Their pursuers' SUV hits a stash of fireworks, which keep exploding around them. As the animals escape, they fly over a group of entranced children, and advise: 'Don't try this at home!'

Then there are films about children or young people. *The Boy Who Could Fly* (1986) is a fantasy about an autistic boy named Eric who can take to the skies. He makes friends with Milly, a girl whose terminally ill father killed himself. The film exploits the magical quality of pyrotechnics as Eric takes Milly flying and they share a kiss, more chaste than Grace Kelly and Cary Grant's, while they watch a firework display from a seat up in the clouds. There is an underlying sadness about the scene to which the celebratory nature of fireworks forms a counterpoint.

Fireworks also provide one of the few bright spots in the award-winning fable *Beasts of the Southern Wild* (2012), set in a dirt-poor Louisiana bayou town called The Bathtub, under threat from rising sea water. A six-year-old girl named Hushpuppy is the main character, and an exhilarating sequence features her joyfully charging through the streets with dozens of others carrying big sparklers as fireworks burst overhead. Another poignant pyrotechnics episode comes in *Fandango* (1985) – the story of a group of American student friends enjoying their last few days of freedom before they are drafted to the Vietnam War. On an eventful road trip, they meet some girls and decide to have a fireworks fight in a cemetery. The only rule of the game appears to be: 'no aiming at the face.' It is a fun, lively sequence, and no one gets hurt but it ends abruptly when two of the boys spot the grave of a corporal aged nineteen who has been killed in Vietnam.

Pyrotechnics perform a triumphant role, though again tinged with sadness, in *Meet Joe Black* (1998). Joe Black is Death, arrived on Earth and taking over a human body in the form of heartthrob Brad Pitt. His assignment is to collect a movie tycoon played by Anthony Hopkins, but he falls in love with Hopkins's daughter. The tycoon's birthday party is to be positively his last appearance, and a top-class fireworks display erupts as he and Joe walk off into the darkness. Then the pyrotechnics become even more dramatic when Joe reappears alone and is reunited with Hopkins's daughter.

Fireworks also mean triumph at the end of *The Natural* (1984), which climaxes with Robert Redford, playing ageing baseball star Roy Hobbs, sweating as he waits an age for the pitcher to hurl the ball at him. When it finally arrives, slowed down in dramatic close-up, Hobbs's bat smashes into it with a thunderous bang, and the ball flies high, crashing into the stadium lights. A dream-like fireworks display suddenly erupts across the sky as Hobbs slow-mos around the bases for a home run, while sparks fall gently in the darkness around him. It is the comeback of a player who was robbed of the best years of his career when he took a bullet from a woman obsessed with shooting the best baseball player in the world. This upbeat ending, incidentally, does not feature in Bernard Malamud's 1952 novel on which the film is based.

In the Oscar-nominated *Avalon* (1990), fireworks represent the wonder America engenders in a new Jewish immigrant. He arrives in Baltimore on the Fourth of July, knowing nothing of Independence Day, to find people carrying sparklers and fireworks exploding in the sky above. 'It was the most beautiful place you have ever seen in your life,' he says, feeling as though the pyrotechnics are a celebration of his arrival.

It is the 14 July Bastille Day fireworks in Paris that burst into *Les Amants du Pont Neuf* (The Lovers on the Bridge, 1991). Juliette Binoche plays a young artist losing her sight and living rough with a vagrant on the Pont Neuf, which is closed for repairs during the two-hundredth anniversary of the French Revolution. It is a headily romantic film, with the plot dismissed as preposterous by some. The pyrotechnics are spectacular as the lovers fire gunshots into the sky and dance along the bridge in an energetically choreographed sequence.

A dazzling fireworks display at Jay Gatsby's party in *The Great Gatsby* (2013) establishes that the hero never does anything by halves. It has the considerable task of not being outshone by the smile Leonardo DiCaprio, in the part of Gatsby, bestows on his neighbour. The neighbour has, in the ear of another guest, been ruing the fact that although he lives next door to Gatsby, they have never met, whispering: 'They say he's third cousin to the Kaiser and second cousin to the devil.' The guest replies: 'I'm afraid I haven't been a very good host, old sport. You see. I'm Gatsby.' Then he raises his glass, and in voiceover, the neighbour says: 'He smiled one of those rare smiles that you may come across four or five times in life. It seemed to understand you and believe in you just as you would like to be understood, and believed in.' The film won an Oscar for best production design.

Pyrotechnics are enlisted to convey bitter irony in Brian De Palma's paranoid thriller *Blow Out* (1981). John Travolta plays a sound recordist gathering effects for a low-budget slasher movie, who stumbles on evidence that a presidential hopeful, apparently killed in a car accident, has actually been murdered. A small-time blackmailer named Sally acquires the only film of the incident, but the man behind the politician's death murders her and destroys the film, and with it any hope that the truth will be revealed. As Travolta cradles Sally's dead body, the American flag and a celebratory firework display appear in the background. Another film in which a fireworks display provides a background for violence is the gay Western *Brokeback Mountain* (2005) when one of the central characters, Ennis, launches a vicious assault on a biker who has made a mocking comment about his relationship with his wife, saying Ennis had 'Probably quit givin' it' to her.

Sometimes directors use fireworks just to make things more chilling. In Martin Scorsese's *Cape Fear* (1991), they provide an alarming backdrop for Robert De Niro's terrifying villain who is pursuing the hero's family, while in the black comedy slasher *Uncle Sam* (1996), Sam, who has risen from the dead as a zombie after being killed in the First Gulf War, uses Fourth of July fireworks as one of the weapons with which he disposes of what he considers undesirable elements such as flag burners, grave desecrators, tax dodgers and lying politicians.

Perhaps it is because pyrotechnics are still a mystery to most of us that they often appear in fantasy films. A crowd wearing Guy Fawkes masks and hats gather at the climax of the dystopian political thriller *V for Vendetta* (2005) to watch fireworks rip through London's Houses of Parliament, blowing them to bits, while the soundtrack plays Tchaikovsky's '1812 Overture', a favourite for the finale of outdoor summer concerts accompanied by pyrotechnics. Based on a graphic novel, the film is the story of V, a mysterious freedom fighter in a Fawkes outfit who overthrows a totalitarian government that has taken over the UK. At the end of the movie, as the people in the crowd take off their masks and hats, the fireworks form a red V in the sky over what is left of the Palace of Westminster. Pyrotechnics play an ingenious role in another dystopian movie, *A Quiet Place* (2018). Blind aliens with very sharp hearing have taken over the world and are killing off the remaining humans. The only way to survive is to keep very quiet, which is extremely inconvenient for Evelyn, played by Emily Blunt, who is about to give birth. Her husband and son set off fireworks to drown out the sound of her cries.

Fantasy coalesces with humour in a spectacular fireworks scene in *The Lord of the Rings: The Fellowship of the Ring* (2001). During a very lively birthday party, two mischievous hobbits steal one of Gandalf the great wizard's fireworks, which is shaped like a dragon. As well as being naughty, the pair are also incompetent, so they set it off inside a tent. It goes up like a rocket, scorching their faces and taking the tent with it, then soars spectacularly into the sky before turning into the form of a dragon that swoops low over the crowd to their initial terror and subsequent delight as it explodes in a host of stars. Gandalf makes the two miscreants do the washing up as punishment.

Another popular fantasy film in which magical fireworks metamorphosize into a dragon is *Harry Potter and the Order of the Phoenix* (2007). Based on J. K. Rowling's novel, it continues the story of Harry's life at Hogwarts School of Witchcraft and Wizardry. While the pupils are sitting an exam, supervised by Harry's adversary, Dolores Umbridge, the Defence Against the Dark Arts teacher, she encounters a tiny little firework weaving crazy patterns in the air. Then two boys wing their way through the hall on broomsticks, letting off pyrotechnics and setting the examination papers flying. Finally the fireworks turn into a dragon that chases Ms Umbridge away.

Along with *Sunrise*, perhaps the most critically acclaimed of all films in which pyrotechnics figure is *Fireworks* (1997), or *Hana-Bi* as it was known in Japan. It was directed by Takeshi Kitano, a television comedian who also carved out a career making and starring in bleak, violent crime films, often playing in art-house cinemas. *Hana-Bi* won the Golden Lion at the Venice International Film Festival in what was described as a 'rare case of a jury verdict wholeheartedly endorsed by the critical cognoscenti'.[41] Typically, Kitano's central character is a world-weary anti-hero, a detective named Nishi, who has to quit the police after an arrest goes wrong, leaving one of his colleagues dead and another two seriously injured. Nishi's wife has leukaemia, and he is forced to borrow from yakuza gangsters to pay for her treatment. When he runs into trouble repaying them, he robs a bank and then shoots dead the yakuza who have been pursuing him. Although there are plenty of metaphorical 'fireworks' in terms of gunfights, literal pyrotechnics play quite a small role in the film as Nishi lets some off one night while he and his wife are on a road trip to iconic Mount Fuji. When one of the fireworks fails to go off, the ex-detective walks over cautiously to investigate, only for it to suddenly take off, knocking him over to his wife's amusement. The outdoor fireworks scene mixes through to a naive painting of fireworks done by one of the detectives injured in the incident that ended Nishi's career. Finally, two of his former colleagues arrive to arrest him, but he asks if he can have a few moments with his wife, and the couple sit down on a beach. Two shots are heard off screen, but we do not see what has happened.

Animated Films

Fireworks are again a prelude to romance in Disney's *Aladdin* (1992) when the street urchin with the lamp watches them with the free-spirited Princess Jasmine. After some sparky verbal sparring, the princess lays her head on Aladdin's shoulder, and then, as he is giving her a lift to her palace on his magic carpet, it suddenly pushes him into a kiss. Pyrotechnics also feature in other Disney animated films, such as *Alice in Wonderland* (1951), *Sleeping Beauty* (1959) and *The Little Mermaid* (1989). In *The Rescuers* (1977), an animal-and-insect rescue group fire them at the villainous Medusa, enabling the orphan girl Penny to escape her clutches, while in *Mulan* (1998), based on an ancient Chinese legend, the eponymous heroine in male disguise and her faithful little dragon use them to blow up the fearsome Hun leader Shan Yu.

Also from the Disney stable was *Toy Story* (1995), the first fully computer-animated film. Some have seen it as a buddy movie about two toys – Sheriff Woody, a traditional cowboy rag doll, and astronaut toy Buzz Lightyear, both owned by a boy named Andy. At first their relationship is rather fraught, because when Buzz arrives, he supplants Woody as Andy's favourite toy. Then just before Andy and his family are about to move house, Woody and Buzz are kidnapped by Sid, the bad boy next door who wrecks toys. Sid straps a rocket to Buzz and is about to launch him when a thunderstorm intervenes, allowing the two toys to escape. But by then the house move is underway. Woody and Buzz pursue the removal van in a toy car but its batteries run out, so they light the rocket that is still strapped to Buzz's back. At first it sends them speeding along the road on the car, then Woody shouts in alarm: 'I just lit a rocket. Rockets explode!' And as they are approaching the open back of the removal truck that contains all Andy's other toys, Buzz and Woody take off from the toy car and fly into the air. Woody exclaims, 'This is the part where we blow up!' but Buzz presses an ejector button on his spacesuit, and they break free from the rocket just in time. They overshoot the removal van and descend through the sunroof of the family car into the toy box on the seat next to Andy. He is thrilled to find them, while his mother assumes they were there all the time and that Andy had just failed to spot them. *Toy Story* was a commercial and critical success, winning an Academy Award for Special Achievement.

If you look at them from the side as they explode in the air, are fireworks round or flat? That is the question that keeps coming up in the

Japanese animated feature *Fireworks* (2017). The film centres on a small glass marble found by a schoolgirl named Nazuna. Throwing it allows people to rewind time and make different choices. The action takes place on the day of a fireworks display at the local shrine, and Nazuna is unhappy because she has just learned that her family will be moving her away from the area before the new school term starts. A group of boys, including one called Norimichi, get involved in a heated discussion about the shape of exploding fireworks. One says a sparkler is clearly round, but another argues that bigger fireworks may be different. They go off to climb a lighthouse so they can view from the side the pyrotechnics that will be going off at the shrine, but Norimichi sneaks off with Nazuna. From the boys' vantage point, the fireworks seem to be flat, but when Norimichi throws the marble, enabling Nazuna and him to go up the lighthouse instead of slipping away, he decides they are round. As they watch a beautiful display together, she says she does not care whether fireworks are round or flat so long as the two of them are together. In the final scene of the film, perhaps they are, because when the school register is taken, Norimichi is absent as well as Nazuna. Two young people also share a beautiful fireworks display in another Japanese animated feature, the intriguingly titled *I Want to Eat Your Pancreas* (2018), but the ending is less happy. Sakura, a girl who is suffering from a fatal pancreatic illness, is befriended by a classmate. They spend lots of time together, ticking off items on her bucket list, until Sakura dies, but not from her disease. Instead she falls victim to an apparently random stabbing.

Fireworks in Music

Not every opera is co-written by a pope-to-be, but *La Vita Humana* (Human Life, 1656) has that distinction. Composed to celebrate the conversion of Protestant Queen Christina of Sweden to Roman Catholicism, its libretto was written by Giulio Rospigliosi, who would become Pope Clement IX, and it concludes with fireworks. The opera is about choosing between the pleasures of the flesh and living devoutly. The fireworks at the end are seen by some as celebrating the triumph of good over evil, and by others as a reminder that the joys of life are fleeting just like the beauty of fireworks. The best-known piece of pyrotechnic classical music is probably Handel's *Music for the Royal Fireworks* (1748), an orchestral suite in five movements composed, as we saw, for the London festivities to celebrate the Treaty of Aix-la-Chapelle, where it was conducted by Handel himself, who was born in Germany but found fame and fortune in England. George II, who commissioned it, had wanted it played only by 'warlike instruments': oboes, bassoons, trumpets, horns, lots of drums, but no strings. Shortly after the first performance, Handel added string parts. Mozart described the piece as 'a spectacle of English pride and joy', and it remains a great favourite.[42]

The Russian composer Igor Stravinsky described his spirited *Fireworks* (1908) as a 'short orchestral fantasy'. It lasts for less than four minutes, but it had an important influence on his glittering career. Many commentators regard it as the piece in which the composer, then aged 26, first found his distinctive voice. Stravinsky wrote it as a wedding present for the daughter of his teacher, Nikolai Rimsky-Korsakov, himself a famous composer. The groom, another of Rimsky-Korsakov's pupils, thought it 'brilliantly scored, if it only proves playable, for it's incredibly hard'.[43] *Fireworks*'s initial public reception was often lukewarm, but pyrotechnics guru Arthur Brock was favourably impressed, saying the work had given him 'great pleasure' because 'with so little use of mechanical realism (I mean trombone and big drum)', Stravinsky had generated 'a wonderful impressionist rendering of pyrotechnic effects . . . with the successive crescendos which we always strive to obtain throughout our firework displays'.[44] The impresario Sergei Diaghilev praised *Fireworks* for its 'witty hints at the reproduction in sound of a sensational explosion of skyrockets'.[45] The story goes that he was sufficiently impressed to commission *The Firebird* (1910), a full-length ballet, from Stravinsky.

Another avant-garde composer, the Frenchman Claude Debussy, also took inspiration from pyrotechnics. The last of the 24 piano preludes he composed between 1909 and 1913 was called 'Fireworks'. In keeping with the artistic theories of the time, each piece was composed with a specific scene or image in mind. 'Fireworks', sometimes regarded as the most technically challenging, is supposed to depict a spectacular display over Paris. Like Diaghilev, the modern British composer Oliver Knussen was very taken with Stravinsky. His own short orchestral work *Flourish with Fireworks* (1988) was described by Knussen as a 'homage' to the Russian. One critic wrote that the piece 'captures the characteristics of every kind of firework imaginable – there are soaring chromatics that fly high like rockets, trills that spin like Catherine Wheels and pizzicato sections that are as bright as sparklers'.[46]

A decade after Debussy's preludes, the Jazz Age was dawning in America, and one of the genre's greatest practitioners, the trumpeter and vocalist Louis Armstrong, was soon recording a catchy, jolly instrumental called 'Fireworks' (1928) with his Hot Five. The tune was composed by Spencer Williams, who also wrote 'I Ain't Got Nobody' and other hits. In 1960s Britain, popular music experienced a rhythm and blues revival, in which one of the most talented artists was the Northern Irish singer and songwriter Van Morrison. He featured fireworks in a ten-minute-long atmospheric song called 'Almost Independence Day' (1972). Recorded in San Francisco, it describes Morrison's feelings as he looks out over the Bay on a cool night. It is contemplative and hypnotic, featuring the singer repeating simple phrases about how he can hear the fireworks and see boats on the water. Otherwise, there is little narrative. One commentator praised it as a voyage of discovery via performance and recording, rather than a work produced by meticulous rehearsal and redrafting.

While 'Almost Independence Day' may be enigmatic, the fireworks are real, but in much of popular music, they play a symbolic role. There is a touch of the psychedelic sound about the American rock band Blue Öyster Cult's 'Fireworks' (1977). It opens with lines about a woman who tries to escape a man, but he follows her to consummate their love. At which point, the earth shakes, and fireworks go off in her head. They are red, which some have been seen as a metaphor for the loss of virginity. Five years later came Siouxsie and the Banshees' 'Fireworks' (1982), a piece of raucous, rumbustious post-punk, melding the belligerence and frustration of punk with strings and more sophisticated instrumentation. The lyrics are not run-of-the-mill, mentioning a face full of cinders, gelignite teeth and a dance of dynamite, while the chorus proclaims that we are all boldly glowing fireworks. If Louis Armstrong gave fireworks an upbeat start in popular music, some later songs about them have been rather angst-ridden. 'Indoor Fireworks' (1986) is a typically plaintive offering about the collapse of a relationship from much-decorated Elvis Costello. Written at a time when his personal life was in turmoil, he seems to use indoor fireworks as a metaphor for things that look safe but are not, warning that even the seemingly harmless can burn your fingers.

As popular music moved into the twenty-first century, the American musician and vegan animal rights activist Moby released a soothing, ethereal instrumental entitled 'Fireworks' (2002) on his album *18*, which got to number one in a dozen countries. Three years later, angst was back with New Model Army's 'Fireworks Night' (2005). It is said to be about the death of the band's former drummer Robert Heaton the previous year, and hints at past tensions in the relationship. The song ponders whether Heaton might be floating above them, looking down, noting that Fireworks Night would be a good time, because he loved to build bonfires that lit up the cold winter nights. The Kaiser Chiefs' 'Indoor Firework' (2016) is much more up-tempo than Elvis Costello's very similarly named piece from thirty years before, but the indie rock band's song also has plenty of angst, with its chorus proclaiming that life is a war.

One of the most successful pyrotechnic pop songs was Katy Perry's more cheerful, metaphorical 'Firework' (2010). It got to number one in America and sold a million copies in the UK. 'Firework' has been seen as inspirational, as it urges listeners to, as it were, search for the firework inside themselves if they are feeling low. If you find the spark and light the light, you will shoot across the sky until your colours burst.

7
Use, Not Ornament

As in so many other spheres, war was crucial in the development of fireworks, but they were not useful only to the military. They would also play a role in rescues at sea, signalling, protecting crops and people, and even delivering mail. The intimacy between military and entertainment pyrotechnics is emphasized by the way so many companies straddled both fields. Some did this permanently, some temporarily, such as Crane's of Warmley, Gloucestershire, who switched to making grenades in the First World War, and Standard, who made items such as non-lethal training ammunition and parachute flares for the Second World War. In 2022 the global pyrotechnic munitions market was reckoned to be worth $3.35 billion.

Military Rockets

Rockets were probably being used in war by the Chinese by the early thirteenth century. A few decades later, they were appearing in Europe, and may have been on Indian battlefields by the fifteenth. As firearms became more accurate, rockets fell out of favour, but they made a comeback in eighteenth-century India. The Sultan of Mysore, Hyder Ali, was said to have a corps of 1,200 'rocketers' by 1766. The number reached 5,000 under his son, Tipu, famous for 'Tipu's Tiger', a mechanical model he had made of a tiger, his personal emblem, savaging a European man, which is now a major attraction at London's Victoria and Albert Museum. Tipu was very into new European technology such as barometers and thermometers, but the Indians stole a march in rockets, putting the propellant in an iron cylinder instead of the usual paper or board. This meant a more powerful mixture could be used, generating greater thrust and carrying the rocket further, up to 1,000 metres. At about 3 metres long, they certainly caused consternation among the British East India Company soldiers whom Hyder and Tipu were fighting in a series of wars. At the Battle of Pollilur in 1780, a rocket set fire to a British ammunition cart, helping to secure a famous victory for the Indians. Nineteen years later, no less a general than the redoubtable Colonel Arthur Wellesley, later the Duke of Wellington and victor of Waterloo, was worsted and his men 'retreated in disorder'. It is said that even after his great triumph over Napoleon, the duke continued to brood over this traumatic episode. Rocketeers had worked their way around to the British rear and then 'threw a great number of rockets at the same instant'. Some burst in the air while others bounced along the ground. There are reports of some being thrown by hand and others being set off from carts with three or four launchers. A young British officer wrote in his diary: 'No hail could be thicker,' as rockets caused 'death, wounds, and dreadful lacerations'.[1] Finally, in 1799, the British prevailed and Tipu was killed.

Word of Tipu's rockets reached the incorrigible inventor Sir William Congreve, whom we last encountered putting on a display to mark the hundredth anniversary of the Hanoverians coming to the English throne. Dubbed 'the ingenious Mr Congreve' by the press, he would take out around twenty patents for inventions including a 'rolling-ball clock' and a colour printing process.[2] In the first years of the nineteenth century, he seems to have been at a bit of a loose end, even dabbling in an anti-government newspaper. His father was comptroller of the Royal Laboratory at Woolwich, and in 1804, at his own expense, William began experimenting on rockets there, following in Indian footsteps to develop an iron case for the propellant. Congreve's father had friends in high places, notably the Prince Regent, later George IV, and soon his son was demonstrating his rockets for the prime minister, William Pitt the Younger. Pitt was sufficiently impressed for them to be rushed into production at the Royal Arsenal and by 1806 more than 13,000 had been made. Congreve reasoned that rockets would be useful for the navy because they eliminated the problem of recoil, which made cannons so tricky to use on ships, and he was present when what became known as 'Congreve rockets' were first used in a naval attack on the French fleet at Boulogne during the Napoleonic Wars in 1805. The operation failed, partly because of the weather, but another attack on Boulogne the following year was considered more successful, although it set fire to the

Congreve rockets were also fired in the bombardment of Algiers in 1816, depicted here by George Chambers Senior in 1836.

town rather than the fleet, which was the real target. Then in 1807, 25,000 rockets rained down on Copenhagen as the city was burned to the ground. Although Wellington professed to be unimpressed by them, the British went on to use Congreve rockets in the Peninsular War, which helped make the duke's reputation.

The Battle of Leipzig in 1813, sometimes known as the Battle of the Nations, was one of the most important of the Napoleonic Wars. The French were decisively beaten by a continental European coalition and Napoleon was forced into his first exile. The Royal Horse Artillery 'rocket brigade' were the only British troops present, but they performed with such distinction that Congreve was decorated by the Russians and the Swedes. Congreve rockets were also used in the Anglo-American war of 1812–14, with mixed results. They could be unreliable and inaccurate, but they made an important contribution to the capture and burning of Washington, DC, by British forces. The Battle of Bladensburg paved the way for the city's fall, and one account speaks of 'a flight of these ungainly projectiles' causing some of the Americans 'to break and flee in wild disorder'.[3] Thanks to another engagement in this war, when British ships pounded an American fort, Congreve's rockets get a mention in America's national anthem, 'The Star-Spangled Banner' – 'the rockets' red glare' being one of the perils the American flag survives. Still, critics were not won over, with the *Morning Chronicle* denouncing the weapons in 1814 as 'tomfoolery'.

After his father died in 1814, Congreve took over as comptroller of the Royal Laboratory. He was an enthusiastic self-publicist and wrote a series of books, claiming that 'the whole system of military tactics' was 'destined to be changed' by the rocket.[4] He kept developing his weapons, fitting them with a variety of warheads – incendiary, explosive, shrapnel – and introducing improvements such as launching them from collapsible wooden frames. He also moved the stick from the side to the centre of the propellant, which was designed to improve accuracy, but he never fulfilled his dream of a stick-free rocket.

By 1825 most major European powers were following Congreve's example and manufacturing military rockets, but when rifling started to improve the accuracy of artillery in the mid-1840s, they faced a new challenge. Another British inventor, William Hale, who had patented an improved version of the windmill among other bright ideas, tried to apply rifling techniques to rocketry, dispensing with the stick and putting angled vents in the rocket's casing, causing it to spin and making it more accurate. He also developed new manufacturing methods at his works near Woolwich. Some of his rockets were as heavy as 45 kilograms, though most of those used by the British military were 11 kilograms or less, with a range of up to 2 kilometres. At first he used iron cases, but later changed to steel. He won some export sales – to Russia, Austria and to the Americans, who used his rockets in the Mexican War of 1846 to 1848. They would also feature in the American Civil War in the 1860s. In 1854 he supplied the British Army in the Crimean War, and thirteen years later the government bought his invention. By then, rockets were again being marginalized by further improvements in artillery, but the British used them in colonial wars up to the end of the century. In the twentieth century, ever more destructive military rockets would be developed, such as Germany's V2 in the Second World War. Later, rocketry would be used to take us into space, but by then pyrotechnics had been overtaken by other means of propulsion.

Other Weapons

As early as 904, there are reports of a Chinese commander, Yang Xingmi, ordering his men to 'shoot off a machine to let fly fire' and burn down the gate of a city he was besieging.[5] Some scholars believe this to mean he was using gunpowder fire-bombs. Whether or not that is true, the Chinese government was soon investing heavily in research and development on gunpowder-based weapons. In 970, a military man named Feng Jisheng demonstrated a new type of gunpowder arrow to the emperor and was handsomely rewarded, as was a soldier called Tang Fu thirty years later when he showed off bombs and other weapons. By the mid-eleventh century, the military manual *Wu jing zong yao* (Collection of the Most Important Military Techniques), published by order of the emperor, was mentioning all sorts of pyrotechnic weapons. One of the most bizarre involved putting a hollowed-out peach stone filled with gunpowder around the neck of a bird in the hope that it would land on some enemy asset, explode and set it alight. There were also plenty of devices with eye-catching names such as the 'ten-thousand fire flying sand magic bomb' and the 'burning heaven fierce fire unstoppable bomb'. For all their terrifying titles, these bombs were not lethal by later standards. At the time, it was hard to procure sufficiently pure ingredients for gunpowder, nor was there the knowledge to mix them in the right proportions, so early weapons tended to be incendiary rather than explosive, and the gunpowder often had to be given a helping hand by other inflammable ingredients such as oil, pitch and resin. With gunpowder being low in the nitrates that provide oxygen, modern experiments have suggested ancient weapons may have worked well only when they could pick it up from an external source, as with an arrow flying through the air. Up to the end of the eleventh century, most Chinese gunpowder was probably still being used for fire arrows. In 1083 the imperial court sent 100,000 to one garrison and a quarter of a million to another.

In the next century, thunderclap bombs, which could be flung from trebuchets, began to feature heavily in descriptions of battles. Though they still had soft casings and contained low-nitrate gunpowder, the Chinese used them to good effect in defending Kaifeng against the Jurchen in 1126, throwing the enemy 'into great confusion. Many fled, howling with fright.'[6] The city eventually fell, but the emperor ordered that all ships be equipped with trebuchets. In 1161 the Chinese employed them to throw thunderclap bombs in a naval battle against the Jurchen on the Yangtze. They added lime to the bomb mixture so enemy soldiers were blinded and 'utterly defeated'.[7] Both sides used gunpowder weapons in the Jurchen siege of the city of Xiangyang in 1206–7. The attackers deployed gunpowder arrows, but the defenders also used fire-bombs and thunderclap bombs, which once again threw the enemy into panic.

Next, more deadly bombs began to appear, with iron cases containing gunpowder richer in nitrates that could blow the casing apart, throwing out shrapnel to devastating effect. In 1221 the Jurchen besieging the city of Qizhou on the Yangtze used them to overwhelm the Chinese defenders: 'Their heads, their eyes, their cheeks were exploded to bits.' The commander of the defending forces said the bombs were 'made with pig iron, about two inches thick, and they cause the city's walls to shake'.[8] These iron bombs were dubbed 'thunder-crash bombs' when the Jurchen used them against the Mongols in a naval battle in 1231. A particularly fearsome version was the 'heaven-shaking-thunder bomb' deployed when the Jurchen found themselves under Mongol siege in Kaifeng the next year. They claimed its explosion could be heard 30 miles away. As Mongol bombs 'rained down' on them, the defenders retaliated by lowering their 'heaven-shaking' bombs down the walls on iron chains so 'the attacking soldiers were all blown to bits, not even a trace being left behind'.[9] Again the bombs were not enough. After more than a year, Kaifeng fell and by 1234 the Jurchen had been completely defeated. An unusual use of an iron bomb came at Jingjiang in 1276 when Chinese soldiers blew themselves up with one rather than surrender.

From the fourteenth century, bombs packed with shrapnel, often contaminated with toxic substances such as faeces, came into favour in China. One was the 'magic-fire meteoric bomb that goes against the wind', which also contained 'blinding' substances, and could be 'so large that it takes draught animals to carry it about or so small it can be thrown by hand'.[10] Land mines, known as 'ground thunder', were also appearing. Made of cast iron, with a gunpowder charge and packed with poisonous and blinding material, they were concealed in places where the enemy was expected to set foot. It is not clear what the trigger mechanism was, and it may be that the mines had to be set off via a long fuse by someone hiding. Chinese use of non-human conscripts was not limited to birds. By 1400 they had the 'rolling thunder-bomb fire-ox', which involved strapping a bomb to the hapless animal and driving it at the enemy, or sometimes they used a wooden human figure on a horse to carry the bomb. The poor horse was encouraged along by firebrands tied to its tail.

Europe seems to have been well behind China in the field of iron bombs, though they were being used by the Burgundians by 1467. By the seventeenth century small iron bombs dubbed hand grenades, a bit bigger than cricket balls, had appeared in Britain. Remains were found on the battlefield of Killiecrankie on Tayside, where in 1689 they had been used by a government force defeated by Jacobite rebels. From the eighteenth century up to the end of the nineteenth, 'carcasses' were the incendiary bomb of choice for the British military. In their earliest form, they were cylindrical canvas containers bound with iron hoops, containing sulphur, saltpetre, turpentine and other ingredients. They got their name because the hoops supposedly resembled a corpse's ribs. Later versions were spheres of cast iron.

Smoke and Light in War

The use of smoke to hamper enemy actions or to hide your own may be as old as war itself. There is said to be evidence going back as far as 2000 BC of armies burning damp straw to achieve the desired effect, and, as we saw, the Chinese were already employing toxic smoke centuries before the birth of Christ. The idea seemed to rub off on Europeans, because in 1622 at the Battle of Macau, the Dutch set fire to damp gunpowder to try to hide a landing they were making. Their Portuguese enemies foiled the manoeuvre by firing into the smoke, and after three days' fighting they emerged victorious. Britain's armed forces also appear to have been using the tactic. In 1760 a report on a military review in Hyde Park said that some novel substance in 'globular form' had been set on fire, causing 'such a smoke as to render all persons within a considerable distance entirely invisible'. It noted that this would be useful 'to secure a retreat'.[11] Smoke balls were still listed in British military inventories a century later, with ingredients that probably had not changed much – gunpowder, coaldust, pitch and tallow – though in 1873 the official handbook *Notes on Ammunition* scoffed that it was doubtful whether they had ever been used in action. Despite this apparent lack of enthusiasm on the part of the establishment, smoke was an important weapon of concealment in both world wars. It was used, for example, by the Germans at the great naval battle of Jutland in 1916, and by the Australians at the Battle of Chuignes on the Western Front in 1918. German aircraft would also drop smoke bombs over suitable targets to help their artillery identify them.

Meanwhile, Wing-Commander Frank Brock of the famous fireworks family who, as we saw, would be killed in action in 1918, devised innovative weapons for British armed forces, such as special bombs for attacking German Zeppelin hangars. (Brock daringly posed as an American tourist to get himself shown around the hangars while tension was building before the war, and even landed illicitly in Germany for more reconnaissance after hostilities began.) Then came the Brock explosive bullet, which brought down airships in flight. He had paid for the initial development costs out of his own pocket. Brock also invented smoke floats for merchant navy vessels, enabling them to lay their own smokescreens to put German submarines off the scent. About 200,000 were issued and they were considered particularly ingenious because

Frank Brock.

Smoke float, *c.* 1922.

when they were thrown overboard, they would be submerged for a time, so the holes from which the smoke would escape had to remain sealed until they came to the surface. They also needed to be easy to use and to survive being stored on deck in all weathers. Brock was killed in heroic action in a raid on Zeebrugge, for which he had fitted out vessels with smoke-making apparatus and designed smoke floats to be anchored in key positions. The Admiral of the Fleet, Lord Keyes, said that without Brock's efforts, 'the operation could not have been successful.'[12] As for the Second World War, according to James C. Bond of the Canadian War Museum, 'all armies made use of smoke screens in their operations to a greater or lesser extent.'[13] In the USA Hitt Fireworks of Seattle produced aerial smokescreens to protect the nearby Puget Sound Naval Shipyard, while smoke was also said to have hampered German air raids on British cities. By then much of it was being generated by non-pyrotechnic means such as crude oil.

Like smoke, pyrotechnic lighting was dual-purpose on the battlefield: it could reveal action being taken by the enemy or help actions of your own. Back in the seventeenth century, in *La Pyrotechnie*, Jean Appier Hanzelet described how the military could use light balls, and over the next couple of centuries their recipe probably changed little. In the 1870s the British military were deploying 'Ground Light Balls' made of saltpetre, sulphur, resin and linseed oil. *Notes on Ammunition* said they were used at night to show up enemy activity, but the publication was as disparaging about light balls as it was about smoke balls, noting that although they had the advantage that water would not put them out, their composition was poor, and 'a few shovelfuls of earth' would do the trick.[14]

The nineteenth century saw the emergence of the parachute light. The idea seems to have originated back in 1820, and soon displays at the Vauxhall Pleasure Gardens were featuring the 'asteroid rocket' that would carry in its cap a light attached to a parachute. When the rocket exploded in the air, the parachute light would drift down to earth. In 1855, to celebrate the fall of Sevastopol in the Crimean War, Captain Boxer of the Woolwich Royal Laboratory demonstrated a shell that could do the same job, but with a much bigger light. The arrival of magnesium soon afterwards meant lights could also be brighter. A highly portable illumination device, the short-barrelled Very pistol, appeared in the last dozen years of the century. Invented by an American naval officer, Edward Wilson Very, it fired a single-star Very light, brightened by aluminium. It was used in the First World War to reveal enemy manoeuvres, and Frank Brock also developed a signalling version that could be employed to establish the identity of a ship. The U.S. Navy produced illuminating projectiles with a range of up to 7 miles, and the Americans also came up with stars that could be dropped from aircraft.

One of the most ambitious uses of illumination in the First World War was Frank Brock's 'Dover flares'. In order to prevent German U-boats coming through the Straits of Dover and wreaking havoc on merchant shipping, the British laid mines in nets underwater, but the U-boats thwarted the ploy by simply waiting until dark, then sailing through on the surface. So Brock developed metre-high flares that illuminated an area with a 3-mile radius for seven and a half minutes, making it, in Churchill's words, 'as bright as Piccadilly'. The government ordered 135,000 from Brocks, and every night a dozen trawlers were sent out to deploy them. Their effect was supplemented by flares suspended from balloons or towed behind motorboats, also devised by Frank Brock. On the first night the Dover flares were used, a U-boat had to dive and was blown to pieces by mines. In all, fourteen were sunk. Keyes said Brock 'worked with the most untiring energy', and in February 1918 he was awarded the OBE.[15] When the war ended, thousands of surplus Dover flares were set off at celebration parties across the country.

During the Second World War, the RAF's Pathfinder Force dropped flares and incendiary bombs to illuminate targets for the bombers that would follow. Flares were also widely used to light landing fields at night or in bad weather. In the Korean and Vietnam Wars, parachute lights were enlisted to illuminate the jungle, but in more recent times weapons have been guided by GPS or laser beams rather than flares and pyrotechnics.

Signalling and Other Military Uses

As far back as the thirteenth century, the Chinese are said to have been firing soft-shelled signal bombs that exploded in mid-air to pass on messages to distant troops, but it was six hundred years years later that a remarkable American woman took pyrotechnic signalling to another level. Born in 1829, Martha Coston had no formal education and was married in her teens to a promising young inventor named Benjamin Franklin Coston, who worked his way up to head of the Naval Laboratory in the Washington Navy Yard. During his time there, among other things, he worked on the development of Hale's rocket, but after a dispute with the military, he left to become president of the Boston Gas Company. Partly because of exposure to hazardous materials in the experiments he conducted there, he died tragically young, leaving Martha a young widow with four small children. Within two years, two of her children had died and she was penniless. Going through some of her husband's old papers one day, she found designs for a pyrotechnic night signal. Martha then remembered he had given some prototypes to an officer at the naval yard to try out, and contacted the man to get them back. Grudgingly they were returned.

Martha approached the Secretary for the Navy, Isaac Toucey, and asked him to get the signals tested. The idea was to have a three-colour flare, to be used in different combinations, each of which would convey a message or instruction from a prearranged list. Toucey agreed to run a trial, but this delivered the disappointing verdict that 'the signals proved utterly good for nothing.' Rather contradictorily, however, the officer who had conducted it also encouraged Martha to keep working on the idea. Toucey concurred, but another test produced more poor results. For a decade, hampered by her lack of pyrotechnic know-how, Martha hired and fired employees as she searched for the recipe to deliver a flare that would burn a patriotic red, white and blue. By 1858 she had a strong white and a good red, but blue was the stumbling block. Then, inspired by a fireworks display celebrating the laying of the first transatlantic cable, she wrote, using a man's name, to some of New York's leading pyrotechnists. The good news was that she got her third colour and the bad news was that she had to settle for green instead of blue, but in 1859 she received a patent for her signal flares.

After a month's intensive tests, Toucey decided the navy should adopt them because they gave 'precision, fullness, and plainness'. Coston hoped the service would buy up her patent, but it declined and orders rather dribbled in, so Coston decided to go into the export market, securing patents in seven European countries. Then, in 1861, the American Civil War broke out, and the navy did buy the patent, though for only half the sum Coston wanted. It tried to manufacture its own Coston signals, but found it could not match the price at which she could make them. Over the course of the war, she provided more than a million flares, but claimed she lost more than $120,000 because wartime inflation was constantly driving up her costs. In the end, the government offered her only $15,000 compensation, leading her to complain bitterly that in the navy there were 'men so small-minded that they begrudged a woman her success, though achieved after long years of struggle and patient industry'. She protested that some of those men had been made rich from her invention through being given financial rewards for capturing blockade-runners – ships trying by night to evade the naval blockade the Union imposed to stop supplies reaching the Confederate States. Not 'in a single instance', she claimed, would any of these have been taken 'without the aid of the Coston Signals'. The flares meant ships could receive messages not only at night but during days when the smoke of battle was thick, and they played a crucial role in the Union's victory at the Battle of Fort Fisher in 1865, which closed the South's last port. In 1875 a former Assistant Secretary of the Navy admitted how vital they were: 'It was the universal testimony of the officers of the navy that the signals were of greatest possible service – indispensable, in fact.'[16]

Pyrotechnics found various other military applications. In the First World War, the Germans used rockets to fire grappling hooks into Allied barbed wire, so it could be pulled out of the way. On D-Day, during the Second World War, Allied soldiers fired rockets carrying ropes attached to grappling hooks to enable them to scale cliffs to a German stronghold overlooking the beaches. Then there were tins of food that a soldier could heat up by means of a firework secreted in a tube inside the can, not to mention mock gun-flashes and shell bursts designed to mislead enemy observers. Imitation bangs and bullets were also used in military training and became an important market for fireworks companies. In the early 1980s they were said to make up half of Brocks' business. Around the same time, the British company Astra built up an important presence in America, the biggest market in the world for simulated military explosives, and when the Gruccis ran into problems in the late 1990s, they got themselves a contract to supply missile simulators for the U.S. military.

Pyrotechnics to the Rescue!

Coston signals were not just for the military. After the American Civil War, they were also used by the United States Life Saving Service, the forerunner of the United States Coast Guard, which supplied them to all its stations to give warnings of danger or to summon rescuers to the scene of a wreck, helping to save thousands of lives. By the time Coston signals appeared, 'blue-light' flares, with a bluish-white light produced by sulphur, saltpetre and arsenic sulphide, were already being used at sea, but the advent of potassium chlorate in the nineteenth century opened the way for more sophisticated coloured signals. After that, magnesium meant they could be made brighter. Like Martha Coston, many companies in the UK took out patents for marine flares, such as Pains in 1873. In 2022 vessels were still required to carry them under the International Convention for the Safety of Life at Sea (SOLAS), though in the UK the rule did not apply to boats shorter than 13.7 metres. Some argued that because of radio and electronic distress signals they were no longer necessary, especially as they can be a hazard. The U.S. Coast Guard said that between 2001 and 2010, fewer than 1 per cent of rescues were initiated by someone seeing a flare.

Pyrotechnics, in the form of maroons, were also used to summon lifeboat crews if there was a ship in trouble, but distress signalling was only part of the story. In 1791 Sgt John Bell of the Royal Artillery was awarded fifty guineas for demonstrating how a mortar could be used to fire a line from a ship in distress to the shore. It travelled 350 metres from a vessel on the river, and embedded itself 50 centimetres into the ground. The sergeant then used it to pull himself and a friend ashore on a raft improvised from chests and casks. Not much seems to have happened with Bell's idea, and sixteen years later a Royal Navy vessel, the *Snipe*, was wrecked just 50 metres off Great Yarmouth in a storm, with the loss of 67 lives. A Norfolk inventor named George William Manby, a lifelong friend of Nelson, saw the disaster and promptly borrowed a mortar from the Board of Ordnance to carry out a few experiments. While Bell had fired a line from ship to shore, Manby decided to go in the other direction, sending a shot with a grappling hook to which a line was attached towards the wreck from land. In February 1808 he used his invention, the Manby mortar, to rescue the crew of a brig that became stranded at almost the same place as the *Snipe*. The Navy Board approved the mortar, and within six years it was in service at 45 places around the coast. It is estimated that by the time Manby died in 1854, his invention had saved 1,000 lives.

While Manby was creating his mortar, Henry Trengrouse, a Cornish cabinet maker, was working on something similar. He too was motivated by a marine disaster he saw. On Christmas Eve 1807, eleven months after the *Snipe* was wrecked, a frigate, the *Anson*, was lost with all hands near Helston, again about 50 metres from shore. The story goes that while he was watching a firework display, Trengrouse was struck with the notion of using a rocket to fire a line to a ship. The Cornishman spent £3,000 of his own money developing his idea, which had various advantages. Manby's mortar weighed over 100 kilograms, whereas Trengrouse's rocket line was fired by a specially adapted musket that could be carried around in a small chest and used from shore or taken aboard a ship. It was also cheaper than Manby's mortar, and there was much less risk of the line breaking, but it was not until 1818 that Trengrouse managed to persuade the navy to accept it. It did not make him rich. The government decided to have the rocket lines made by its own ordnance department,

The Manby mortar, 1821.

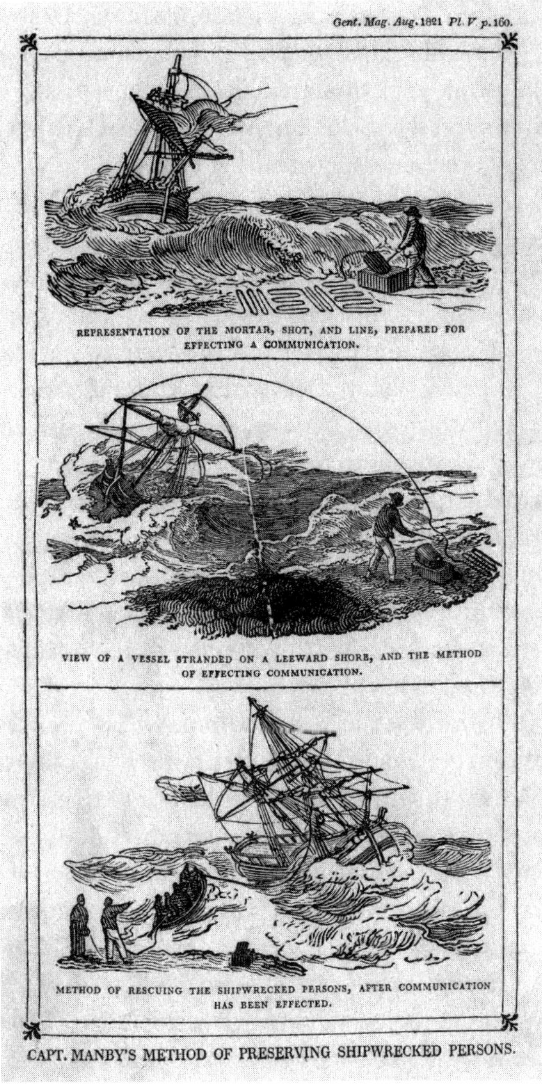

and paid the cabinet maker £50 compensation, though Trengrouse did receive various awards, including a diamond ring from Tsar Alexander I of Russia, who had adopted his invention enthusiastically.

In 1830 John Dennett, a civil engineer from the Isle of Wight, built on Trengrouse's ideas by using an improved rocket with an iron case. It was supplied to coastguard stations as well as being exported. Dennett tried to get greater range by attaching two rockets side by side on the same pole, but without success. In 1855 another Isle of Wight man, Colonel Edward Boxer, superintendent of the Royal Laboratory at

Woolwich, created the Boxer rocket, which arranged two rocket cases head to tail so that when the first had burned out, it was thrown off, and the second took over, enabling the rocket to fly further. The next inventor to take on the rocket line was a sailor named William Schermuly, who spent ten years experimenting before he launched his invention in 1897. Schermuly's ambition was to provide a compact unit that could be carried on every ship. Like Bell, he decided his line would go from sea to land, reasoning that the shore represented an easier target than a ship. One of his innovations was a new method of winding a long line into a small space. Initial takers were few, but by 1920, working with his son, he had developed a version with greater range and accuracy that could be fired from a pistol. Nine years later, the British government ordered that every ship over 500 tons must carry line-throwing equipment. Nineteen days after, William Schermuly died. His family company went on manufacturing what became known as the Schermuly Pistol Rocket Apparatus until in 1973 it was taken over by Pains Wessex, which would stop manufacturing in the UK early in the twenty-first century. Between 1871 and 1962 the tally of lives at sea saved by rocket lines was said to have risen to 15,000.

As early as the 1840s, maroons were being fastened to the tracks on Britain's railways. When a train went over them, they would detonate, warning the driver of an accident or of track work ahead. Two decades later came a more ambitious idea for railway pyrotechnics. Britain suffered what is said to have been its first murder on a train in 1864. In those days, carriages were often divided into completely isolated compartments, and the crime led to demands for a way for passengers to raise the alarm. Brocks came up with a plan to have a Roman candle protruding through the roof of each compartment so that, in an emergency, the firework could be lit by means of a mixture spread on each ticket. Perhaps the least surprising thing about this ambitious scheme is that it was not adopted, but flares have been used on the railway to warn drivers about dangers ahead, as they have on the roads.

One of Britain's first air crashes happened at Eastbourne in 1911, when a pilot clipped the branches of a tree and struck a lamp post as he tried to land. The aircraft was badly damaged, but no one was hurt. Frank Brock visited the resort most weekends, and there has been speculation that it was this accident that inspired him to produce 'smoke rockets', which were ignited on the ground to guide an aircraft to where it was meant to land. The Wild West showman and air pioneer Samuel Cody is supposed to have been the first person to use them, on a flight from London to Manchester. (Cody would be killed in an air crash in 1913.) Maroons were fired to deliver air raid alarms in the First World War, and during the Cold War they were given the ultimate warning mission when thousands of them, many manufactured by Pains Wessex, were distributed to 12,000 sites around the UK to alert people in the event of a nuclear attack.

Taming Nature

As we saw, a fifteenth-century Italian traveller in India remarked on how scared elephants were of fireworks, and a couple of hundred years later the French traveller and physician François Bernier noted that in Delhi and Agra local people used pyrotechincs to control elephant fights. These bouts were put on as entertainment at festivals, with Bernier remarking: 'The fight of these noble creatures is attended with much cruelty,' though he was more concerned about the many humans who got injured than the suffering of the elephants. If things got out of hand, wrote the Frenchman, 'the animals can be separated only by means of *cherkys*, or fireworks, which are made to explode between them; for they are naturally timid and have a particular dread of fire.' A note in a nineteenth-century edition of his *Travels in the Mogul Empire, AD 1656–1668* adds that *cherkys* are 'catherine wheels on the end of a stick',[17] while George Plimpton speculates that they were more like cherry bombs and that the Indians also used them to stop elephants charging.[18]

In West Africa, too, Arthur Brock used pyrotechnics as protection against potentially dangerous animals, developing the tripflare by attaching flares to trip wires, so that soldiers or hunters camping in the wild would be warned if beasts or people came close. They are still used today, particularly by the military, while in Canada the leading fireworks company, Hands, produced polar bear scaring devices. But smaller creatures than polar bears can be a problem. Seattle's Hitt company made a special firecracker called Doggone to protect postmen from unfriendly canines. Then there are birds. Between 2003 and 2012 the International Civil Aviation Organisation reckoned that more than four hundred people had died in plane crashes caused by bird strikes. Companies including France's Etienne Lacroix make pyrotechnic cartridges that can be fired to scare birds away from airfields and flight paths. Honolulu International Airport was one of many which had a device that let off regular bangs, but a journalist who visited it in 2012 reported on the 'shellcracker', an even more basic pyrotechnic solution. A recalcitrant egret had defied all the airport's safety measures and was flying along the runway. A 'biological-science technician with the U.S. Department of Agriculture's Wildlife Services' airport wildlife-management program', helpfully translated by the reporter as 'a bird-scarer', took off in his pick-up truck. Often the racing truck would be enough to scare away the egret, but not this time. So the technician tried 'pyroing the bird', using his shotgun to send a shellcracker high into the air, where it went off with a flash and a noise like a supercharged firecracker. The egret flinched, but stuck to its course. The same happened with the second shot, and it was only with shellcracker number three that the bird banked away from the runway.[19] But, especially for the inexpert, pyrotechnic methods of controlling pests have their dangers. In 2017 a Florida man was killed when his sister threw a firecracker at a rodent and set their mobile home on fire.

Nowadays talk of whaling is likely to provoke shudders of horror, but in the nineteenth century it was big business, with these giants providing raw materials for candles, skirt hoops, corset stays and lighting and lubrication oils. Harpooners were skilled and well paid for doing a very dangerous job. The traditional harpoon was not meant to kill the whale. Its job was to stop the creature escaping the small boats into which ships' crews decanted when prey was sighted and from which the harpoons were flung. They had to be attached to long lines because the whale's first reaction was often to dive deep. There then followed a long battle, with the whale dragging the boat along at speeds of 20 miles an hour or more until it tired and the pursuers were able to close in and finish off their prey with lances. Losses of men and boats were frequent, and pyrotechnics seemed to promise a way of making the deadly hunt more efficient. Sir William Congreve took out a patent for a rocket harpoon, while George Manby of the life-saving mortar explored the possibilities of killing whales with shells. By the 1870s, one of the best-known rocket harpoons was the Roys–Liliendahl, developed by two Americans, a whaling captain named Thomas Welcome Roys and Gustavus A. Liliendahl, an explosives expert. The *Pacific Rural Press* sang its praises in 1879, describing it as 'the most destructive implement ever devised for the purpose of killing whales'. The point of the harpoon carried a 'bomb' which 'when projected into the whale by the rocket, explodes, inflicting a fatal wound'. The *Press* said it could kill a whale at 50 metres, 'very much further' than the range of an ordinary harpoon. It was 2 metres long, and had to be fired from the shoulder using a 'peculiar rest' with a shield, to protect the operator.[20] But as whaling grew more and more industrialized, rocket harpoons fired from small boats were made redundant by harpoon guns mounted on the prows of steam ships.

As well as protecting aircraft, pyrotechnics have long been used in agriculture to save crops. One method was to attach firecrackers at regular intervals to a slow-burning fuse to scare off pests, but there have also been more ambitious ideas, such as changing the weather. Hailstorms have always been a hazard for winemakers and in 1896 one of their number, an Austrian named Albert Stiger, tried firing a hail cannon into the clouds to stop them. The theory was that the cannon would cause shock waves in the atmosphere that would prevent hailstones from forming. By 1900 more than 10,000 of these cannon were in use, and some still are, but after a series of scientifically supervised experiments in Italy and Austria they were dismissed as useless. So how about using rockets? Shortly after the Second World War, a French general developed a competitively priced short-range model carrying an explosive charge that a farmer could point at any cloud he did not like the look of. They were very popular, but experiments in Switzerland between 1948 and 1952 demonstrated no difference between areas where rockets were deployed and those where they were not. In more recent times, the Soviet Union claimed success from using rockets to fire silver iodide or lead iodide crystals up into the clouds, the plan being to create many more nuclei around which hailstones would form, making them more numerous, but smaller and less destructive. Once again, scientists were sceptical, as tests in the West were unable to reproduce the Russian results. Still the idea survived the collapse of the USSR, and in 2016 it was reported from Georgia that a hundred rockets had been fired to try to stop a hailstorm that was threatening vines and other crops. In 1921, incidentally, Arthur Brock had taken part in an experiment to use fireworks to create rain on Hampstead Heath. Several tons were let off, and journalists reported that 'within a few moments', there were '30 or more clouds in the sky', but no raindrops.[21]

Vehicles and Mail

We are used to rockets powering flight, but between the wars they were also tried out on land vehicles such as cars and motorcycles. Behind many of the initiatives was the German industrialist Fritz von Opel, whose family gave its name to the car company, and who was himself a successful competitor in motor, motorcycle and motorboat racing. In 1928 he commissioned the world's first rocket-powered car, the Opel-RAK 1, a racing vehicle in which the engine was replaced by six rockets. It reached 55 miles an hour, and then, when more rockets were added, 70. Opel himself took the next rocket car, the Opel-RAK 2, fitted with 24, up to 143 mph. The company also experimented with a rocket car on rails which got to 160 mph before it came off the track and crashed, and they attached half a dozen rockets to a motorbike and called it 'The Monster'. The authorities banned it after a few trial runs. In 1984 a rocket-powered car would be clocked at more than 386 mph at the Santa Pod Raceway in Bedfordshire, but after that, speed records would start falling to jet-powered vehicles.

The twenty-first century has seen drones being used to make deliveries, but back in the late nineteenth century South Sea Islanders had a go at something similar using rockets. Getting mail to Niuafo'ou in the Tonga group was especially difficult because of its rough waters and volcanic reefs. It had become known as Tin Can Island because the favoured method of delivering letters was for passing ships to put them in watertight containers and drop them in the sea for locals to swim out and collect. Then the Tongan postal service got its hands on some Congreve rockets from New Zealand, left over from wars between the British and the Maoris, and in 1882 it decided to try them out on the post. It was not a success. Sometimes rockets flew off in the wrong direction; some cans burst open in mid-flight, and others on impact with the water. Rocket mail then went pretty quiet until the late 1920s, when an Austrian engineer named Friedrich Schmiedl enters the story. He lived in the Alps, where two villages might be close as the crow flies, but an up-hill-down-dale journey between them could take the best part of a day. Schmiedl started making rockets equipped with parachute landing systems and in 1931 one successfully delivered 102 letters. Over the next two years he carried hundreds more, but in 1934 the Austrian Post Office banned private mail services. When war broke out five years later, he destroyed all his equipment to stop the Nazis using it.

Meanwhile, in Germany in 1933, Gerhard Zucker demonstrated a 4-metre projectile to a big crowd at Duhnen on Germany's North Sea coast. It was meant to reach Heligoland, nearly 30 miles offshore, and there were roars of laughter when, having hardly begun its journey, it belly-flopped into mudflats. The Nazis forbade any further experiments, so in 1934 Zucker travelled to England and met a German stamp dealer named C. H. Dombrowski. Together they formed the British Rocket Syndicate, but immediately ran into a problem when Germany forbade the export of the rocket propellant Zucker had been using. He had to buy Brocks' powder instead and he put it in a much smaller rocket, just 1 metre long. In June 1934 he and Dombrowski went to Rottingdean in Sussex. According to contemporary reports, their rocket was loaded with 'upwards of 3,000 letters' bearing special stamps sold by the syndicate. Launched from rails lubricated with butter, it rose in the air, travelled about a mile, then fell back to earth. The letters ended up being delivered by local Post Office staff.

Unabashed, Zucker claimed his rocket post could provide a vital lifeline for the Western Isles off the coast of Scotland, another place where rough seas could easily disrupt the mail. This time he planned to send a rocket across the mile of water that separated the islands of Scarp and Harris. The letters it carried bore 'Western Isles Rocket Post' stamps costing about twenty times the price of normal postage, but it proved not to be a giant leap for mail delivery. The projectile had travelled only a few metres when there was a 'terrific explosion' as it blew up. A second attempt went no better, with the rocket exploding again and scattering 'scorched and blackened' letters like confetti.[22] Zucker reportedly fainted.

A final effort from Lymington in Hampshire in December 1934 was meant to reach the Isle of Wight, but it was blown off course, and managed only a mile and a half in the wrong direction, never leaving the mainland. By then the British authorities had had enough and warned Zucker and Dombrowski they could face criminal prosecution if they attempted any further flights, while expressing suspicion that the whole enterprise had been primarily devised to sell their expensive stamps. One MP remarked that Zucker's rockets had 'shown a remarkable tendency to convey letters to anywhere but their proper destination', and the would-be pioneer was deported back to Germany.[23] There he did time in prison for fraud and embezzlement over selling stamps for rocket flights that never happened before being wounded when serving in the Luftwaffe. After the war, he became a furniture dealer, but in 1964 the rocket mail bug bit again. This time his projectile exploded over a crowd, scattering shrapnel and killing two schoolboys. Zucker went back to gaol and the authorities banned any further experiments.

Perhaps it was thanks to the example of Tipu that while Zucker's letter-carrying rockets were flopping in Europe, in India a dentist named

Stephen H. Smith was doing rather better. Said to have been inspired by carrier pigeons, in September 1934 he fired a projectile made by Calcutta's Oriental Firework Company carrying 143 letters from a ship to the island of Sagar in the Ganges delta. It is said the rocket exploded in mid-air, but most of the letters were saved. Over the next ten years, Smith would manage eighty successful mail deliveries by rocket, some produced in Calcutta and some by Pains in the UK, before he graduated to making his own from thick cardboard, leather and tin. In June 1935 it was not just letters but a live cock and hen, named Adam and Eve, that he sent over the Damodar River in West Bengal. The birds, claimed to be the first living creatures to be transported by rocket, apparently landed none the worse for wear though a little 'restive'. In recognition of their achievement, they were spared the pot and allowed to live out their days at a private zoo in Calcutta. Smith was partly bankrolled by a rich businessman and his wife, who was a great airmail enthusiast, and by a local ruler, the king of Sikkim, who could see the benefits for his mountain realm of a mode of mail delivery that could cut out a lot of that trudging up peaks and down valleys. The king's secretary wrote that the rockets were particularly useful 'during flood or landslides', mentioning one that delivered 'medicines, cigarettes, tea and sugar in small quantities . . . without any damage to the contents'.[24] This was regarded as another world record for Smith – the first ever parcel post by rocket. In an echo of Zucker, he helped to finance his experiments by selling special souvenir covers for the letters his rockets carried, some of which are now very valuable. His last flight was in 1944.

By then America was in the game. In 1936 the McAllen, Texas, branch of the war veterans' organization the American Legion were looking for

Commemorative Indian stamp for Stephen Smith, 1992.

a way of paying off the mortgage on their new building when someone came up with the idea of sending a mail rocket across the Rio Grande to Reynosa in Mexico, and, yes, selling special stamps. The projectile was pretty basic – made of laminated cardboard and powered by powder emptied out of firecrackers. The first one blew up soon after take-off, but the second landed outside a bar in Reynosa. That was not exactly where it had been meant to come to earth, but it did mean it was the first ever successful cross-border rocket mail delivery. The branch launched other mail rockets and managed to raise the money they needed.

Rocket mail had a final flurry in 1959 when the U.S. Postal Service fired a cruise missile stuffed with 3,000 souvenir letters from the deck of a navy submarine to Florida 700 miles away. The postmaster general was ecstatic, declaring: 'before man reaches the moon, mail will be delivered within hours from New York to California, to Britain, to India or Australia by guided missiles. We stand on the threshold of rocket mail.'[25] But the threshold was as far as the U.S. Postal Service got. There were no further flights, and suspicion grew that the real point had been to impress the Russians with the prowess of American missiles.

References

1 From Origins to Guy Fawkes

1 Joseph Needham, with Ho Ping-Yü, Lu Gwei-Djen and Wang Ling, *Science and Civilisation in China*, vol. V: *Chemistry and Chemical Technology*, part VII: *Military Technology: The Gunpowder Epic* (Cambridge, 1986), p. 129.
2 Ibid.
3 Ibid., p. 130.
4 Harry Smee and Henry Macrory, *Gunpowder and Glory: The Explosive Life of Frank Brock* OBE (Oxford 2020), p. 1.
5 Thomas Glick, Steven J. Livesey and Faith Wallis, eds, *Medieval Science, Technology and Medicine: An Encyclopedia* (New York, 2005), p. 211.
6 Clive Ponting, *Gunpowder: An Explosive History* (London, 2006), p. 234.
7 Smee and Macrory, *Gunpowder*, p. 3.
8 George Plimpton, *Fireworks* (New York, 1984), p. 164.
9 Robert Friedel, *A Culture of Improvement: Technology and the Western Millennium* (Cambridge, MA, 2010), p. 85.
10 Needham, *Military Technology*, p. 138.
11 Ibid., p. 131.
12 Robert K. G. Temple, *The Genius of China: 3,000 Years of Science, Discovery and Invention* (New York, 1986), p. 237.
13 Ponting, *Gunpowder*, p. 33.
14 Needham, *Military Technology*, p. 135.
15 Nandini Rathi, 'A Brief and Crackling History of Fireworks in India', http://indianexpress.com, 14 November 2020.
16 Ibid.
17 Heena Khandelwal, 'The Pyrotechnic Saga', http://dnaindia.com, 4 November 2018.
18 Simon Werrett, *Fireworks: Pyrotechnic Arts and Sciences in European History* (London, 2010), p. 17.
19 Ibid., p. 17.
20 Ibid., pp. 19–20.
21 Kevin Salatino, *Incendiary Art: The Representation of Fireworks in Early Modern Europe* (Los Angeles, CA, 1997), p. 80.
22 Ibid., p. 77.
23 Charlotte A. Eaton, *Rome in the 19th Century* (London, 1892), vol. II, pp. 208–10.

24 Werrett, *Fireworks*, p. 18.
25 Plimpton, *Fireworks*, p. 48.
26 Ibid., p. 50.
27 Giambattista della Porta, *Natural Magic* (London, 1658), p. 289.
28 Ibid., p. 4.
29 Werrett, *Fireworks*, p. 61.
30 Alan St H. Brock, *A History of Fireworks* (London, 1949), p. 32.
31 John Eliot Hodgkin, *Rariora* (London, 1902), p. 187.
32 Brock, *History*, p. 32.
33 Alan St H. Brock, *Pyrotechnics: The History and Art of Firework Making* (London, 1922), p. 17.
34 George Whetstone, *The History of Promos and Cassandra* (London, 1578), Act I, Scene vi.
35 R. Chambers, ed., *The Book of Days. A Miscellany of Popular Antiquities* (London, 1864), vol. II, p. 24.
36 Joseph Strutt and John Charles Cox, *The Sports and Pastimes of the People of England* (London, 1903), p. 295.
37 Brock, *History*, p. 33.
38 Ibid., p. 34.
39 Strutt, *Sports and Pastimes*, p. 296.
40 John Wolfe, *The Honourable Entertainment Given to the Queen's Majesty in Progress, at Elvetham in Hampshire* (London, 1591), https://google.co.uk/books.
41 Edward Arthur Brayley Hodgetts, *The Rise and Progress of the British Explosives Industry* (London, 1909), p. 123.
42 Henry Dircks, *The Life, Times, and Scientific Labours of the Second Marquis of Worcester* (London, 1865), pp. 517–18.
43 Strutt, *Sports and Pastimes*, p. 296.

2 From Guy Fawkes to an Explosion of Colour

1 Eva Griffith, *A Jacobean Company and Its Playhouse: The Queen's Servants at the Red Bull Theatre (c. 1605–1619)* (Cambridge, 2013), p. 113.
2 Robert Folkestone Williams, ed., *The Court and Times of James the First* (London, 1848), vol. I, p. 67.
3 Alan St H. Brock, *A History of Fireworks* (London, 1949), p. 35.
4 Ibid., p. 36.
5 Alan St H. Brock, *Pyrotechnics: The History and Art of Firework Making* (London, 1922), p. 27.
6 Brock, *History*, p. 37.
7 Ibid., p. 41.
8 John Babington, *Pyrotechnia; or, A Discourse of Artificial Fire-works* (London, 1635), https://wellcomecollection.org/.
9 Katie Birkwood, '"Light the Blue Touchpaper . . .": Fireworks in 17th Century England', https://history.rcplondon.ac.uk, 4 November 2016.
10 Brock, *History*, p. 191.
11 Simon Werrett, *Fireworks: Pyrotechnic Arts and Sciences in European History* (London, 2010), p. 25.
12 Ibid., p. 21.

13 J. R. Mulryne, ed., *Europa Triumphans: Court and Civic Festivals in Early Modern Europe* (Aldershot, 2004), p. 150.
14 Bram van Oostveldt, ed., *Performing Arts in the Austrian 18th Century* (Ghent, 1999), p. 76.
15 Kevin Salatino, *Incendiary Art: The Representation of Fireworks in Early Modern Europe* (Los Angeles, CA, 1997), p. 19.
16 Ibid.
17 Ibid., p. 34.
18 Harry Smee and Henry Macrory, *Gunpowder and Glory: The Explosive Life of Frank Brock* OBE (Oxford 2020), p. 7.
19 Clive Ponting, *Gunpowder: An Explosive History* (London, 2006), p. 223.
20 Piers Wauchope, 'Sir Martin Beckman', www.oxforddnb.com, 3 January 2008.
21 Brock, *History*, p. 44.
22 Edward Wedlake Brayley, *Londiniana* (London, 1829), vol. IV, p. 56.
23 John Milton, '*In Quintum Novembris*' (London, 1645).
24 Edward Arthur Brayley Hodgetts, *The Rise and Progress of the British Explosives Industry* (London, 1909), p. 132; Samuel Pepys, *Diary and Correspondence: With a Life and Notes by Richard Lord Braybrooke* (London, 1858), vol. I, p. 231.
25 Pepys, *Diary*, vol II, p. 430.
26 Birkwood, 'Blue Touchpaper'.
27 Henry Chamberlain, *A New and Compleat Survey of the Cities of London and Westminster* (London, 1770), p. 258.
28 The Rev. Ronald Lancaster, *Fireworks Principles and Practice* (New York, 1998), p. 14.
29 *Littell's Living Age*, 5th series (Boston, MA, 1878), vol. XXII, p. 256.
30 'An Account of the Burning the Pope at Temple-bar in London, November 17. 1679', https://quod.lib.umich.edu.
31 Brock, *Pyrotechnics*, p. 58.
32 William III, 1697–8: 'An Act to prevent the throwing or firing of Squibbs Serpents & other Fire works', http://british-history.ac.uk.
33 Brock, *Pyrotechnics*, p. 58.
34 Roy Porter, ed., *Myths of the English* (Cambridge, 2002), p. 78.
35 J. A. Sharpe, *Remember, Remember: A Cultural History of Guy Fawkes Day* (Cambridge, MA, 2005), p. 141.
36 Porter, *Myths*, p. 79.
37 *The Times*, 5 November 1790, p. 5.
38 Gavin Morgan, 'The Guildford Guy Riots (1842–1865)', https://archaeologydataservice.ac.uk, p. 61.
39 Simon Werrett, 'Green Is the Colour: St Petersburg's Chemical Laboratories and Competing Visions of Chemistry in the Eighteenth Century', www.discovery.ucl.ac.uk, May 2013, p. 12.
40 Ibid., p. 15.
41 Werrett, *Fireworks*, p. 181.
42 John Bell, *Travels from St Petersburg in Russia to Various Parts of Asia* (Edinburgh, 1788), vol. II, p. 88.
43 Athanasius Kircher, *Antiquities of China* [1677], www.quod.lib.umich.edu. p. 426.
44 Werrett, *Fireworks*, p. 181; Brock, *History*, p. 57.

45 Brock, *History*, pp. 24–5.
46 'Meaning of Hanabi: A Brief History of Fireworks in Japan', www.koloajodo.com, 7 July 2020.
47 P. K. Gode, *The History of Fireworks in India between* AD *1400 and 1900* (Basavangudi, 1953), pp. 21–3.
48 Werrett, *Fireworks*, p. 55.
49 John Smith, *Travels. History of Virginia* (Cambridge, 2012), p. 162.
50 Thomas Harriott, *A Brief and True Report of the New Found Land of Virginia* (New York, 1903), www.college.cengage.com.
51 Werrett, *Fireworks*, p. 55.
52 Abigail Adams, *Familiar Letters of John Adams and His Wife Abigail Adams, during the Revolution* (New York, 1876), pp. 193–4.
53 Helen Thompson, '14 Fun Facts about Fireworks', www.smithsonianmag.com, 4 July 2014.
54 James R. Heintze, *The Fourth of July Encyclopedia* (London, 2007), p. 97.
55 William Bray, ed., *Diary and Correspondence of John Evelyn* (London, 1850), vol. II, p. 245.
56 Kevin Matthew Carr, 'A Theater of the Senses: A Cultural History of Theatrical Effects in Early-Modern England', www.diginole.lib.fsu.edu, 2013.
57 A. Boyer, *The Political State of Great Britain* (London, 1719), vol. VI, p. 23.
58 Brock, *History*, p. 49.
59 Ibid., pp. 49–50.
60 George Plimpton, *Fireworks* (New York, 1984), p. 41.
61 Ibid., p. 48.
62 Robert Cochrane, ed., *The British Letter Writers: A Collection of the Best English Letters* (Edinburgh, 1882), p. 134.
63 Charles A. Knight, *A History of England* (London, 1783), vol. VI, p. 183.
64 James Earle, *Commodore Squib: The Life, Times and Secretive Wars of England's First Rocket Man, Sir William Congreve, 1772–1828* (Newcastle upon Tyne, 2010), p. 70.
65 Pamela H. Smith and Benjamin Schmidt, *Making Knowledge in Early Modern Europe: Practices, Objects, and Texts, 1400–1800* (London, 2007), p. 83.
66 Robert Jones, *Artificial Fire-Works, Improved to the Modern Practice* (London, 1766), www.gutenberg.org.
67 *An Account of the Celebration of the Jubilee* (Birmingham, 1809), pp. 18–20.
68 Francis L. Clarke, *The Life of His Grace Arthur Duke, Marquis, and Earl of Wellington* (London, 1814), vol. III, p. 564.
69 'The Jubilee', *The Times*, 2 August 1814.
70 Charles Lamb, *The Works of Charles Lamb* (New York, 1850), vol. I, p. 161.
71 Jonathan Conlin, ed., *The Pleasure Garden, from Vauxhall to Coney Island* (Philadelphia, PA, 2013), p. 49.
72 'The Wellington Connection: Vauxhall Gardens', www.numberonelondon.net.
73 John Ashton, *The Fleet: Its River, Prison, and Marriages* (New York, 1888), p. 145.
74 John Green, *Odds and Ends about Covent Garden and Its Vicinity* (London, 1866), p. 40.
75 Brock, *History*, p. 57.

76 Warwick William Wroth and Arthur Edgar Wroth, *The London Pleasure Gardens of the Eighteenth Century* (London, 1896), p. 98.
77 'Wellington Connection'.
78 'Entertainment at the Royal Surrey Zoological Gardens, 1854', www.bl.uk.
79 William John Pinks, *The History of Clerkenwell* (London, 1881), p. 740.
80 Philip H. Highfill, Kalman A. Burnim and Edward A. Langhans, *A Biographical Dictionary of Actors, Actresses, Musicians, Dancers, Managers and Other Stage Personnel in London, 1660–1800* (Carbondale, IL, 2006), p. 421.
81 Fanny Burney, *Evelina; or, The History of a Young Lady's Entrance into the World* (London, 1861), p. 264.
82 Samuel Johnson, *The Works of Samuel Johnson* (London, 1854), vol. II, p. 420.
83 James Boswell, *Boswell's Life of Johnson* [1791], www.gutenberg.org.
84 Highfill et al., *Biographical Dictionary*, p. 348.
85 Brock, *History*, pp. 64–5.
86 Smee and Macrory, *Gunpowder*, p. 131.
87 Ibid., p. 130.
88 Warwick William Wroth, *Cremorne and the Later London Gardens* (London, 2022).
89 Brock, *History*, p. 66.
90 Playbill, 5 May 1828, www.collections.vam.ac.uk.
91 Jean-Baptiste Du Halde, *The General History of China* (London, 1736), vol. II, p. 168.
92 Werrett, *Fireworks*, p. 181.
93 Brock, *Pyrotechnics*, pp. 105–7.
94 Ibid.
95 Werrett, 'Green', p. 16.
96 Ibid., pp. 15–18.
97 Werrett, *Fireworks*, p. 229.
98 Ibid., p. 181.
99 Joseph Needham, with Ho Ping-Yü, Lu Gwei-Djen and Wang Ling, *Science and Civilisation in China*, vol. V: *Chemistry and Chemical Technology*, part VII: *Military Technology: The Gunpowder Epic* (Cambridge, 1986), p. 144.
100 Brock, *History*, p. 156.
101 *American Journal of Science and Arts* (1824), p. 132; Brock, *History*, p. 157.
102 Smee and Macrory, *Gunpowder*, pp. 19–20.

3 From the Coming of Colour to Electrical Firing

1 Harry Smee and Henry Macrory, *Gunpowder and Glory: The Explosive Life of Frank Brock* OBE (Oxford 2020), p. 23.
2 Ibid.
3 Alan St H. Brock, *A History of Fireworks* (London, 1949), p. 160.
4 Alan St H. Brock, *Pyrotechnics: The History and Art of Firework Making* (London, 1922), pp. 46–7.
5 George Plimpton, *Fireworks* (New York, 1984), p. 62.
6 Brock, *History*, p. 88.
7 Smee and Macrory, *Gunpowder*, p. 25.

8 Ibid., p. 27.
9 Ibid., p. 59.
10 *Punch*, 24 July 1869, p. 29.
11 'Crystal Palace', *The Times*, 24 September 1888.
12 Frederick Willis, *A Book of London Yesterdays* (London, 1960), p. 32.
13 Smee and Macrory, *Gunpowder*, p. 26.
14 Ben Weinreb, ed., *The London Encyclopaedia* (London, 2008), p. 295.
15 Edward Arthur Brayley Hodgetts, *The Rise and Progress of the British Explosives Industry* (London, 1909), p. 343.
16 For example, see 'Armada Celebration at Hastings', *The Times*, 21 September 1888.
17 Weinreb, *Encyclopaedia*, p. 295.
18 Brock, *Pyrotechnics*, pp. 44–5.
19 'Government by Shows – The Paris Fetes', *Illustrated London News*, 21 August 1852.
20 'The Versailles Fete', *Illustrated London News*, 1 September 1855.
21 'Festivities at Parsonstown Castle', *Illustrated London News*, 15 February 1851.
22 Brock, *History*, pp. 95–6.
23 Smee and Macrory, *Gunpowder*, p. 32.
24 'Nostalgia: Glorious Fireworks for Queen Victoria's Diamond Jubilee', www.thewestmorlandgazette.co.uk, 11 January 2014.
25 Brock, *History*, p. 103.
26 Smee and Macrory, *Gunpowder*, p. 50.
27 'Pain's Benefit', *The Times*, 10 September 1907.
28 Fred and Mary Fried, *America's Forgotten Folk Arts* (New York, 1978), p. 195.
29 Brock, *History*, p. 97.
30 Smee and Macrory, *Gunpowder*, p. 40.
31 Victoria C. Gardner Coates, ed., *Antiquity Recovered: The Legacy of Pompeii and Herculaneum* (Los Angeles, CA, 2007), p. 195.
32 Sir John Francis Davis, *The Chinese: A General Description of the Empire of China and Its Inhabitants* (London, 1836), vol. I, pp. 304–6.
33 Brock, *Pyrotechnics*, p. 9.
34 Brock, *History*, p. 108.
35 Smee and Macrory, *Gunpowder*, p. 227.
36 Brock, *History*, p. 104.
37 Michael Diamond, *Victorian Sensation* (London, 2004), p. 30.
38 Smee and Macrory, *Gunpowder*, p. 54.
39 Plimpton, *Fireworks*, p. 202.
40 Smee and Macrory, *Gunpowder*, p. 60.
41 'Brock's Benefit', *The Times*, 23 September 1904.
42 Ibid.
43 Smee and Macrory, *Gunpowder*, p. 45.
44 'Fireworks at the Crystal Palace', *The Times*, 22 May 1891.
45 Brock, *Pyrotechnics*, p. 47.
46 J. Corbet Anderson, *The Great North Wood* (London, 1898), p. 87.
47 Emily Inverso, 'The Gruccis: How Fireworks' "First Family" Has Kept the Spark Alive for Six Generations', www.forbes.com, 2 July 2015.
48 'Standard Fireworks Co.', in *Illustrated New York: The Metropolis of Today* (New York, 1888), p. 113.

49 James R. Heintze, *The Fourth of July Encyclopedia* (London, 2007), pp. 98–100.
50 Brock, *History*, p. 131.
51 William Hone, *The Every-Day Book and Table Book* (London, 1826), vol. I, pp. 1433–4.
52 Roy Porter, ed., *Myths of the English* (Cambridge, 2002), p. 80.
53 R. Chambers, ed., *The Book of Days* (London, 1864), vol. II, p. 550.
54 Porter, *Myths*, p. 80.
55 Hone, *Every-Day Book*, pp. 1435–6.
56 Porter, *Myths*, p. 79.
57 Gavin Morgan, 'The Guildford Guy Riots (1842–1865)', www.archaeologydataservice.ac.uk, 1985, pp. 62–4.
58 Porter, *Myths*, p. 84.
59 John Bohstedt, *The Politics of Provisions* (Farnham, 2010), p. 252.
60 Porter, *Myths*, p. 85.
61 Jeremy Goring, *Burn Holy Fire: Religion in Lewes since the Reformation* (Cambridge, 2003), p. 130.
62 Brock, *History*, p. 132.
63 Goring, *Burn*, pp. 144–5.
64 'Guy Fawkes' Day', *Life*, 10 December 1945.
65 Goring, *Burn*, p. 157.
66 'A Brief History of Battle Bonfire', www.battelbonfire.co.uk, accessed 25 August 2023.
67 Daniel Defoe, *A Tour Thro' the Whole Island of Great Britain* [1724–7], www.archive.org, vol. I, p. 154.
68 Jenny Gilbert, 'Fire in Their Bellies: Meet Sussex's Traditional Bonfire Societies', www.independent.co.uk, 3 November 2013.
69 Porter, *Myths*, p. 86.
70 'The Visit of the French Fleet', *The Times*, 9 August 1905.
71 Smee and Macrory, *Gunpowder*, p. 85.
72 Brock, *History*, p. 116.
73 W. C. Sellar and R. J. Yeatman, *1066 and All That* (London, 1999), p. 122.
74 Smee and Macrory, *Gunpowder*, p. 221.
75 'Shipwreck Scene in Fireworks', *The Times*, 16 July 1921.
76 'Whitsuntide Bank Holiday', *The Times*, 21 May 1929.
77 Sean Delaney, 'From Disney to the Olympic Games', www.kentonline.co.uk, 5 November 2019.
78 'The One Day a Year Fireworks Industry', *The Times*, 3 November 1959.
79 Rev. Ronald Lancaster, *Fireworks Principles and Practice* (New York, 1998), p. 13.
80 'Divine Light', www.theguardian.com, 2 November 1973.
81 Cassandra Tate, 'Hitt's Fireworks: Lighting Up the Skies from Columbia City (Seattle)', www.historylink.org, 9 June 2001.
82 Plimpton, *Fireworks*, p. 12.
83 Ibid., pp. 12–14.
84 Sally Simon Stitch, 'You Could Call It a Hall of Flame', www.chicagotribune.com, 4 July 1988.
85 Mark Wilkerson, *Who Are You? The Life of Pete Townshend* (London, 2009).
86 'Investigations. Illegally Manufactured Explosive Devices', New Hampshire Department of Safety, www.nh.gov/safety, accessed 23 August 2023.

87 Andrea Swalec, 'DC to Send Firework Safety Teams onto Streets for Holiday Weekend', www.nbcwashington.com, 1 July 2020.
88 Brock, *History*, p. 25.
89 Izumiya Gensaku, 'Fireworks by "Hanabishi" Masters Blossom in the Night Sky', www.nippon.com, 7 July 2014.
90 Plimpton, *Fireworks*, p. 78.
91 Lisa Jardine, 'How Fireworks Became Linked with Freedom', www.bbc.co.uk, 13 August 2010.
92 Plimpton, *Fireworks*, p. 175.
93 'Fête du Lac Annecy – A Pyrotechnic Wonder', www.apassion.com, 6 August 2013.
94 'Kenneth Tynan on Valencia', www.247valencia.com, January 2019.
95 Michael Palin, *Michael Palin's Hemingway Adventure* (London, 2010).
96 Ibid.
97 Lancaster, *Fireworks Principles*, p. 58.
98 Kenneth Tynan, *The Sound of Two Hands Clapping* (London, 1975), p. 245.
99 'Spectators in Mexico Run from Dangerous Fireworks During Traditional Display', www.greenocktelegraph.co.uk, 20 August 2018.
100 Marian Harvey, *Mexican Crafts and Craftspeople* (London, 1987), p. 131.
101 Mark Stachiew, 'Surviving a Taiwanese Fireworks Festival Where Rockets Are Fired at You', https://.o.canada.com, 17 June 2019.
102 Helen Davidson, 'Gods, Fireworks and Plague', www.theguardian.com, 26 February 2021.
103 Ida Liberkowski and Cynthia Malizia, *Along the Amalfi Drive* (self-published, 2006), p. 104.
104 Ellen Castelow, 'Bonfire Night in the 1950s and 1960s', www.historic-uk.com, accessed 26 August 2023.
105 Delaney, 'Disney'.

4 Bigger, Brighter, Louder: Electricity, Electronics and Computers

1 Revd Ronald Lancaster, *Fireworks Principles and Practice* (New York, 1998), p. 44.
2 Omar Sattaur, 'The Dark Secret of Fireworks', *New Scientist*, 31 October 1985.
3 Comment from former Astra worker, www.pyrosociety.org.uk, 26 January 2008.
4 Robin Young, 'Not with a Bang But a Whimper', *The Times*, 28 July 1981.
5 Mark Meredith, 'Fierce Scramble to Be First Up in Smoke', *Financial Times*, 4 November 1983.
6 Rebecca Smith, 'Meet the Merchants of Boom', *Daily Mirror*, 29 October 1995.
7 Jay Rayner, 'It'll Be All Bright on the Night', *The Times*, 2 November 1991.
8 Mark Rowe, 'British Fireworks Industry Fizzles Out', *Independent on Sunday*, 1 November 1998.
9 Caroline Bloom, 'Pennies for the Guy', *Daily Mirror*, 4 November 1994.
10 Ruth Metzstein, 'Tried and Tested: Brightest Sparks', *The Independent*, 22 October 1995.

11 Damian Whitworth, 'Bonfire Night Proves a Damp Squib as Firework Sales Dive', *The Times*, 6 November 1997.
12 Rowe, 'Fizzles Out'.
13 'Jobs Lost as Firework Firm Ceases Trading', *Hunts Post*, 27 February 2019.
14 Smith, 'Merchants of Boom'.
15 Hansard, 28 February 2003, column 510.
16 'Founder John Culverhouse Recalls 35 Years of Fantastic Fireworks', www.fantasticfireworks.co.uk, accessed 26 August 2023.
17 Roy Hodson, 'Family Company Starts to Sparkle', *Financial Times*, 4 November 1989.
18 *Time*, CXLI/1–8, p. 24.
19 Charles Passy, 'Summer Planning Starts Now for Covid-Hit Businesses', *Wall Street Journal*, 5 March 2021.
20 Randy James, 'The Art of Fireworks', www.content.time.com, 3 July 2009.
21 Scott Horsley, 'For Independence Day Fireworks, U.S. Depends on China', www.npr.org, 3 July 2018.
22 Philip Wen and Thomas Suen, 'China's Millennium-Old Fireworks Hub Grapples with Bans and Shifting Traditions', reuters.com, 11 February 2018.
23 George Plimpton, *Fireworks* (New York, 1984), p. 156.
24 Polly Schneider, 'All Fired Up', *CIO*, 1 July 1999.
25 Anthony Gardner, 'Revolutions in Pyrotechnic Magic', *The Times*, 31 October 1992.
26 Sabine Durrant, 'Outside Edge', *The Independent*, 13 August 1993.
27 Pascale Hughes, 'The Art and Science behind Those Spectacular New Year's Eve Fireworks Displays', www.inews.co.uk, 29 December 2017.
28 Plimpton, *Fireworks*, p. 81.
29 Lancaster, *Fireworks Principles*, pp. 53–5.
30 Ibid., pp. 55–6.
31 Harry Smee and Henry Macrory, *Gunpowder and Glory: The Explosive Life of Frank Brock* OBE (Oxford 2020), p. 222.
32 Emerson Rosenthal, 'Watch These Two Churches Go to Battle with Fireworks', www.vice.com, 30 June 2015.
33 Cannes Fireworks Festival and Competition: 2023 Guide, www.iconicriviera.com, accessed 26 August 2023.
34 James, 'Art of Fireworks'.
35 Plimpton, *Fireworks*, p. 72.
36 Ibid., p. 71.
37 Marilyn E. Weigold, 'Grucci, Felix James, Sr. ("Pops")', www.encyclopedia.com, accessed 26 August 2023.
38 Roy Bongartz Jr, 'Bombs Bursting in Air', *Popular Mechanics*, July 1980.
39 'Pyrotex Fireworx', www.local.standard.co.uk, accessed 26 August 2023.
40 Molly Dowrick, 'British Firework Championships in Plymouth Is Returning in August 2021', www.plymouthherald.co.uk, 25 March 2021.
41 Plimpton, *Fireworks*, p. 81.
42 Ibid., p. 86.
43 Ibid., pp. 95–100.
44 Mike White, 'Grucci Family Sets World Fireworks Record on New Year's Eve in the UAE', www.greaterlongisland.com, 4 January 2018.

45 John Voket, 'Newtown Pyrotechnist Sets World Record with Recent Firework Launch', www.newtownbee.com, 24 February 2020.
46 Derek Maiolo, '"We haven't given up": Steamboat Fireworks Aficionado to Make 2nd World Record Attempt', www.steamboatpilot.com, 4 February 2020.
47 'About the Church of Perfect Liberty', www.perfectliberty.org, accessed 26 August 2023.
48 Plimpton, *Fireworks*, p. 130.
49 Ibid., pp. 138–9.
50 'Ras Al Khaimah Marvels the World with Spectacular New Year's Eve Gala', www.businesswire.com, 1 January 2020.
51 Kevin Lynch, 'Dubai Smashes Largest Fireworks Display World Record with New Year's Spectacular', www.guinnessworldrecords.com, 13 January 2014.
52 Emily Inverso, 'The Gruccis: How Fireworks' "First Family" Has Kept the Spark Alive for Six Generations', www.forbes.com, 2 July 2015.
53 Koray Erol and Alexander Ward, 'World's Biggest Sparkler?', www.epicfireworks.com, 18 January 2016.
54 Rachel Swatman, 'How One Man Launched 642 Fireworks from a Homemade Pyrotechnics Suit', www.guinnessworldrecords.com, 4 May 2018.
55 John Culverhouse, '2009 – The Bournemouth Rocket Disaster', www.fantasticfireworks.co.uk, accessed 26 August 2023.
56 Steve Pile, ed., *Unruly Cities* (London, 1999), p. 218.
57 Ellie Dudley, 'From Fireworks to Festivals, Here's How to End the Decade with a Bang', www.smh.com.au, 29 December 2019.
58 Rachel Eddie, 'How Do the New Year's Eve Fireworks Work?', www.smh.com.au, 29 December 2019.
59 Tegan Jones, 'How Australia Is Transforming the World of Fireworks', www.gizmodo.com.au, 6 November 2017.
60 'Dynamite Dynasty', www.irishtimes.com, 20 February 1999.
61 'More Fireworks in the Family', www.abc.net.au, 20 November 2017.
62 Jones, 'Transforming'.
63 Plimpton, *Fireworks*, p. 41.
64 Mary Dejevsky, 'London's Far Too Exclusive Already, So Don't Start Charging People for the New Year's Eve Fireworks', www.independent.co.uk, 18 September 2014.
65 Fantastic Fireworks, 'London's First Ever New Year's Eve Fireworks', www.youtube.com, accessed 26 August 2023.
66 Ben Proctor, 'New Year Kicks Off with Bang', *The Sun*, 1 January 1998.
67 Mark Henderson and Dominic Kennedy, 'Spin-Doctors Blamed for River of Fire Hype', *The Times*, 3 January 2000.
68 John Harlow and Roland White, 'The World Lights Up in a Blaze of Competition', *Sunday Times*, 2 January 2000.
69 Matt Wells, 'River of Fire That Fizzled Out', www.theguardian.com, 3 January 2000.
70 Henderson and Kennedy, 'Spin-Doctors'.
71 'Thousands Crowd Riverside for New Year Fireworks at the London Eye', www.london-se1.co.uk, 1 January 2007.

72 'London's Olympic Year to Start with Fireworks at the London Eye', www.london-se1.co.uk, 20 November 2011.
73 Helen Bushby, 'London 2012: How New Year Fireworks Dazzled', www.bbc.co.uk, 3 January 2012.
74 Keith Perry, 'Crowds in London Enjoy a Fruit-Flavoured Firework Display', *Daily Telegraph*, 2 January 2014.
75 'Multisensory Fireworks – Embankment, New Years Eve 2013/2014', www.bompasandparr.com, accessed 26 August 2023.
76 'The Studio', www.bompasandparr.com, accessed 30 June 2021.
77 Perry, 'Fruit-Flavoured'.
78 Jack Slater, 'How Much Does London's New Year's Eve Fireworks Show Cost?', www.metro.co.uk, 1 January 2020.
79 Dejevsky, 'Too Exclusive'.
80 'Promise + Proof = Experience Brand', www.jackmorton.com, accessed 26 August 2023.
81 'The World's Smallest Fireworks Display at Legoland Windsor', www.titaniumfireworks.com, accessed 26 August 2023.
82 'London 2012: Opening Ceremony – Reviews', www.theguardian.com, 29 July 2012.
83 Sarah Oliver, 'He's Set Fire to the Rain for Adele', www.dailymail.co.uk, 27 January 2018.
84 'The London 2012 Olympic Ceremonies', www.titaniumfireworks.com, accessed 26 August 2023.
85 Oliver, 'Adele'.
86 'Darryl Fleming', www.titaniumfireworks.com, accessed 25 May 2021.
87 Sara Townsend, 'Bangs for Their Bucks: Which City Has the Biggest New Year's Eve Fireworks?', www.theguardian.com, 30 December 2014.
88 Oliver, 'Adele'.
89 Chris York, 'Sadiq Khan Trolled Brexiteers during London's New Year Fireworks and They're Not Happy', www.huffingtonpost.co.uk, 1 January 2019.
90 Martin Robinson and Jemma Carr, '"Disgusting waste of money": London Assembly Members Slam Sadiq Khan's £1.5million New Year's Eve Light Show', www.dailymail.co.uk, 4 January 2021.
91 Rayner, 'All Bright'.
92 Jeremy Goring, *Burn Holy Fire: Religion in Lewes since the Reformation* (Cambridge, 2003), p. 157.
93 Ibid., p. 158.
94 'Lewes Bonfire Night Effigies Include a Urinating Boris Johnson', www.bbc.co.uk, 5 November 2019.
95 Matt Southam, 'Bangers Are a Part of Bonfire Tradition', www.ryeandbattleobserver.co.uk, 19 November 2010.
96 Bruce Haring, 'Disney Changes Fireworks Show Announcement to More Inclusive Message, Setting Off Some Conservatives', www.deadline.com, 2 July 2021.
97 Emily Ferguson, '"Mickey Mouse goes woke!" Disney Brutally Mocked for Ditching "Boys and Girls" Greeting', www.express.co.uk, 3 July 2021.
98 Plimpton, *Fireworks*, pp. 158–9.
99 Ibid., p. 236.

100 David Agren, 'Despite Accidents, Mexicans Continue to Honor Saints with Fireworks', www.cruxnow.com, 15 March 2017.
101 'Illegal Fireworks Makers Outnumber the Legal Ones in Tultepec', www.greenocktelegraph.co.uk, 27 June 2018.
102 Agren, 'Despite Accidents'.
103 Alan St H. Brock, *A History of Fireworks* (London, 1949), p. 128.
104 Adriana Bishop, 'Behind the Scenes of Malta's Impressive Fireworks Tradition', www.guidemalta.com, accessed 28 August 2023.
105 Lancaster, *Fireworks Principles*, p. 73.
106 Andrew Ellul, 'Record-Breaking Catherine Wheel', www.timesofmalta.com, 24 June 2011.
107 'Indoor Fireworks: Harder Than It Looks', www.ukfr.com, 24 March 2022.
108 Ibid.
109 'The Rise of the Firework Cake', www.epicfireworks.com, 16 July 2021.
110 Christopher Jobson, 'Artist Cai GuoQiang Sends a 500-Meter Ladder of Fire into the Sky', www.thisiscolossal.com, 12 August 2015.
111 Y-Jean Mun-Delsalle, 'Contemporary Artist Cai Guo-Qiang Paints the Sky Using Gunpowder', www.homeanddecor.com.sg, 29 April 2021.
112 Dodie Bellamy, 'Up in Smoke', artforum.com, 26 October 2021.
113 'Guinness World Record Title for "Highest Altitude Fireworks Display"', www.epicfireworks.com, 3 May 2021.
114 'Corporate Team Building Events', www.howardsfireworks.com.au, accessed 5 March 2021.
115 'Go Out with a Bang', www.howardsfireworks.com.au, accessed 5 March 2021.
116 'Helping to Celebrate the Life of a Loved One or Friend with Fireworks', www.heavenlystarsfireworks.com, accessed 6 March 2021.

5 Accidents, Disasters, Rules and Regulations

1 John Bond, *The Hazards of Life and All That* (London, 1996).
2 Craig J. Spence, 'Accidents and Response: Sudden Violent Death in the Early Modern City, 1650–1750', PhD thesis, Royal Holloway, University of London, https://pure.royalholloway.ac.uk, 2013.
3 Clive Ponting, *Gunpowder: An Explosive History* (London, 2006), p. 233.
4 Alan St H. Brock, *Pyrotechnics: The History and Art of Firework Making* (London, 1922), p. 61.
5 Philip H. Highfill, Kalman A. Burnim and Edward A. Langhans, *A Biographical Dictionary of Actors, Actresses, Musicians, Dancers, Managers and Other Stage Personnel in London, 1660–1800* (Carbondale, IL, 2006), p. 340.
6 'Scott v Shepherd', www.masonlec.org, accessed 26 August 2023.
7 Thomas Beven, *Negligence in Law* (London, 1895), vol. I, p. 52.
8 Henry A. Chamberlain, *A New and Compleat Survey of the Cities of London and Westminster* (London, 1770), p. 390.
9 Joseph Strutt and John Charles Cox, *The Sports and Pastimes of the People of England* (London, 1903), p. 376.

10 *Gentleman's Magazine*, XXXIII, p. 311.
11 Kevin Salatino, *Incendiary Art: The Representation of Fireworks in Early Modern Europe* (Los Angeles, CA, 1997), p. 41.
12 *Eclectic Review* (London, 1825), vol. XXIV, p. 533.
13 Simon Werrett, 'Green Is the Colour: St. Petersburg's Chemical Laboratories and Competing Visions of Chemistry in the Eighteenth Century', *Ambix*, LX/2 (2013), pp. 122–38, p. 132.
14 Henry Sutherland Edwards, *Old and New Paris: Its History, Its People, and Its Places* (London, 1893), vol. I, p. 146.
15 Alan St H. Brock, *A History of Fireworks* (London, 1949), pp. 168–9.
16 Revd Ronald Lancaster, *Fireworks Principles and Practice* (New York, 1998), p. 25.
17 Wendy Neal, *With Disastrous Consequences: London Disasters, 1830–1917* (Enfield Lock, 1992), p. 75.
18 Brock, *History*, p. 172.
19 *The Times*, 5 September 1825, p. 2.
20 Brock, *Pyrotechnics*, p. 65.
21 Neal, *Disastrous Consequences*, p. 78.
22 Brock, *Pyrotechnics*, p. 144.
23 Jennifer Latson, 'The Dark History of Fireworks', www.time.com, 3 July 2015.
24 Colonial Williamsburg Foundation, *Colonial Williamsburg* (Williamsburg, VA, 1995), vol. XVIII, p. 61.
25 Niraj Chokshi, 'A History of Fireworks Mayhem on the Fourth of July', www.nytimes.com, 1 July 2016.
26 James R. Heinze, *The Fourth of July Encyclopedia* (London, 2013), pp. 99–100.
27 'Fireworks Blow Up', *Atlanta Constitution*, 8 April 1894.
28 David Nasaw, *The Chief: The Life of William Randolph Hearst* (New York, 2000).
29 Michael Waters, 'The 1900s Movement to Make the Fourth of July Boring (But Safe)', www.smithsonianmag.com, 2 July 2019.
30 Ibid.
31 Ibid.
32 Cassandra Tate, 'Hitt's Fireworks: Lighting Up the Skies from Columbia City (Seattle)', www.historylink.org, 9 June 2001.
33 Gianni DeVincent Hayes, *Zambelli: The First Family of Fireworks* (New York, 2003), p. 121.
34 Brock, *History*, pp. 175–6.
35 'Firework Accident in Campania', *The Times*, 5 August 1926.
36 'Firework Factory Explosion', *The Times*, 22 June 1932.
37 Brock, *History*, p. 177.
38 'Blasts Wreck Three Fireworks Plants', www.fireengineering.com, 10 September 1926.
39 'Four Killed in Fireworks Plant Fire', www.fireengineering.com, 12 June 1929.
40 'Devon, PA Fireworks Plant Explosion', *Cumberland Evening Times*, 3 April 1930.
41 Brock, *History*, p. 175.
42 'The One Day a Year Fireworks Industry', *Times*, 3 November 1959.
43 'Firework Factory Explosion', *Times*, 13 December 1955.

44 'Fireworks Safety Campaign ahead of Bonfire Night', www.manchestereveningnews.co.uk, 1 November 1968.
45 Marianne Curphey, 'Imported Fireworks Fill Displays with Danger', *The Times*, 5 November 1994.
46 George Plimpton, *Fireworks* (New York, 1984), pp. 147–8.
47 '12 Avril 1977 – 12 Avril 2017 Monteux se souvient', www.monteux.fr, accessed 26 August 2023.
48 Claudia Calleja, 'Thirty Years On: Recalling Tragedy That Shook Nation', *Times of Malta*, 8 September 2014.
49 Brock, *History*, p. 177.
50 Antonio Cano, 'Tragedia en México al incendiarse un alamacén de cohetes', www.elpais.com, 12 December 1988.
51 Teoh Pei Ying and Lim Xin Ying, 'The Bright Sparklers Tragedy', www.nst.com, 4 August 2020.
52 'Sivakasi: India's Dangerous Fireworks Capital', www.bbc.co.uk, 23 September 2012.
53 Jaya Menon, 'In Sivakasi, Caste Holds the Fireworks', www.indianexpress.com, 26 April 2006.
54 Graham Johnson, 'Child Victims of the Firework Factories', *Sunday Mirror*, 29 October 2000.
55 'Sivakasi: Fireworks Capital'.
56 'Kerala State Disaster Management Plan', 2016, www.sdma.kerala.gov.in, pp. 73–4.
57 'Kollam Temple: India Fireworks Blast Kills at Least 100', www.bbc.co.uk, 10 April 2016.
58 David Agren, 'Mexican Town Pays Tribute to Firework Blast Victims with Pyrotechnic Display', www.theguardian.com, 10 March 2017.
59 Missy Ryan, 'Over 200 Die in Peru Fireworks Blaze', www.theguardian.com, 31 December 2001.
60 Owen Amos, 'The U.S. State That Bans Sparklers but Not Guns', www.bbc.com, 1 November 2017.
61 'Restrict Firework Use to Four Days a Year: Pet Lovers', www.bbc.com, 17 May 2016.
62 Saffron Otter and Lea Nakache, '"Please Think of the Animals": How Fireworks Caused Puppy to "Die of Fright"', www.dailypost.co.uk, 4 November 2019.
63 'New Year Fireworks: Why Don't More People Use Quiet Pyrotechnics?', www.bbc.com, 31 December 2019.
64 Tim Quantrill, 'Public Asked for Say on Fireworks by Bradford Council', www.thetelegraphandargus.co.uk, 21 January 2020.
65 Daniel Jaines, 'Lincoln Council Reminded of Veterans' Health as Fireworks Controls Tightened', www.thelincolnite.co.uk, 22 January 2020.
66 Jez Hemming, 'North Wales Retailers "Should Stock Quieter Fireworks"', www.dailypost.co.uk, 23 January 2020.
67 John Merrow, 'Fireworks from a Different Perspective', www.vineyardgazette.com, 1 July 2021.
68 'New Year Fireworks'.
69 'Our Low Noise Firework Displays Prove Noisier Isn't Always Better', www.flashpoint-fireworks.co.uk, accessed 26 August 2023.

70 'New Year Fireworks'.
71 Geoffrey Lean, 'Bonfire Night "Saved" from New Pollution Law', *Independent on Sunday*, 5 November 1995.
72 Teresa Moreno, 'Effect of Fireworks Events on Urban Background Trace Metal Aerosol Concentrations: Is the Cocktail Worth the Show?', *Journal of Hazardous Materials*, CLXXXIII/1–3 (15 November 2010), pp. 945–9.
73 'Trafalgar Fireworks' ECO Sparklers', www.ukfr.com, 12 May 2022.

6 Fireworks in the Arts

1 William Shakespeare, *Love's Labour's Lost*, Act v, Scene i.
2 Ben Jonson, *Every Man in His Humour*, Prologue, www.gutenberg.org.
3 Kevin Matthew Carr, 'A Theater of the Senses: A Cultural History of Theatrical Effects in Early-Modern England', PhD thesis, The Florida State University, 2013.
4 Matthew Steggle, *Speed and Flight in Shakespeare* (Cham, 2022), p. 112.
5 Samuel Johnson, *The Beauties of Samuel Johnson: Maxims and Observations* (London, 1804), p. 37.
6 William Makepeace Thackeray, *Vanity Fair*, www.gutenberg.org.
7 William Makepeace Thackeray, *Pendennis*, www.gutenberg.org.
8 Charles Dickens, *Sketches by Boz*, www.gutenberg.org.
9 Charles Dickens, *Nicholas Nickleby*, www.gutenberg.org.
10 Charles Dickens, *Bleak House*, www.gutenberg.org.
11 George Gissing, *The Nether World*, www.gutenberg.org.
12 Thomas Hood, 'Sonnet to Vauxhall', www.theguardian.com, 27 November 2017.
13 Robert Browning, *The Ring and the Book*, Book XII, www.en.wikisource.org.
14 Johann Wolfgang von Goethe, *Elective Affinities*, https://oll.libertyfund.org.
15 Anton Chekhov, *The Bishop and Other Stories*, www.en.wikisource.org.
16 Oscar Wilde, *The Remarkable Rocket*, www.users.uoa.gr.
17 James Joyce, *Ulysses* (London, 1969), pp. 362–4.
18 Ibid., p. 364.
19 Alain-Fournier, *Le Grand Meaulnes*, trans. Frank Davison (London, 2000), pp. 15–17.
20 Amy Lowell, 'Fireworks', www.thereader.org.uk, 10 November 2014.
21 Ernest Hemingway, *For Whom the Bell Tolls* (Harmondsworth, 1970), p. 84.
22 Ernest Hemingway, *Fiesta* [*The Sun Also Rises*] (London, 1949), pp. 116–17.
23 Ibid., p. 136.
24 Iris Murdoch, *Under the Net* (London, 2002), pp. 62–4.
25 Ibid., pp. 60–61.
26 Philip Pullman, *The Firework-Maker's Daughter* (Reading, 1996), pp. 1–3.
27 Ibid., pp. 9–11.
28 Ibid., p. 33.
29 Ibid., p. 62.
30 Ibid., pp. 88–91.
31 Ibid., p. 91.
32 Ibid., pp. 98–102.
33 Alfred Hickling, '*The Firework-Maker's Daughter* – Review', www.theguardian.com, 24 March 2013.

34 Kevin Salatino, *Incendiary Art: The Representation of Fireworks in Early Modern Europe* (Los Angeles, CA, 1997), p. 43.
35 Ibid., p. 49.
36 Barbara H. Weinberg, 'James McNeill Whistler (1834–1903)', www.metmuseum.org, April 2010.
37 Frances Fowle, '*Nocturne: Black and Gold: The Fire Wheel*', www.tate.org.uk, 4 December 2000.
38 K. Flint, 'Fireworks', *Interdisciplinary Studies in the Long Nineteenth Century*, www.bbk.ac.uk, 2017.
39 'Homage to Destruction: Jean Tinguely', www.tate.org.uk, 1 September 2009.
40 Anna McNay, 'Dennis Oppenheim: Thought Collision Factories', www.studiointernational.com, 27 November 2013.
41 David Rooney, '*Hana-Bi* Gets Gold at Venice', www.variety.com, 8 September 1997.
42 Tim Bouverie, *Perfect Pitch* (London, 2021).
43 John Mangum, '*Fireworks*. Igor Stravinsky', www.laphil.com, accessed 27 August 2023.
44 'Mr Brock on "Fireworks"', *The Times*, 2 March 1914.
45 Mangum, '*Fireworks*'.
46 'Six of the Best . . . Pieces of Music for Firework Night', www.classical-music.com, 5 November 2021.

7 Use, Not Ornament

1 Roddam Narasimha, 'Rockets in Mysore and Britain, 1750–1850 AD', National Aeronautical Laboratory, Bangalore, project document DU 8503, 1985.
2 Roger T. Stearn, 'Sir William Congreve', *Oxford Dictionary of National Biography*, 10 February 2022.
3 Narasimha, 'Rockets'.
4 Stearn, 'Congreve'.
5 Peter Frankopan, 'A Devilish Instrument of War', www.spectator.co.uk, 12 March 2016.
6 Joseph Needham, with Ho Ping-Yü, Lu Gwei-Djen and Wang Ling, *Science and Civilisation in China*, vol. V: *Chemistry and Chemical Technology*, part VII: *Military Technology: The Gunpowder Epic* (Cambridge, 1986), p. 165.
7 Philip Ball, *The Water Kingdom: A Secret History of China* (Chicago, IL, 2017), p. 200.
8 Tonio Andrade, *The Gunpowder Age: China, Military Invention and the Rise of the West in World History* (Princeton, NJ, 2016), p. 42.
9 Needham, *Science and Civilisation*, p. 171.
10 Ibid., p. 180.
11 Edward Walford, *Old and New London* (London, 1891), vol. IV, p. 389.
12 Roger Keyes, *The Naval Memoirs of Admiral of the Fleet Sir Roger Keyes: Scapa Flow to the Dover Straits, 1916–1918* (New York, 1935), p. 404.
13 James C. Bond, 'The Fog of War: Large-Scale Smoke Screening Operations of First Canadian Army in Northwest Europe', *Canadian Military History*, XIII/1 (1999), p. 41.
14 Alan St H. Brock, *A History of Fireworks* (London, 1949), p. 240.

15 Harry Smee and Henry Macrory, *Gunpowder and Glory: The Explosive Life of Frank Brock* OBE (Oxford, 2020), pp. 157–9.
16 Denise E. Pilato, 'Martha Coston', *International Journal of Naval History*, 1/1 (2001).
17 François Bernier, *Travels in the Mogul Empire,* AD *1656–1668*, trans. Irving Brock (London, 1891), p. 277.
18 George Plimpton, *Fireworks* (New York, 1984), p. 230.
19 David Thompson, 'The Bird Scarers of Honolulu International Airport', www.honolulumagazine.com, 3 April 2012.
20 'Hunting Whales with Gunpowder', *Pacific Rural Press*, 19 April 1879.
21 Smee and Macrory, *Gunpowder*, p. 220.
22 Joanna Espin, 'Rocket Mail: Prankster or Visionary?', www.postalmuseum.org, 13 March 2019.
23 Christopher Turner, 'Letter Bombs. Gerhard Zucker's Rocket Post', www.cabinetmagazine.org, Fall 2006.
24 Amal Kumar Bose, 'Stephen Smith Story', ISDA *Journal*, 2 (1992), pp. 5–9.
25 Jamie Rigg, 'The Rise and Fall of Rocket Mail', www.engadget.com, 2 February 2019.

Bibliography

Books

Alain-Fournier, *Le Grand Meaulnes*, trans. Frank Davison (London, 2000)
Andrade, Tonio, *The Gunpowder Age: China, Military Invention and the Rise of the West in World History* (Princeton, NJ, 2016)
Bacon, Sir Francis, *The New Atlantis* (1626), www.gutenberg.org
Bernier, François, *Travels in the Mogul Empire, AD 1656–1668*, trans. Irving Brock (London 1891)
Brock, Alan St H., *A History of Fireworks* (London, 1949)
—, *Pyrotechnics: The History and Art of Firework Making* (London, 1922)
Buchanan, Brenda J., *Gunpowder, Explosives and the State: A Technological History* (Abingdon, 2006)
Chase, Kenneth, *Firearms: A Global History to 1700* (Cambridge, 2003)
Conlin, Jonathan, ed., *The Pleasure Garden, from Vauxhall to Coney Island* (Philadelphia, PA, 2013)
David, Robert C., and Garry R. Marvin, *Venice, the Tourist Maze: A Cultural Critique of the World's Most Touristed City* (Berkeley, CA, 2004)
Dickens, Charles, *Nicholas Nickleby* (1839), www.gutenberg.org
—, *Sketches by Boz* (1839), www.gutenberg.org
Edwards, Henry Sutherland, *Old and New Paris: Its History, Its People, and Its Places* (London, 1893)
Gissing, George, *The Nether World* (1889), www.gutenberg.org
Gode, P. K., *The History of Fireworks in India between AD 1400 and 1900* (Basavangudi, 1953)
Goethe, Johann Wolfgang von, *Elective Affinities* (1809), www.oll.libertyfund.org
Goring, Jeremy, *Burn Holy Fire: Religion in Lewes since the Reformation* (Cambridge, 2003)
Griffith, Eva, *A Jacobean Company and Its Playhouse: The Queen's Servants at the Red Bull Theatre (c. 1605–1619)* (Cambridge, 2013)
Gristwood, Sarah, *Elizabeth and Leicester* (London, 2008)
Harvey, Marian, *Mexican Crafts and Craftspeople* (London, 1987)
Heinze, James R., *The Fourth of July Encyclopedia* (London, 2013)
Hemingway, Ernest, *Fiesta* [*The Sun Also Rises*] (London, 1949)
Highfill, Philip H., Kalman A. Burnim and Edward A. Langhans, *A Biographical Dictionary of Actors, Actresses, Musicians, Dancers, Managers and Other Stage Personnel in London, 1660–1800* (Carbondale, IL, 2006)

Hone, William, *The Every-Day Book and Table Book* (London, 1826), www.gutenberg.org
Illustrated New York: The Metropolis of Today (New York, 1888)
Lancaster, the Revd Ronald, *Fireworks Principles and Practice* (New York, 1998)
Livingstone, Ken, *You Can't Say That: Memoirs* (London, 2011)
Murdoch, Iris, *Under the Net* (London, 2002)
Neal, Wendy, *With Disastrous Consequences: London Disasters, 1830–1917* (Enfield Lock, 1992)
Needham, Joseph, with Ho Ping-Yü, Lu Gwei-Djen and Wang Ling, *Science and Civilisation in China*, vol. V: *Chemistry and Chemical Technology*, part VII: *Military Technology: The Gunpowder Epic* (Cambridge, 1986)
Palin, Michael, *Michael Palin's Hemingway Adventure* (London, 1999)
Partington, J. R., *A History of Greek Fire and Gunpowder* (Baltimore, MD, 1999)
Phillips, Henry Pratap, *The History and Chronology of Gunpowder and Gunpowder Weapons (c. 1000 to 1850)* (Chennai, 2016)
Plimpton, George, *Fireworks* (New York, 1984)
Ponting, Clive, *Gunpowder: An Explosive History* (London, 2006)
Pullman, Philip, *The Firework-Maker's Daughter* (Reading, 1996)
Russell, Michael S., *The Chemistry of Fireworks* (Cambridge, 2009)
Salatino, Kevin, *Incendiary Art: The Representation of Fireworks in Early Modern Europe* (Los Angeles, CA, 1997)
Sharpe, James, *Remember, Remember: A Cultural History of Guy Fawkes Day* (Cambridge, MA, 2005)
Smee, Harry, and Henry Macrory, *Gunpowder and Glory: The Explosive Life of Frank Brock* OBE (Oxford 2020)
Strutt, Joseph, *The Sports and Pastimes of the People of England from the Earliest Period* (London, 1801)
Thackeray, W. M., *Pendennis* (1850), www.gutenberg.org
—, *Vanity Fair* (1848), www.gutenberg.org
Werrett, Simon, *Fireworks: Pyrotechnic Arts and Sciences in European History* (London, 2010)
Withington, John, *London's Disasters: From Boudicca to the Banking Crisis* (Stroud, 2010)

Articles

'Brazil Nightclub Fire: Four Convicted over Blaze That Killed 242', www.bbc.co.uk, 11 December 2021
'Festive Fireworks Create Harmful Pall of Pollution', www.forbes.com, 31 December 2019
'Fireworks Legislation and Impacts: International Evidence Review', www.gov.scot, 4 October 2019
'Gods, Fireworks and Plague', www.theguardian.com, 26 February 2021
'Guy Fawkes' Day', *Life*, 10 December 1945
'Kollam Temple: India Fireworks Blast Kills at Least 100', www.bbc.co.uk, 10 April 2016
'Owner Jailed over Deadly 2009 Russia Nightclub Fire', www.bbc.co.uk, 30 April 2013
'The Rise of the Firework Cake', www.epicfireworks.com, 16 July 2021

Agren, David, 'Despite Accidents, Mexicans Continue to Honor Saints with Fireworks', www.cruxnow.com, 15 March 2017
Amos, Ilona, 'Scottish Skies Lit with Fireworks over 500 Years Ago', www.scotsman.com, 31 August 2015
Amos, Owen, 'The U.S. State That Bans Sparklers but Not Guns', www.bbc.com, 1 November 2017
Andersen, Ross, 'The Strange and Wonderful Origins of Rocketry', www.theatlantic.com, 25 July 2012
Bantoey, Nilobon, 'Finland Won a Trophy at Da Nang International Fireworks Festival 2019', www.scandasia.com, 8 July 2019
Bellwood, Tom, 'Mario Balotelli Firework Damage Revealed', www.dailymail.co.uk, 31 October 2014
Bishop, Adriana, 'Behind the Scenes of Malta's Impressive Fireworks Tradition', www.guidemalta.com
Biswas, Arun Kumar, 'Epic of Saltpetre to Gunpowder', *Indian Journal of History of Science*, XL/4 (2005), pp. 539–71
Bond, James C., 'The Fog of War: Large-Scale Smoke Screening Operations of First Canadian Army in Northwest Europe', *Canadian Military History*, XIII/1 (1999), p. 41
Bongartz Jr, Roy, 'Bombs Bursting in Air', *Popular Mechanics* (July 1980), pp. 63–6
Bradley, Michael, 'A Very Derry Halloween: A Carnival of Frights, Fireworks and Parades', www.theguardian.com, 24 October 2018
Bushby, Helen, 'London 2012: How New Year Fireworks Dazzled', www.bbc.co.uk, 3 January 2012
Calleja, Claudia, 'Thirty Years on: Recalling Tragedy That Shook Nation', *Times of Malta*, 8 September 2014
Cano, Antonio, 'Tragedia en México al incendiarse un alamacén de cohetes', www.elpais.com, 12 December 1988
Carr, Kevin Matthew, 'A Theater of the Senses: A Cultural History of Theatrical Effects in Early-Modern England', PhD thesis, The Florida State University, 2013
Carroll, Nadine, 'Hundreds of Birds Drop Dead after the Fireworks Ban in Rome Was Ignored', www.uk.finance.yahoo.com, 4 January 2021
Carroll, Rory, 'Argentinian Band Convicted over Nightclub Fire', www.theguardian.com, 21 April 2011
Catherman, Caroline, and David Williams, 'A Colorado City Has Set Off the World's Largest Firework', www.edition.cnn.com, 11 February 2020
Changnon, Stanley A. Jr, and J. Loreena Ivens, 'History Repeated: The Forgotten Hail Cannons of Europe', *Bulletin of the American Meteorological Society*, LXII/3 (1981), pp. 368–75
Chokshi, Niraj, 'A History of Fireworks Mayhem on the Fourth of July', www.nytimes.com, 1 July 2016
Cohen, Jennie, 'Fireworks' Vibrant History', www.history.com, 3 July 2019
Curphey, Marianne, 'Imported Fireworks Fill Displays with Danger', *The Times*, 5 November 1994
Davies, Ross, 'Derrick Worthington, Pyrotechnician', *The Times*, 26 October 1981
Delaney, Sean, 'From Disney to the Olympic Games, Exploring the History of Dartford's Wells Fireworks Factory', www.kentonline.co.uk, 5 November 2019

Douglas, Elliot, 'Can Fireworks Ever Become Eco-Friendly?', www.ecowatch.com, 30 December 2020

Ellul, Andrew, 'Record-Breaking Catherine Wheel', www.timesofmalta.com, 24 June 2011

Erol, Koray, and Alexander Ward, 'World's Biggest Sparkler?', www.mirror.co.uk, 18 January 2016

Espin, Joanna, 'Rocket Mail: Prankster or Visionary?', www.postalmuseum.org, 13 March 2019

Ferrari, Marco, 'Falmouth Woman's Ashes Spread by Firework above Pendennis Point', www.falmouthpacket.co.uk, 23 January 2020

Gilbert, Jenny, 'Fire in Their Bellies: Meet Sussex's Traditional Bonfire Societies', www.independent.co.uk, 3 November 2013

Greenberger, Alex, 'Feminist Pioneer Judy Chicago's Seminal Fireworks Art Heads to Nevada', www.artnews.com, 19 May 2020

Helmenstine, Anne Marie, 'The Chemistry behind Sparklers', www.thoughtco.com, 30 November 2019

Henderson, Mark, and Dominic Kennedy, 'Spin-Doctors Blamed for River of Fire Hype', *The Times*, 3 January 2000

Hickling, Alfred, '*The Firework-Maker's Daughter* – Review', www.guardian.com, 24 March 2013

Holland, Clare, and John Nairn, 'Blast Them! – Police Must Give These Firework Shops a Rocket', *Sunday Mail*, 29 October 1995

Horsley, Scott, 'For Independence Day Fireworks, U.S. Depends on China', www.npr.org, 3 July 2018

Inverso, Emily, 'The Gruccis: How Fireworks' "First Family" Has Kept the Spark Alive for Six Generations', www.forbes.com, 2 July 2015

James, Ben, 'Battle for Bonfire Night', www.theargus.co.uk, 4 November 2014

James, Randy, 'The Art of Fireworks', www.time.com, 3 July 2009

Johnson, Graham, 'Child Victims of the Firework Factories,' *Sunday Mirror*, 29 October 2000

Khare, Vineet, 'Sivakasi: India's Dangerous Fireworks Capital', www.bbc.co.uk, 23 September 2012

Knee, Karen, 'Pa. Company Works to Make Fireworks Greener', www.philly.com, 4 July 2009

Lean, Geoffrey, 'Bonfire Night "Saved" from New Pollution Law', *The Independent*, 5 November 1995

Lin, Chi-Chi, 'A Review of the Impact of Fireworks on Particulate Matter in Ambient Air', *Journal of the Air and Waste Management Association*, LXVI/12 (2016), pp. 1171–82

Lynch, Kevin, 'Official: Dubai Smashes Largest Fireworks Display World Record with New Year's Spectacular', www.guinnessworldrecords.com, 13 January 2014

McNay, Anna, 'Dennis Oppenheim: Thought Collision Factories', www.studiointernational.com, 27 November 2013

Maune, Tess, '30 Years Later, Man Returns to Scene of Pawnee County Fireworks Explosion', www.newson6.com, 25 June 2015

Metzstein, Ruth, 'Tried and Tested: Brightest Sparks', *The Independent*, 22 October 1995

Morgan, Gavin, 'The Guildford Guy Riots (1842–1865)', www.archaeologydataservice.ac.uk
Mun-Delsalle, Y-Jean, 'Contemporary Artist Cai Guoqiang Paints the Sky Using Gunpowder', www.asiaone.com, 30 April 2021
Nalewicki, Jennifer, 'In Switzerland, an Exploding Snowman Helps Predict Spring', www.smithsonianmag.com, 12 April 2016
Narasimha, Roddam, 'Rockets in Mysore and Britain, 1750–1850', National Aeronautical Laboratory, Bangalore, project document DU 8503, 1985
Nicholls, Arthur, 'Glorious Fireworks for Queen Victoria's Diamond Jubilee', www.thewestmorlandgazette.co.uk, 11 January 2014
Oliver, Sarah, 'He's Set Fire to the Rain for Adele', www.dailymail.co.uk, 27 January 2018
Paletta, Damian, and Emily Rauhala, 'The Fireworks King', *Washington Post*, 27 June 2018
Penman, Andrew, '50 Per Cent More Injuries since Firework Rules Relaxed', *Daily Mirror*, 4 November 1996
Perry, Keith, 'Crowds in London Enjoy a Fruit-Flavoured Firework Display', *Daily Telegraph*, 2 January 2014
Pilato, Denise E., 'Martha Coston', *International Journal of Naval History*, 1/1 (2001)
Rayner, Jay, 'It'll Be All Bright on the Night', *The Times*, 2 November 1991
Rooney, David, '*Hana-bi* Gets Gold at Venice', www.variety.com, 8 September 1997
Ryan, Missy, 'Over 200 Die in Peru Fireworks Blaze', www.theguardian.com, 31 December 2001
Shen Ke, ed., 'China's Millennium-Old Fireworks Hub Grapples with Bans and Shifting Traditions', www.shine.cn, 12 February 2018
Simpson, Andrew G., 'Fireworks Facts', www.insurancejournal.com, 2 July 2018
Stachiew, Mark, 'Surviving a Taiwanese Fireworks Festival Where Rockets Are Fired at You', www.o.canada.com, 17 June 2019
Sullivan, David A., 'Coney Island History: The Story of Pain's Manhattan Beach Fireworks Shows', www.heartofconeyisland.com, 2015
Thompson, David, 'The Bird Scarers of Honolulu International Airport', www.honolulumagazine.com, 3 April 2012
Trevena, Lowie, 'Fireworks Believed to Cause Death of Young Zebra', www.bristol247.com, 10 November 2020
Verney, Joseph, 'Lincolnshire Pet Owner's "Firework Rules" Petition Gains over 960k Signatures', www.thelincolnite.co.uk, 2 January 2022
Waters, Michael, 'The 1900s Movement to Make the Fourth of July Boring (But Safe)', www.smithsonianmag.com, 2 July 2019
Werrett, Simon, 'Full Colour Fireworks', www.bshs.org.uk
Xiang Jing, ed., 'Lidu Fireworks', www.cctv.com, 23 September 2004

Acknowledgements

I would like to thank Dr Lee Banting, former Senior Lecturer in Chemistry at the University of Portsmouth, and Dr Thomas Withington, author and my son, for kindly reading the manuscript and offering expert comments and suggestions. Any errors are my responsibility.

Photo Acknowledgements

The author and publishers wish to express their thanks to the sources listed below for illustrative material and/or permission to reproduce it. Some locations of artworks are also given below, in the interest of brevity:

British Library: p. 108; The British Museum: pp. 47, 60, 61, 287; from Alan St. H. Brock, *Pyrotechnics: The History and Art of Firework Making* (London, 1922): pp. 68, 115, 280, 281; Columbus Museum of Art: p. 104 top (Museum Purchase: Howald Fund II); Creative Commons: pp. 14 (Giovanni Grevembroch/Public Domain), 18 (Huangdan2060/CC BY-SA 3.0 Unported), 20 (mattbuck/CC BY-SA 2.0 Generic), 23 (Kang Byeong Kee/CC BY-SA 3.0 Unported), 26 (Public Domain), 27 (Peter van der Sluijs/CC BY-SA 3.0 Unported/CC BY-SA 2.5 Generic/CC BY-SA 2.0 Generic/CC BY-SA 1.0 Generic), 35 (HathiTrust/Public Domain), 51 (Paul Sandby/Public Domain), 65 (*Illustrated London News*/HathiTrust/Public Domain), 82 (Ebenezer Landells/Public Domain), 90 (Science History Institute/Public Domain), 97 (Public Domain), 100 (Van Gogh Museum, Amsterdam/Public Domain), 102 top (Buffalo AKG Art Museum/Sailko/CC BY-SA 3.0 Unported), 120 (Edwinsilvester/CC BY-SA 3.0 Unported), 130 (Carlos Sancho/ CC BY-SA 2.0 Generic), 131 (Simon Burchell/CC BY-SA 4.0 International), 145 (Tiverton: Tiverton Rugby Club – Bonfire Night by Lewis Carke/CC BY-SA 2.0 Generic), 176 (Ragespinloss/CC BY 2.0 Generic), 197 (Science History Institute/Public Domain), 202 top (Adam J. W./CC BY 3.0 Unported), 202 bottom (Bengin Ahmad from Dubai, United Arab Emirates/CC BY 2.0 Generic), 203 (Domenic Camilleri/CC BY-SA 4.0 International), 204 top (Kyrill Poole/CC BY-SA 2.0 Generic), 204 bottom (Gaetan Lee from London, UK/CC BY 2.0 Generic), 205 (AlejandroLinaresGarcia/CC BY-SA 3.0 Unported), 206 top (SIMarsden/CC BY-SA 4.0 International), 206 bottom (Jason Zhang/CC BY-SA 3.0 Unported), 207 top (Roland zh/CC BY-SA 3.0 Unported), 207 bottom (Tim Hipps, U.S. Army/Public Domain), 208 top (Korean Culture and Information Service (Korean Olympic Committee)/CC BY-SA 2.0 Generic), 208 bottom (Leeds Castle: Public firework display by Michael Garlick/CC BY 2.0 Generic), 213 (Toledo-Lucas County Public Library/Public Domain), 275 (National Maritime Museum, London/Public Domain), 294 (http://postagestamps.gov.in/Stamps_List.aspx (GODL-India)); Detroit Institute of Arts: p. 103 (Gift of Dexter M. Ferry, Jr); The J. Paul Getty Museum, Los Angeles: p. 98; Klassik Stiftung Weimar: p. 99 bottom; Library of Congress, Washington, DC: p. 87; Metropolitan Museum of Art, New York: pp. 28 (Bequest of Phyllis Massar, 2011), 32 (Harris Brisbane Dick Fund, 1953), 42 (Harris Brisbane Dick Fund, 1953), 45 (Harris Brisbane Dick Fund, 1953), 101 (Purchase, Joseph Pulitzer Bequest, 1918), 253 (Harris Brisbane Dick Fund, 1953) 257 (Harris Brisbane Dick Fund, 1938), 258 (Rogers Fund, 1919); National Portrait Gallery, London: p. 38; New York Public Library: pp. 99 top, 254; Philadelphia Museum of Art, PA: p. 109 (Gift of Robert A. Taub); Roger-Viollet/TopFoto: p. 125 (Jacques Boyer); Shutterstock.com: p. 29 (Stefano Cellai); Shutterstock: pp. 222 (Sipa), 228 (Reinier van Willigen), 229 (El Universal via ZUMA Wire), 231; from Tate Britain: p. 104 bottom; Walker Art Gallery: 102 bottom (Gift from Robert Neilson, 1880); Wellcome Collection: p. 15.

Index

Page numbers in *italics* indicate illustrations